Maps of the World

MAP
0.1
THE WORLD'S GEOGRAPHICAL BORDERS

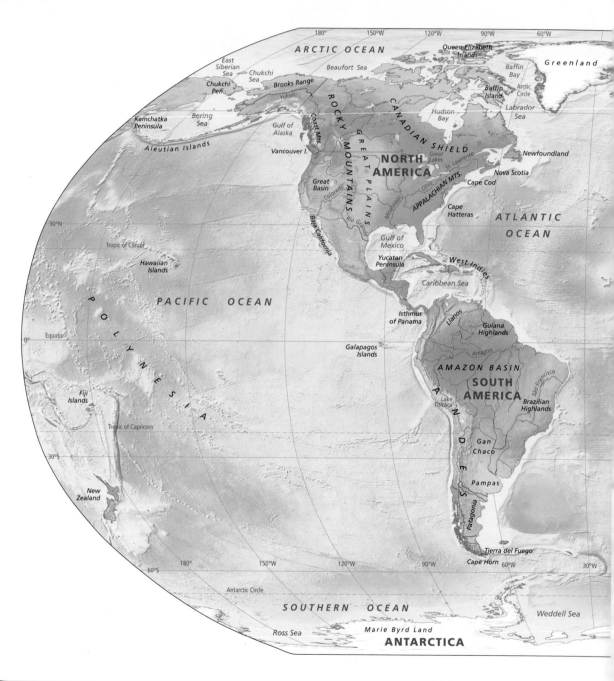

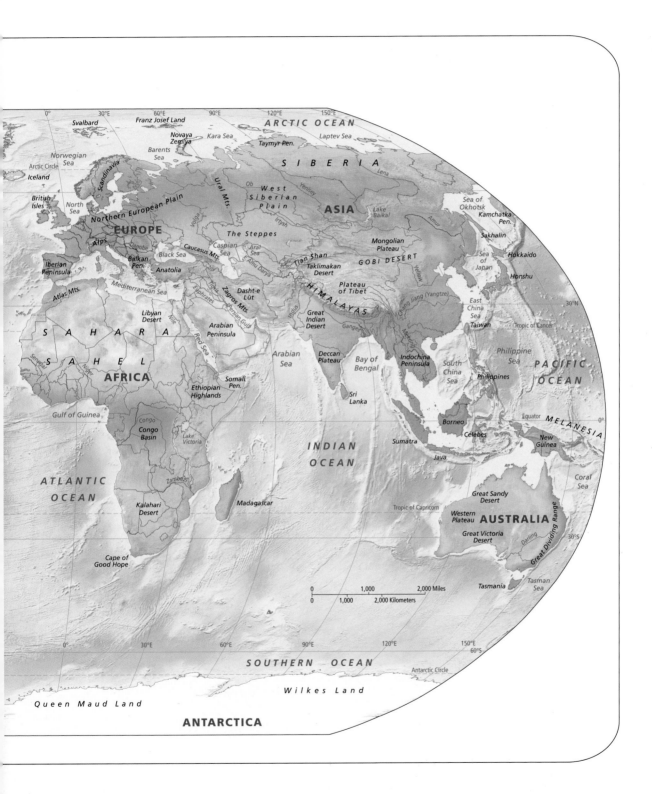

MAP
0.2

THE WORLD'S POLITICAL BORDERS

ARCTIC OCEAN

Beaufort Sea

Greenland
(DENMARK)

RUSSIA

Yukon

Arctic
Circle

Bering
Sea

Gulf of
Alaska

Hudson
Bay

CANADA

Great
Lakes

St. Lawrence

ATLANTIC

UNITED STATES

Colorado

Ohio

Mississippi

OCEAN

30°N

Tropic of Cancer

Rio Grande

Gulf of
Mexico

BAHAMAS

MEXICO

ST KITTS AND NEVIS
ANTIGUA AND BARBUDA
DOMINICA
ST LUCIA
ST VINCENT AND
THE GRENADINES
BARBADOS
GRENADA
TRINIDAD AND TOBAGO

CUBA

DOM.
REP.

Puerto
Rico

HAITI

CAPE
VERDE

BELIZE

JAMAICA

PACIFIC   OCEAN

GUATEMALA
EL SALVADOR

HONDURAS

Caribbean Sea

NICARAGUA

MARSHALL
ISLANDS

COSTA RICA

VENEZUELA

SURINAME

PANAMA

GUYANA

French Guiana
(FRANCE)

COLOMBIA

0°

Equator

ECUADOR

Amazon

NAURU

KIRIBATI

BRAZIL

São Francisco

PERU

SAMOA

Lake
Titicaca

BOLIVIA

VANUATU

FIJI

TONGA

Tropic of Capricorn

PARAGUAY

30°S

ARGENTINA

NEW
ZEALAND

CHILE

URUGUAY

60°S

180°

150°W

120°W

90°W

60°W

30°W

Antarctic Circle

SOUTHERN   OCEAN

Weddell Sea

Ross Sea

ANTARCTICA

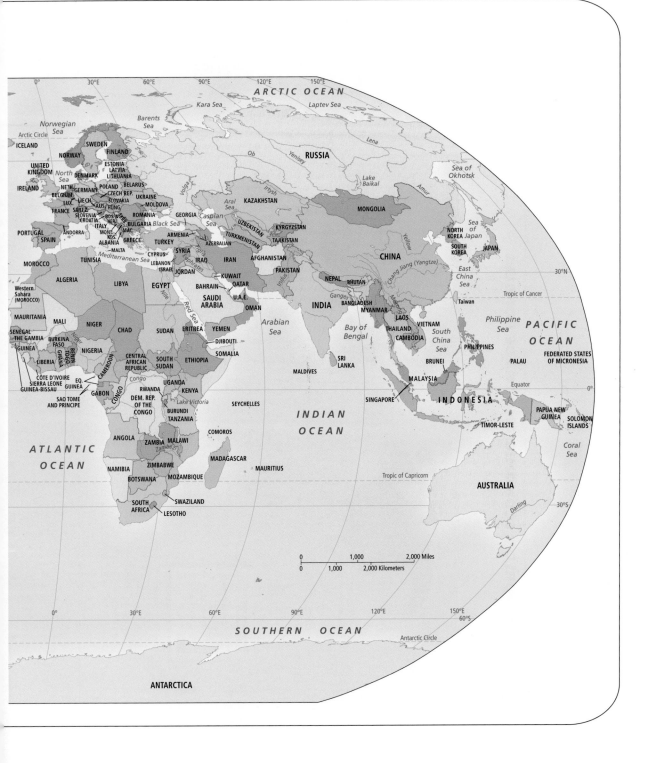

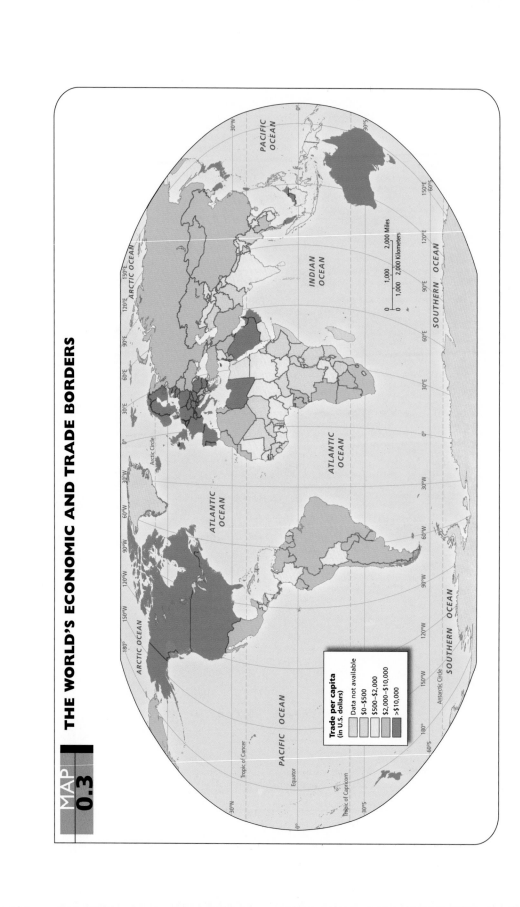

MAP
0.3

THE WORLD'S ECONOMIC AND TRADE BORDERS

Trade per capita
(in U.S. dollars)

Data not available
$0–$500
$500–$2,000
$2,000–$10,000
>$10,000

MAP
0.4

THE WORLD'S SOCIAL BORDERS

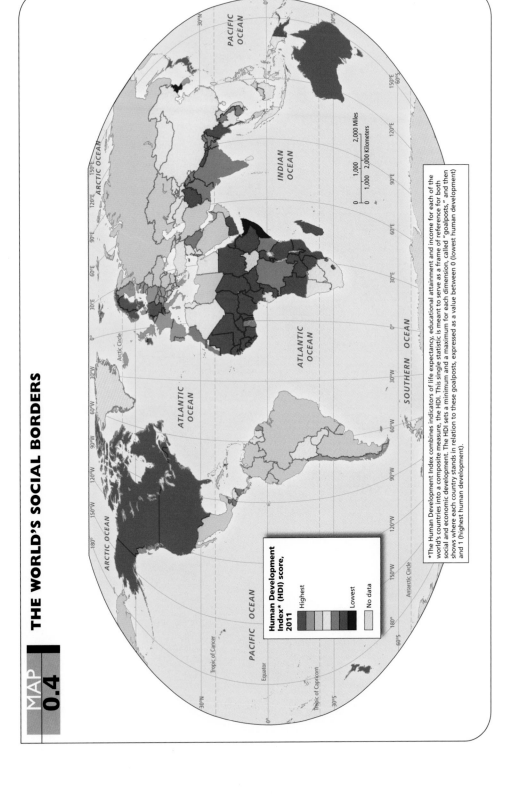

Human Development Index* (HDI) score, 2011

Highest

Lowest

No data

*The Human Development Index combines indicators of life expectancy, educational attainment and income for each of the world's countries into a composite measure, the HDI. This single statistic is meant to serve as a frame of reference for both social and economic development. The HDI sets a minimum and a maximum for each dimension, called "goalposts," and then shows where each country stands in relation to these goalposts, expressed as a value between 0 (lowest human development) and 1 (highest human development).

MAP
0.5

THE WORLD'S CULTURAL BORDERS

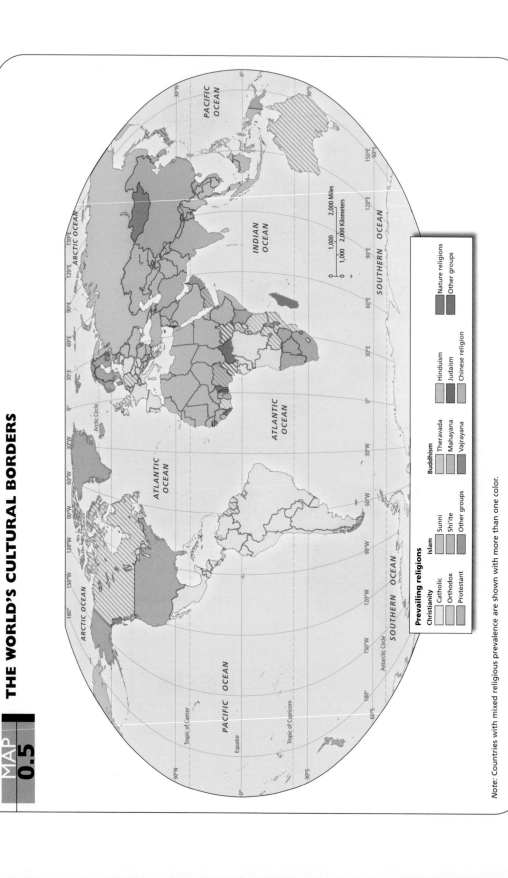

Prevailing religions

Christianity
- Catholic
- Orthodox
- Protestant

Islam
- Sunni
- Shi'ite
- Other groups

Buddhism
- Theravada
- Mahayana
- Vajrayana

- Hinduism
- Judaism
- Chinese religion

- Nature religions
- Other groups

Note: Countries with mixed religious prevalence are shown with more than one color.

CQ Press, an imprint of SAGE, is the leading publisher of books, periodicals, and electronic products on American government and international affairs. CQ Press consistently ranks among the top commercial publishers in terms of quality, as evidenced by the numerous awards its products have won over the years. CQ Press owes its existence to Nelson Poynter, former publisher of the *St. Petersburg Times,* and his wife Henrietta, with whom he founded Congressional Quarterly in 1945. Poynter established CQ with the mission of promoting democracy through education and in 1975 founded the Modern Media Institute, renamed The Poynter Institute for Media Studies after his death. The Poynter Institute (*www.poynter.org*) is a nonprofit organization dedicated to training journalists and media leaders.

In 2008, CQ Press was acquired by SAGE, a leading international publisher of journals, books, and electronic media for academic, educational, and professional markets. Since 1965, SAGE has helped inform and educate a global community of scholars, practitioners, researchers, and students spanning a wide range of subject areas, including business, humanities, social sciences, and science, technology, and medicine. A privately owned corporation, SAGE has offices in Los Angeles, London, New Delhi, and Singapore, in addition to the Washington DC office of CQ Press.

CROSSING BORDERS
INTERNATIONAL STUDIES FOR THE 21ST CENTURY

To our families whose support has been critical to the completion of this project

CROSSING BORDERS

INTERNATIONAL STUDIES FOR THE 21ST CENTURY

HARRY I. CHERNOTSKY
The University of North Carolina at Charlotte

HEIDI H. HOBBS
North Carolina State University

SAGE | **CQPRESS**

Los Angeles | London | New Delhi
Singapore | Washington DC

Los Angeles | London | New Delhi
Singapore | Washington DC

FOR INFORMATION:

CQ Press

An Imprint of SAGE Publications, Inc.

2455 Teller Road

Thousand Oaks, California 91320

E-mail: order@sagepub.com

SAGE Publications Ltd.

1 Oliver's Yard

55 City Road

London EC1Y 1SP

United Kingdom

SAGE Publications India Pvt. Ltd.

B 1/I 1 Mohan Cooperative Industrial Area

Mathura Road, New Delhi 110 044

India

SAGE Publications Asia-Pacific Pte. Ltd.

3 Church Street

#10-04 Samsung Hub

Singapore 049483

All maps in the color insert were drawn by International Mapping Associates. Photo credits (listed by page number): 1: REUTERS/David Moir. 3: REUTERS/Adnan Abidi. 12: AP Photo/Eric Draper. 13: Personal photo by Elaine M. Chernotsky. 25: NASA and the National Space Science Data Center. 30: Image courtesy of the National Snow and Ice Data Center, University of Colorado, Boulder. http://nsidc.org/arcticseaicenews/. 31: UNHCR/Brendan Bannon. 35: AP Photo/Mohamed Sheikh Nor. 40: AP Photo/Kyodo News. 45: Source: Carbon Footprint LTD website, http://www.carbonfootprint.com/calculator.aspx. 47: Personal photo by Rozita Singh. 51: AP Photo/Muhammed Abu Zaid. 54: Underwood & Underwood/Corbis; Daisy Cooper/Corbis. 56: Nicolas Perez. 57: Bettmann/Corbis. 60: Joseph Sohm/Visions of America/Corbis. 69: Personal photo by John McGregor. 75: Peter Turnley/Corbis. 84: Hulton-Deutsch Collection/Corbis. 87: Hansi-Krauss/AP/Corbis. 89: Rex features via AP Images. 97: AP Photo/US Air Force. 101: Les Stone/Sygma/Corbis. 102: Alessio Romenzi/Corbis. 103: Personal photo by Mor Green. 109: AP Photo. 117: AP Photo/Rajanish Kakade. 120: Bettmann/Corbis. 126: Bill Ross/Corbis. 134: Sherwin Crasto/Reuters/Corbis. 147: Maximilian Stock Ltd/Science Fiction/Corbis. 154: Michael S. Yamashita/Corbis. 161: Bettmann/Corbis. 162: AP Photo/Wilfredo Lee. 165: Personal photo by Puneet Gupta. 171: Eric Nathan/arabianEye/Corbis. 173: © Trustees of the British Museum. 185: Danny Lehman/Corbis. 190: Mathew Ashton/AMA/Corbis. 195: Howard Davies/Corbis. 200: Personal photo by Asli Akbas. 202: Patrick Robert/Sygma/Corbis. 203: Marcus Bleasdale/VII/Corbis. 209: AP Photo/Str. 213: Ocean/Corbis. 216: Michael Kooren/Reuters/Corbis. 224: Ton Koene/Visuals Unlimited/Corbis. 228: Jacques Langevin/Sygma/Corbis. 237: Les Stone/Sygma/Corbis. 245: Personal photo by Leah McManus. 248: Image Source/Corbis. 249: Imaginechina/Corbis. 252: Scott Houston/Corbis. 257: Credit Diversity Abroad. 263: Michael Reynolds/epa/Corbis. 265: The Peace Corps. 271: Leah Gardner.

Printed in the United States of America

A catalog record of this book is available from the Library of Congress.

ISBN 978-1-6042-6956-7 (paperback)

This book is printed on acid-free paper.

Certified Chain of Custody
Promoting Sustainable Forestry
www.sfiprogram.org
SFI-01268

SFI label applies to text stock

Acquisitions Editor: Elise Frasier

Production Editor: Laureen Gleason

Copy Editor: Cate Huisman

Typesetter: C&M Digitals (P) Ltd.

Proofreader: Gretchen Treadwell

Indexer: Michael Ferreira

Cover Designer: Jeffrey Everett/El Jefe Design

Marketing Manager: Jonathan Mason

Permissions Editor: Adele Hutchinson

12 13 14 15 16 10 9 8 7 6 5 4 3 2 1

About the Authors

Harry I. Chernotsky is chair of the Department of Global, International and Area Studies and professor of political science at the University of North Carolina at Charlotte. He has a PhD in political science from Rutgers University.

Heidi H. Hobbs is the director of the Master of International Studies program and an associate professor of political science in the School of Public and International Affairs at North Carolina State University. She has a PhD in international relations from the University of Southern California.

Brief Contents

Detailed Contents

Tables, Figures, and Maps

TABLES

FIGURES

MAPS

Preface

The proliferation of international studies majors at colleges and universities across the United States has created both a new frontier for understanding the world and a problem for those of us who are expected to identify the key concepts associated with these programs. We are asked to structure distinct disciplines into a coherent multidisciplinary major, where learning outcomes and objectives are most often in the eye of the beholder. Not only is this difficult intellectually, it is challenging administratively as well. International studies is the intersection of anthropology, political science, geography, culture, language, science, technology, art, health, and so many other disciplines. Historically, it has lacked an integrative framework. This eclectic scheme of organization is reflected in the way international studies has developed in colleges and universities. While the growth of majors and minors has been fueled by an increasing interest in all that is "international," it is the "studies" aspect that has varied from one academic institution to the next. As a result, it has become quite difficult to define a core curriculum.

This book addresses this challenge by providing a framework for students that is built upon an understanding of the many borders that define the international system. In adopting this view, we are able to address the many different fields that constitute international studies and provide instructors a starting point from which they can pursue their own disciplinary interests. The challenge for students majoring in international studies is less about what anthropology, political science, or sociology *is* and more about what each of these disciplines *does* to contribute to their understanding of the world.

The notion of global citizenship as an organizing concept for international studies is critical to our perspective. Whatever the focus of international studies may be at your college or university, we are dedicated to the belief that students must have a greater understanding of the world around them and the role they will play in it. This sense of cosmopolitanism will be critical as they navigate their daily lives and consider the range of career opportunities available to them. We have designed this work to provide a dialog between academic frameworks and to include practical components that suggest how students can put an international studies degree to work. The book is organized to reflect these goals by including chapters on both the various disciplines that address international studies and the global challenges we must all confront. The book concludes with a how-to guide for students that offers suggestions for study abroad, internships, service learning, and future training. We hope it will serve as a road map for students to better understand the world and to become important actors in it.

Acknowledgments

The broad nature of this subject matter has been difficult to capture in a text, and we are very grateful to the people who have played important roles in this process. First, we must thank Darin Van Tassell for his many intellectual contributions to this manuscript, most notably that fated conversation in Starbucks that really laid out the borders theme we would subsequently adopt and his contributions to Chapter 1. Thanks to those who have thoughtfully worked on the conceptualization of international studies and to the participants in the many International Studies Association (ISA) panels on this topic, especially Ann Kelleher, Rob Blanton, Barron Boyd, and Marijke Breuning. Thanks also to our academic homes, the University of North Carolina at Charlotte and North Carolina State University, which have supported us through this endeavor.

Pulling from so many disciplines has been challenging. The work of several teaching assistants in the Master of International Studies program at North Carolina State has been critical from the early days with Shirreef Loza, Lisa Sands Shelton, and Carl Booksing, and on to include Sarah Cowles, Margaret Jackson, Chantell LaPan, Leah McManus, Chris Sawyer, Shari Tate, and Nicole Zapata. Most noteworthy is the input of Leah Gardner, who contributed significantly to the completion of the final manuscript and development of teaching resources.

We are indebted to the editors and staff of SAGE Publications and CQ Press for their support and assistance. We appreciated the initial enthusiasm of Charisse Kiino for this project. It was contagious. We thank Elise Frasier for all her efforts in moving us along, Karen Fein for her editorial contributions, and Laureen Gleason and Cate Huisman for their production work.

Finally, we are grateful to our families for their patience through this process. They stuck with us and encouraged us through the thick and thin of it all. Harry sends his love and thanks to his wife and partner, Elaine, and children, Rena and Chris. Heidi extends her love and appreciation to her husband, Steve, and children, Perry and Madison. We could not have done this without them!

August 2012

CROSSING BORDERS

INTERNATIONAL STUDIES FOR THE 21ST CENTURY

Getting Your Global Bearings
Navigating the World

CHAPTER 1

"Don't panic."

—Douglas Adams's 1979 science fiction classic,
The Hitchhiker's Guide to the Galaxy[1]

You can't escape it. The world has become smaller as the food you eat, the clothes you wear, and the products you use come from all around the globe. Your own daily routines are closely connected to the world beyond your doorstep. As distances shrink and traditional borders become fuzzy, we have to learn to think differently. In Douglas Adams's science fiction classic, *The Hitchhiker's Guide to the Galaxy*, the protagonist, Arthur Dent, is thrust into a tour of the galaxy and is relieved upon receiving his *Hitchhiker's Guide* emblazoned with the words, "Don't panic."

Anyone embarking on a journey to understand the world today might benefit from similar advice. You must embrace the many changes taking place, but you might want some help in planning your trip. What is therefore needed to set you at ease is a "hitchhiker's guide to the global arena" that will provide a road map for the world of today and the people who inhabit it. This book will serve as your guide as it lays out the foundations of international studies and describes the knowledge, skills, and experience you will need to get your global bearings to navigate the world.

These Circus Oz performers at a festival in Edinburgh have no trouble navigating their terrain. Our job in this book is to introduce you to equally exciting ways to traverse borders. Some of them may be familiar to you, but others will be new and potentially strange. But don't panic—this book will be your resource through the entire journey.

TOWARD A WORKING DEFINITION OF INTERNATIONAL STUDIES

The goal of international studies is to prepare students for meeting the challenges of a rapidly changing world. A working definition of **international studies** is "a field of inquiry that examines the broad array of human relationships that involve cross-border interactions." International studies is one of the fastest growing majors in the United States today, in large part because students and teachers alike recognize that we live in a rapidly changing landscape and know that we need a new set of tools to engage with it. It is different from traditional studies of international relations and their narrower emphasis on politics in that it offers a unique and broader way to examine the challenges of a global world order. For instance, whereas a focus on politics helps us think about how countries around the world interact with one another, it does not tell us very much about how ordinary people are connected to or affected by the world around them and how they in turn affect it.

international studies
a field of inquiry that examines the broad array of geographic, political, economic, social, and cultural interactions and relationships that cross borders.

As a course of study, international studies therefore draws upon multiple disciplines and perspectives. These may include anthropology, business, communication, economics, geography, health care, history, languages, literature, political science, religion, and sociology. Relationships among these different disciplines are often hard to manage for academic institutions, but the changing nature of the international system and the ability to understand it requires looking at the world through these multiple lenses. Ultimately, international studies is designed to help students forge a new identity for themselves that is responsive to their environment.

DIFFERENT WAYS OF LOOKING AT THE WORLD'S BORDERS

Each of the academic disciplines devoted to the study of the world's people and systems has a different way of looking at the world. Each is focused on a particular aspect of the world and is primarily interested in that unit of analysis. For our purposes, we can think of those units as making up different kinds of "borders," the features that most strongly define the various parts of any given system (see Table 1.1). We will be concerned in this book with five major types of borders: geographic, political, economic, social, and cultural.

In the classic view of earth from outer space, it appears as a tranquil blue globe distinguished by landmasses and bodies of water. Upon closer inspection, we can begin to identify rivers, deserts, and mountain ranges (see Map 0.1 in the color insert). Even the lithosphere, the stratosphere, and the ozone layer become important distinctions that form the earth's ecological system. These **geographic borders** affect how and where humans have settled and the degree to which they interact with one another.

geographic borders
borders that delineate the physical world (mountains, oceans, rivers, deserts, ozone) and affect how and where humans have settled and the degree to which they interact with one another.

Over time, these geographic borders have changed, shifted, expanded, and shrunk. Volcanoes, glaciers, earthquakes, and meandering rivers transform the landscape. Geographic borders are also altered by the environmental impact of melting polar ice caps, retreating wetlands, and expanding deserts. Furthermore, such borders have shifted because people increasingly live in large groups today, where they once did not. The valleys subject to monsoon flooding in Bangladesh and the converted

TABLE 1.1 — THE BORDERS OF INTERNATIONAL STUDIES

Type of Border	Main Unit of Analysis	Primary Academic Field of Study
geographic	physical earth	geography
political	states	political science
economic	markets	economics
social	class	sociology
cultural	nations	anthropology

deserts and now wildfire-prone areas of Southern California are examples of two such areas where large numbers of people now live.

While geographic borders may shift, they are still fairly simple to identify. The rest of the "borders" of international studies, however, are distinguished in a more nuanced manner. Looking at a modern map of the world (see Map 0.2 in the color insert), we see a series of recognizable lines and boundaries. These lines represent the **political borders** of the world. These political borders form states, arguably the most powerful actors in the world today. Defined largely by governments in control within these boundaries, states remain a primary focus for students of international studies.

The sheer number of states is important to recognize as well. Today, there are almost 200 independent states. Only 100 years ago, roughly 50 states existed. By the start of World War II, there had been little change. Because the end of World War II brought incredible devastation to the European continent and consequently ended the formal trappings of colonialism, some 36 new states had come into existence by 1960. The existence of so many relatively new political entities itself is important to recognize, particularly when observing that these new political borders sit on top of—and often divide— very old cultures.

International studies involves much more than government members sitting around a table discussing issues of war and peace. Beyond political borders that form states, the existence of **economic borders**—those that form markets—is central to the relationships among states, nations, and individuals (see Map 0.3). Markets, or the exchange of goods and services within a given system, represent dynamic forces that provide almost everyone with the items they consume. As a result, the emergence of a global marketplace is driven not just by states, but by other actors, such as transnational private corporations and individuals.

Think about your morning routine:

> You may have woken up to the sounds of an alarm clock/radio assembled in Mexico, gotten out of a bed that had been made with linens from Egypt or Malaysia, and struggled to the kitchen, outfitted with appliances manufactured in China. There perhaps you made a cup of Brazilian coffee or tea grown in Sri Lanka. You might have even had a banana from Costa Rica or an orange from Morocco. Next, you headed into the shower with the fixtures possibly made in Germany. Then, you slipped into your Levi's, made in Vietnam, T-shirt made in India, and Reeboks made in Indonesia, and headed for school in your Toyota, assembled in Kentucky. You stopped to buy gas, imported from Saudi Arabia or Venezuela, arrived on campus, and then searched for a parking place—a problem confronted worldwide!

The ability to purchase goods across international borders has much to do with economic success. A central question revolves around the resources available to individuals for their advancement. Goods and services and the resources needed to produce them are not distributed equally—they go to those who can

political borders
borders that delineate the governing entities of the world and that are distinguished on the basis of territory, population, governments, and recognition by others.

economic borders
borders that delineate the markets that promote the exchange of goods and services across the world.

social borders
borders that delineate the class divisions of the world that are formed by inequality of opportunity.

cultural borders
borders that delineate the nations of the world that form identities in terms of language, religion, ethnicity, or a common historical experience.

afford them and who have access to them—and this uneven distribution and access produces a divide along **social borders** (see Map 0.4). In other words, it separates people into different social classes. Karl Marx is the best known advocate of using class as an important means of analysis. His ideas were implemented by some of his most prominent followers—Lenin and Stalin in Russia and Mao in China—in the formation of governing bodies to oversee political states. But social divisions remained even in these proposed utopian societies, and such divisions are even more pronounced today along the north-south line formed by the equator, such that societies to the south of the equator, the Global South, are less economically viable than those to the north. The inherent structure of the world's political and economic systems creates a world of haves and have-nots that furthers class distinctions.

But international studies is about more than just states and markets. To add another layer, the next borders that must be considered are the **cultural borders** that form nations. Nations can be defined in terms of language, religion, ethnicity, or a common historical experience. Such cultural distinctions provide us with some of the most important insights into the world's people. There may be some 200 different states, but there are well over 6,000 languages, dozens of global religions, countless folk religions, and hundreds of different ethnic groups (see Map 0.5).

Though governments decide who belongs or has membership (generally referred to as *citizenship*) in a state, it is largely up to individuals to determine their cultural identity. The language of international studies makes these distinctions between political and cultural borders confusing. The countries that are members of the United Nations, for example, are referred to as *nation-states*; with this term there is an implicit assumption that political borders and cultural borders generally coincide. But such is not always the case, and the African continent offers an excellent example. There are 54 African states and over 300 distinct nations on the sub-Saharan African continent. Many of the problems surrounding the violence, leadership, and economic stagnation in that region must begin with the recognition that there are many new states that have been formed that split very old nations.

The independence movement in the Québec province of Canada provides another example. The Québequois, who embrace a French culture, believe they are being stifled by the Canadian political system and more rightfully should be independently aligned with France. They have reluctantly stayed in the Canadian federal system but not without great debate and consternation. The instability in Iraq is also instructive of the challenges posed by political and cultural borders. One of the more glaring issues that the government of Iraq faces is that most of the people living within its political

HOW DO YOU CONNECT?

HOW DO YOU DEFINE YOURSELF?

By your . . .

a. country
b. state or town
c. religion
d. language
e. race or ethnic group
f. some combination of all

borders define themselves first as a part of the Sunni, Shi'a, or Kurdish nation rather than as Iraqi citizens.

One of the striking characteristics of the emerging century is that the globe's inhabitants now routinely cross these borders, and it is largely the impact of **technology** and technological innovation that has transformed the relationship between individuals and their political, economic, and cultural affiliations. Perhaps best exemplified by the telecommunications revolution and the presence of the World Wide Web, these technological developments permit much of the world's people to be connected with one another in ways unimaginable only a few years ago. In just over 100 years, the transition from horse and buggy to cars and planes made people more physically mobile, while communications, through radio and television, transformed society. In the twenty-first century, it is the access to computers and cell phones that is bridging these divides, particularly as the cost and size of computers and cell phones continue to shrink while their capabilities grow.

HOW DO YOU CONNECT? | **WHAT IS ONE ITEM YOU COULD NOT LIVE WITHOUT?**

a. cell phone
b. computer or tablet
c. iPod or MP3 player
d. books or other printed media

technology
the practical application of science.

THE EVOLUTION OF GLOBALIZATION

The most popular way to understand what is happening in the world today is the concept of **globalization**, a relatively new buzzword that emerged with the end of the Cold War and the ensuing interconnectedness of the international arena. Originally coined by Theodore Levitt in a 1983 *Harvard Business Review* article entitled "The Globalization of Markets," it referred to changes in behaviors and technology that allowed companies to sell the same products around the world.[2] Today, the definition is much broader. Generally, the term is used to describe the political, economic, social, and cultural flows across the international system. It includes a broad range of interactions, from trade and financial relationships to the integrated communication networks that have developed to facilitate those connections.

A Buddhist monk adjusts a television satellite dish affixed to a rooftop at a monastery in remote northeastern India. Increasingly we are connected via technologies such as these, even in the most hard-to-reach areas of the world.

globalization

the political, economic, social, and cultural flows across the international system. The term includes a broad range of interactions, from trade and financial relationships to the integrated communication networks that have developed to facilitate those connections.

hyperglobalization

the view that emphasizes the progressive erosion of the borders that have differentiated national economies and sustained the centrality of nation-states.

There is still some controversy, however, as to the extent and impact of this connectivity. Some have argued that the most recent acceleration marks the beginning of the end of the current global system—that something even bigger than globalization is happening. They point to the emergence of a new era of **hyperglobalization**, as it has come to be called, with the progressive erosion of the borders that have differentiated national economies and sustained the centrality of nation-states. They argue that this development has resulted in a significantly altered environment as defined by the following changes:

1. The nation-state is in steady decline and is now merely one of a growing number of players or actors on an increasingly multilevel world stage, where the practical limits to sovereignty have become more pronounced.

2. There are a growing number of issues that are global in scope and cannot be dealt with effectively by individual countries or even small groups of countries without some overarching system of global governance.

3. The mobility of capital has produced new patterns of finance and commercial exchange that do not necessarily correspond to flows that fit neatly within existing political borders.

4. The future will be marked by an increasing number of transnational interactions and institutions that will lead to a widening and deepening of integration processes—politically, economically, and socially.[3]

Not everyone agrees with this assessment. Skeptics point to the resiliency and political endurance of the nation-state system and the continuing capacity of states to regulate the global economy. While not disputing some of the important changes that are bringing disparate parts of the world closer together, these critics are less certain of the uniqueness or overarching significance of these developments. The expansion of trade and investment, they argue, is occurring within prevailing structures and continues to be shaped by existing borders. While more and more trade across the world is between transnational companies, trade balances are still measured on a country to country basis. In addition, the role of nationalism and other more restricted forms of identity in shaping relationships across the globe suggests potential limits to the cooperative spirit required to nurture and maintain these connections.

Similar patterns have developed previously, only to be strained or even severed due to emerging conflicts. The high levels of trade and investment that characterized the global economy of the late nineteenth century, for example, came to an abrupt halt with the outbreak of World War I in 1914. The volume of trade had risen sharply, with merchandise exports rising from 5 percent of the world's **gross domestic product** (GDP) in 1870 to 8.7 percent in 1913.[4] Merchandise trade represented 12 percent of the **gross national product** (GNP) for developed countries, a level unmatched until the 1970s.[5] Postwar efforts to revive the global economy and political order were hindered by lingering distrust and failure to devise an effective collective security system. A repetition of this pattern is not outside the realm of possibility today, particularly in light of the efforts of some states to limit their international exposure following the global financial crisis of 2008.

The inconsistent patterns evident across the global political and economic arenas are reflected in what some have labeled the *third wave* of globalization theory.[6] This view, often referred to as the *transformationalist* perspective, emphasizes the complexity of globalization. Its proponents see globalization as an extended historical process that goes back as far as the early "globalizers" who traveled the Silk Road trade route in the third century BCE linking the Chinese and Roman Empires. This initial wave was followed by a more pronounced period in the 1500s with the rise of European metropolitan centers and merchant classes. The activities of the Dutch and British East India trading companies marked the expansion of these centers into previously uncharted areas.

Transformationalists view the more recent trends that have been stimulated by major advances in technology as unprecedented in terms of their growth and intensity and serving to alter fundamental political, economic, and social relationships. The lines between what is domestic and what is international have become increasingly blurred. The national origin of particular products, for example, may be difficult to discern given the multiple sources of inputs or assembly. This is portrayed quite vividly by business professor Pietra Rivoli, who follows the life cycle of a T-shirt from its origins in a Texas cotton field to its manufacture in a Shanghai factory and its eventual appearance at a used clothing market in Tanzania.[7] Similar challenges present themselves when it comes to music, food, and fashion, as they have become increasingly influenced by styles and tastes originating in many places.

Even as the sovereign authority of states has diminished and the world economy has become increasing deterritorialized, third-wave theorists emphasize the importance of recognizing the uneven patterns and different responses to these globalizing trends.[8] Nation-states still enjoy the legal right to sovereignty, while territorial boundaries maintain both their political and commercial significance despite the fact that they may no longer serve as the "primary markers of modern life."[9] Crops are raised and goods and services are produced locally, and countries across the global economy tend to operate within regional contexts that often serve to limit contacts or integration outside those networks. While there are considerable and mutual stakes in sustaining these ties and relationships, their strength will be affected by the behaviors and policy choices of international actors.

gross domestic product (GDP)

the quantification of a country's production of goods and services at home.

gross national product (GNP)

the quantification of the value of all the goods and services produced in an economy, plus the value of the goods and services imported, less the goods and services exported.

GLOBALIZATION: WINNERS AND LOSERS

Given these disagreements and differing interpretations, what are the strengths and weaknesses of globalization? Who benefits from the increasingly connected world in which we live? In fact, globalization has become a contentious process. While many argue that everyone benefits from these changes—as the saying goes, a rising tide raises all boats—that has not always been the case. Consumers may gain from access to more goods and lower prices, but they have become more vulnerable to political and economic fluctuations abroad. As economic interdependence moves the free trade economic model to a global arena, the private sector will succeed or fail as a result of its ability to compete. Moreover, competition is not simply domestic in nature but with everyone around the world. People are living and interacting with their global neighbors on a level unprecedented in human history, but they are apprehensive when such interactions are perceived to threaten their traditions and customs.

It is possible that overall standards of living can be improved through access to more goods produced around the world. In terms of purchasing power for everyday items, consumers benefit from global competition that can provide access to cheaper goods. Items once considered luxuries are now more widely available. Diversification of manufacturing can create jobs in places where there were limited opportunities before. For example, workers in China, Sri Lanka, Indonesia, and Mexico have benefited from these developments. The heart of this argument is that globalization promotes a better quality of life for a greater number of people.

Proponents of globalization further believe that it empowers individuals both economically and politically. Advances in communications and greater opportunities to travel and experience places around the world, coupled with the heightened migration of peoples, increase people's awareness of many of the challenging issues facing the world. This recognition may serve as a catalyst in promoting cooperative and collaborative efforts at both the local and global levels.

the golden straitjacket
a term used by journalist Thomas Friedman to describe what states must do to participate competitively in the global market.

While everyone in the world may be directly or indirectly affected by this new system, not everyone benefits equally from it. This reality has produced a backlash by people who feel frustrated by their inability to control their destiny. In his first book on globalization, *The Lexus and the Olive Tree, New York Times* columnist and best-selling author Thomas Friedman talked about the difficulties societies may have keeping up with globalization or adapting to its demands—what he referred to as a hardware/software type of problem—and went on to address reasons for broader social and political resistance to the process.[10] Ultimately, he came to label the policies that would be required to get with the globalization program and reap its benefits "**the golden straitjacket**," whereby a state would need to balance its budget, cut state bureaucracy, promote the private sector, and encourage free trade to compete effectively in the global market. Even in a Western-based, politically democratic and freer trade economic system, these objectives are hard to achieve. For many of the less affluent people of the world, such objectives may not even be necessarily advisable.

As a result, they see themselves as being left behind. They believe that transnational corporations (TNCs) manipulate their economic status and ignore local concerns. Consequently, this loss of economic control makes states susceptible to decisions that are made in faraway places that do not necessarily take local interests into consideration. This trend has prompted many to argue that while globalization may well expand the economic pie, it is also contributing further to the divide between rich and poor.

Examples of such antiglobalization forces abound in both developed and developing countries. Some opponents cite the transfer or outsourcing of jobs as manufacturing moves from traditional industrial countries to offshore locations. While relocation may create jobs where they did not previously exist, employment conditions are often questionable or unsafe, resembling the sweatshops of a bygone era. Furthermore, outsourcing is not limited to manufacturing.

One of the fastest-growing areas is in information technology (IT). It is estimated that approximately 28 percent of outsourced jobs are related to this sector.[11] India has been the prime beneficiary to date, owing largely to its large pool of trained professionals and relatively low labor costs. By the end of 2010, three of India's largest IT services firms—Wipro, Infosys, and Tata—employed a combined 359,000 workers.[12]

The result is the creation of new jobs in other countries that are drawing people from rural areas to the city, contributing to the increasing urbanization of the world. As people move to the emerging megacities of Latin America, Asia, and Africa to take advantage of these jobs, living conditions for those at the lower end of the economic ladder are often below acceptable human standards. The problems of sanitation, inadequate housing, overcrowding, and serious health care issues are pervasive.

Opposition to globalization has become more public and pronounced, resulting in large-scale protest demonstrations. One of the first was in late November 1999, when trade ministers from 135 countries assembled in Seattle, Washington, to launch a new round of global trade talks. Delegates to the World Trade Organization (WTO) meeting were greeted by tens of thousands of demonstrators who disrupted the proceedings. The "**Battle of Seattle**," as it was quickly dubbed, became a debate about more than trade. It turned into a broader discussion about globalization. Since that time, similar protests have occurred almost every time there has been a meeting of a major international organization associated with promoting the globalization agenda.

Globalization also has a significant cultural impact. It is difficult to protect what is unique about different cultures, and this has prompted the question as to whether the world is becoming too homogenized. This question is an important one for many people, particularly when they believe their traditional ways

Battle of Seattle
the first major large-scale protest against globalization that occurred during the WTO meeting in Seattle, Washington, in November 1999.

At what came to be called the "Battle of Seattle," Seattle police use gas to push back World Trade Organization protesters in the city's downtown area. The protests delayed the opening of the WTO third ministerial conference. Protests have since been staged at nearly every WTO conference.

of living are threatened by forces that might erase their local identity.

In short, there is a feeling among those who question globalization that with the focus on competitiveness and efficiency, too little attention is given to the impact on the human condition. Despite the emphasis on cooperation and the growth of international organizations, there is a sense that the needs of many go unmet. While it may not be particularly useful to think of globalization as good or bad, it has become increasingly apparent that there have been winners and losers.

What then might be the alternatives for those who do not see their interests served? Throughout history, states have turned inward when they thought the intrusion of the outside world would jeopardize their way of life. They believed that minimizing contact would limit their vulnerability. China tried it twice. The first was during the fifteenth century under the Ming Dynasty with the decision to ground all seagoing vessels to protect the Chinese base of knowledge. Later, under Mao Zedong in the 1960s, the Cultural Revolution was instituted to shield the country from outside forces that were deemed responsible for perverting the basic principles and ideology of the communist revolution. Iran moved to a more protectionist posture after the revolution in 1979 and the establishment of an Islamic republic. Under the leadership of Ayatollah Khomeini, Iran's government sought to sever all ties to Western influences to strengthen its Islamic hold on the country.

The United States also has a history of avowed isolationism (with the notable exception of its intervention in Latin America) that can be traced from the farewell address of President George Washington to the events following World War I. America was reluctant to enter World War I, and when it did, then-president Woodrow Wilson characterized it as "the war to end all wars." Immediately thereafter, Wilson advocated the creation of a League of Nations to provide collective security for its members. His colleagues in the US Senate did not agree, however. When the Treaty of Versailles that ended the war and embraced Wilson's ideals came to them for ratification, they did not approve it.

In all of these cases, and to varying degrees, isolation did not work. Today, China has adopted an open economic strategy while remaining tied to a closed political system. Its current trading prowess is impressive, with an economy growing an average of 10 percent annually and a strong trading surplus.[13] Over time, Iran has rejected isolationism as well and is presently seeking to bolster its influence and prestige through its ongoing development of nuclear capabilities. Despite efforts by the Senate to prevent US involvement in world affairs after World War I, the ensuing turbulent years punctuated by the financial crash of 1929 and the rise of extreme nationalist political ideologies led to the outbreak of World War II and the return of the United States to an activist role in the international arena.

Today, technological innovation, the integration of markets, and overlapping financial networks preclude effective isolation. We cannot build up the walls, disconnect the computers, cut the phone lines, take out the satellite networks, and turn off the TV indefinitely. There is an emerging set of challenges—more commonly known as **global issues**. They are global not simply because they are happening all over the world, but because they transcend state boundaries and require a collective response. No single entity (government, transnational corporation, nation, organization, group, or individual) possesses the ability to deal with, much less solve, these issues by itself. While this is not an exhaustive list, global issues include protection of the physical environment, terrorism, development of alternative energy, protection of human rights, growth in the human population, creation of wealth and alleviation of poverty, and halting the spread of weapons of mass destruction.

global issues
challenges that transcend state boundaries and require a collective response. No single entity possesses the ability to deal with or solve these issues by itself.

The difficulty of addressing these issues is compounded by the fact that they are experiencing exponential growth. The metaphor of the lily pond used by Lester Brown—borrowing from the philosopher Jean Boudin—illustrates the use of a riddle to teach schoolchildren the nature of exponential growth.[14] A lily pond contains a single leaf. Each day the number of lily pads doubles—two leaves the second day, four leaves the third day, eight leaves the fourth day, and so on. If the pond is one-fourth full on Day 28, on what day is the pond half full? The answer is actually the next day—Day 29. It is completely full by Day 30, and the lilies will overflow beyond the pond after that, such that the resources of the pond will be tapped out, and the lilies will begin to die. By that time, the nature of the pace of growth and change is so great, there is no longer the capacity for a solution, and so it is for global issues.

The lily pond in Giverny, France, that served as inspiration for the famous French impressionist artist Claude Monet.

Further, the growing interdependence of the global system compounds the difficulty in responding to these issues. Governments and other actors can no longer disregard what happens in the rest of the world, as there is a growing reality that no one country has the capability to solve the world's problems.

Issues have become linked from one country to another. The conceptual challenges are especially daunting if the goals are to minimize violence, maximize human rights, maximize social justice, and rehabilitate the environment, as working on one may make another worse off. Such is the nature of the interdependent world.

The metaphor of a spider's web is also useful in conceptualizing today's global problems and challenges. Touch that web anywhere, even lightly, and it vibrates everywhere. Similarly, the reach of global problems resonates beyond any immediate environment. As University of Chicago psychologist Mihaly Csikszentmihalyi has suggested, it is imperative to recognize the actual interconnections of causes and effects.[15]

One example is the debate over the environment. As corporations use the Amazonian rain forests to generate wealth, subsistence farmers also are clearing them to survive. While these actions may be justifiable in the short term, they are contributing to the destruction of the world's vital oxygen supply. Experts estimate that

> we are losing 137 plant, animal and insect species every day due to rainforest deforestation. That equates to 50,000 species a year. As the rainforest species disappear, so do many possible cures for life-threatening diseases. Currently, 121 prescription drugs sold worldwide come from plant-derived sources. While 25 percent of Western pharmaceuticals are derived from rainforest ingredients, less than 1 percent of these tropical trees and plants have been tested by scientists.[16]

People across the world are part of an emerging global order and share in its successes and failures.

THE CHANGING DEFINITION OF CITIZENSHIP IN A GLOBAL ERA

What do rock star and U2 front man Bono, Muhammad Yunus, and Wangari Maathai have in common? All have taken it upon themselves to participate directly in efforts to protect the earth, promote prosperity, and advocate for peace. Rock star Bono has championed the plight of Africa's poor, cofounding the nonprofit organization, DATA (Debt, AIDS, Trade, Africa) to fight poverty and disease. As director of the Grameen Bank in Bangladesh, Muhammad Yunus received the Nobel Peace Prize in 2006 for pioneering the microlending movement that provides loans to the poorest of the poor. Wangari Maathai of Kenya was awarded the Nobel Peace Prize in 2004 for her activities on behalf of the Green Belt Movement, an organization seeking to reduce poverty and protect the environment through community-based tree planting. She continued to work tirelessly to improve the lives of others until her death in 2011.

Understanding the contributions of renowned rock stars, bankers, and environmentalists is one thing, but where do regular individuals fit in? What role can they play in the global community? Beyond having a framework for understanding the globalized world of the twenty-first century, we also need to make a personal connection to it. One way to realize this relationship is to take a fresh look at the idea of **citizenship**.

Traditional notions of citizenship date back to the time of the ancient Greek city-state and have focused on membership in distinctive political communities that are very much tied to a particular place. Since the mid-seventeenth century, that place has been the state. In return for certain protections and rights, citizens are expected (and often compelled) to assume responsibilities and obligations to the state. While not necessarily prevented from acting in venues or on behalf of ideals that might transcend the state, citizens may do so only if those actions are deemed consistent with state interests. Primary political loyalties and identities have been defined by a connection to a particular physical space and differentiated on the basis of territorial boundaries.[17] In the early days, the Romans came from Rome and owed their allegiance to their state and its leaders.

But people across the world are reconsidering these matters. Much of the turmoil that can be observed today can be traced, in part, to a fundamental rethinking of both individual and collective identity and belonging. In addition to an increasing number of states that cannot sustain themselves, such as Somalia and Sudan, the limited capacity of countless others to fulfill various responsibilities to their citizens has added to the uncertainty.

People are also moving around at an accelerated and unprecedented rate. The United Nations Global Commission on International Migration has estimated that by 2009, there were between 185 and 200 million people living in countries other than their own.[18] The migration phenomenon has touched every region of the world and has had considerable impacts. Access to citizenship rights and privileges for noncitizens has become controversial in many countries. Such challenges are exemplified by the European Union (EU), which has gone a long way toward redefining citizenship by extending entitlements available to citizens of member states residing elsewhere in the Union—for instance, a citizen of France, one of the EU member states, can travel freely throughout Germany by virtue of both states' membership in the EU. The arrival of increasing numbers of refugees, asylum

citizenship
the duties, rights, privileges, and responsibilities of individuals to and in the community in which they reside.

HOW DO YOU CONNECT? | **WHERE DO YOU COME FROM?**

Have you ever moved?
 a. yes
 b. no

Have you lived in another state?
 a. yes
 b. no

Have you lived in a country other than where you were born?
 a. yes
 b. no

seekers, and displaced persons from outside the EU has produced some backlash while producing new challenges that have proven difficult to resolve.[19]

Once again, the question of borders must be addressed. Matters of national or regional security fuel support for more exclusionary policies. Increasingly, there are relationships between people, ideas, and problems that are not defined or confined by existing borders. Consider the experience of Nathan, a young professional from Charlotte, North Carolina, working as an analyst at a major US financial institution. While sitting on his couch with laptop at hand, Nathan is actively involved in the global microfinancing effort to assist budding entrepreneurs across the developing world. As noted earlier, this movement has been spurred by the work of the Grameen Bank and its founder, Muhammad Yunus. Nathan participates by interfacing with Kiva (www.kiva.org), a web-based organization originating in San Francisco, to match aspiring business-people with prospective lenders across the globe. He is able to review the business plans and check the repayment records of potential recipients and to execute secure online loans. After a satisfactory first pass, which consisted of $25 loans to four separate borrowers, Nathan is considering a significant increase in his lending activities. He is also encouraging many of his friends to get involved.[20]

By his own admission, Nathan was drawn to this activity as an opportunity to broaden his experience and to sharpen his professional skills. He had also been affected by the extreme poverty he observed during a visit to Mexico and was looking for an outlet to address that concern. In his own way, Nathan is stretching the boundaries of his citizenship by exploring new ways to express his connection to the world. He is not alone.

As Nathan and others come to grips with the realities of an increasingly inter-connected world, the idea of global citizenship has gained popularity. What does it mean to be a **global citizen**? Nigel Dower suggests that global citizens are indi-viduals who see themselves as members of a global community and who con-front the challenges we face from a global perspective.[21] From this vantage point, global citizenship is about belonging and taking responsibility. Global citizens are seen as those with the knowledge, skills, and desire to act on behalf of a set of beliefs and ideals to bring about a more just and compassionate world.

Oxfam, a British nongovernmental organization noted for its extensive devel-opment and relief activities, has offered one of the more widely cited definitions of global citizenship. It defines a global citizen as someone who

- is aware of the wider world and has a sense of their own role as a world citizen

- respects and values diversity

- has an understanding of how the world works

- is outraged by social injustice

global citizens

individuals who perceive themselves as members of a global community. Such people are aware of the wider world, respect and value diversity, and are willing to act to make the world a more equitable and sustainable place.

- participates in the community at a range of levels, from the local to the global

- is willing to act to make the world a more equitable and sustainable place

- takes responsibility for their actions[22]

While advocates of global citizenship seek to encourage the acquisition of knowledge and skills to promote proactive involvement in dealing with the challenges of the world, their efforts have generated considerable controversy. Critics argue that the very notion of global citizenship is vague and does not really have much meaning to most people, particularly those who do not think of themselves in these terms and have no effective means to become engaged in these matters. Moreover, with no institution in place to confer such citizenship— no global organization that can say, "Congratulations, you're now a citizen of the world!"—the very idea is seen to lack serious practicality.

Others have not been so quick in dismissing the possibility of a growing interest in this new thinking; rather, they view global citizenship as problematic and have been quite pointed in their criticisms. Global citizenship, they suggest, can undermine the foundations of national citizenship. It provides a rationale for the strengthening of global institutions and forms of global governance that might threaten state sovereignty. Perhaps most disconcerting to critics, however, has been the notion that global citizenship emphasizes issues such as global social justice, the protection of human rights, and environmental conservation, which tend to promote a partisan political agenda. Opponents of a global identity resist an approach that elevates certain sets of values that may not necessarily correspond to the interests of all affected parties. The creation of organizations or institutions designed to impose policies reflecting these values, no matter how reasonable or lofty they might appear, remains the source of their concern.[23]

Supporters of the global citizenship concept answer these detractors by noting the increasing number of issues requiring common approaches and mutually derived solutions. The development of plausible strategies, they argue, would benefit greatly from a generally acceptable ethic or set of values upon which to build cooperative action. Discussion of this concept has been around for a while. The 1993 Parliament of World Religions offered a useful example of this approach. It suggested the need to adopt a global ethic that included a commitment to a culture of nonviolence, a just economic order, tolerance, and equal rights. Similarly, the 1995 Commission on Global Governance urged the inclusion of an ethical dimension that incorporated respect for the rights of all people and shared responsibilities to contribute to the common good based on the values of justice and equity.[24]

At first glance, adherence to these principles might not seem particularly problematic. However, opposition has been significant. Critics have questioned the assumption that it is possible to identify some set of universally acceptable values or common obligations. Others have gone even further by charging that the presumption of a global ethic smacks of cultural imperialism and does not account sufficiently for the different ways these ideals might be defined or applied in various societies around the globe.[25] A perfect example would be the debate surrounding what constitutes basic or universal human rights. This controversy illustrates the difficulty of moving forward to address the challenges that lie ahead.

Does the notion of global citizenship pose a threat to national interests and potentially undermine the foundation of our current international order? The world has been brought closer together through an expanding number of formal and informal networks as well as governmental and nongovernmental contacts. The destinies of people across the world have become more closely linked, and individual actions—no matter how limited or trivial they may appear—can impact others in profound ways. Our consumption of resources, our interface with our environment, our efforts to limit the costs of production, and our responses to those under siege will go a long way in shaping the world of the future.

It can further be argued that at least some of the controversy surrounding the idea of global citizenship stems from its terminology. For many proponents, a *global* citizen implies nothing much more than a globally oriented or globally minded person who is both sensitive to many of the effects of globalization and interested in some form of personal engagement. Rather than posing any threat or danger to commonly accepted forms of existing citizenship, this view offers the possibility for additional outlets for expression and action. Globalization has not rendered national citizenship obsolete. It may be seen as presenting avenues for the expression of multiple citizenships that reflect the different stages and venues—local, regional, national, global—that many people find themselves occupying these days.[26]

Broader acceptance of this mindset might, at the very least, help to guard against the extreme forms of ethnic nationalism that have characterized so many recent conflicts. It could also encourage a greater willingness to seek a commonality of purpose when approaching the many vexing problems that threaten the tranquility and security of the world. Martha Nussbaum, a leading contributor to the discussion of citizenship and a proponent of this more expansive view, strongly suggests the need for cosmopolitan education to enable us to realize this potential. She argues that it is critical to recognize our obligations to the rest of the world and forge a set of clear global values to make progress in solving problems that require broad-based cooperation.[27]

HOW DO YOU CONNECT?	HOW DO YOU DEFINE YOUR CITIZENSHIP?
a. local	d. global
b. regional	e. some combination of the above
c. national	

WHERE DO WE GO FROM HERE?

International studies must introduce the perspectives and competencies required to prepare for citizenship in the global community of the twenty-first century. This book responds to that need by addressing the following objectives:

1. It will enhance understanding of the issues, actors, institutions, cultures, ideologies, and policy instruments, as well as the relationship among them, all of which condition and affect the primary issues and events confronting the peoples of the world. In short, it will help readers to understand the interdependent nature of the contemporary world.

2. It will provide an opportunity to develop an appreciation for how scholars, policymakers, and ordinary individuals living in various regions of the world understand and explain the various topics covered here, and to consider and evaluate the impact of the various policies that have attempted to address these issues.

3. It will consider and evaluate alternative explanations and interpretations as to what drives the policy process, and help the reader develop an awareness of the realities of the workings of the contemporary world we live in.

4. Finally, it will sharpen critical thinking, analytical abilities, and effective communication skills as a way to prepare for the changing definition of citizenship in a global era.

To achieve these objectives, this book will embark upon a journey that crosses the borders of the world and those that define international studies in a way that will help develop a better understanding of the global community. Following this introduction, Chapter 2 delineates the geographical conceptualization of borders. The way physical borders have been understood and mapped has changed throughout history and colors the way the world is perceived. Today, more than ever, people are cognizant of planet earth as a finite resource and the challenges it faces. Chapter 3 provides the jump start to this trip by noting how technology has become the means for making border crossings more accessible for many while simultaneously dividing further those who are without the latest tools of innovation.

The next six chapters begin to launch the trip in earnest, as the various borders to be crossed and the issues that confront them are introduced. For each of the borders that must be crossed, there is a group of challenges that must be addressed, and we take these up in alternating chapters. Chapter 4 introduces the political borders of the world and the nation-state system. Security of these borders is a critical concern and has frequently led to conflict. A set of cases in

Chapter 5 examine the security issues faced by nation-states in terms of conflict and war, weapons of mass destruction, and terrorism. Chapter 6 defines the economic borders that have emerged over time, from barter economies to the transnational financial networks that operate around the clock today. The challenges facing economic interests, most notably in the areas of trade, investment, finance, and development, are addressed in Chapter 7. In Chapter 8, identity and the importance of social and cultural borders are examined. This section concludes with a closer look at the challenges to identity posed by the roles of religion, ethnic conflict, and failed states, in Chapter 9.

We then take the journey beyond borders to look for areas of global cooperation. Chapter 10 explores the transformations that have occurred in recent years that promote a more global view of the world, including the expansion of international law and the proliferation of international organizations. Chapter 11 explores some of the issues that transcend borders and require a more global response: poverty, disease, and human rights, while also examining the possibility of global governance.

The journey ends in Chapter 12 with a road map for what you can do—where you can go from here. This chapter addresses the role individuals can play in this new global order and what students must do to connect to the world and become effective citizens. It includes an overview of the career opportunities that students can pursue to respond to the challenges presented throughout the book.

Chapters 4, 6, and 8 define the borders and open with a historical view of their subject matter and continue with a delineation of how various academic fields have grown to study them. Prominent scholars who have shaped these fields are introduced, and each chapter includes a section where these scholars tell the reader about their perspectives in a feature called "In Their Own Words." Chapters 5, 7, and 9 discuss the challenges generated by the many borders that exist and close with a section called "What Can Be Done." Three features in these chapters place the various borders and their challenges in a broader context and bring the chapters to life:

- "How Do You Connect?" boxes ask questions and offer ideas about participation in civil society: What organizations are you a member of? Do you buy counterfeit goods? Have you participated in political or social movements?

- "Where Do You Stand?" boxes outline controversial issues in crossing borders and invite you to take a position on global issues.

- "So What?" boxes showcase interviews with current and former international studies students from around the world reflecting on their experiences.

There is a popular saying suggesting that everything local is global, urging us to "think globally and act locally." The essence of this comment is embodied in international studies. It is not enough simply to acknowledge the linkages that exist; it is necessary to derive an action plan for individuals to embrace those connections, not only for their own benefit but as citizens of an increasingly complex world. The goal of this book is to offer you a plan to do exactly that—to provide you with an intellectual map that will show you the many borders you must cross and the tools you will need to be an effective citizen of the world. "Don't panic!"

KEYConcepts

Battle of Seattle 11
citizenship 15
cultural borders 6
economic borders 5
geographic borders 4
global citizens 16
global issues 13
globalization 8

golden straitjacket 10
gross domestic product (GDP) 9
gross national product (GNP) 9
hyperglobalization 8
international studies 4
political borders 5
social borders 6
technology 7

TO LEARNMore

Books and Other Print Media

CQ Researcher, *Global Issues: Selections from the CQ Researcher 2012* (Washington, DC: CQ Press, 2012).

This book is compiled annually by CQ Press and provides an in-depth look at current issues affecting the global arena. The CQ Researcher is available online and can be accessed through many university libraries: http://library.cqpress.com/cqresearcher.

J. Michael Adams and Angelo Carfagna, *Coming of Age in a Globalized World: The Next Generation* (Bloomfield, CT: Kumarian Press, 2006).

Adams and Carfagna offer insight into the forces that have transformed the boundaries of the world and make a strong case for the need to develop new appreciations and perspectives to deal effectively and productively with these changes.

Nigel Dower, *An Introduction to Global Citizenship* (Edinburgh, UK: Edinburgh University Press, 2003).

Dower provides a theoretical and historical context for considering the idea of global citizenship and suggests how it may be applied in dealing with an array of current global issues.

Pietra Rivoli, *The Travels of a T-Shirt in the Global Economy* (Hoboken, NJ: John Wiley & Sons, 2005).

This is a story of a T-shirt from its origins in the cotton fields of Texas to its final destination in the second-hand clothing market in East Africa, with many stops along the way. It offers an interesting and close-up look at the intricacies of today's global trade system.

Thomas L. Friedman, *The Lexus and the Olive Tree* (New York: Farrar, Straus, and Giroux, 1999).

This best seller offers a comprehensive look at the dynamics of globalization and highlights the tensions between the forces of change and the desires of some to maintain traditional ways of life.

The World Bank, *The Global Citizen's Handbook: Facing Our World's Crises and Challenges* (New York: Harper Collins, 2007).

This is a visual guide to some of the critical issues affecting global political, economic, and social development. The text is filled with useful statistical information and many charts and graphs that present the material in a clear fashion.

Websites

Center for Strategic and International Studies (CSIS), www.csis.org/.

A good primer on international issues, the CSIS website provides users with information on particular topics and regions as well as on international studies programs and leading experts.

International Forum on Globalization, www.ifg.org/.

The International Forum on Globalization is an international organization that analyzes and critiques the effects of globalization on culture, society, politics, and the environment.

International Monetary Fund, "Key Issues: Globalization," www.imf.org/external/np/exr/key/global.htm.

The International Monetary Fund provides an overview of globalization and then delves into specific issues with regard to the effects of globalization on finance, trade, and labor.

SUNY Levin Institute, "Globalization 101," www.globalization101.org/.

This website is a project of the Levin Institute in the State University of New York (SUNY) system. It provides a very good overview of what globalization is and the issues that are related to it. It also includes a series of expert videos.

The Yale Center for the Study of Globalization, "Yale Global Online," http://yaleglobal.yale.edu.

The Yale Center for the Study of Globalization publishes this extensive online resource, which includes the online magazine *YaleGlobal* as well as scholarly articles and multimedia presentations by globalization experts from around the world.

Videos

Babel (2006).

Winner of the Golden Globe award for Best Motion Picture, this movie depicts a cross-cutting set of events taking place in Morocco, Japan, and Mexico that highlight the global interconnectedness of world problems.

Borders (Frontières) (2001).

A group of refugees leaves Senegal and crosses the Sahara, Algeria, and the Strait of Gibraltar in an attempt to enter Spain.

Life 8 (2009).

A 16-part series about the effects of globalization on people around the world. An excellent opportunity to see how the global economy impacts directly on the lives of people. Programs from previous series are also available.

Life in a Day (2010).

From National Geographic, this documentary is unique in that it was created from 80,000 clips submitted to YouTube depicting daily life from 192 nations on July 24, 2010. http://movies.nationalgeographic.com/movies/life-in-a-day/

Gordon Brown on Global Ethic vs. National Interest (2009).

Former British Prime Minister Gordon Brown discusses the concept of global citizenship, nationalism and patriotism, how the interests of one country are the interests of another, and how the people of the world have a responsibility for one another. www.ted.com/talks/lang/en/gordon_brown_on_global_ethic_vs_national_interest.html

Point of Departure
Planet Earth

"*Our interconnectedness on the planet is the dominating truth of the 21st century.*"

—Jeffrey Sachs, Director, Earth Institute at Columbia University[1]

As noted Harvard economist Jeffrey Sachs suggests, we are connected to planet earth in fundamental ways that are critical to our future. Everyone has responsibility for the earth as a common resource, and we all must work together to maintain it. It is a shared resource that represents a **global commons**, a natural asset of the earth that is available to all. Clean air, a healthy environment, and access to the oceans and outer space all fall into this category. But sharing this global commons requires that all people must use it in a responsible way to protect not only their individual interests but those of future generations as well.

Ecologist Garrett Hardin captured the tension between individual interests and shared resources in his famous essay, "The Tragedy of the Commons," first published in *Science* magazine in 1968.[2] Hardin posed a hypothetical scene in which a village of herdsmen shares a common

pasture for grazing their sheep. If each herdsman adds a sheep, he alone will benefit from future sales, but the costs of grazing for that sheep will be shared by all. An individual herdsman will add sheep, because he does not feel the negative effects by himself. The benefits to him are great, but everyone shares the negative impacts, so they are not as great on an individual level. The incentive then would be for each herdsman to increase his personal flock at the expense of the others. The ultimate result, however, would be overgrazing of the commons until there was nothing left and hence, the tragedy of the commons. Hardin concludes his assessment with the sobering truth that following this logic will result in ruin: "Ruin is the destination toward which all men rush, each pursuing his own best interest in a society that believes in the freedom of the commons. Freedom in a commons brings ruin to all."[3] In the real world, we see the potential for devastation all the time in terms of finite resources, population pressures, and pollution, to name just a few examples.

The problem of the tragedy of the commons helps us focus on the issue of **sustainable development**. The term *sustainable development* can be traced back to the World Commission on Environment and Development, better known as the Bruntland Commission, convened by the United Nations General Assembly in 1983 to address growing concerns about the deterioration of the environment as a consequence of economic and social development.[4] The Commission's 1987 report, *Our Common Future,* would provide what has become the most widely used definition of sustainable development: "Development that meets the needs of the present without compromising the ability of future generations to meet their own needs."[5]

This familiar NASA image is the most requested photo of the earth, depicting it as a watery blue marble floating alone in a sea of space. Viewed this way, it is easy to see how important stewardship of our global commons is for our mutual well-being. In this chapter we will explore a variety of other ways of looking at and understanding the earth—the starting point for our journey.

global commons
a natural asset of the earth that is available to all.

sustainable development
"Development that meets the needs of the present without compromising the ability of future generations to meet their own needs," as defined by the World Commission on Environment and Development.

How this concept has been addressed globally is critical to our understanding of the borders that must be crossed. This chapter explores our connection to earth as the starting point of our journey toward understanding international studies. First, the study of geography will be introduced as a way to understand the earth and the ways in which it is depicted through maps. Geography is the basis for our understanding of the planet. Human settlements are elementary units for us to understand ourselves. There are reasons why settlements spring up in some areas but not in others, or why some flourish and some do not, and underlying those reasons is geography. Some of the critical challenges that threaten our global well-being will then be examined: settlement patterns, population growth, food production, energy, and climate change. Finally, we will give you some ideas about what you can do to sustain the earth for future generations.

GETTING OUR HEADS AROUND THE EARTH: GEOGRAPHY AS A FIELD OF STUDY

Viewed from space, the earth appears as a physical mass marked by oceans, mountains, deserts, rivers, forests, and fields. From this perspective, it appears static, when in fact it is not. Over the course of time, the borders that have differentiated this mass have been changed by natural events, from continental drift thousands of years ago to more recent hurricanes, wildfires, earthquakes, tsunamis, droughts, and floods. The earth's physical attributes, such as where arable land or mineral riches or waterways are located, have to a large extent determined where people have settled and what they do. The fundamental challenge of **geography** has been that there is no one place that any of us can stand on the planet in order to observe the whole thing at once. It is also nearly impossible for any one person to conceive of all of the ways people are connected to one another and to the planet. Our image of what the earth as a whole even looks like has changed radically over time and has been profoundly shaped by technological developments.

geography
the study of the earth and its characteristics.

Scholarly attempts to understand the world in a meaningful way date back to the earliest philosophers. For starters, we owe the word *geography* to Greek scholar Eratosthenes, who was born about 275 BCE. Eratosthenes was very interested in writing and learning about the earth, and the term he coined for this activity came from the Greek language—*geo* meaning earth and *graphos* meaning description.[6] His greatest accomplishment in this regard was the first scientific calculation of the circumference of the earth based on his observations of the sun.

One of the earliest scholars whose impressions had lasting effects was Claudius Ptolemy. Born sometime late in the first century CE, Ptolemy was of Greek origin but lived in Alexandria, Egypt. Two of the major texts he produced, *Geography* and

Almagest, were efforts to map the world in a system of degrees that measured distances from the equator.[7] Relying on limited knowledge of the world, Ptolemy created a map that introduced the concepts of latitude and longitude. While his calculations were off and much of the world was not known to him at the time, his contribution to measurement was significant and enduring.

The modern discipline of geography developed many years later in the mid-1800s. Alexander von Humboldt (1769–1859) was a German naturalist who is often called the "father of modern geography" for his contributions not only to an understanding of the physical world but to the relationship of humans to their environment as well.[8] His great work, *Cosmos,* was a multivolume examination of nature that included some of the first systematic observations about climate and its relationship to geography. Juxtaposing a review of ancient writings about the natural universe with the technologies emerging during his time, von Humboldt sought a scientific way to understand the earth.

> There dwells an irresistible charm, venerated by all antiquity, in the contemplation of mathematical truths—in the everlasting revelations of time and space, as they reveal themselves in tones, numbers, and lines. The improvement of an intellectual instrument of research—analysis—has powerfully accelerated the reciprocal fructification of ideas, which is no less important than the rich abundance of their creations. It has opened to the physical contemplation of the universe new spheres of immeasurable extent in the terrestrial and celestial regions of space, revealed both in the periodic fluctuations of the ocean and in the varying perturbations of the planets.[9]

IN THEIR OWN WORDS   **Alexander von Humboldt**

Today the discipline of geography is generally divided into two branches: physical and human geography. **Physical geography** refers to the study of the earth and its resources. **Human geography** refers to how humans interface with the physical environment and how political, economic, social, and cultural factors influence these connections.

The study of maps or **cartography** refers to how both these physical and human borders are depicted. They can show **topography**—any of the earth's physical features, including mountains, rivers, lakes, and streams and their relationships to one another in terms of location and elevation. They can also depict political borders, which are frequently influenced by topography but fundamentally drawn by people to serve political interests. Many modern states, for example, are the artificial constructs of former colonial powers and do not necessarily accommodate the diversity of interests and needs of their inhabitants. Another type of map can show economic distinctions, such as the location of resources and trade routes. Social and cultural division can also be depicted where ethnic and cultural identities overlap with political and economic borders. Even cooperation across borders can be mapped in terms of regional and international organizations. The following maps illustrate these distinctions.

physical geography
the study of the earth and its resources.

human geography
the study of the way that humans interface with the physical environment and how political, economic, social, and cultural factors influence these connections.

cartography
the depiction of physical and human-made borders.

topography
the depiction of earth's physical features and their relationships to one another in terms of location and elevation.

MAP
2.1 **CHINA: ONE COUNTRY, MANY VIEWS**

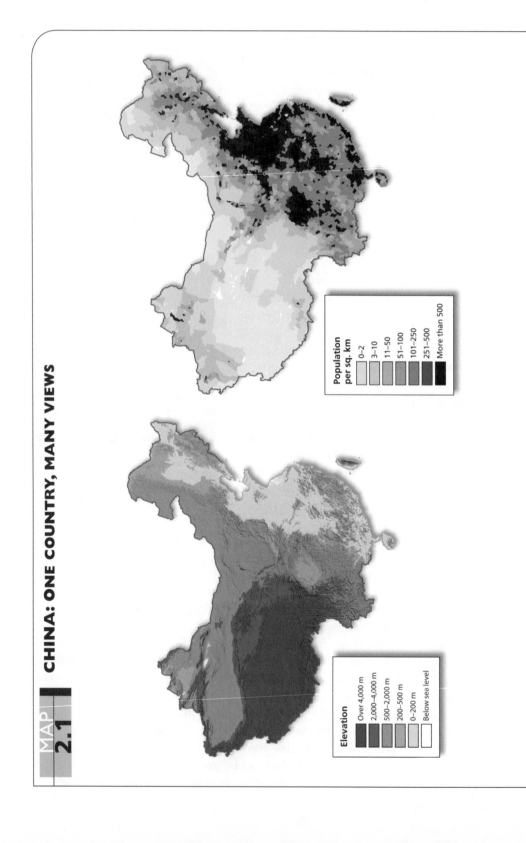

**Population
per sq. km**

0–2
3–10
11–50
51–100
101–250
251–500
More than 500

Elevation

Over 4,000 m
2,000–4,000 m
500–2,000 m
200–500 m
0–200 m
Below sea level

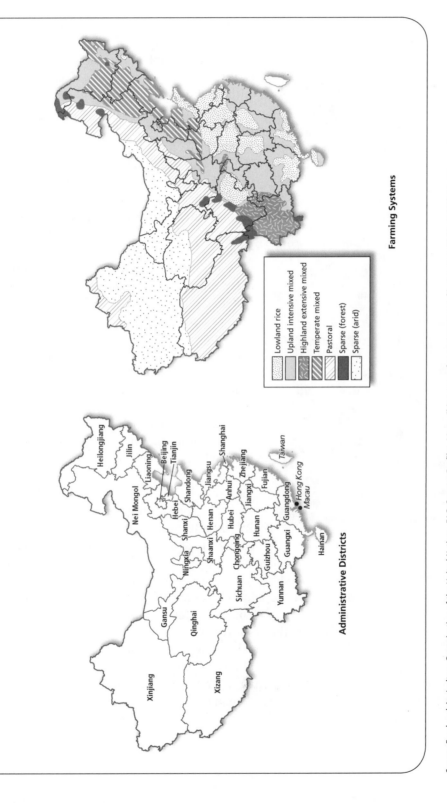

Farming Systems

Lowland rice
Upland intensive mixed
Highland extensive mixed
Temperate mixed
Pastoral
Sparse (forest)
Sparse (arid)

Heilongjiang
Jilin
Nei Mongol
Beijing
Tianjin
Liaoning
Hebei
Shandong
Jiangsu
Shanghai
Shanxi
Henan
Anhui
Zhejiang
Ningxia
Shaanxi
Hubei
Jiangxi
Fujian
Gansu
Chongqing
Hunan
Guangdong
Hong Kong
Macau
Qinghai
Sichuan
Guizhou
Guangxi
Xinjiang
Yunnan
Hainan
Xizang
Taiwan

Administrative Districts

Source: Food and Agriculture Organization of the United Nations, FAO Country Profiles, Maps, China, www.fao.org/countryprofiles/maps.asp?is03=CHN&lang=en.

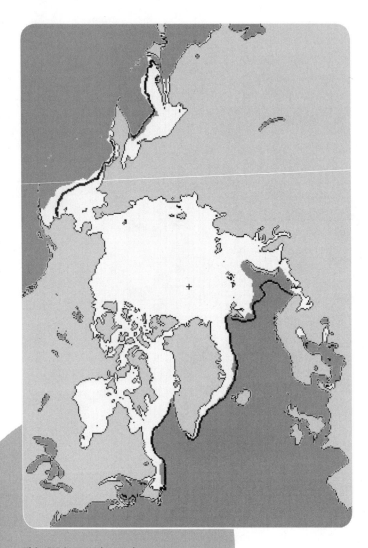

This GIS image shows the extent of Arctic sea ice in April 2012, at which time it covered 14.73 million square kilometers. The black line shows the 1979 to 2000 median extent for April. The black cross in the center of the ice field is the geographic North Pole.

Modern technologies have changed the field of geography and how mapping occurs. Geographic information systems (GIS) combine the power of computers with satellite imagery to produce new ways of understanding spatial relationships and include new technologies such as Google Earth and global positioning systems (GPS). These technologies are able to utilize different kinds of information about geography, from physical dimensions to human interventions, to track changes in the environment.[10] As a result, they are able to give a much more comprehensive view of the earth and the changes taking place today than was available before these systems were put into use. This is particularly critical in understanding some of the challenges we face. For example, the National Snow and Ice Data Center has used Google Earth to track changes in the polar ice cap over time.[11] Countries are also using GIS technology for more strategic purposes that include pinpointing the location of military installations, potential improvised explosive devices (IEDs), or even the whereabouts of suspected terrorists.

Technological innovation and our ability to better understand the world around us has made us more sensitive to the finite nature of the planet on which we live. This capacity to know more has also led us to be more conscious of the challenges that can affect everyone and are not specific to any one area on the globe. The earth is a finite resource, and the charge must be to extract and utilize the resources we need to sustain our lives while not inflicting undue harm that might threaten the sustainability of the planet itself. The historical record suggests that we have not done a particularly good job in managing these resources. The following sections address some of the challenges of managing resources and how they have been handled.

CHALLENGES TO THE PLANET: WHERE WE LIVE

As a starting point, it is important to understand that where people settle is not always a choice made freely. In that sense, the borders that shape where we live are human-made. People can be displaced by conflict and forced to flee their homes. They may have few or no options as to where they resettle and under what terms and circumstances, and they may end up having to live in inhospitable environments. Large refugee tent cities can grow up overnight in response to violence and sometimes continue to exist for years. For example, the world's largest refugee camp, Dadaab in Kenya, is run by the United Nations (UN). It has supported those fleeing violence in Somalia for 20 years, but it is now running out of room.[12] People in these camps are susceptible to natural dangers ranging from wild animals attacking small children who have invaded their environment to flooding from the annual rains. The temperatures in this area can soar well above 100 degrees, and the camps offer the only hope for shelter, food, and water.

Economic pressures can also lead people to relocate to areas where they can find work but where human habitation is not sustainable over time. People lose their jobs and have to find alternative employment. They move to areas, often along borders, where factories have been built. Shanty towns are constructed with homes built from cardboard and any other spare materials that can be found. People are overcrowded in these areas, and there is often no electricity, no running water, and no way to manage sewage and waste. The result is a systematic degradation of the environment fostered by the need to meet the challenges of competition.

> **HOW DO YOU CONNECT?**
>
> **WHAT TYPE OF MAPS DO YOU USE?**
>
> a. traditional maps
> b. Google Maps or other map service
> c. GPS in your car
> d. GPS on your phone

A view of just a small section of the Dadaab refugee camp in Kenya, currently home to 450,000 refugees, the majority of them from Somalia. According to the World Food Program, around 75,000 people have arrived since June 2011, fleeing the famine in the south of the country. In 2010, the UN refugee agency, the UN High Commission on Refugees (UNHCR), estimated that 43.3 million people had been displaced by force throughout the world.

HOW DO YOU CONNECT? | **WHERE HAVE YOU BEEN?**

How many countries have you been to?

a. I have never traveled outside of my home country.

b. 1–3 countries

c. 4–6 countries

d. 7 or more

Have you ever lived in a country other than your own?

If you could go to any country right now, where would you go?

Living and working in this environment can further deepen and aggravate social and cultural divisions. While those who move to cities for work frequently have rising expectations about their futures, they may easily find themselves relegated to marginal status. Particularly in many of the world's lesser developed countries, poverty is persistent, and the success that was so eagerly anticipated often goes unrealized. These conditions can last for generations, as there is no easy way out.

WILL POPULATION EXCEED CAPACITY?

One of the underlying factors in perpetuating this uneven development has been the rapid growth of the world's population. As more and more people come to inhabit the planet, protecting and managing shared resources will become even more challenging. Burgeoning populations are consuming natural resources at unprecedented rates. As a result, there is a delicate balance with the environment that must be considered. Whether intentional or not, the actions of this growing population have significantly impacted the earth, from the destruction of natural habitats and extinction of animal and plant life to the pollution of the atmosphere.

To put this growth in perspective, in one hour, the population on earth increases by 8,726 people. In just one minute, it increases by 145 new inhabitants with a growth rate of 2.4 people per second.[13] It is important to note that population growth is uneven such that the more significant increases often occur in those regions or countries that are least able to provide for it. The vast majority of global population growth, roughly 97 percent, is coming from Africa, Asia, the Middle East, and Latin America.[14] Table 2.1 shows the most populous countries in 2010 and their projected growth by 2050. In 2010, the top 10 account for 58.7 percent of total world population; it is estimated they will account for 53.5 percent in 2050.

What are the factors that affect these disparities? There are several that can be examined. One of the most frequently cited is education. For example, in the largest, least educated and most populous Indian state of Uttar Pradesh, the proportion of women using birth control is less than 30 percent, where the national average is 48.5 percent. Moreover, the average woman in this region will bear up to four children and be challenged to feed them.[15] Despite general declines in the overall birth rates for India, from six children per family to three, the population still grew by 1.4 percent over the last five years, and it is anticipated that India will surpass China in population by 2050.[16] Cultural values also continue to push births in the area, as the desire for a boy is great, and rural parents are still influenced by the need for large families to support them. Table 2.2 indicates where the greatest growth in population is occurring—primarily in sub-Saharan Africa, as seen below—by measuring crude birth rate, which is commonly the most dominant factor in determining population growth rates.

China has taken an interesting path in addressing this issue through its governmental policy of one child per family. Only those families living in rural areas are allowed to have more children to support their agricultural needs. There has been considerable criticism of this policy by human rights activists due to the limits it places on individual choice, as well as the unintended consequences that have occurred. Female babies are abandoned or even killed by Chinese parents who, like those in India, want a boy. This prioritization has resulted in a disproportionate number of males, which has both practical and political consequences. Many young Chinese men have difficulty finding wives, are underemployed, and often feel alienated from society. As a result, they are seen as a potential source of political opposition by the government.

These trends have additional implications. In China, families traditionally cared for their aging parents. Now there is a shortage of care providers due to an aging population and the strict controls that have been placed on reproduction. The number of Chinese people over age 65 is expected to triple by 2050, and the mechanisms for their care simply do not exist.[17] In contrast, many developing countries find themselves coping with a population that is very young. The median age in Afghanistan is 18, and in Somalia it is just 17; in contrast, it is almost 37 in the United States and 40 in the UK.[18] The political unrest in the Middle East in the spring

| TABLE 2.1 | THE WORLD'S MOST POPULOUS COUNTRIES |

		2010	Projected, 2050
1.	China	1,330,141,295	1,303,723,332
2.	India	1,173,108,018	1,656,553,632
3.	United States	310,232,863	439,010,253
4.	Indonesia	242,968,342	313,020,847
5.	Brazil	201,103,330	260,692,493
6.	Pakistan	184,404,791	276,428,758
7.	Bangladesh	156,118,464	233,587,279
8.	Nigeria	152,217,341	264,262,405
9.	Russia	139,390,205	109,187,353
10.	Japan	126,804,433	93,673,826
Top 10 Countries		4,016,489,082	4,950,140,178
TOTAL WORLD		6,845,609,960	9,256,342,700

Source: Data are from internetworldstats.com, with data from US Census Bureau, www.internetworldstats.com/stats8.htm.

| TABLE 2.2 | COUNTRIES WITH LEADING POPULATION GROWTH RATES, 2011 |

		Births/1000 Population
1.	Niger	50.54
2.	Uganda	47.49
3.	Mali	45.62
4.	Zambia	44.08
5.	Burkina Faso	43.59
6.	Ethiopia	42.99
7.	Angola	42.91
8.	Somalia	42.71
9.	Burundi	41.01
10.	Malawi	40.85

Source: nationmaster.com, with data from CIA World Factbook 2011, www.nationmaster.com/graph/peo_bir_rat-people-birth-rate.

of 2011 was led by youth, who represent a significant demographic shift. They are a new generation that has found innovative ways to communicate and bring about change.

WHAT ARE THE CHALLENGES? THE POTENTIAL FOR TRAGEDY

carrying capacity
earth's ability to meet the needs of its population.

Can the earth adequately provide for this growing population? Human efforts to sustain ourselves and to develop and progress have strained the earth's **carrying capacity**. In other words, our needs have placed considerable strain on the world's ecosystems, thereby threatening the global commons and suggesting the possibility of a potential tragedy as envisioned by Hardin.

Too Little Food, and Too Many Mouths to Feed

First and foremost, it is important to recognize that people require access to sufficient amounts of food and clean water to ensure their survival. This is the most basic physiological need of humans, as noted by psychologist Abraham Maslow when he delineated his hierarchy of needs in the 1940s. While Maslow identified five levels of needs (to be discussed more thoroughly in Chapter 11), critical to the point here is that the first level was the most basic—the need for food and water. Only once these bodily needs are met can people move up the pyramid to assure safety, belonging, esteem, and ultimately self-actualization.[19] Therefore, sustenance is critical to development, and the ability to produce enough food to provide for a growing population while protecting the environment poses great challenges.

The idea that population could exceed food supply is not new. Thomas Malthus (1766–1834), an English economist who was very interested in demographics, wrote of this possibility in his work, "An Essay on the Principle of Population," first published anonymously in 1798 and later revised to include more detail. Malthus speculated that the growth of the world's population would be geometrical compared to the production of food, which could only increase arithmetically.[20] This notion is referred to as the **Malthusian dilemma**. More recent interpretations have suggested that, in today's terms, what Malthus's prediction might mean is a population of over nine billion people by the year

HOW DO YOU CONNECT?	**HOW MANY SIBLINGS DO YOU HAVE?**
a. none	c. 3–4
b. 1–2	d. 5 or more

2050 with agricultural resources significantly short of being able to provide for them.[21] There is simply not enough arable land to meet that need, according to Columbia University's Earth Institute, and even the best efforts could not recover lands that have been devastated by deforestation to allow for adequate agricultural production.

Malthusian dilemma
the conflict inherent in the idea that the growth of the world's population increases geometrically whereas the production of food can only increase arithmetically.

Appropriate use of the land is critical. Specifically, the production of food is closely related to geographic changes taking place, both natural and human-made. For example, natural disasters—from forest fires to drought—that destroy crops and render lands unviable are just one impediment to the production of food resources adequate to address the growing population. Environmental degradation through the overuse of arable land and fertilizers also has a negative effect. Nor are the challenges limited to production. The availability of food can also be impacted by war due to the disruption of supply and distribution lines. Together, these factors play a considerable role in influencing both the price and safety of our food. A closer look sheds light on these concerns.

Despite Malthus's forecast, food production has increased over time, but the ability to feed a growing population has been undermined by other factors. The use of pesticides and certain chemicals designed to increase crop yields over the short term, for example, can have longer-term adverse effects on the soil. The greatest need for food is in developing countries. Current figures suggest that of the 850 million people in the world suffering from hunger, nearly 840 million are living in these areas. India (224.6 million) and China (129.6 million) are the countries with the largest numbers of people affected.[22] Countries facing these conditions are not able to produce enough food or adequately distribute food provided to them from other sources. Natural conditions such as drought may exacerbate the situation, as does the need evident in some cases to earn money through exporting much of the food that is produced locally. For example, the African country of Lesotho suffered from heavy rains in 2010 and 2011, resulting in a large decline in its production of cereal, a major source of food for the area.[23] In contrast, severe drought in Somalia has left over three million people in need of food assistance.[24]

Internally displaced Somali children line up to receive food aid at a food distribution center in Mogadishu, Somalia. The center is run by a Somalia-based nongovernmental organization called SAACID (Somali for "to help") and is funded by the United Nations World Food Programme in Somalia.

Hunger is not simply about having enough food, it is also about nutrition. Those who endure hunger may not be starving but are suffering from undernourishment. Ultimately, the impact can be devastating and can result in death. The Food and Agriculture Organization of the United Nations (FAO), which monitors global food issues, refers to this condition as **food insecurity** and defines it as "a situation that exists when people lack secure access to sufficient amounts of safe and nutritious food for normal growth and development and an active and healthy life."[25] It is estimated that chronic undernourishment and the lack of vitamins and minerals that result from it contribute to more than five million child deaths annually. Undernourishment is defined as dietary energy consumption that is continuously below the minimum dietary energy requirement for maintaining a healthy lifestyle. Table 2.3 identifies those countries with the greatest percentage of their populations suffering from undernourishment.

Why not just send food to those in need? There are many efforts to provide food aid, coordinated by both governmental and nongovernmental entities. Internationally, the United Nations World Food Programme (WFP) is a key actor in emergency food aid response. While welcomed, this aid is frequently hard to get to the people who need it most. Deliverability is limited by many factors. Perhaps one of the greatest inhibitors is conflict. The safe transportation and distribution of food in countries ravaged by conflict can be almost impossible due to the lines of battle or even the logistics of navigating often vastly overcrowded refugee camps. This situation is particularly problematic in sub-Saharan Africa. Due to ongoing civil conflict in Darfur, for example, it is estimated that Sudan needs food aid for almost six million people. Chad hosts large numbers of refugees from Sudan and Central African Republic (over 350,000) but is without the food to feed them. Similarly large numbers of refugees in Congo, Ivory Coast, and Democratic Republic of the Congo require food assistance.[26]

The total amount of food aid (in terms of annual tonnage) has fallen steadily over the past decade. Table 2.4 indicates the top 10 countries that accepted food aid in 2010; they accounted for nearly 70 percent of total food aid in that year. Five major donors contributed to approximately 75 percent of food aid deliveries (US, Japan, European Commission, Canada, and UK). Emergency food aid is the most significant category, accounting for 73 percent of total deliveries.

Cost is also a factor in limiting the supply of food to those in need. Food is a primary commodity, and

TABLE 2.3	THE WORLD'S MOST UNDERNOURISHED POPULATIONS, 2005–2007	
		Undernourished Population, by Percent
1.	Democratic Republic of the Congo	69%
2.	Eritrea	64%
3.	Burundi	62%
4.	Haiti	57%
5.	Comoros	46%
6.	Zambia	43%
7.	Angola	41%
8.	Ethiopia	41%
9.	Central African Republic	40%
10.	Mozambique	38%

Source: "Food Security Data and Definitions," United Nations Food and Agriculture Organization, www.fao.org/economic/ess/ess-fs/fs-data/ess-fadata/en/.

commodity prices can vary widely. They are often not regulated in the same way as industrial goods. The FAO has reported a significant increase in costs over time. More recently, prices spiked in 2008 due to the global financial crisis and again to even higher levels in 2011.[27] Growing demand, coupled with production limitations and increasing levels of investor speculation in commodities markets to offset low interest rates, have pushed prices upward. Figure 2.1 documents these trends in food prices.

There are many ways to address these issues, most notably through international organizations like the FAO and the World Trade Organization (WTO). The FAO monitors food prices internationally and develops multiple paths to address hunger issues. The WTO has also addressed agricultural prices and the stability of the food supply over the course of many years but with little effect.[28] Agriculture has been an issue on the agenda of various rounds of WTO negotiations over the years but with little progress due to the highly politicized nature of these concerns, particularly those relating to the rights of governments to subsidize their farmers and to manage production in ways that maintain higher prices for their food-related exports.

Scientifically, there are efforts to be more effective in food production through utilization of genetically modified organisms (GMOs). The idea here is to use modern biotechnology for greater agricultural productivity. Crops can be made more resistant to pests and more nutritious through genetic manipulation. The fear about this modification, however, is that it may undermine natural biological processes and have a long-term harmful effect.[29]

TABLE 2.4	THE WORLD'S LEADING FOOD AID RECIPIENTS, 2010		
		Metric Tons	*Percent of Total*
1.	Ethiopia	1,415,454	24.9%
2.	Pakistan	763,436	13.4%
3.	Sudan	475,532	8.4%
4.	Haiti	266,237	4.7%
5.	Kenya	258,069	4.5%
6.	Bangladesh	193,805	3.4%
7.	Congo, DR	192,914	3.4%
8.	Niger	158,675	2.8%
9.	Afghanistan	139,883	2.5%
10.	Chad	110,982	2.0%
	TOTAL	5,682,070	100.0%

Source: "Food Aid Flows 2010 Report," United Nations World Food Programme, www.wfp.org/content/food-aid-flows-2010-report.

Unsustainable Energy Sources: Burning the Candle at Both Ends

Beyond the need for food and some of the consequences of efforts and activities in this regard, the earth is also being compromised by lifestyle and consumption choices. The use of energy offers an important example of the dilemma. One of the key components of sustainable development is that it does no harm to future generations. The global demand for coal, oil, and other nonrenewable

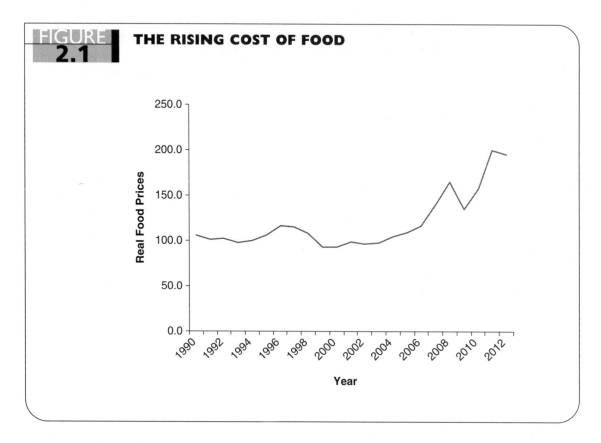

FIGURE 2.1   **THE RISING COST OF FOOD**

Source: Data are from FAO's food price index, www.fao.org/worldfoodsituation/wfs-home/foodpricesindex/en/.

Note: The FAO food price index is a measure of the monthly change in international prices of a basket of food commodities. It consists of the average of five commodity group price indices (representing 55 quotations), weighted with the average export shares of each of the groups for 2002–2004.

sources of energy taxes the environment and calls attention to the fragile nature of the world's resources.

Persistent demands for economic development have exacerbated this problem as the need for energy continues to grow. The world has relied extensively on oil for its industrial development, but the oil supply is limited. One alternative has been the development of nuclear energy. Although it was once popular with the United States, Japan, and parts of Europe as a source of cleaner and more efficient energy, there have always been concerns about its safety and potentially severe or even catastrophic human and environmental impacts. Among the more notable examples of the possible consequences were the nuclear plant meltdowns in the United States at Three Mile Island in Pennsylvania in 1979 and the far more serious malfunctions in Ukraine at Chernobyl in 1986, which had severe health implications for thousands of inhabitants and rendered a significant amount of surrounding land unusable and uninhabitable due to contamination. The more recent meltdowns in Japan resulting from the 2011 tsunami, however, may prove to be an important watershed in terms of support for the nuclear energy option, due to concern over the limits of efforts to ensure the safety of these production facilities. Not long after the Japanese tragedy, Germany announced that it would severely curtail its nuclear energy activities and move to phase out nuclear energy production by 2022. A number of other countries have indicated that they may follow suit.

Energy disasters are not limited to the nuclear arena and can affect both air and water supplies as well. The harvesting of natural resources for energy has had its own set of challenges and disasters. A gas plant leak in Bhopal, India, in 1984 killed 3,800 people and sickened several thousand.[30] The more recent explosion on the BP Deepwater Horizon oil rig in the Gulf of Mexico in 2010 killed 11 workers and resulted in roughly five million barrels of oil spilled into the water.

HOW DO YOU CONNECT? | **WHAT DO YOU EAT?**

Have you ever grown your own food?

   a. Yes, my garden is my main source of vegetables.

   b. Yes, I plant a few herbs.

   c. no

Where do you shop for your food?

   a. local grocery store

   b. local wholesale store

   c. local superstore

   d. specialty markets

   e. farmer's market

How many times do you go to the grocery store a week?

   a. once

   b. twice

   c. three or more times

How much of your food is fresh, and how much of it is packaged?

   a. almost all fresh

   b. half fresh, half packaged

   c. mostly packaged

Do you buy organic foods?

   a. Yes, I buy organic fresh and packaged foods.

   b. Yes, I buy organic fresh foods such as vegetables.

   c. Yes, I buy organic packaged foods.

   d. No, I don't buy organic.

THE HUMAN FACTOR: CONTRIBUTING TO THE TRAGEDY

In our efforts to sustain ourselves and to provide for our basic needs, we have both purposefully and inadvertently contributed to the fouling of our environment. Among the more significant ways this destruction has occurred has been through the progressive depletion of our rainforests, the desertification of

A large ship sits among rubble after it was hit by a tsunami in Kesennuma, northeastern Japan, on Saturday March 12, 2011, one day after a giant quake and tsunami struck the country's northeastern coast. The tsunami also caused massive, albeit less visible, damage to nuclear reactors in Fukushima, Japan, prompting the government shutdown of all 50 of the country's nuclear facilities until full safety checks could be completed.

arable land, the pollution of our water supply, and the compromising of our air quality. Perhaps the greatest of these impacts is in the area of global warming and the subsequent climate changes that are occurring around the world. A closer look at these actions illustrates their effect.

It is estimated that every hour, 4,500 acres of tropical forest are plowed, burned, or cut down.[31] Population growth has contributed significantly to this loss of trees, as the clearing of forests provides opportunities for cultivating crops and grazing animals. The activities of commercial logging companies seeking to capitalize on the worldwide demand for timber have also added to this devastation. The consequences are significant, not only for the destruction of the land but also the wildlife that resides there. Perhaps most important, trees play a critical role in maintaining the balance of the ecosystem by storing carbon. Removal of trees releases carbon, thereby contributing to global warming and climate change. While the rate of deforestation is slowing down, it is still considered by the FAO to be alarmingly high, with losses of approximately 5.2 million hectares per year over the past decade, and the biggest damage in tropical regions. Table 2.5 identifies these declines by region.

A related consequence of human activities changing the landscape is desertification. Desertification is degradation of land in "arid, semi-arid and dry sub-humid areas" that is the result of variations in the climate and human activities.[32] It is estimated that a third of the earth's land surface is threatened, affecting more than 250 million people and putting another one billion at risk. Many of these people are among the world's poorest. The results of desertification are less food production, increased downstream flooding, and reduced water quality. In Africa alone, 36 countries are affected, and an estimated 75 percent of the continent's farmland has lost capacity for growing crops.

Similar problems exist for water, perhaps the most critical resource for human survival. Estimates suggest that globally, 884 million people lack access to safe

| TABLE 2.5 | THE WORLD'S FOREST AREAS, ANNUAL CHANGE 1990–2010 |

	Percentage of World Total	Change* 1990–2000	Percentage Change, 1990–2000	Change* 2000–2010	Percentage Change, 2000–2010
Africa	16.7%	–4,067	–0.56%	–3,414	–0.49%
Asia/Pacific	18.3%	–703	–0.10%	1,404	0.19%
Europe	24.9%	877	0.09%	676	0.07%
Latin America & Caribbean	22.0%	–4,534	–0.47%	–4,195	–0.46%
Near East	3.0%	–518	–0.42%	90	0.07%
North America	16.8%	32	0.01%	188	0.03%
TOTAL WORLD	100.0%	–8,334	–0.20%	–5,216	–0.13%

*All figures in these columns are in thousands of hectares.

Source: "State of the World's Forests 2011," 3–25, Food and Agriculture Organization of the United Nations, www
.fao.org/docrep/013/i2000e/i2000e.pdf.

water supplies, and 3.58 million people die each year from water-related disease.[33] As noted earlier, the quest for energy resources has frequently fouled water sources through oil spills and nuclear tragedies. Human activity has contributed to this pollution, from bodies of water being used as waste disposal sites for animals and trash to runoffs from agriculture and industry that bring toxic pollutants into the water supply. As a result, fresh water is becoming scarcer. At times, the competition for access to this water becomes highly politicized. In the Middle East, for example, some have suggested that future conflict may be as much about access to water as it is about competing claims to the land.

Human activity has also damaged the atmosphere, perhaps irreparably. Air pollution from industrial output and the burning of fossil fuels combined with the devastation of the rainforest, which naturally absorbs carbon emissions, has resulted in a situation commonly referred to as the **greenhouse effect**. While the release of greenhouse gasses—that is, gasses that trap heat in the atmosphere[34]—occurs naturally, the amount of these gasses in the atmosphere has expanded significantly due to the burning of fossil fuels. As a result, the average temperature of the earth has increased. From 1990 to 2003, the average temperature increased 1.31 degrees Fahrenheit, and another increase

greenhouse effect
the rise in the earth's temperature due to greenhouse gases that trap heat in the atmosphere.

of 1.41 degrees occurred between 2004 and 2008.[35] The effects are most evident in what has been termed *global warming*. For many years a highly contentious and controversial subject due to the unwillingness of some scientists and politicians to acknowledge its existence, global warming stems largely from the large-scale emissions of carbon dioxide and other greenhouse gasses into the atmosphere. Table 2.6 identifies the largest carbon dioxide emitters in 2009.

THE GLOBAL RESPONSE

There has been an array of international efforts to address these issues, beginning with the Earth Summit in 1992. Organized by the UN Conference on Environment and Development in Rio de Janeiro, this meeting brought together both governmental and nongovernmental actors in the largest gathering ever held on global environmental issues to adopt guiding policies that would slow down and perhaps someday eliminate pollution of the earth. Subsequent meetings would seek further agreements, such as the Kyoto Protocols developed in 1997 that included specific guidelines for greenhouse gas emissions.

Delegates met in Copenhagen, Denmark, in December 2009 to move forward a more aggressive agenda. Perhaps most significant, the gathering went beyond the debate over whether global warming is occurring. While consensus was reached on limiting global warming to 3.5 degrees Fahrenheit above pre–Industrial Revolution levels, the final accord remained vague in terms of committing individual countries to specific targets or legally binding timetables.[36]

In all of these meetings, there has not been complete agreement due to the conflicting interests of the participating nation-states and the tension among them. Ultimately, what states will agree to may be far from the broad sweeping actions needed to significantly reduce current trends. The following *CQ Researcher* Pro/Con demonstrates these tensions.

TABLE 2.6 — THE WORLD'S LARGEST CARBON DIOXIDE EMITTERS, 2009*

		Million Metric Tons	Percentage of Total
1.	China	7,706.8	25.4%
2.	United States	5,424.5	17.9%
3.	India	1,591.1	5.3%
4.	Russia	1,556.7	5.1%
5.	Japan	1,097.9	3.6%
	TOP FIVE TOTAL	17,377.0	57.3%
	WORLD TOTAL	30,313.2	100.0%

*Includes carbon dioxide emissions from consumption of petroleum, natural gas, and coal and from flaring of natural gas.

Source: "International Energy Statistics," US Energy Information Administration, www.eia.gov/cfapps/ipdbproject/IEDIndex3.cfm?tid=90&pid=44&aid=8.

PRO/CON

Is the Copenhagen Accord a meaningful step forward in halting climate change?

PRO	CON
Ban Ki-moon Secretary-General, United Nations. From opening remarks at press conference, UN Climate Change Conference, Copenhagen, December 19, 2009	**Nnimmo Bassey** Nnimmo Bassey, Chair, Friends of the Earth International. Written for *CQ Global Researcher*, February 2010

PRO

The Copenhagen Accord may not be everything that everyone hoped for. But this decision of the Conference of Parties is a new beginning, an essential beginning.

At the summit I convened in September, I laid out four benchmarks for success for this conference. We have achieved results on each.

- All countries have agreed to work toward a common, long-term goal to limit global temperature rise to below 2 degrees Celsius.
- Many governments have made important commitments to reduce or limit emissions.
- Countries have achieved significant progress on preserving forests.
- Countries have agreed to provide comprehensive support to the most vulnerable to cope with climate change.

The deal is backed by money and the means to deliver it. Up to $30 billion has been pledged for adaptation and mitigation. Countries have backed the goal of mobilizing $100 billion a year by 2020 for developing countries. We have convergence on transparency and an equitable global governance structure that addresses the needs of developing countries. The countries that stayed on the periphery of the Kyoto process are now at the heart of global climate action.

We have the foundation for the first truly global agreement that will limit and reduce greenhouse gas emission, support adaptation for the most vulnerable and launch a new era of green growth.

Going forward, we have three tasks. First, we need to turn this agreement into a legally binding treaty. I will work with world leaders over the coming months to make this happen. Second, we must launch the Copenhagen Green

(Continued on next page)

CON

The Copenhagen Accord is not a step forward in the battle to halt climate change. Few people expected the Copenhagen climate talks to yield a strong outcome. But the talks ended with a major failure that was worse than predicted: a "Copenhagen Accord" in which individual countries make no new serious commitments whatsoever.

The accord sets a too-weak goal of limiting warming to 2 degrees Celsius, but provides no means of achieving this goal. Likewise, it suggests an insufficient sum for addressing international solutions but contains no path to produce the funding. Individual countries are required to do nothing.

The accord fails the poor and the vulnerable communities most impacted by climate change. This non-agreement (it was merely "noted," not adopted, by the conference) is weak, non-binding and allows false solutions such as carbon offsetting. It will prove completely ineffective. Providing some coins for developing countries to mitigate climate change and adapt to it does not help if the sources of the problem remain unchecked.

The peoples' demands for climate justice should be the starting point when addressing the climate crisis. Instead, in Copenhagen, voices of the people were shut out and peaceful protests met brutal suppression. Inside the Bella Center, where the conference took place, many of the poor countries were shut out of back-room negotiations. The accord is the result of this anti-democratic process.

The basic demands of the climate justice movement remain unmet. The U.N. climate process must resume, and it must accomplish these goals:

- Industrialized countries must commit to at least 40 percent cuts in emissions by 2020 by using clean

(Continued on next page)

PRO/CON (Continued)
Is the Copenhagen Accord a meaningful step forward in halting climate change?

Pro	Con
Climate Fund. The U.N. system will work to ensure that it can immediately start to deliver immediate results to people in need and jump-start clean energy growth in developing countries. Third, we need to pursue the road of higher ambition. We must turn our back on the path of least resistance. Current mitigation commitments fail to meet the scientific bottom line. We still face serious consequences. So, while I am satisfied that we have a deal here in Copenhagen, I am aware that it is just the beginning. It will take more than this to definitively tackle climate change. But it is a step in the right direction.	energy, sustainable transport and farming and cutting energy demand. • Emission cuts must be real. They cannot be "achieved" by carbon offsetting, such as buying carbon credits from developing countries or by buying up forests in developing countries so they won't be cut down. • Rich countries must make concrete commitments to provide money for developing countries to grow in a clean way and to cope with the floods, droughts and famines caused by climate change. Funding must be adequate, not the minuscule amounts proposed in the accord. Wealthy nations are most responsible for climate change. They have an obligation to lead the way in solving the problem. They have not done so with the Copenhagen Accord.

Source: *Reed Karaim, "Climate Change," CQ Global Researcher 4, (2010): 25–50, http://library.cqpress.com/globalresearcher/.*

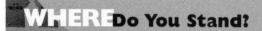

WHERE Do You Stand?

1. Is climate change an issue that pits rich countries against poor countries?
2. Is it possible for states to put aside their individual interests and come together to protect the environment?

While there have been efforts to protect the earth through international conferences and treaties, they have not been sufficient to mitigate these threats. As illustrated in the difficulty of gaining agreement in Copenhagen, there have often been difficult trade-offs. In June of 2012, the UN Conference on Sustainable Development met for the Rio+20 Conference to mark the twentieth anniversary of the 1992 Earth Summit. They renewed their commitment to a common vision in the closing outcome document, "The Future We Want." But many challenges remain. As the world's population increases, as countries in the Global South such as China and India grow economically, and as the pressures of maintaining the global economy increase, environmentally related pressures will persist. Without more directed activity to protect this global commons, we may find ourselves even further challenged to sustain ourselves.

WHAT CAN YOU DO?

Even if nation-states cannot gain agreement on how to address these issues, the interconnected nature of the environment necessitates that people recognize the global consequences of their personal actions. There has been considerable attention directed toward alternative and renewable energy resources since the oil crisis of the 1970s, when gas prices quadrupled due to the outbreak of war in the Middle East. These renewable sources include solar technologies, harnessing wind for energy production, and geothermal energy generated from the heat of the earth. Progress has been slow and sporadic due to the cost involved and the reluctance of governments and major energy consumers to absorb that cost. While somewhat greater progress has been evident with regard to conservation, impacts are just beginning to be felt and remain limited. Some examples of conservation include the use of appliances with Energy Star consumption ratings, hybrid automobiles that use both gas and electricity, and fluorescent and LED lightbulbs.

The success of these alternatives depends upon the choices we as individuals can make that will have a positive impact on the environment and its sustainability for future generations. Here are just a few examples of what you can do.

In regard to energy, you can see how well you are doing by calculating your **carbon footprint**. Carbon footprint is a measurement of the amount of greenhouse gases produced daily through the use of fossil fuels for electricity, heating/air conditioning, and transportation. The carbon footprint calculator shown in the screenshot above asks you about your use of natural resources to heat and cool your home, about how you get around town, and even about your food preferences to help you identify areas where you can reduce your impact on the global system.

Another way you can make a difference is to follow the three *Rs*—reduce, reuse, recycle. *Reduce* refers to the amount of waste you generate, particularly in terms of disposable goods that cannot be recycled. According to the US Environmental Protection Agency, between 1960 and 2009 in the United States alone, the amount of waste each person generated rose from 2.7 to 4.3 pounds per day![37] This is particularly problematic for waste that is not biodegradable. One of the most significant causes is the greater reliance on packaged goods. This trend is an even greater challenge for less developed countries that do not have waste disposal systems in place to manage this increased production. More and more, they find themselves buried in this waste with no place to dispose of it.

One area of tremendous concern in this regard is electronic waste. With anticipated sales of electronic products expected to rise significantly in Africa and Latin

---

This website, like numerous others, offers individuals and businesses an easy way to measure their impact on the environment by calculating their "carbon footprint."

Source: Carbon Footprint LTD website, www.carbonfootprint.com/calculator.aspx.

carbon footprint

a measurement of the amount of greenhouse gases produced daily through the use of fossil fuels for electricity, heating/air conditioning, and transportation.

HOW DO YOU CONNECT? | REDUCE, REUSE, RECYCLE

What kind of grocery bags do you use?

a. always reusable

b. reusable, but sometimes I forget them

c. plastic

d. paper

Do you recycle?

a. yes

b. no

What is your carbon footprint?

How do you get to school?

a. I drive myself.

b. I carpool with friends.

c. My parents take me.

d. I take the bus.

e. I walk.

f. I ride a bike.

How often do you travel using public transportation?

a. daily

b. a few times a week

c. a few times a month

d. a few times a year

e. never

Do you drink bottled water or tap water?

a. bottled water

b. tap water

Do you have a reusable water bottle?

a. Yes, and I use it.

b. Yes, but I never use it.

c. no

Do you use incandescent lights or fluorescent lights?

a. incandescent lights

b. fluorescent lights

America, as they already have in countries like India and China, the United Nations Environment Programme (UNEP) has raised concern about the hazards of e-waste disposal. In "Recycling—from E-Waste to Reduction," they report that in China, by the year 2020, e-waste from old computers will increase by 200 to 400 percent, and in India it will increase by up to 500 percent. By 2020, e-waste in the form of discarded mobile phones will be 7 times higher than 2007 levels in China, and in India, 18 times higher.[38] The significance of these developments is a proliferation of hazardous waste that can have not only serious environmental effects but health consequences as well. The UNEP report examines 11 vulnerable countries around the world and then offers examples of best practices to develop national recycling programs that can address these issues.

The second *R* stands for *reuse* as a way of reducing waste. The concept of reusable materials applies to salvaged goods from buildings that are torn down; these recycled goods are used to construct new buildings or are reused in other ways. For example, the nonprofit organization Habitat for Humanity has established ReStore resale outlets in the United States and Canada that take donated home improvement goods and resell them; the proceeds support the construction of Habitat homes in local communities.[39] Another example is playground safety surfaces that consist of rubber mulch made from recycled tires.

The success of these programs depends on the third *R*—recycle. Recycling allows materials that would otherwise be waste to be transformed into useable items. It can be as simple as putting a plastic water bottle or newspaper in a recycling bin or as complicated as purchasing goods made from recycled materials. It can include sharing with others through charitable donations of useable goods or simply swapping clothes with friends.

There is a challenge to recycling that occurs in developing countries, particularly among the urban poor—waste picking.[40] In poor urban centers, many people survive by salvaging recyclable goods from trash piles. One source suggests this is a way of life for as many as 15 million people, or 1 percent of the urban population in developing countries.[41] Particularly at risk are children who may be directly involved in this process. Brazil has undertaken a national campaign supported by the World Bank that provides health care and gives parents a cash credit if their children attend school. The money compensates for the revenue lost from not having the children picking the waste.

SOWhat? COMPOSTING IN INDIA

By Rozita Singh, Sustainable Development Graduate Student, New Delhi, India

Two years back, I watched a documentary called *Don't Rubbish It*, and little did I know that the 9-minute documentary would shape my 'interest area'—Solid Waste Management. A minute or so in the documentary was devoted to composting. It was then that I got to know about this lovely organization called Daily Dump in Bangalore (http://dailydump.org). The Director, Ms. Poonam Bir Kasturi, has designed a series of products suitable for household composting. I fell in love with the three-tier *khamba* model—it was beautiful, could be kept anywhere (veranda or balcony), and what I liked the most: It made composting so much more easier!

As part of British Council's Climate Champion Programme, I decided to take this up as my project. It is part of the National Action Project (NAP) and has been selected to receive a grant. I am a part of a group called Social Action Team under NAP and though my fellow climate champions are based in different cities, we have taken up waste management as our agenda and are working towards it simultaneously from different places.

As urbanization increases, the problem of mounting garbage in the cities increases. With land fast becoming a scarce commodity, how long can we depend on landfills? The idea is to promote the habit of segregation at the source among the urban households in New Delhi, India. The technique is aerobic composting using terracotta pots designed by the Daily Dump organization, which converts organic kitchen waste into manure in a very simple way. The intended outcome is to sensitize urban residents about the problem of increased solid waste generation and show them a sustainable solution to tackle the problem. Using the pots will decrease the pressure on existing landfills by offsetting the organic waste that currently constitutes roughly 60-70 percent of the total waste generated in an ideal household. My ultimate dream/mission is to convince the urban residents to adopt the practice of composting so that we handle our own waste responsibly.

I believe in the power of the "one"—the individual. As an eco-lover and Master's student of Sustainable Development Practice, I feel that I should emulate the teachings of sustainable living. Moreover, this project is the perfect example of the 3Rs (re-use, reduce and recycle). Turning your waste into compost is good for the environment and good for your soul. It is also a logical step because it doesn't make sense for organic waste to be sent to the landfill! On an average an urban Indian household generates 0.5 kg (1.1 lb.) of waste each day. When this mixed waste ends up in the landfill, it produces methane, a greenhouse gas. Do the calculation on how many emissions you can save by not sending this waste to the landfill, instead turning it into manure, which in turn could support green-belt development and develop carbon sinks.

If you would like to learn more, please visit me on my blog at http://come-n-post.blogspot.in/. Happy Composting!

What is clear from these observations is the interconnectedness of the environment and the responsibility everyone must share for it. Individual decisions will be an important first step, but a global response is really required. The need for sustainability and the reality that people are dependent on their physical environment to survive is critical. Technology links people around the world and offers ways to work together on these issues. The next chapter, on technology, allows us to jump start our trip across the other borders dividing the world today.

KEYConcepts

carbon footprint 45
carrying capacity 34
cartography 27
food insecurity 36
geography 26
global commons 26

greenhouse effect 41
human geography 27
Malthusian dilemma 35
physical geography 27
sustainable development 26
topography 27

TO LEARNMore

Books and Other Print Media

Al Gore, *An Inconvenient Truth: The Planetary Emergency of Global Warming and What We Can Do About It* (New York: Rodale, 2006).

Former vice president Al Gore's famous book and documentary trace the pattern of global warming and its consequences.

Dan Smith, *The Penguin State of the World Atlas*, 8th ed. (New York: Penguin Books, 2008).

Smith's book offers multiple ways of looking at the world through very different types of maps.

Marvin Soroos, "The Tragedy of the Commons in Global Perspective," in *The Global Agenda: Issues and Perspectives*, ed. Charles W. Kegley and Eugene Wittkopf (Boston, MA: McGraw Hill, 1998), 473–486.

In this article, Soroos connects the Tragedy of the Commons to global environmental issues.

R. Karaim, "Climate Change," *CQ Global Researcher* 4 (2010): 25–50, http://library .cqpress.com/globalresearcher.

This article looks at the science of climate change and its effects around the world.

Thomas L. Friedman, *Hot, Flat and Crowded: Why We Need a Green Revolution—and How It Can Renew America* (New York: Picador, 2009).

In this book, Friedman examines the global thirst for oil and its future environmental impact.

Websites

The Climate Hub, www.theclimatehub.com/.

This website hosts information about climate change, including information about the science and evidence behind climate change and interactive climate models and maps.

The Global Education Project, "Earth: A Graphic Look at the State of the World," www
.theglobaleducationproject.org/.

A Canadian NGO offering high quality graphics, with a section called "Earth" related
to environmental issues.

National Aeronautics and Space Administration, "Earth," www.nasa.gov/topics/earth/
index.html.

This website features data and information, including high-quality video, photos, and
maps of earth-related science topics, including many interactive features and other
visualization tools.

The United Nations Environment Programme, "GRID-Arendal," www.grida.no/.

Based in Norway, this is the UN's website to communicate information and data
about the environment. It features excellent data and maps.

The US Department of Agriculture, "Natural Resources Conservation Service," www
.nrcs.usda.gov/wps/portal/nrcs/main/national/home.

This service of the USDA features data and coverage of topics like land use, soils,
water, and air. It also houses many maps at http://soils.usda.gov/use/worldsoils/
mapindex/index.html showing natural and human effects on soil and land.

Videos

An Inconvenient Truth (2006).

Former vice president Al Gore argues the case that we've reached a tipping point in
climate change.

Chris Jordan Pictures Some Shocking Stats (2008).

Artist Chris Jordan shares his work depicting the unintentional environmental and
social effects of our unconscious behaviors. www.ted.com/talks/chris_jordan_
pictures_some_shocking_stats.html

The Lorax (2011).

An animated feature based on the book by Dr. Seuss (1972) that explores the impact
of overconsumption, environmental degradation, and personal responsibility.

Manufactured Landscapes (2006).

This award-winning documentary features the work of Ed Burtynsky, who traveled
throughout China and documented how humans have altered their landscapes,
bringing up questions of ethics and environmentalism.

Planet Earth (2006).

This Discovery Channel series features extensive coverage of all aspects of the
earth's nature.

Yann Arthus-Bertrand Captures Fragile Earth in Wide-Angle (2009).

French photographer and environmentalist Yann Arthus-Bertrand shares some of his
aerial photographs of the earth, depicting our relationship with changing ecosystems and
some startling facts and statistics about our impact on the environment. www.ted
.com/talks/lang/en/yann_arthus_bertrand_captures_fragile_earth_in_wide_angle.html

Jump Starting the Trip

The Role of Technology

CHAPTER 3

"I think the world is flat."

—American political commentator Thomas Friedman, 2005[1]

Nearly 500 years ago, in the course of circumnavigating the globe, Renaissance explorer Ferdinand Magellan demonstrated that the earth was round. He was part of a broader scientific and technological revolution that took place during that era, one that ultimately transformed the world. In this new era of technological revolution, Thomas Friedman has turned Magellan's observation on its head by proclaiming, paradoxically, that the world is flat. Friedman argues that modern technologies make economic and social relationships between people,

businesses, and coun-
tries "flatter"—less
hierarchical—and claims
that they have opened up
important new opportuni-
ties for advancement and
development. Borders separating countries have become
far more porous.

Throughout history it has been
technology—from the invention of
the wheel and the printing press to
more modern modes of transportation and
communication—that has increased the flow
of people across the world's borders. Today, people
around the world are more mobile than ever, and that
mobility is clearly aided by technology. Cars and airplanes take
us physically to the same places that cell phones and cyberspace allow us
to visit virtually. As a result, technology transcends the borders that define our identity both at home and in the workplace—what we are able to do and how we communicate, travel, and learn.

These developments offer new ways to communicate across borders and affect
how people define themselves and relate to others. Through modern technologies,
individuals are on the cutting edge of political change and social interaction. They
have the ability to organize quickly to influence the political process. Groups that
were once outsiders now impact policymaking. Social networks have launched
national revolutions, and videos taken with mobile phones are often the best
sources of information about what is going on in conflict situations. The technology that has allowed information to be converted to computer-ready formats—
digitization—has fundamentally altered communication to provide more broad-
based methods of delivery.

The events in the Middle East in 2011 that transformed the Egyptian, Tunisian, and
Libyan governments and have seriously challenged the Syrian government—the Arab
Spring—are an excellent example. Protestors organized massive events through digital

Army police in Cairo,
Egypt, detain a
number of people
who were blocking
Tahrir Square with
razor-wire and
barricades, while
onlookers take photos
with their cell phones.
Egyptians and others
across the Middle East
made widespread use
of digital media and
cellular technologies
during the Arab
Spring to organize
protests and share
information with the
rest of the world
about events
happening within
their countries.

51

media, using social networks and mobile phone messaging. The rest of the world saw them unfold using the same modes of participation, watching eyewitness videos of the gatherings and the violence they frequently encountered. With this firsthand knowledge, empathy for the protestors grew.

This **information revolution** has enhanced our ability to communicate via multiple sources. We are truly living in a **digital age**. But is the world really flat, as Friedman would have us believe? The forces that define Friedman's argument include geographical border shifts—the tearing down of the Berlin Wall—as well as computer and software developments and shifts in commercial operations, trade, and worker productivity.[2] They include sharing of information across borders through the Internet, outsourcing of commercial operations to other countries for greater efficiency, and supply chain innovation to move products or services around the world quickly from production to the consumer. Technological innovation is the "steroid" that drives the "flatteners" at work today. It is a major force in transforming the world and people's relationships. Yet, is technology really leveling the world?

Friedman's analysis is based on observations about the economic powerhouses of China and India. Not all countries have had their same opportunities and access to innovation. Another way to really understand the digital age is to recognize that the impact of technology is divided between those who have access and those who do not. Globally, there is a significant **digital divide**. For example, while it may seem like we are all connected by the Internet, in fact, less than 35 percent of the world is actually online.[3] Figure 3.1 illustrates

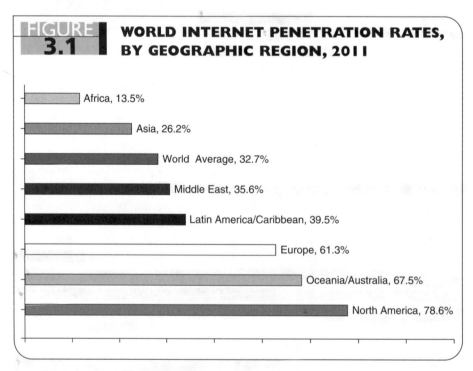

FIGURE 3.1 WORLD INTERNET PENETRATION RATES, BY GEOGRAPHIC REGION, 2011

Africa, 13.5%

Asia, 26.2%

World Average, 32.7%

Middle East, 35.6%

Latin America/Caribbean, 39.5%

Europe, 61.3%

Oceania/Australia, 67.5%

North America, 78.6%

Source: Data are from Internet World Stats, www.internetworldstats.com/stats.htm.

Internet usage by geographic region in terms of the percentage of the population with access to the Internet. Accessibility varies widely around the globe—most notably deficient are Africa (only 13.5 percent of the continent's population has access), Asia (26.2 percent), and the Middle East (35.6 percent).[4]

This chapter explores the development of technology, its applications, and its relationship to the changes taking place in the world. The underlying power of technological innovation has been critical to our understanding of the world not just today but throughout history. A brief account of the development of modern technology sets the stage for how it is used to cross borders.

TECHNOLOGY IN THE MODERN ERA

Thousands of years ago, travel on foot limited people by and large in their contact and interactions to their immediate surroundings. Hundreds of years ago, advancements in maritime technology allowed people to travel greater distances, but they spent months or even years on the high seas to exchange goods and ideas. Today, technological innovation has expanded to the point that space tourism has emerged as a new industry. While orbital space tourism opportunities remain limited and expensive, with only the Russian Space Agency providing transport thus far, its very existence marks an unprecedented level of technological sophistication. Guy Laliberte, founder of the Montreal-based Cirque du Soleil, paid $35 million for a 12-day trip aboard a Russian Soyuz spacecraft in 2009.[5] Virgin Atlantic mogul Sir Richard Branson is hoping to get into the business of space tourism with the creation of his company, Virgin Galactic, and its Spaceship Two, which will provide transport for up to six passengers and two pilots.[6] This development suggests the expanding reach of globalization even beyond our own planet! Hollywood actor Ashton Kutcher was the 500th customer to reserve a $200,000 spot for space travel with Virgin Galactic, which expects to begin offering commercial service in 2013.[7]

While most of us will not be going to outer space any time soon, technology has radically transformed our ease and accessibility of transportation. Since the nineteenth century, people have been traveling by train, a mode of transportation that is changing significantly. The newest bullet train, called the CRH380A, will go 236 miles per hour. It went into service in June of 2011, linking Beijing and Shanghai, and cutting travel time from 10 hours to just over 4 hours.[8] Air travel for the public has been in existence since the 1930s but was initially available only to a wealthier clientele. Today, air travel has become financially accessible to the masses, both domestically and abroad. In 2011, the world's airlines

Five hundred fifty years ago, the printing press (left) gave us the book as we have long known it—gatherings of printed pages set within a binding. E-book readers like the Kindle and the iPad (right) were invented in the late 2000s, and within just a few short years, the majority of book sales switched to digital from print. Are you reading this book on an e-reader?

flew 1.46 million scheduled flights into and out of the United States and carried over 164.6 million passengers.[9] The number of automobiles operated globally has also increased significantly, particularly in countries where sales were once limited. For example, as China becomes the world's second-largest consumer market, the Chinese are outpacing other countries in sales of automobiles. In 2010, China surpassed the United States, buying 13.5 million cars in comparison to the 11.6 million purchased by Americans.[10]

The series of industrial and information innovations that have brought us to these new frontiers began in the mid-fifteenth century with Johannes Gutenberg's invention of the printing press. While information had previously been passed along verbally or written and copied by hand, the press allowed information to circulate more freely around the world. It gave more people the opportunity to become literate and allowed information to reach a wider audience. Across long distances, people could read the same words and develop common interests. And it moved very quickly! James Burke sheds light on this phenomenon noting that "From the single Mainz press of 1457, it took only 23 years to establish presses in 110 towns: 50 in Italy, 30 in Germany, nine in France, eight in Spain, eight in Holland, four in England, and so on." [11]

HOW DO YOU CONNECT?   DO YOU DOWNLOAD MEDIA?

a. I download music.
b. I download movies.
c. I download books.
d. I download television shows.

Today books have gone digital. With the advent of e-readers such as the Nook and the Kindle, a person can buy and read a book without ever having gone to the bookstore and without ever having picked up an actual book. This shortens the supply chain process and has great implications for how people think and use books. In 2012, the Pew Internet and American Life Project found that almost 30 percent of Americans age 18 and older owned either a tablet or an e-book reader for e-book reading.[12] Books are even being converted to formats that can be read on a mobile phone, particularly by the Chinese, whose character language lends itself to the condensation of thought by presenting small pictures or concepts with each character.[13]

THE INDUSTRIAL REVOLUTION

Starting in the eighteenth century, a transformation took place that introduced the machinery of the modern age. The **Industrial Revolution** brought about the transition from an economy based on the labor of humans and animals to one based on machines. Key inventions included spinning machines that converted wool and cotton into spools of yarn, steam engines and their application to trains and boats, and the mechanization of iron production.[14] The first steam engine was created in England and registered in 1698 by Thomas Savery. Thomas Newcomen would move it forward, and James Watt would improve upon the design to provide a model for the engine that would become a commercial success. So significant was Watt's contribution that a unit of power—the Watt—was named after him. It is equal to 1/746 horsepower, or one volt times one amp.[15] If we look back to Thomas Savery's expectations as he writes about the uses for his steam engine, we can understand how the measurement of horse power evolved—how many horses could the use of this engine replace?

Trains would use the steam engine for transit, and the expansion of the railroads began. Critical to the Industrial Revolution, they facilitated the movement of goods and services across previously insurmountable distances. Raw materials could now be easily transported to manufacturing sites, thereby fostering the development of trade relationships. Eventually, large freight containers would be created that would move an unprecedented amount of resources and products around the globe, using existing rail networks, shipping, and cross-country roadways. The growth of this trade has been extraordinary. Prior to the economic slowdown in 2008, more than

Industrial Revolution
the eighteenth century transformation from a human- and animal-based labor economy to one based on machines.

> I have only this to urge, that water, in its fall from any determinate height, has simply a force answerable and equal to the force that raised it. So that an engine which will raise as much water as two horses working together at one time in such a work can do, and for which there must be constantly kept ten or twelve horses for doing the same....I say, such an engine will do the work or labours of ten or twelve horses.[16]

IN THEIR OWN WORDS   **Thomas Savery**

Pictured here is a Watt double-acting steam engine, which sparked the Industrial Revolution and greatly expanded the horizons for trade across world borders. Steam engines are still utilized today, as steam turbine engines are used to produce much of the world's electrical power.

short message service (SMS)
the technology that allows cell phone users to text messages up to 160 characters to one another.

$16 trillion of freight was transported around the world using large container ships, airplanes, trucks, and trains. The top three global merchandise exporters were China, Germany, and the United States, which together accounted for 26 percent of the total value of freight exports around the world.[17]

A second industrial revolution, which began in the latter part of the nineteenth century, brought electricity, mechanization of production, and experiments with aviation. These advances underlie the great twentieth-century transformations. The advent of an affordable car that could carry people long distances on their own initiative gave way to some new modes of transportation and the downfall of others, most notably the rail system in the United States. The telegraph and telephone enabled instantaneous communication over long distances and fostered economic growth. With the technology behind the telegraph, inventors created a "wireless" system for radio signals.[18] Initially protected by patents for military use in World War I, the release of those patents after the war allowed for the mass availability of the radio that brought information directly into people's homes. Access grew quickly, and it is estimated that 60 percent of American families bought radios between 1923 and 1930.[19] Telephone technology was also related to the telegraph, but progress was slow. By the 1930s, only 30 percent of US households had telephones, and the percentage was even less in rural areas of the United States and significantly less in other countries.[20]

Today, the number of landline phones in use has diminished significantly as mobile phones have taken their place. In the United States, the number of landlines decreased by over 26 percent from 1995 to 2008, as mobile phone subscriptions increased by 699 percent over the same period of time![21] Globally, mobile phone subscriptions have more than tripled in the last 10 years with large countries like India and China representing millions of subscribers. In 2010, China reported over 859 million subscribers, and India had 752 million. These figures translated to 64 phones per 100 persons for China and 61 per 100 for India compared to 89 per 100 for the United States.[22] Concurrent with the proliferation of mobile phones has been the development of **short message service (SMS)** technology that allows cell phone users to text messages of up to 160 characters to one another. This is perhaps one of the more pervasive new modes of communication, as texting has become a part of daily life for millions of people around the globe.

ENTER THE COMPUTER

The creation of the computer during World War II and subsequent expansion of that technology to business and home uses revolutionized access to information. While the first programmable computer had been built by German engineer, Konrad Zuse, in 1936, John Presper Eckert and John W. Mauchly would invent the electronic numerical integrator and computer (ENIAC) in 1946 in association with the US Army.[23] ENIAC was able to manage unheard of volumes of information at one time and would serve as the forerunner to UNIVAC, the first commercial computer, also created by Eckert and Mauchly in 1951.[24]

The development of the machine we know today as the personal computer was piecemeal and took place over several decades. Jack Kilby and Robert Noyce made the first critical addition through the development of the microchip in 1958.[25] Microchips are now ubiquitous, integrating circuits on almost every piece of technology. Even your pets may have microchips in them for tracking in case they get lost. Intel invented two additional components: the dynamic RAM chip, which increased memory and operating speeds, and the microprocessor, the first central processing unit. [26,]

This 1984 IBM AT computer—*AT* stood for "advanced technology"—was among the first personal computers (PCs), effectively the "great-grandparent" of the computer you likely use or own. Though revolutionary at the time, it was not without its flaws and frequently crashed.

In other developments, Alan Shugart and IBM (International Businesses Machines) created the floppy disk in 1971. The first floppy disks were eight inches square and could only hold 79.7 kilobytes of data. The last one developed by IBM was the 3½-inch HiFD in 1998–99, which holds only 150–200 megabytes. In comparison, we use thumb drives today, small portable memory cards that store large volumes of data that can hold up to 32 gigabytes, and some companies manufacture portable hard drives that can contain 2 terabytes of data. In other words, a 2-terabyte hard drive can hold the same information that 10,000 200-megabyte 3½-inch floppies can![27]

IBM would take these technologies to an even broader commercial application and be one of the first to enter the home computer market in 1981 with the IBM personal computer—the PC.[28] The home computer revolution had begun, and soon the term *PC* would become a part of our everyday language. The operating system on these computers was Microsoft's MS DOS (Microsoft disk operating system), which uses text commands and was developed by Bill Gates, the founder of Microsoft. Gates wrote the first BASIC (beginner's all-purpose symbolic instruction code) interpreter for IBM in 1980 that would evolve to the Windows operating system by 1985. Windows technology is now in its seventh generation.[29]

Beyond hardware innovations, the creation of communications technology for their operation has also been significant. The Internet has provided a way to communicate rapidly across borders and provides an unlimited repository for information. While US vice president Al Gore famously claimed responsibility for the Internet in an interview with CNN's Wolf Blitzer in 1999, stating, "During my service in the United States Congress, I took the initiative in creating the Internet,"[30] in fact, the Internet today is a global network connecting computer networks (a network of networks) that use the **transmission control protocol/internet protocol** or **TCP/IP standard**. It is built on the idea of packet switching (communications method of sending content back and forth in the form of packets, in contrast with circuit switching). TCP/IP was standardized in 1982, and interconnected TCP/IP networks became known as the Internet.[31]

transmission control protocol/internet protocol—TCP/IP standard
the communications method of sending content back and forth in packets that underlies the Internet.

The World Wide Web came into being in 1990, when a researcher at CERN, the European Organization for Nuclear Research, Tim Berners-Lee, developed hypertext markup language (HTML).[32] HTML is all about standards, and users could connect to the Internet through the World Wide Web using standards such as URL (uniform resource locator) and HTTP (hypertext transfer protocol).[33] Internet browsers, such as Netscape, connected people to the World Wide Web and the Internet. Netscape was introduced in 1995 and was the first Internet browser, soon followed by Microsoft Internet Explorer. Today Netscape is no longer around, but people can pick from many browsers, including Mozilla's Firefox, Google Chrome, and Apple's Safari.[34]

The next step would be to provide a guide to the web. In 1994, Yahoo was founded by Jerry Yang and Dave Filo as a search engine for the World Wide Web.[35] The idea was to create a way to navigate the information superhighway, which was growing exponentially daily. Google would follow in 1998, founded by Larry Page and Sergey Brin. Both of these groups merged the machines, or hardware that provided a platform, with the operating systems and software that made them run into a new form of communication that allowed immediate access to a world beyond. Information on just about anything was now at your fingertips. You could look up facts and find old friends or learn about distant places with the click of a mouse. A new form of mail developed, e-mail, that allowed you to send a message to someone instantaneously, where previously a paper letter would have taken several days to arrive. A new era of communication had begun.

THE PACKAGING OF TECHNOLOGY: THE SECOND ERA OF COMPUTING

As IBM and Bill Gates developed their hardware and software technology, an upstart company out of the Bay Area of California founded by Steve Wozniak and Steve Jobs was really running on a parallel track. The first Apple computers were developed in the late 1970s, but it would be a few years more before the war between Microsoft and Apple would officially begin. Apple would revolutionize the computing industry in 1983 and 1984, when it introduced first the Lisa computer—the first home computer with a **graphical user interface** (**GUI**)—and then the Macintosh computer, the most affordable home computer with a GUI.[36] A GUI allowed users to interact with their computers through images rather than text commands and gradually overtook the text based MS DOS system. GUIs have been adopted by PC users as well, and they are what we use today. Common GUI features include the icons you can click on to access browsers like Firefox, applications like iTunes, software such as Word, and other folders on your desktop, calendars, and dashboards.

graphical user interface (GUI)

images that provide for interaction with the computer without text, such as icons, that originated with Apple computers and are now found on PCs as well.

What the Apple revolution provided was a way to connect people to their computers in new and innovative ways. Steve Jobs was able to see things differently, and that led to the development of many products that would change how information was shared across multiple mediums. When asked about the role of creativity in how Apple's innovations came about, Steve Jobs was quite clear.

Jobs saw that the technology of computing could be applied to directly connect people to their machines. From the creation of the alternative operations systems that continue to pit PCs against its computers, Apple has been on the cutting edge of electronic breakthroughs, particularly as they apply to individual uses. These innovations have included the iMac computer, the iPod portable media player, the iPhone, and the iPad, a personal

> Creativity is just connecting things. When you ask creative people how they did something, they feel a little guilty because they didn't really do it, they just saw something. It seemed obvious to them after a while. That's because they were able to connect experiences they've had and synthesize new things. And the reason they were able to do that was that they've had more experiences or they have thought more about their experiences than other people.
>
> Unfortunately, that's too rare a commodity. A lot of people in our industry haven't had very diverse experiences. So they don't have enough dots to connect, and they end up with very linear solutions without a broad perspective on the problem. The broader one's understanding of the human experience, the better design we will have.[37]

IN THEIR OWN WORDS | **Steve Jobs**

In Kenya's Lewa Wildlife Conservancy, about 275 kilometers northeast of Nairobi, this Masai man passes some time listening to his iPod.

computer operated from a tablet. The iPod and the accompanying iTunes application allow people all over the world to share a market space. There they can purchase music and many other types of recordings, television shows, documentaries, and movies. Moreover, they have something in common with users all over the world as the concept of a portable media player has changed how people think about acquiring and listening to music.

A similar transformation has occurred with phones. While the technology to connect phones with the Internet existed prior to 2007 in the form of the Blackberry, it did not really take off until June 2007, when Apple introduced the first iPhone. The iPhone provided a simple way to connect through a touch-based screen driven by images. And it continues to make huge leaps forward. For example, recent iPhones, starting with the iPhone 4s, include Siri software, a voice-activated assistant. You can literally ask your phone anything, and it will respond to you.[38] Apple's largest competitor is the Android operating system from Google, which is offered on phones from HTC, Samsung, and other companies.

The term *smartphone* is now used to refer to these phones that are built on mobile computer operating systems, such as Apple's iOS or Google's Android. Users can load any number of applications (apps) on their smartphones, which now act as miniature computers, and do many of the same things they do on their home computers—for example, banking, online shopping, instant messaging, checking e-mails, and even word processing. Some of the most popular apps include Googlemaps, Facebook, and theWeatherchannel.com.[39]

If the smartphone screen is not big enough for you, the iPad, a computer that operates on a thin tablet, can help you out. Featuring a touch screen, it is revolutionizing computing today. It performs many of the same applications as a laptop, and many users have supplemented or replaced their laptops with tablets. A close runner-up to the iPad is the Samsung Galaxy Tab, which runs on the Android system.

HOW DO YOU CONNECT?   WHAT ELECTRONICS DO YOU OWN?

a. cell phone or smartphone

b. tablet (Galaxy Tab, iPad, etc.)

c. e-book reader (Kindle, Nook, etc.)

d. video game system (PS3, Xbox, etc.)

e. MP3 player

Finally, many of us find ourselves in the clouds today. **Cloud computing** essentially removes the burden of running applications and programs from a computer and places it in a system of servers. It is a web-based service run by remote machines. Use of smartphones and tablets is enhanced by cloud computing, as it serves multiple devices. For example, Google offers a suite of applications and services, including Gmail and Google Calendar, that can be synced from any compatible device. You can enter an appointment on your calendar from your Google Android phone, and this same information can be accessed from your computer, laptop, or tablet. Likewise, you can check your e-mail from any device, as long as the accounts are linked among devices. It is a very significant shift in how people use computers. What makes the cloud important is the ubiquity of smartphones, tablets, and laptops. It provides general access to information from virtually anywhere.

> **HOW DO YOU CONNECT?**
>
> **HOW DO YOU COMMUNICATE WITH YOUR FRIENDS?**
>
> a. telephone calls
> b. texting
> c. instant messaging
> d. e-mail
> e. Skype
> f. social media networks
> g. a combination of the above

cloud computing
the delivery of web-based content via remote servers to multiple devices.

THE ROLE OF TECHNOLOGY IN CROSSING BORDERS

The result of this acceleration in information sharing, as well as in the movement of people and products, is that political, economic, social, and cultural borders have opened up. The development of means of communication that are not constrained by borders is probably the single most significant contribution to the restructuring of the global arena. Global access to information 24/7 has empowered individuals, businesses, and governments to forge new opportunities and methods of operation that would have been unimaginable just 10 or 20 years ago. Taken together with the expansion of the Internet, these new modes of communication have a significant role in crossing international divides. These technologies are connecting the world's population in new and revolutionary ways, across traditional borders and boundaries. As a result, people are crossing borders every day without even leaving home!

Political Borders

Communications technology has become a source of political change, as citizens orchestrate revolutions through the Internet—messaging, texting, and tweeting the location of gathering places to interested parties, and uploading video as fast as events happen. It can be particularly beneficial in the hands of those who have few other political resources. The usages can range from recruitment of participants and mobilization of political sympathizers to the late

Osama Bin Laden's use of a thumb drive to communicate with al-Qaeda operatives. The Internet can be used to spread knowledge of how to create destructive weapons, challenging national security. The 9/11 attacks were coordinated by cell phone. Map 3.1 shows global Internet usage rates and provides a list of terrorist groups who use websites.

This same technology can also be used to prevent change, as those in power manipulate it to retain their control. China restricts access to Internet sites and monitors usage. The internationally strong search engine Google originally was willing

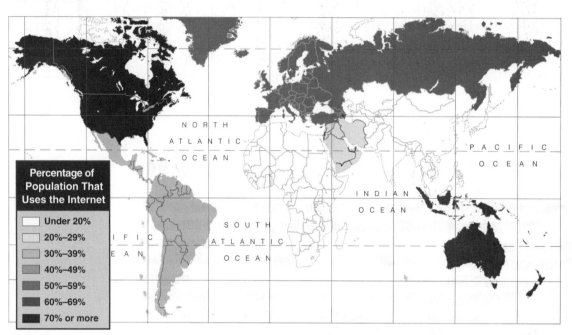

MAP 3.1   INTERNET OFFERS POTENTIAL FOR SPREADING TERROR.

Percentage of Population That Uses the Internet

- Under 20%
- 20%–29%
- 30%–39%
- 40%–49%
- 50%–59%
- 60%–69%
- 70% or more

The Internet has opened global communication channels to anyone with computer access, creating a simple and cheap venue for spreading terrorist ideology. Interestingly, the regions with the largest concentrations of terrorist groups—the Middle East and Asia—have some of the lowest Internet usage rates. The highest rates are in developed countries, such as the United States, Canada, Australia and New Zealand.

Major Terrorist Groups With Websites, by Region

Middle East: Hamas, Lebanese Hezbollah, al-Acsa Martyrs Brigades, Fatah Tanzim, Popular Front for the Liberation of Palestine, Palestinian Islamic Jihad, Kahane Lives Movement, People's Mujahidin of Iran, Kurdish Worker's Party, Popular Democratic Liberation Front Party, Great East Islamic Raiders Front

Europe: Basque Euskadi Ta Askatasuna, Armata Corsa, Real Irish Republican Army

Latin America: Tupac.Amaru,Shining Path, Colombian National Liberation Army, Armed Revolutionary Forces of Colombia, Zapatista National Liberation Army Asia: Al Qaeda, Japanese Supreme Truth, Anser al Islam, Japanese Red Army, Hizb-ul Mujahidin, Liberation Tigers of Tamil Eelam, Islamic Movement of Uzbekistan, Moro Islamic Liberation Front, Lashkar-e-Taiba, Chechnyan rebel mavement

Source: Barbara Mantel, "Terrorism and the Internet," *CQ Global Researcher 3* (2009): 285–310, http://library.cqpress.com/globalresearcher/.

to self-censor to accommodate these limitations, but Google and China had a falling out in 2010. Google accused the Chinese of hacking into their databases and indicated they would no longer put limits on searches. As a result, they lost significant market share, and the Chinese competitor, Baidu, has grown significantly.[40]

Hacking has also facilitated a whole new type of terrorism—**cyberterrorism**—whereby groups or individuals unlawfully attack and manipulate Internet information to further either their personal or group's gains.[41] These include hacking of websites, gaining access to classified information, and compromising the activities of governments and businesses. The activities of Wikileaks are a case in point.

Wikileaks was launched in 2007 as a nonprofit organization that brings tightly held information to the general public.[42] Accepting secret information from anonymous sources, Wikileaks has brought to light many classified documents that raise questions about governmental actions and policies. In 2011, it published many classified US government documents on the wars in Iraq and Afghanistan that included embarrassing cables among US embassies around the world.

cyberterrorism
the unlawful attack and manipulation of Internet information to further a personal or group's gain.

PRO/CON

Is cyberterrorism a significant global threat?

The extent to which actions like those taken by Wikileaks constitutes a global security threat is subject to debate. The following arguments explore these concerns.

PRO	CON
Mohd Noor Amin Mohd Noor Amin, Chairman, International Multilateral Partnership Against Cyber Threats, Selangor, Malaysia. Written for *CQ Global Researcher*, November 2009	**Tim Stevens** Tim Stevens, Associate, Centre for Science and Security Studies, King's College London. Written for *CQ Global Researcher*, November 2009
Alarm bells on cyberterrorism have been sounding for more than a decade, and yet, hacktivism aside, the world still has not witnessed a devastating cyber attack on critical infrastructure. Nothing has occurred that caused massive damage, injuries and fatalities resulting in widespread chaos, fear and panic. Does that mean the warnings were exaggerated?	Cyberterrorism is the threat and reality of unlawful attacks against computer networks and data by an individual or a nongovernmental group to further a political agenda. Such attacks can cause casualties and deaths through spectacular incidents, such as plane crashes or industrial explosions, or secondary consequences, such as crippled economies or disrupted emergency services.
On the contrary, the convergence of impassioned politics, hacktivism trends and extremists' growing technological sophistication suggests that the threat of cyberterrorism remains significant—if not more urgent—today. Although hacktivists and terrorists have not yet successfully collaborated to bring a country to its knees, there is already significant overlap between them. Computer-savvy	We have seen many attempts to disrupt the online assets of governments, industry and individuals, but these have mercifully not yet caused the mass casualties predicted by the term "cyberterrorism." The assumption that terrorists might use cyberspace in such attacks is not in question, but the potential threat that cyberterrorism poses is accorded disproportionate weight in some circles.
(Continued on next page)	*(Continued on next page)*

PRO/CON (Continued)
Is cyberterrorism a significant global threat?

Pro	Con
extremists have been sharpening their skills by defacing and hacking into Web sites and training others to do so online. Given the public ambitions of groups like al Qaeda to launch cyber attacks, it would be folly to ignore the threat of a major cyber assault if highly skilled hackers and terrorists did conspire to brew a perfect storm.	Cyberterrorism resulting in civilian deaths is certainly one possible outcome of the convergence of technology and political aggression. That it has not happened yet is a function of two factors. First, the ongoing vigilance and operational sophistication of national security agencies have ensured that critical infrastructure systems have remained largely unbreached and secure. And second, like all self-styled revolutionaries, terrorists talk a good talk.
Experts are particularly concerned that terrorists could learn how to deliver a simultaneous one-two blow: executing a mass, physical attack while incapacitating the emergency services or electricity grids to neutralize rescue efforts. The scenario may not be so far-fetched, judging from past cyber attacks or attempts, although a certain level of technical skill and access would be needed to paralyze part of a nation's critical infrastructure. However, as shown by an oft-cited 2000 incident in Australia, a single, disgruntled former employee hacked into a wastewater management facility's computer system and released hundreds of thousands of gallons of raw sewage onto Sunshine Coast resort grounds and a canal. Vital industrial facilities are not impenetrable to cyber attacks and, if left inadequately secured, terrorists and hackers could wreak havoc. Similarly, the 2008 cyber attacks that caused multicity power outages around the world underscore the vulnerabilities of public utilities, particularly as these systems become connected to open networks to boost economies of scale.	Although a terrorist group might possess both the intent and the skill-sets—either in-house, or "rented"—there is little evidence yet that any group has harnessed both to serious effect. Most attacks characterized as "cyberterrorism" so far have amounted to mere annoyances, such as Web site defacements, service disruptions and low-level cyber "skirmishing"—nonviolent responses to political situations, rather than actions aimed at reaping notoriety in flesh and blood.
	It would be foolish, however, to dismiss the threat of cyberterrorism. It would also be disingenuous to overstate it. Western governments are making strides towards comprehensive cyber security strategies that encompass a wide range of possible scenarios, while trying to overcome agency jurisdictional issues, private-sector wariness and the fact that civilian computer systems are now seen as "strategic national assets."
If this past decade of terrorist attacks has demonstrated the high literacy level, technological capability and zeal of terrorists, the next generation of terrorists growing up in an increasingly digitized and connected world may hold even greater potential for cyberterrorism. After all, if it is possible to effect visibly spectacular, catastrophic destruction from afar and still remain anonymous, why not carry it out?	As it becomes harder to understand the complexities of network traffic, identify attack vectors, attribute responsibility and react accordingly, we must pursue integrated national and international strategies that criminalize the sorts of offensive attacks that might constitute cyberterrorism. But designating the attacks as terrorism is a taxonomic firewall we should avoid.

Source: Barbara Mantel, "Terrorism and the Internet," *CQ Global Researcher* 3 (2009): 285–310, http://library.cqpress.com/globalresearcher/.

WHERE Do You Stand?

1. Do you think the United States should spend more money on monitoring cyberterrorism?
2. Should hackers and cyberterrorists face greater criminal punishment for their actions?
3. Do you believe censorship tactics like those used by China are beneficial to Internet security?

Economic Borders

In terms of economic borders, technology has truly transformed the nature of global transactions. From a personal perspective, we can buy goods from the far corners of the world without leaving our homes and have them delivered to us sometimes even the next day! How does this happen? Technology has promoted the mobility of production processes, facilitating the movement of goods around the world. Remember the journey taken by a T-shirt introduced in Chapter 1? The cotton it was made from was grown in Texas, it then traveled to China where the T-shirt was made, the shirt was sold in the United States at a retail outlet, and ended up in an African market.

The outsourcing of production—moving the creation of a good to a third party provider—and offshoring of communications and online servicing through call centers is a product of innovation. Through interfaces that include e-mail, instant messaging, and real-time face-to-face interaction through Skype, people can go to a meeting sitting at home in their pajamas or answer your call when a dishwasher is not working to set up a repair. Moreover, large transnational corporations can export advanced workflow software technology to different places around the globe to enhance their productivity by allowing teams to work on the same project around the clock. The project manager software giant, SAP, has made a name for itself in this regard, offering a service that "keeps projects rolling around the clock, around the globe."[43]

One company that has been at the cutting edge of these initiatives is Infosys, an international technology services firm that was founded in 1981.[44] It is headquartered in Bangalore, India, a city known as an information technology (IT) hub in India. Infosys is important because, as a leading firm in a growing IT sector in India, it provides resources for industry worldwide, thereby supporting Friedman's ten flatteners (especially outsourcing). Friedman, in fact, came upon his realization that the world is flat after visiting Bangalore, a city that includes regional headquarters for Accenture, Compaq, IBM, Sun Microsystems, Texas Instruments, and Wipro Infotech, just to name a few.[45]

Infosys provides IT services for many different industries, including aerospace and defense, communication services, education, energy, financial services, health care, industrial manufacturing, and resource industries.[46] They provide call center services for several companies.[47] If you have ever had to call Microsoft customer service, you probably contacted someone with Infosys.[48] This relationship with Microsoft represents one of Infosys's largest partnerships.

A key project they are working on is the development and implementation in business environments of Microsoft SharePoint, collaboration software that allows industries like oil and gas to operate across six continents. These connections speak to another of Friedman's flatteners—the idea that business practices are integrated such that people can work together simultaneously and respond quickly to change from anywhere in the world.

Internet technology has also transformed global financing in both positive and negative ways. Billions of dollars are now transmitted electronically 24 hours a day, facilitating the flow of capital around the world. This has had some important impacts in terms of making capital available quickly to those who are in most need of it, in dire times of disaster, or simply through regular remittances to families back home from convenience stores all over the world by MoneyGram or Western Union. But it has also invited criminal activity, such as hiding assets and embezzling funds. The former governor of Nigeria's Delta State, in the oil-rich region of that country, was given a 13-year prison sentence in 2012 for taking an estimated $250 million of US aid funds and using them for his own personal spending. A special team created by the United Kingdom's government to track such crimes around the world was able to identify his actions and bring him to justice.

Terrorists take advantage of rapid transfers of money to support their agendas, moving money quickly online and having it withdrawn from ATMs around the world with a very scant recorded trail back to its origins. Governments frequently detect terrorist activities by following the money. The activities of Somali refugees and expatriates living in Kenya have come under scrutiny in this regard for suspected transfers of cash to al-Qaeda through an allied organization operating in the area, al-Shabaab.[49] Alternative remittance systems (ARS) or *hawala,* an Arabic term that means "transfer," allow money to move electronically through grey areas without being identified by source.

When political actions are deemed contrary to international norms, the interconnectedness of financial information can allow a quick freeze of assets. For example, in response to unrest in Libya in 2011, the United States, the European Union, and other countries moved to freeze the assets of the late Libyan leader Muammar Qaddafi.[50] Anticipating this move, Qaddafi deposited nearly $5 billion with a private wealth manager based in London and was able to protect some of his holdings prior to his capture and subsequent death.

Social and Cultural Connections

Social and cultural borders are crossed every day as social media create communities of individuals that spontaneously can come together. The critically acclaimed movie *The Social Network* touched a popular nerve in telling the story of Facebook's creation. Originally launched in 2004, Facebook provides connections for 650 million people worldwide with the click of a mouse. Its format is popular in countries around the world, some of which have created their own social networking environments. For example, Studivz.com is a German version of Facebook popular with students, and MiGente.com appeals primarily to Latin Americans. The powerhouse search engine, Google, is getting into the arena now with its Google+ that challenges Facebook as a social network site.

MAP
3.2
GLOBAL MAP OF SOCIAL NETWORKING

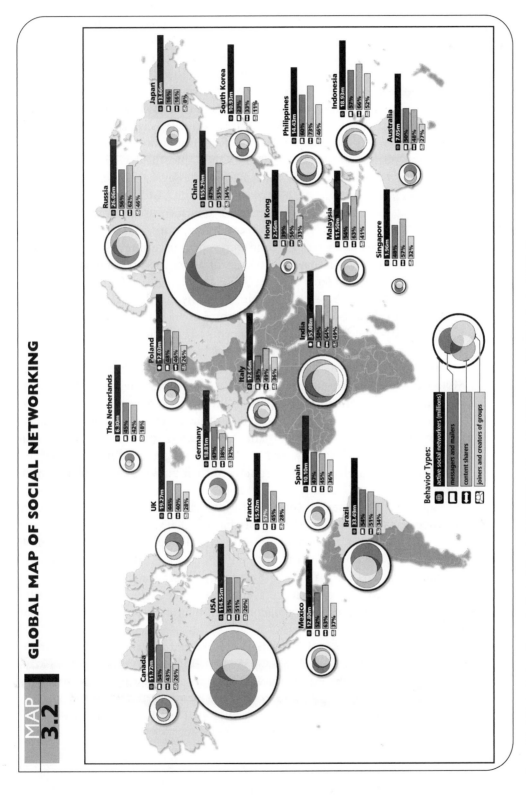

Behavior Types:
- 🌐 active social networkers (millions)
- ▪ messagers and mailers
- ▫ content sharers
- ▨ joiners and creators of groups

Canada 🌐 11.72m ▪ 54% ▫ 43% ▨ 26%

USA 🌐 114.55m ▪ 51% ▫ 51% ▨ 20%

Mexico 🌐 12.80m ▪ 52% ▫ 63% ▨ 37%

Brazil 🌐 33.49m ▪ 54% ▫ 51% ▨ 34%

UK 🌐 19.27m ▪ 44% ▫ 40% ▨ 28%

France 🌐 15.92m ▪ 57% ▫ 45% ▨ 28%

Spain 🌐 10.10m ▪ 47% ▫ 45% ▨ 36%

Germany 🌐 18.81m ▪ 47% ▫ 38% ▨ 32%

The Netherlands 🌐 6.30m ▪ 45% ▫ 42% ▨ 18%

Poland 🌐 12.03m ▪ 48% ▫ 46% ▨ 26%

Italy 🌐 12.66m ▪ 38% ▫ 49% ▨ 36%

Russia 🌐 26.06m ▪ 56% ▫ 62% ▨ 46%

China 🌐 155.29m ▪ 47% ▫ 53% ▨ 34%

India 🌐 35.08m ▪ 50% ▫ 64% ▨ 49%

Japan 🌐 13.66m ▪ 16% ▫ 16% ▨ 8%

South Korea 🌐 10.93m ▪ 23% ▫ 33% ▨ 11%

Hong Kong 🌐 2.56m ▪ 39% ▫ 56% ▨ 33%

Malaysia 🌐 11.50m ▪ 56% ▫ 63% ▨ 41%

Singapore 🌐 1.59m ▪ 49% ▫ 57% ▨ 32%

Philippines 🌐 14.43m ▪ 60% ▫ 73% ▨ 46%

Indonesia 🌐 18.93m ▪ 57% ▫ 66% ▨ 52%

Australia 🌐 7.05m ▪ 50% ▫ 48% ▨ 27%

Source: http://globalwebindex.net/wp-content/uploads/downloads/2011/06/Global-Map-of-Social-Networking-GlobalWebIndex-June-20112.pdf

67

HOW DO YOU GET THE NEWS?

a. in print (local newspaper, *The New York Times*, etc.)

b. televised (local news, CNN, etc.)

c. radio (NPR, BBC, etc)

d. online (CNN, RSS feeds, etc)

e. other method

f. I don't read the news.

The strength of Google+ will be its ability to manipulate groups of friends into circles and its potentially superior photo, video, and mobile applications.[51]

The activity of social networkers by country around the world is illustrated in Map 3.2. What this map tells us is that countries use this mode of communication differently. In the United States and the United Kingdom, the focus is on messaging, while faster-growing markets like China, India, and the Philippines are using this medium for sharing content and creating groups. These activities have changed the focus of social media networking from a purely social usage to a more activist orientation that can have significant effects on political, economic, social, and cultural borders.

Social media can be significant in elections, as they create an identity among political supporters. In his election bid in 2008, Barack Obama was one of the first major political candidates to rely heavily on social media outlets to grow his message and gather potential voters. Iran's 2009 elections pitted incumbent president Mahmoud Ahmadinejad against Mir Hossein Mousavi. Mousavi chose the color green—representing Islam and hope—to symbolize the movement that supported him.[52] The reelection of Mahmoud Ahmadinejad was a great disappointment to the green movement, and allegations of election fraud were rampant. The green revolutionaries took to the streets in protest, organizing their meetings through social media, especially Twitter and Facebook, and sending news of their activities out globally in the same way.

Another new resource for communication that has rapidly crossed borders is YouTube. Created as a video sharing platform in 2005, YouTube today connects people through both personal and informational videos. A home video can go viral in just a few hours, as it is watched around the world. YouTube has even included auditions for a YouTube Symphony Orchestra with musicians from numerous countries participating. The group performed in March 2011 at the Sydney Opera House in Australia, conducted by the music director of the San Francisco Symphony.

These developments as they relate to cultural borders can be significant. On the one hand, they can offer ways to preserve traditional mores and norms as practices are documented for future generations. Languages can be preserved and histories shared as groups form around traditional identities. Many groups have webpages and Facebook sites that celebrate their history and identity.

SOWhat? TECHNOLOGY 24/7

By John McGregor, International Studies Graduate Student and Soccer Blogger

New technology has completely changed the way I operate both inside and outside the classroom. My personal life and education are driven by these technological advances. It is the best way to keep in contact with friends and family now spread out all over the globe. In school, I use the Internet to conduct research and to communicate with my professors. While I still use the library for research, I usually identify the material I need online, even if I review or acquire it through the library. All my assignments are prepared on the computer, and are usually sent directly to my professors online. I have my computer or iPad with me for note taking in all my classes.

Thanks to developments in New Media, I obtain roughly 90% of my local, national, and international news from Twitter. It gives me the opportunity to follow an infinite number of journalists and news publications that deliver news and opinions constantly on a 24-hour cycle. The brevity of Twitter allows me to consume a large amount of news very quickly, while almost every post features a link that leads to a more in-depth story. The ability to tailor my news experience in a very personalized way allows me to pick sources that I know to be credible. As someone who is constantly on the go and relying on a mobile device, there is no more efficient way to stay informed.

I rely on my iPhone more than any piece of technology that I currently own. It plays a vital role in my daily routine, from supplying the alarm that wakes me to allowing me to check multiple email accounts in seconds. It also lets me check Twitter to see what has been going in the world over the few hours I slept, all while downloading up to the minute weather reports that help me plan my day. It lets me stay in touch with friends through text messaging, video conferencing, and old-fashioned phone conversations. The iPhone certainly plays a vital role in my life, and its absence would greatly alter how I live on a day-to-day basis.

The biggest way that technology has led me across international borders is through my love of soccer. The Internet and Social Media have not only allowed me to connect to fans all over the world, but to interact directly with the journalists and media sources dedicated to covering the sport. As someone who writes about soccer, it is an invaluable resource to be able to directly communicate with some of the best writers in the industry, who all have a significant presence with Social Media. This resource has increased both my knowledge and love for the sport, as well as continuing to make me a better writer.

On the other hand, technological innovation and communication across borders can bring new styles of food, dress, music, and sports that become universal as opposed to specific to a state, nation, or people. World music, global hip hop, and even the popularity of designer blue jeans are examples of cultural identity changing in response to technological innovation that allows the selling of ideas, images, and goods readily across traditional borders. The nonprofit organization TED (Technology, Entertainment, Design) supports a series of talks—TED talks—that are short observations on "ideas worth spreading." They are currently translated into 86 languages, with 93 additional language translations in progress.[53] Talk about sharing ideas with the world!

New languages can even emerge. Language can adapt through interactions, such as the popularity of Spanglish—a cross between English and Spanish that is spoken in many parts of the Spanish and English speaking world today. Even texting and tweeting have created a new universal language of acronyms and emoticons, such as LOL, TTYL, and :) that people around the world are using daily.

A FINAL THOUGHT ON TECHNOLOGY PRIOR TO THE JOURNEY

New technologies have changed how we live and interact with one another. Despite the technological divide, the spread of the Internet and satellite communications has brought the world together. The rapid way in which information can be shared globally gives states access to the same information and allows them to easily share their needs and concerns. When disaster strikes, the world can be there. Even the technology corporations that we have met here have come together to help people. When Haiti suffered a devastating earthquake in 2010, Google was one of the first to say it would donate $1 million in relief supplies.[54] Infosys has a philanthropic mission beyond IT through the Infosys Foundation, which was established to lift the people of India out of poverty. They emphasize education, especially in the hard sciences and mathematics. The Bill and Melinda Gates Foundation has been at the forefront of providing mosquito nets around the world to prevent malaria. And our friend Nathan, who we met in Chapter 1, used these new technologies to invest in people around the world from the comfort of his couch.

The extent to which we can use technology to promote greater cooperation will depend on our understanding of the divisions that exist and the challenges we face. The task is complicated by the borders that continue to separate us. The remainder of this book will provide you with a road map to traverse the globe across these political, economic, social, and cultural borders. Pack your bags, the course has been set, and let the journey begin!

KEY Concepts

cloud computing 61
cyberterrorism 63
digital age 52
digital divide 52
digitization 52
graphic user interface (GUI) 59

information revolution 52
Industrial Revolution 55
short message service (SMS) 56
transmission control protocol/
internet protocol—TCP/IP
standard 58

TO LEARN More

Books and Other Print Media

Aravind Adiga, *White Tiger* (New York: Free Press, 2008).

Aravind Adiga's debut novel, *White Tiger,* is about the letters from an Indian call center worker, Balram, to the Chinese prime minister in advance of an upcoming state visit. Balram wants the prime minister to know his story and how Indian society has been transformed by technological innovation.

Guy Klemens, *The Cellphone: The History and Technology of the Gadget that Changed the World* (Jefferson, NC: McFarland, 2010).

This book tells the story of the cellphone, from its earliest conceptions to the technology that continues to develop today.

Leslie Chang, *Factory Girls* (New York: Spiegel & Grau, 2008).

This nonfiction account by journalist Leslie Chang tells the story of an emerging culture in China that has developed around the girls who travel to the cities to work in the large factories there. Their pursuit of work and income has estranged them from their family life in the villages such that they can never really go home again, yet they don't quite fit in the city either.

Thomas L. Friedman, *The World Is Flat* (New York: Farrar, Strauss, and Giroux, 2005).

Friedman analyzes ten forces that have contributed to the deepening globalization of the world and have created new opportunities for China, India, and other emerging countries.

Walter Isaacson, *Steve Jobs* (New York: Simon & Schuster, 2011).

Isaacson presents an intriguing biography of Steve Jobs, one of the most important pioneers in personal computers and devices.

Websites

Cable News Network, "CNN Tech," www.cnn.com/TECH/index.html.

CNN offers updates on technology trends around the world today. Regular features updated weekly focus on the web, gadgets and gaming, mobile news, social media, and technology innovation.

Computer History Museum, www.computerhistory.org/.

This website is the home of the Computer History Museum, located in Mountainview, California—in Silicon Valley, where it all began. It provides a history of the computer as well as the people who were the pioneers of the industry.

Facebook (www.facebook.com), LinkedIn (www.linkedin.com), and Twitter (www.twitter.com).

These are major social networking sites, which you have probably already joined!

Popular Science, www.popsci.com/.

Popular Science magazine has been documenting technology news since its inception in 1872. Today it offers insight into the latest technologies and their applications.

Wired, www.wired.com.

The online version of the print magazine, *Wired*, covers cutting-edge technologies and frequently explores their social, cultural, political, and economic implications.

Videos

Burma VJ: Reporting from a Closed Country (2008).

This documentary about the 2007 protests against the military junta in Burma (Myanmar) centers around the role of video journalists and features footage shot on hand-held cameras, some of which was smuggled out of the country.

Four Principles for the Open World (2012).

Canadian businessman and author Don Tapscott discusses how the Internet is transforming the world into a more open and transparent society and touches upon four principles to guide this process. www.ted.com/talks/don_tapscott_four_principles_for_the_open_world_1.html

How Web Video Powers Global Innovation (2010).

Chris Anderson addresses the growth and impact of the Internet video and the phenomenon of *crowd accelerated innovation,* a cycle of learning that could change how people connect and how ideas spread. www.ted.com/talks/chris_anderson_ how_web_video_powers_global_innovation.html

I Lost My Job (2012).

This film addresses the growing phenomenon of technological unemployment, or when manual labor is displaced by new machines and computers, and its economic and social effects.

Internet Rising (2011).

This documentary explores the connections between technology and humans and addresses some of humanity's greatest questions, including our search for meaning and mindfulness. http://internetrising.net/

The Social Network (2010).

A popular and award-winning movie, *The Social Network* tells the story of Mark Zuckerberg's rise from Harvard dropout to creator of the world's most powerful "social network"—Facebook.

Searching for Security

The Political World

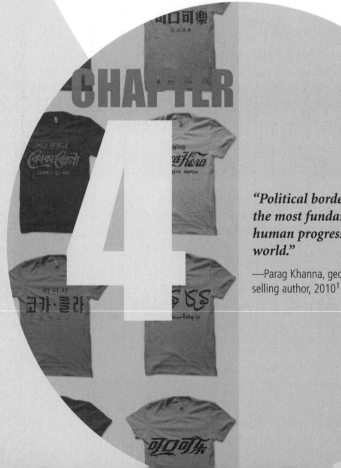

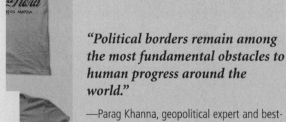

CHAPTER

4

"*Political borders remain among the most fundamental obstacles to human progress around the world.*"

—Parag Khanna, geopolitical expert and best-selling author, 2010[1]

The search for security is driven by many factors, from the fear of war and terrorist attacks to the general concern that leads people to feel they must lock their doors at night. Political entities have provided the structures that respond to these needs, but they are no longer able to do it alone. The political borders that we have come to rely on may not be the best framework for responding to the demands of modern society, particularly when some of the forces that threaten our physical security do not stop at the border, such as communicable diseases and tainted waters.

Globally acclaimed geostrategist Parag Khanna puts forth an interesting proposition as he questions the role political borders play. He believes stubborn adherence to these borders poses significant challenges for progress in the current world order. He even goes

so far as to suggest that the problems facing the world today require a new way of responding that builds upon other conceptions of power. It is political boundaries, however, that have had an enduring impact on the way in which the global arena operates. While there has been great talk in the era of globalization that nation-states are on the way out, to paraphrase Mark Twain—rumors of their death are greatly exaggerated.

Even as protestors took to the streets of Chicago at the 2012 summit of the North Atlantic Treaty Organization (NATO) in opposition to its activities, the gathering of the 28 member countries that view this military alliance as central to their security tells us the story remains the same. Long-standing rivalries remain, even as organizations like the NATO alliance cope with changing relationships and the emergence of new states that challenge the status quo. Security remains a vital concern that perpetuates these disputes.

In the *Summit Declaration on Defence Capabilities* that looked toward what NATO would be in 2020, the opening statement reiterates this core mission: "We are determined to ensure that NATO retains and develops the capabilities necessary to perform its essential core tasks of collective defence, crisis management and cooperative security—and thereby to play an essential role promoting security in the world."[2] But NATO is fundamentally a military alliance whose members are nation-states in Europe and the United States. They have come together for security in a world where serious threats remain. How then does the rest of the world seek security in a changing global order? The continued reliance on political borders remains crucial.

In 1990, as the Berlin Wall dividing East and West Berlin, Germany, was being dismantled, an East German border guard shook hands with a West German woman through a hole in the wall. The Berlin Wall symbolizes the type of border that states sometime erect, dividing populations of people who otherwise might share the same state, society, and culture.

DEFINING POLITICAL BORDERS: THE ORIGINS OF THE MODERN STATE SYSTEM

The study of politics dates back to the writings of the earliest philosophers. Both Plato and his student Aristotle considered many of the fundamental questions that must be addressed by groups of people as they sought to govern themselves in the fourth century BCE. People have always pursued the security of groups for safety as well. Some of the earliest forms of governance, kingdoms and city-states, were determined by their leaders. How they related to one another was critical and based on an assessment of relative power.

The Athenian general and historian Thucydides is often considered one of the first proponents of power politics. He argues in *The History of the Peloponnesian War*, written in 431 BCE, that leaders who ignore the pursuit of power invite conflict.[3] His Melian Debate is famous for elucidating this notion as it captures the Athenians' view that the people of Melos, the Melians, could not remain neutral in the face of conflict. When the Melians refused to take up arms, the Athenians attacked without mercy.

Since these earliest days, states have been prone to violence. They have often resorted to war to settle conflicts that defy more peaceful resolution. Disputes over land and resources have been particularly common. These clashes can be traced, in part, to the importance of territorial control in determining the relative status and positioning of states and their capacity to protect their sovereign rights and interests. Hopes for revenge or reversing the outcome of previous struggles have fanned the fires of hatred between peoples and added to the longevity of their conflicts. The artificial nature of many political borders has contributed further to this pattern. It has not been uncommon for rival ethnic, religious, or tribal groups to be thrown together politically within a designated space.

Joseph Nye identifies three forms of world politics that have emerged over time: imperial systems, feudal systems, and anarchic systems.[4] **Imperial systems** are characterized by the domination of a single power. Examples include the Roman Empire, Spain in the sixteenth century, France in the seventeenth century, and the British Empire in the nineteenth century. Other examples include ancient empires that were more regional in scope, such as those of the Aztecs, Incas, and Egyptians, who sought to control their contiguous environments.

A second way that international political borders have been delineated is **feudal systems**. Here political loyalties were based on allegiance not to the land but to the land owner or local lord. In some cases, this obligation might have even been to a more distant ruler or religious leader. Such a system was particularly common after the collapse of the Roman Empire. As Nye suggests, these political ties

imperial system
political organization in which one government is dominant over most of the world with which it has contact.

feudal system
political organization in which loyalty and political obligations take precedence over political boundaries.

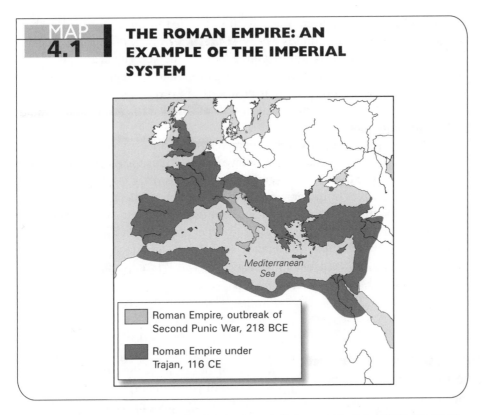

MAP 4.1 THE ROMAN EMPIRE: AN EXAMPLE OF THE IMPERIAL SYSTEM

Mediterranean Sea

Roman Empire, outbreak of
Second Punic War, 218 BCE

Roman Empire under
Trajan, 116 CE

Source: Henry R. Nau, *Perspectives on International Relations: Power, Institutions, and Ideas,* 3rd ed. (Washington, DC: CQ Press, 2012), 77.

were determined to a large extent by what happened to one's superiors. If a ruler married, an area and its people might find their obligations rearranged as part of a wedding dowry. Townspeople born French might suddenly find themselves made Flemish or even English.[5]

The third form of political borders that Nye distinguishes is an **anarchic system of states**. This is a system composed of political units operating in an environment with no higher central authority. The city-states of Greece were organized in this way. The international political system we are familiar with today is also considered an anarchic system of states. The Treaty of Westphalia, which ended the Thirty Years' War (1618–1648) in Europe, is generally regarded as the origin of this system. This war was primarily a religious conflict that divided combatants along Protestant and Catholic lines. Its outcome would change the political landscape of the area.

The writings of Niccolo Machiavelli in the early 1500s captured the creation of the anarchic system of states quite well. Machiavelli was an official in Florence serving under the rule of Piero Soderini. When the Medici family ousted

anarchic system of states

organization of political units that are relatively cohesive but with no higher government above them.

realism
political philosophy that sees
the struggle for power and the
potential for conflict as a
necessary evil in the pursuit of
national interest.

Soderini and came to power, Machiavelli was exiled to the countryside, where he would write his most famous work—*The Prince.* A man of the city relegated to farm life, Machiavelli sought to gain favor with the new rulers and get his job back. He put forward a series of recommendations and strategies for the leaders of the day, princes, to preserve their positions of power. His message was clear and reflected the conventional wisdom—all means were appropriate in pursuing the desired end.

Machiavelli's perspective can be characterized as an early conceptualization of **realism**, a perspective that many believe best captures the essence of international politics since the days of ancient Greece. Realism argues that power is the most critical element in understanding the character of international relations. The state is the most powerful actor in the international system and its pursuit of power drives its choices in relation to other states. Such a notion of using power to achieve political dominance was clearly in line with Machiavelli's worldview. Niccolo Machiavelli's advice from *The Prince* that it is better to be feared than loved reflects this perspective.

If you have a choice, to be feared is much safer than to be loved. For it is a good general rule about men, that they are ungrateful, fickle, liars and deceivers, fearful of danger and greedy for gain. While you serve their welfare, they are all yours, offering their blood, their belongings, their lives, and their children's lives, as we noted above—so long as the danger is remote. But when the danger is close at hand, they turn against you. Then, any prince who has relied on their words and has made no other preparations will come to grief; because friendships that are bought at a price, and not with greatness and nobility of soul, may be paid for but they are not acquired, and they cannot be used in time of need.[6]

IN THEIR OWN
WORDS   **Niccolo Machiavelli**

The Westphalian accords in 1648 placed states at the center of a new European order. It defined states on the basis of territory and populations within their boundaries, the existence of a system of government, and the recognition of other governments. The system revolved largely around the notion of **sovereignty**, which provided states with the right to self-determination—to attend to their own affairs without the interference of other states. The signatories thought that this system would provide a solid basis for a relatively stable order. In practice, however, it was difficult to realize, as individual states and their leaders had their own agendas.

Napoleon is a good example of such a leader, as he sought to extend France's reach as the nineteenth century began, posing a threat to the Westphalian system. He went too far in his quest for domination and was ultimately defeated by a coalition of Austria-Hungary, Britain, the Netherlands, Prussia, Russia, and Spain. The Napoleonic challenge revealed the fragile nature of this new order. It also illuminated the character of the system as it would evolve over the next 200 years. **Nationalism**—the commitment to and support of the interests of one's nation—emerged as a significant force. It brought diverse people together in pursuit of a common purpose but also created rifts between them, often providing the rationale for conflict and war.

THE BALANCE OF POWER SYSTEM: ITS FAILURES AND THE OUTBREAK OF WAR

Degrees of power would define the world order that emerged. Europe had come to dominate the international system, owing largely to the technological advances that had spurred the Industrial Revolution and the expansion of its colonial empires. Driven by the search for new riches and religious zeal, Spain and Portugal had been the first to expand outward, as they colonized the Americas prior to the mid-1700s. The British, Germans, Dutch, and French constituted the second wave, which lasted from about 1750 to 1870. Initially, these colonists went forth in pursuit of trade and markets. To continue growing, the industrial success that defined Germany and Great Britain at the beginning of the nineteenth century required raw materials and new markets. The less charted territories of Africa and Asia provided new ground. After 1870, economic necessity drove the exploitation of colonies.

While political control in the first two waves of colonialism had not been an overriding objective, it gained prominence in the latter part of the nineteenth century as the means to assure cooperation. This was certainly the case with Great Britain's colonial empire, which encompassed large parts of the Indian subcontinent, Africa, and Southeast Asia. The French were actively engaged in colonial expansion in Africa and Southeast Asia. Italy, Germany, and Belgium also joined the scramble for territory during this period. Colonial expansion wrought havoc on the African continent, as the European intruders uprooted indigenous groups and native cultures. The imperialist nations ignored African cultural identities in their pursuit of economic gain. Among the many legacies of colonialism are political borders that do not necessarily correspond to existing cultural borders. These colonial borders cut across land occupied by existing tribes, ethnic groups, and nations.

Preserving peace among the Europeans as they jockeyed for colonial empires required the maintenance of a fragile **balance of power**. Relying on transitory alliances to balance relationships, nation-states were able to prevent conflict while minimally cooperating with one another. Two major alliances emerged from these relationships—the Triple Alliance formed by Italy, Germany, and Austria-Hungary in 1882, and the Triple Entente formed in 1907 by France,

sovereignty
the right of states to self-determination—to attend to their own affairs without being subjected to the unwanted interference of others.

nationalism
commitment to and support of the interests of one's nation.

balance of power
a system of states that relies on shifting alliances to balance relationships and prevent conflict.

Great Britain, and Russia. These alliances solidified the political order, and as a result, undermined the flexibility states needed to assure peace. Increasingly, states also wanted more power for themselves, and this desire outweighed their need to cooperate with others. No longer was it simply enough for one alliance to balance another.

The result was that the balance of power that had stabilized the international system began to erode. While the Austro-Hungarians sought to maintain their influence, particularly in the Balkans, other countries began chipping away at their power. The Germans were intent upon expanding their power and prestige, sparking a naval arms race with Britain in the early part of the twentieth century. The French wanted revenge for their 1871 defeat in the Franco-Prussian War, and Russia wanted a show of force to offset perceptions that it had lost its ability to exert influence in the international arena.[7] In all of these instances, cooperation as a means to peaceful relationships lost credibility. The final blow, which triggered all-out conflict, came on June 28, 1914, with the assassination of Archduke Ferdinand, the heir to the Austro-Hungarian throne, by a Serbian nationalist. Within a month, the first full-scale world war had broken out.[8]

The discipline of **political science** developed about this time, as scholars tried to be more systematic in their understanding of the forces that were driving state interests. Up until the late 1800s, political studies were tied to history and to some extent economics. The founding of the American Political Science Association in 1903 is considered a turning point for the origins of the current field. The objective was to apply a more rigorous standard to understanding political behavior.

Intellectually, new perspectives were emerging as well. While the power politics notion was clear from historical experience, there were efforts to promote cooperation that relied on a more moderate view. In contrast to realism and its emphasis on conflict, **liberalism** emerged from the democratic tradition, emphasizing the potential for cooperation that exists among states. This notion would greatly inform US president Woodrow Wilson, himself a political scientist with a PhD from Johns Hopkins University, as he contemplated the turmoil in Europe.

Wilson entered World War I cautiously and only after US interests were directly under attack. Guided by the liberal tradition that placed a high value on the extension of democracy and cooperation, Wilson did not believe that war was the best method to resolve conflict. He justified the US entry into the conflict by arguing it would be "the war to end all wars." He outlined his intentions in his Fourteen Points Speech to Congress in 1917. In this address, Wilson argued for a new world order. He saw strong possibilities for the emergence of an enlightened leadership in the postwar era that would work together toward world peace. This approach came to be known as **idealism**—some would even call it utopianism—and it represented a view that would be difficult to attain. Idealism assumed cooperation would triumph over conflict. Enlightened leaders would jointly establish a world order defined by group effort as opposed to individual interest. The following excerpt from President Woodrow Wilson's

political science

the systematic study of political behavior institutionalized at the turn of the twentieth century.

liberalism

political philosophy from the democratic tradition that emphasizes the potential for cooperation among states.

idealism

a political philosophy that emphasizes cooperation to establish a peaceful world order.

Fourteen Points Speech delineates his vision for a new kind of cooperation.

Central to Wilson's utopian idealism was the notion of collective security. Each state would reduce its military preparedness with the understanding that all would act together in the event of an attack against any one state. Education and cross-cultural understanding would be emphasized as a way of gaining trust. Peaceful coexistence and cooperation would be encouraged through an institutionalized international organization, the League of Nations.

Unfortunately, Wilson's plan was not sufficient to resolve the conflict. The Treaty of Versailles that ended the war created the League, but an isolationist US Senate, wary of undertaking new international commitments, would not ratify it. This defeat was quite a blow to its creator, President Wilson, and undermined the League's power from the start. Moreover, the notion of cooperation that underlay not only the League, but also the ideal world that Wilson envisioned, was not realized. Wilson had hoped for a liberal order in which peace among states prevailed, reliant on the innate spirit of people to cooperate. International institutions would maintain that peace, and individual states would cooperate through those institutional mechanisms.

> It will be our wish and purpose that the processes of peace, when they are begun, shall be absolutely open and that they shall involve and permit henceforth no secret understandings of any kind. The day of conquest and aggrandizement is gone by; so is also the day of secret covenants entered into in the interest of particular governments and likely at some unlooked-for moment to upset the peace of the world. It is this happy fact, now clear to the view of every public man whose thoughts do not still linger in an age that is dead and gone, which makes it possible for every nation whose purposes are consistent with justice and the peace of the world to avow now or at any other time the objects it has in view.[9]

IN THEIR OWN WORDS   **Woodrow Wilson**

These assumptions proved naïve, as the uneasy peace was jeopardized by the Russian Revolution, which overthrew the Tsarist regime and marked the emergence of a communist Union of Soviet Socialist Republics (generally referred to as either the USSR or the Soviet Union) in the early 1920s. It bent further under the weight of global financial instability following the US stock market crash of 1929 and the aggressive military expansion of Germany and Japan. Tensions escalated on many fronts, threatening the sovereignty of many countries and the very existence of Jews and other groups. The peace shattered completely with the outbreak of World War II in 1939.

In the early days of World War II, the United States chose to operate on the sidelines. It entered the fray only following the Japanese attack on American forces and facilities at Pearl Harbor, Hawaii, in 1941. The United States joined its European allies and its rival, the Soviet Union, to defeat a common German enemy as well. The war confronted the United States with a series of new security challenges that required significant changes in its previous isolationist philosophy and policy.

By the time the war was over, the array of states had changed completely. States that had previously dominated the anarchic system lay in financial, political, and physical ruin. The war had taken its toll. Atomic bombs dropped on Hiroshima and Nagasaki devastated Japan, Germany was divided into two countries—East Germany and West Germany—and many European cities had been leveled by airstrikes. The world needed leadership in order to move beyond the wreckage. The United States had not suffered any physical destruction and emerged from the war as the world's only creditor country. A considerable segment of the US population believed that the future security of the country rested on its willingness and ability to restructure the pattern of international relations. Despite considerable controversy over whether it should do so, the United States took on a leadership position.

The United States assumed this responsibility somewhat reluctantly but did not take it lightly. The decision to return to a more isolationist posture after World War I had been a failure. The geopolitical strategies that had fueled the fires of many countries in their pursuit of power were now clear. The United States hoped to soften these inclinations with a cooperative spirit that might provide for a lasting peace. In short, it intended to move forward with a blend of realist and idealist approaches.

The creation of the United Nations (UN) in 1945 reflected this thinking. The victors of World War II crafted the organization to restore a sense of collective responsibility for maintaining the peace. Power politics was still important, however, necessitating the need to grant special privileges and authority to a Security Council of five designated Great Powers (China, France, the Soviet Union, the United Kingdom, and the United States) to assure their participation. Unlike the League of Nations, the UN attracted a wide range of eligible states to its ranks by limiting its mandate and its ability to take definitive action without the unanimous consent of its strongest members. This veto power of the "Big Five," as the permanent members of the Security Council came to be called, seriously undermined the body's overall effectiveness in the years ahead. The first 10 years of the organization were marred by a rivalry between the United States and the Soviet Union that played out in the Security Council, preventing effective action.

During this time, realists honed their views of state relationships to reflect the divisions of the day. Political scientist Hans Morgenthau defined the political realism that characterized the emerging dynamics of the post–World War II period in his 1948 treatise, *Power among Nations: The Struggle for Power and Peace.* Morgenthau's views connected Machiavelli's and Thucydides's understandings of power and impulse with the modern world. The Great Powers' failure to create a cooperative international environment after World War II required a reevaluation of the motivations that guided state interaction.[10] Ultimately, individual states returned to the pursuit of power as a guiding principle.

THE COLD WAR

Even as the United States was poised to assume leadership of the world, it was forced to confront the emerging power of its wartime ally, the Soviet Union. The Soviets had broad political aspirations and were unwilling to relinquish power to support the collective security interests of the rest of the world. Two relatively equal centers of power, the United States and the Soviet Union, became the dominant players in a **bipolar** world. As both sides recognized the need to avoid the potentially dire consequences of a heated or direct military confrontation, this period became known as the Cold War era. Each side expressed its animosity toward one another in low intensity conflicts around the globe.

The Cold War was both an ideological struggle between economic and moral ideas (capitalism vs. communism) and a political competition where both sides sought, at the very least, to establish alliances that would extend their influence across the world. For its part, the United States pursued a strategy that came to be known as **containment**. Diplomat George Kennan explained it as a defensive strategy designed to limit Soviet efforts to extend their influence. The US leadership saw it as the best way to preserve a global balance of power. The Truman Doctrine, a policy put forth by US president Harry Truman to support Greece and Turkey economically and militarily against Soviet aggression, would be extended many times over.

The Soviet Union put forward its policies in similar fashion. Each side viewed the intentions of the other with considerable distrust and suspicion. The first major confrontation came in the crisis over divided Berlin in 1948. Soviet leader Joseph Stalin sought to isolate the US zone of western Berlin through a blockade. The United States responded with a massive airlift in 1949, forcing the Soviets to lift their siege of the city.

Initially, the Cold War was mainly a European phenomenon, with the postwar division of Germany capturing the essence of the superpower rivalry. The Berlin Wall, built in 1961 to separate East Berlin from West Berlin, served as its most poignant symbol. The United States sought both to promote and protect the military security of its allies through the North Atlantic Treaty Organization (NATO); the Soviets put forward an equivalent strategy by creating the Warsaw Treaty Organization (WTO), more commonly referred to as the Warsaw Pact.

In 1949, the establishment of a communist government in China under the leadership of Mao Zedong extended the struggle. With the support of the Soviet Union, China began to emerge as a power in its own right as evidenced by its involvement in the Korean War in 1950. Under the auspices of the UN, the United States intervened in that conflict, ending a military and political stalemate. Meanwhile, the Russians and the Chinese soon found themselves embroiled in a rivalry of their own. They split by the early 1960s over

bipolar
a type of interstate system where two states hold the most significant power.

containment
the policy of the United States during the Cold War that checked aggressive Soviet actions by military alliances.

American soldiers stand near one of the checkpoints of the Berlin Wall in February 1961.

ideological differences. To counter communist efforts across Asia, the United States moved to cement ties with Japan, its former enemy.

The basic intent of the two superpowers remained quite consistent throughout the Cold War era (1945–1989). Different phases periodically changed the way the game was played. The stakes were high as the specter of a mushroom-shaped cloud, embodying the risk of a nuclear confrontation, loomed. Soviet efforts to consolidate power came in several phases in relation to their new East European partners. In November 1956, low tolerance for dissention led to the invasion of Hungary to counter what had become a spontaneous revolt against the Soviet-dominated government. A similar action was taken against Czechoslovakia in August of 1968 following the Prague Spring, a period during which more liberal political freedoms had been granted under the leadership of Alexander Dubcek.

The 1959 Cuban Revolution was especially critical, as it threatened the US political monopoly in the hemisphere by extending Soviet influence to within 90 miles of American soil. Following a failed US effort to overthrow Cuban leader Fidel Castro through an invasion at the Bay of Pigs, the Soviet Union attempted to install nuclear missiles on the island. The United States learned of the undertaking prior to the completion of the project, setting up what was to become the defining moment of the Cold War. The 1962 Cuban Missile Crisis was the first (and only) direct superpower confrontation that threatened to involve the use of nuclear weapons. After a two-week standoff resulting from a US-imposed blockade of all traffic—air and naval—into the island, President John F. Kennedy and Soviet premier Nikita Krushchev resolved the situation diplomatically.

Each power tried to mold political events across the world. At times, this led to interventions with unpredictable outcomes. The US involvement in Vietnam in the 1960s is a good example. Driven to prevent the fall of pro-Western governments to communist insurgencies across Southeast Asia (by the so-called domino theory—if one fell, then the next would follow), the United States fought a difficult and highly controversial war that lasted for over a decade and failed to achieve its objectives. When it was all over, the United States had lost considerable political and military prestige.

Not all states became parties to the Cold War, however, and many colonies endeavored during this period to assert their independence. Most notable was

India, the jewel in the crown of the British Empire. While the movement had been growing in the interwar years, the divisiveness of World War II and the weakening of British influence globally that followed opened the door for a formal declaration of independence in 1950. Pakistan followed in 1956. Given its newfound independence, India quickly moved to declare itself "nonaligned" with either axis of power—the United States or the Soviet Union. Other states soon joined India, including Indonesia, Yugoslavia, Egypt, and Ghana. This group has endured and expresses its common interests in occasional nonaligned summits. Politically, the group functions today as a voting bloc in the UN, with over 100 members.

As the burdens of the Cold War mounted, both major powers attempted to lessen their ongoing confrontations. By the late 1960s, veteran cold warriors US president Richard Nixon and Soviet premier Leonid Brezhnev had assumed leadership of their respective countries and had the political credentials to pursue a new approach. They designed a policy of **détente** that promoted opportunities for US-Soviet cooperation, even while the broader rivalry persisted. These efforts produced some worthwhile results, most notably in the area of arms control through the negotiation of two Strategic Arms Limitation Treaties (SALT I and SALT II). But the relaxation in tension was short lived. Détente could not get the two sides to agree on the basic principles of acceptable behavior—especially when it came to dealing with political unrest in Africa, Asia, Latin America, and the Middle East.

détente
a policy designed in the late 1960s by US president Richard Nixon and Soviet premier Leonid Brezhnev to promote opportunities for US-Soviet cooperation, even while the broader rivalry persisted.

By the 1980s, the Cold War was heating up once again. Following a period of considerable Soviet meddling in other countries and limited response from a United States weary from its Vietnam experience, US president Ronald Reagan assumed a more aggressive strategy to turn the tide. The Reagan Doctrine signaled a renewed willingness to assert US interests where the Soviets had been active, such as Nicaragua and Afghanistan. Reagan also took steps to bolster US nuclear and conventional weapons capabilities. These policies were met with trepidation by both European allies and Latin American neighbors.

Meanwhile, the decades of global engagement had taken their toll on the Soviet Union. Difficulties in managing leadership succession, a stagnant economy, prolonged war in Afghanistan, and growing political unrest in many of the Soviet republics themselves contributed to the eventual demise of the communist regime. Across much of Eastern Europe, pro-democracy movements ultimately led to the toppling of many governments that the Soviets had installed and supported. Just as the Berlin Wall had come to epitomize the Cold War, its fall in 1989 marked the end of this era. By 1991, the Soviet Union itself ceased to exist. The bipolar structure rapidly gave way to a more multipolar one with new centers of power.

As the lone remaining superpower, the United States appeared poised to preside over what President George H.W. Bush declared to be a "new world order" that would require less in the way of active manipulation and management of the global arena. It did not take long for that optimism to fade. Despite its many dangers, the US-Soviet rivalry of the Cold War had provided a degree of predictability and stability to international relations. Neither side anticipated the challenges to international security that the demise of their rivalry would create.

THE POST–COLD WAR WORLD

The world that emerged after the Cold War saw significant changes to the international order. The demise of the Soviet Union and the many new countries that were created resulted in a new distribution of power. The former communist state of Yugoslavia, for example, became engulfed in a civil war. It broke apart as Slovenia, Croatia, and later Bosnia and Herzegovina asserted their rights to sovereignty. While the dominant Serbians were able to accept the new states of Croatia and Slovenia, there were not willing to let Bosnia and Herzegovina go as easily, and a protracted battle ensued.

Political instability continued in the Middle East, erupting in war in 1991. Iraqi President Saddam Hussein, hoping to acquire control over additional territory and oil, invaded neighboring Kuwait. Despite warnings from the

MAP 4.2 YUGOSLAVIA: BEFORE AND AFTER 1991

Source: Bruce Bueno de Mesquita, *Principles of International Politics,* 3rd ed. (Washington, DC: CQ Press, 2005), 123.

United States, Saddam anticipated little if any response. He guessed wrong, and Iraqi troops were forced into a hasty retreat as President George H. W. Bush authorized a massive US invasion with support from an impressive coalition of governments worldwide.

This first Gulf War was significant for a number of reasons. First, it forced states to reconsider the ways regional balances could be preserved without the counterpositioning of opposing superpowers. Second, US efforts to gain the approval of the UN and countries with a stake in the outcome appeared to offer the promise of multilateral management of future crises. The international coalition that formed in response to the Iraqi invasion of Kuwait was unprecedented. Finally, the decision of the United States to leave Saddam in power rather than risk protracted involvement indicated a reluctance to extend commitments beyond those to address direct threats to American interests.

A UN soldier is shown here guarding Somalis near a UN food distribution site in Mogadishu, Somalia, on July 4, 1993.

The African continent was not left unscathed, as conflicts unfolded in the African countries of Somalia and Rwanda. By 1992, Somalia's ongoing civil conflict left no one effectively in charge, as small groups of warlords fought for control of the country. The majority of the citizens were starving to death after a failed crop season. The United States spearheaded a coalition of forces that intervened for humanitarian and peacekeeping purposes. Given the coalition troops' limited mandate, which did not allow engaging in military action, they found themselves in a compromised position. As a result, they suffered gut-wrenching casualties that included the dragging of a dead US soldier through the streets of Mogadishu. The movie *Black Hawk Down* (2001) captured the intensity of the conflict.

Rwanda posed an even more difficult challenge, as feuding ethnic groups took their animosities to the extreme in a blood bath in 1994. Hutu extremists sought restitution against the Tutsis for past wrongs in a killing rampage that lasted over 100 days. International attention to the tragedy was limited, as the Somali experience weighed heavily in the decision to avoid Rwanda altogether, despite widespread atrocities that resulted in the slaughter of an estimated 800,000 civilians. The result was an outflow of refugees to neighboring countries that are still bearing the burden of the conflict.

HOW DO YOU **CONNECT?**	**HAVE YOU OR A FAMILY MEMBER EVER SERVED IN THE MILITARY?**

a. Yes, I have served in the military.

b. Yes, someone in my family has served in the military.

c. No, neither I nor anyone in my family has served in the military.

HOW DO YOU CONNECT?

WHAT IS YOUR EXPERIENCE WITH POLITICAL UNREST?

Have you ever been in a place at a time when it was experiencing political unrest?

   a. yes

   b. no

Have you ever had to leave your home due to political unrest?

   a. yes

   b. no

Beyond these realignments, the most significant event that would restructure the post–Cold War world was 9/11. On the morning of September 11, 2001, hijacked airplanes crashed into the twin towers of New York's World Trade Center and into the Pentagon in Arlington, Virginia. A fourth hijacked plane, targeting Washington, DC, was brought down by passengers in a crash landing in Pennsylvania. No one survived. These attacks, orchestrated by Osama bin Laden and his Islamic al-Qaeda network, revealed the dangerous undercurrents jeopardizing the world's political stability. The United States and an array of partners responded forcefully, with President George W. Bush declaring a global war on terror that started with an invasion of Afghanistan in 2001.

The war in Afghanistan pitted the United States against a government controlled by the Taliban, an Islamic fundamentalist group with close ties to al-Qaeda—the organization that claimed responsibility for the 9/11 attacks. The Taliban were deposed early on, but the political restructuring process proved difficult and unwieldy. The NATO–led international security force, composed largely of US military personnel, found it difficult to bring order to the country or to fully guarantee the future of the Afghan government against a continuing insurgency led by Taliban and al-Qaeda forces. The conflict dragged on and the outcome was in doubt. Finally, in 2012, there was an agreement to turn over the bulk of responsibility for security to Afghan forces by mid-2013 and to remove NATO combat forces by 2014.[11] The political future of the country remains uncertain.

Fear that a former adversary, Saddam Hussein, had access to weapons of mass destruction would extend the war on terror into Iraq, as the United States invaded in 2003. There was insufficient evidence from the outset to document the existence of weapons of mass destruction, undermining the credibility of the intervention. Critics charged that the invasion was an American effort to settle an old score with Saddam for his earlier invasion of Kuwait and for his alleged role in a plot to assassinate the president's father. A long, protracted conflict would begin that ultimately resulted in not only the overthrow of Saddam but also his trial and subsequent death sentence. Efforts to forge a political balance among Iraq's competing groups (Shi'a Muslims, Sunni Muslims, and Kurds) were met with stiff resistance, and the war continued. In 2011, a deal was struck that paved the way for the removal of US combat forces and for moving forward with the complex task of rebuilding the country.

The post–Cold War world was evolving, with traditional powers seeking to hold on to their influence and new ones aspiring to acquire greater leverage of their own. Although the United States assumed a central role, Russia made it clear that it did not intend to recede into the background. Russia worked to parlay considerable military strength and wealth generated by ample oil and gas reserves into a position where it could extend its political and military reach. Vladimir Putin, the country's dominant political figure, took firm control in directing the effort. After completing the constitutionally mandated limit of two terms as Russia's president (2000–2008), Putin stepped down but was then reelected for a new term in 2012. He had engineered a constitutional change to extend presidential terms to six years and was poised to move forward with his goal of returning Russia to international prominence.

If Russia symbolized the attempt to recapture past glory, China represented the potential of the future. The world's fastest-growing economy, China, was well positioned to become a major global military and political power. It significantly enhanced its military capabilities, built a lucrative weapons export industry, actively supported economic development projects in Africa and Latin America, and nurtured ties with troublesome regimes such as those of North Korea and Iran. While avoiding volatile confrontations that could jeopardize its broad commercial interests, China bristled at periodic US criticisms of its human rights policies and made it clear that it would do things its own way and according to its self-interest.

Meanwhile, the efforts of some other states to assert themselves and to wield their influence threatened the stability of the international order. North Korea provided an important test. Although in many respects a failed state incapable of sustaining its own people, North Korea launched a nuclear weapons development program and indicated its intention to move forward aggressively with the effort. Diplomatic attempts to persuade North Korea to suspend these activities did not succeed, and the potential for conflict remained considerable, particularly in light of the continuing tensions between North and South Korea dating back to the war of the early 1950s.

Demonstrators take part in a protest at Tahrir Square in Cairo, Egypt. One of the watershed events of the Arab Spring of 2011, these protests led to the resignation of long-time Egyptian president Hosni Mubarak in February 2011 and helped spark revolution and protests in other Middle East countries.

Iran posed an even greater challenge to the peace. The country's considerable political agenda included the desire to extend its political clout across the Persian Gulf, facilitate the spread of fundamentalist Islamic ideology, destroy Israel, and develop a nuclear capability. While Iran claimed that its nuclear aspirations were confined to peaceful purposes only, the United States was not convinced and moved to impose economic sanctions such as limiting purchases of oil and freezing access to Iranian assets held in American banks.[12] The UN sought to broker a deal that would subject Iran's nuclear program to international monitoring, but found it difficult to reach agreement. Iran's ambitions were not derailed, and the country continued to pursue a path that would broaden the scope of its influence—both within the region and beyond.

In many respects, traditional notions of power politics continued to dominate the global political scene. However, changing conditions also gave voice to the hopes of people looking to gain greater control over their own lives. The dramatic events that unfolded across North Africa and the Middle East in 2011 spoke directly to these dreams. The decision of a street merchant to burn himself to death to protest treatment by police set off protests across Tunisia calling for the resignation of its authoritarian leader. Prodemocracy demonstrations quickly spread to other countries across the area during what became popularly known as the Arab Spring. By the time it was over, a number of longstanding rulers were gone. Perhaps most noteworthy was the forced resignation of Hosni Mubarak, the president of Egypt since 1981, and the killing of Muammar Gaddafi, who ruled Libya for 42 years.

The events of the Arab Spring did not produce uniform results. In Syria, for example, the regime of Bashar al-Assad strongly resisted efforts to unseat it, and a protracted and bloody civil war ensued. In Egypt, the transition to democracy was rocky, as the military sought to retain its political leverage, and many different political groups vied for power.

The desire for democracy was reflected in political changes occurring in other parts of the world as well. In Bolivia and Peru, for example, leaders gained power by appealing to people's hopes for more open political processes and policies to address severe economic inequalities. Despite varying circumstances and outcomes, these situations were all driven, in part, by the actions of people demanding to have their voices heard and to participate in selecting those who governed them.

What is the significance of these events and the realignment of the world that has occurred? What tools are available to help us understand them? Political scientists have introduced a new way of thinking about the international order, **constructivism**, which emphasizes the role of ideas and the meaning given to those ideas. They argue that the underlying forces frequently driving decisions in the international system are based on artificially constructed perceptions and the historical and emotional baggage attached to them, what international

---

HOW DO YOU CONNECT? | HOW DO YOU PARTICIPATE POLITICALLY?

Do you vote?

  a. yes, in almost all elections

  b. yes, in elections of particular interest to me

  c. No, I choose not to vote.

  d. No, I come from a place where elections are not held.

Are you a member of a political organization?,

  a. Yes, I am affiliated with a political party.

  b. Yes, I am affiliated with other organizations.

  c. No, I am not affiliated with any political organization.

Have you ever participated in a political campaign?

  a. yes, on a national level

  b. yes, on a local level

  c. yes, both on a national and local level

  d. No, I have not participated in a political campaign.

Have you ever been a part of a political protest or demonstration?

  a. yes

  b. no

---

constructivism
a view of the global order that sees the state and the rules that govern it as an artificial construct.

relations scholar Nicholas Onuf has called "a world of our making."[13] The development of feminist views of international relations has emerged from this perspective, giving rise to feminist critiques of the masculine images of world order. Feminist scholar Ann Tickner employs a gendered perspective to challenge the way in which we understand issues in the post–Cold War era, comparing the feminist view to more traditional perspectives.[14] Still, the reliance on power politics and alliances as a way to promote security agendas in the current era, even though significant changes in the international system have occurred, is an example of how we have held on to traditional concepts. The following debate on the role of the NATO alliance reflects this concern.

PRO/CON
Should the NATO alliance continue?

PRO	CON

Xenia Dormandy
Xenia Dormandy, Senior Fellow, US International Role, Chatham House, London. Written for *CQ Researcher*, March 2012

Justin Logan
Justin Logan, Director of Foreign Policy Studies, CATO Institute, Washington. Written for *CQ Researcher*, March 2012

PRO

Among other factors, new technologies, diverse communications channels, more-integrated problems and a rising number of actors are all increasing the complexity and speed of change in the world today. Amid this cacophony and potential confusion, it would be only sensible to propose that the methods of responding to today's events need to be updated.

The United Nations will be 67 this year. NATO will be 63. While there are many valid questions regarding their constituent memberships, given their relatively broad inclusiveness and their long and respected histories, their activities invoke a certain legitimacy.

Nations will continue to choose, where possible, to undertake operations under the banner of these institutions according to the situation and their specific capabilities, responsibilities and strategic concerns. Recent efforts by European, Gulf and U.S. powers to gain a U.N. resolution on Syria are indicative of this. However, these efforts also demonstrate that such institutions, precisely because of their broad membership, can be dysfunctional.

CON

The United States should form military alliances to fight wars. NATO was formed because after World War II Western Europe was devastated, and Washington feared that Moscow might be able to plunge into Western Europe and capitalize on the devastation.

In 1951, however, President Dwight D. Eisenhower remarked that "if in 10 years, all American troops stationed in Europe for national defense purposes have not been returned to the United States, then this whole project will have failed." According to Ike, the purpose of NATO was to help the Western European countries "regain their confidence and get on their own military feet."

NATO's broader purpose in Europe was summed up in an apocryphal quote attributed to Lord Ismay: The alliance was to keep "the Russians out, the Americans in and the Germans down." The Russians are out, and they are going to stay out. Poland faces no threat of Russian attack, to say nothing of countries to her west.

(Continued on next page)   *(Continued on next page)*

PRO/CON (Continued)
Should the NATO alliance continue?

PRO	CON
Different values and ideologies can stymie decisions and progress on vital issues.	Instead, today NATO constitutes a system of transfer payments from U.S. taxpayers (and their Chinese creditors) to bloated European welfare states. It also serves as a make-work project for the think tankers, bureaucrats and journalists who make a living off the "trans-Atlantic relationship."
If international institutions are to continue to be effective tools for multilateral action, they will have to find new ways of working. The likely path will mirror patterns already seen in structures like the Proliferation Security Initiative (PSI) or the post-2004 East Asian tsunami response, in which five countries came together to provide immediate relief as the U.N. mounted its operations and subsequently disbanded when its job was done. These are ad hoc groups of nations with the will, capabilities and interests to act to achieve specific objectives, which, when attained, break up. The future lies with such groups.	All of this might be waved off as harmless had the alliance not expanded eastward three times to include an array of countries that no major member has any intention of defending militarily, should it come to that. There simply aren't the funds in member-state accounts to cover the checks NATO has written.
If current organizations like the U.N. and NATO want to continue to remain effective, they too will have to adopt similar mechanisms. We are already seeing this to be the case. The operation in Libya had NATO cover but involved only a subset of NATO members in its activities, in coordination with some non-NATO actors. The ISAF (International Security Assistance Force) operations in Afghanistan are another such example.	In the past decades there has been talk in Europe of promoting autonomous European defense capabilities. (Indeed, talk of autonomous European cooperation goes back nearly to the founding of NATO.) However, Washington has consistently scuppered European attempts at creating a third force because it views NATO as a vehicle for controlling Europe's security policy. The result has been a militarily infantile Europe that found it impossible even to fulfill its desire to change the regime of Moammar Gadhafi without help from Washington.
NATO is already finding ways to act effectively according to this new ad hoc method, within its more formal constructs. It is unlikely, however, that the members will formalize this methodology, instead letting it take place implicitly. One should not expect the current debate within NATO for all members to "pull their weight" to end anytime soon.	Despite Washington's misgivings, a more powerful, more autonomous Europe would be a good thing for America. It would allow the United States to shrink its armed forces and save money. Sixty years after Eisenhower's admonition, surely it is time to declare the alliance a relic of the past and put NATO out to pasture.

Source: R. Flamini, "U.S.-Europe Relations," *CQ Researcher*, 22 (March 23, 2012): 277–300, http://library.cqpress.com/cqresearcher/.

WHERE Do You Stand?

1. Are military alliances important in a globalized world?
2. Should the membership of NATO be expanded?
3. Do you believe NATO should be disbanded altogether?

CONCLUSION: THE QUEST FOR SECURITY

Political borders, such as those separating rival powers and major military blocs, have constituted the principal fault lines of international politics throughout our history. World War I, World War II, and the Cold War between the United States and the Soviet Union provide recent examples. For some, political boundaries have lost their significance, as struggles today fall along ethnic, racial, religious, linguistic, caste, and class lines. This erosion of the building blocks of the political world represents a growing problem, as countries used to be easier to define and differentiate. To better understand the changing international system, we need to recognize other boundaries.

The conflicts that have emerged in this new political environment pose some unique challenges. As technology has brought the world closer together, it has also made it more difficult to limit the spillover from situations that threaten the peace. The failure to reduce animosities or to address ongoing frustrations has added to the chaos. Liberalism suggests that the more people cross political borders, the more their interactions provide opportunities for a more peaceful planet. However, realists would remind us that there are numerous conflicts throughout the world at any given time. Constructivists argue that we must rethink our traditional ways of conceptualizing the world to better understand one another.

As we noted at the outset of this chapter, states remain the most powerful actors in the global arena; however, globalization has introduced new challenges that confront them. The ability of states to address problems that are increasingly global in nature will require a broader view that takes into account multiple pressures on these political borders. The roles that conflict, dangerous weapons of mass destruction, and terrorists will play cannot be overlooked, and creative responses must be crafted to address them.

KEYConcepts

anarchic system of states 77
balance of power 79
bipolar 83
constructivism 90
containment 83
détente 85
feudal system 76

idealism 80
imperial system 76
liberalism 80
nationalism 79
political science 80
realism 78
sovereignty 79

TO LEARNMore

Books and Other Print Media

Alexander Wendt, *Social Theory of International Politics* (Cambridge, UK: Cambridge University Press, 1999).

Wendt offers a cultural theory of international politics that forms the basis of constructivism.

Cynthia Enloe, *Bananas, Beaches and Bases: Making Feminist Sense of International Politics* (Berkeley: University of California Press, 2000).

Enloe lays the foundation for a feminist perspective on international relations, illustrated by many examples of power relations between genders and other groups.

Hans Morgenthau, *Politics Among Nations: The Struggle for Power and Peace* (New York: Knopf, 1948).

Morgenthau's assessment of the post–World War II world that was emerging remains a classic for understanding the way in which power politics and political realism has guided international relations.

John Mearsheimer, *The Tragedy of Great Power Politics* (New York: W. W. Norton, 2001).

Mearsheimer outlines his theory of offensive realism, including its basic assumptions, its roots in early realism, how power shifts among state actors, and what it could all mean for the future of international relations.

Niccolo Machiavelli, *The Prince*, 2nd ed. (New York: W. W. Norton, 1992).

Machiavelli's prescriptions for how a prince should behave provide an excellent view not only of the political machinations of the day but the practical realities of governing.

Parag Khanna, *The Second World: How Emerging Powers are Redefining Global Competition in the 21st Century* (New York: Random House, 2008).

Khanna offers a view of the changing world order that focuses on the US, Europe, and China.

Websites

Carnegie Endowment for International Peace, www.carnegieendowment.org/.

The Carnegie Endowment for International Peace is a global think tank that produces reports on the issues that affect the search for peace.

Foreign Affairs, www.foreignaffairs.com/.

Foreign Affairs is an American journal published by the Council on Foreign Relations that aims to promote discussion on American foreign policy and global affairs.

Foreign Policy, www.foreignpolicy.com/.

Foreign Policy is an American journal owned by *The Washington Post* that covers issues of global politics and economics and publishes the Top 100 Global Thinkers and Failed States Index annually.

IR Theory, www.irtheory.com/.

The International Relations Theory website gives an overview of the various theories that inform the way in which international relations scholars view the world.

World Politics Review, www.worldpoliticsreview.com/.

World Politics Review is a web-based news organization that offers news and opinions on many topics, including global politics, economics, culture, security, and environmental issues.

Videos

Black Hawk Down (2001).

This popular movie, based on real events, tells the story of the Battle of Mogadishu, in which an elite group of US soldiers seek to capture the Somali leader and find themselves engaged in a fierce battle for their lives.

A Historic Moment in the Arab World (2011).

Wadah Khanfar speaks about the forces that sparked the Arab Spring and moved the revolution forward and offers a positive view of the future. www.ted.com/talks/wadah_khanfar_a_historic_moment_in_the_arab_world.html

The Hurt Locker (2008).

This Academy award-winning movie, based on true events, follows the story of a sergeant in charge of a bomb disposal team in Iraq.

Joseph Nye on Global Power Shifts (2010).

Nye discusses how power shifts between state actors and the relationship between the United States and China. www.ted.com/talks/joseph_nye_on_global_power_shifts.html

Why Nations Should Pursue "Soft" Power (2009).

Shashi Tharoor discusses how nations can influence the international political system through soft power and the sharing of their culture through food, music, and technology. www.ted.com/talks/lang/en/shashi_tharoor.html

Challenges to Security

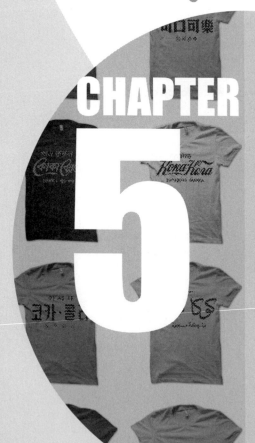

The combination of nuclear weapons and terrorist activities place the world today at significant risk. US senator Sam Nunn and media mogul Ted Turner founded the Nuclear Threat Initiative organization in 2001 to prevent the use of nuclear, biological, and chemical weapons and strengthen global security. They believe these weapons pose the greatest threat to peace in the world today. In fact, conflict is always present due to the nature of nation-states, the people who live in them, and the way in which these people define their interests. The potential for destruction has never been greater, given the unstable political climates in many areas of the world. As a result, the most fundamental global political challenges relate to matters of war and peace and the arsenal of weapons readily available to both states and terrorists alike.

Since its earliest days, the nation-state system has been prone to violence. Nationalism has been a contributing factor. State leaders have often used symbols of pride and purpose to mobilize support and to justify actions, particularly

"The greatest threat we face in the world is the threat of nuclear terrorism, and the best way to protect against that threat is to secure nuclear material wherever it exists and to get rid of as much material as possible."

—Sam Nunn, former US senator and cofounder of the Nuclear Threat Initiative, 2012[1]

in response to perceived threats or injustices. Nationalism has served as an important tool of governments to defend, protect, or advance state interests. It has also been used to both promote and rationalize aggressive or belligerent behaviors.

Unfortunately, states have often resorted to war to settle conflicts, even before they may have exhausted all possibilities for a more peaceful resolution. Disputes over land and resources are particularly common. Such conflict can be traced, in part, to the importance of ownership and control in determining the relative status and positioning of states, as well as their capacity to protect their sovereign rights and interests. The long history of many territorial conflicts in the Balkans, the Middle East, and elsewhere adds to their endurance. Hopes for revenge or reversing outcomes of previous encounters often fan the fires of hatred between peoples and make it difficult to find common ground for peaceful coexistence.

The artificial nature of many boundaries and borders has contributed further to this pattern. It is not uncommon for rival ethnic, religious, or tribal groups to be thrown together politically within a designated space. Such delineations have proven especially troublesome in the developing world, where the end of colonialism led to the creation of new states—which sat on top of and often crossed over much older nations—without much consideration for historical differences and grievances. The results are predictable. Civil wars erupt, and governments fall apart easily. Rwanda, Somalia, Yugoslavia, Iraq, and many other places have suffered catastrophic human tolls. When a particular group is separated and seeks to come together to claim their sovereign rights that other powers do not recognize, such as the Kurds in Iraq, Iran, and Turkey, matters are further complicated. The ongoing conflicts in much of the Middle East illuminate these challenges.

A giant column of dark smoke rises more than 20,000 feet into the air after the second atomic bomb ever used in warfare explodes over the Japanese port and town of Nagasaki, on August 9, 1945. Dropped by the US Army Air Force's B-29 plane "Bockscar," the bomb killed more than 70,000 people instantly, with tens of thousands dying later from effects of the radioactive fallout. This photo was made three minutes after the atom bomb struck Nagasaki. Almost 70 years later, nuclear weapons, as well as biological and chemical weapons, remain amongst the biggest challenges to world security.

CONFLICT IN THE MIDDLE EAST

While protests across the region in spring 2011 altered the political landscape, the long-standing tension between Israel and the Palestinians lies at the heart of the instability in the Middle East. The conflict goes back to biblical times and incorporates a number of the issues that have caused disputes among other people elsewhere—land, resources, religion, the desire for revenge. The roots of the conflict today can be traced to the early twentieth century, when Britain became the latest in a long succession of great powers to control the area.

After World War I and the defeat of the Turkish Ottoman Empire, the British administered Palestine—the territory that today comprises Israel and Jordan. They put forward their vision for the future of the area in the 1917 **Balfour Declaration**, which called for the eventual creation of a Jewish national home in Palestine while still preserving the rights of non-Jewish communities.[2]

Balfour Declaration
the 1917 British plan calling for the eventual creation of a Jewish national home in Palestine.

Britain presided over Palestine through a mandate of the League of Nations but had a difficult time maintaining order. It increasingly resorted to force to counter the activities of both Arab and Jewish militias looking to advance their respective political power and to undermine the British occupation. Meanwhile, the demographic balance of Palestine changed considerably in the 1930s with the arrival of thousands of European Jews escaping the scourge of the Holocaust that would subsequently claim more than six million victims.

The effort to implement the spirit of the Balfour plan proceeded in 1947, with the decision by the United Nations (UN) to endorse the partition or division of Palestine into independent Jewish and Arab states with Jerusalem as an international city. In 1948, the state of Israel was established—welcomed by Jews as the miracle of independence and regarded by Arabs as *al-nakba,* the catastrophe. Setting a pattern that was to characterize much of the future between these rivals, a war ensued that engulfed many countries across the region. When the fighting stopped, the situation on the ground was quite different from that envisioned by the UN. Israel survived, but the country was smaller geographically. The city of Jerusalem was divided, and Jordan gained control of additional territory on the West Bank of the Jordan River that was home to significant numbers of Palestinian Arabs.

Other wars would occur as the years progressed, but the one in 1967 would have the most profound implications for Israeli-Palestinian relations. The Six-Day War, as it came to be called, established Israel's sovereignty over all of Jerusalem and the West Bank territories. Israel also gained control over Gaza, a narrow strip of land off the Mediterranean coast that had belonged to Egypt, as well as some other strategic terrain (the Sinai Desert, also acquired from Egypt, and the Golan Heights from Syria).

While enhancing Israel's physical security, its possession of these lands added to the animosities and political stalemate. Diplomatic efforts failed to secure a

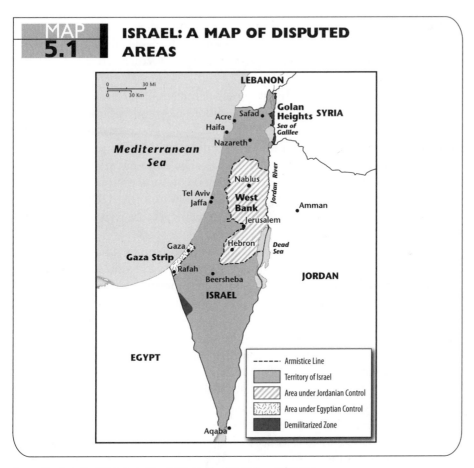

MAP 5.1 | ISRAEL: A MAP OF DISPUTED AREAS

Source: Ellen Lust, *The Middle East,* 12th ed. (Washington, DC: CQ Press, 2010), 253.

deal that would involve the exchange of land in return for peace guarantees. Palestinians did not accept the legitimacy of the state of Israel, and Israel did not accept the right of Palestinians to have their own state in the occupied territories. The precarious coexistence of the two sides was often marked by significant outbursts of violence.

With no government of their own, many Palestinians turned to a political movement born in the 1960s to lead the fight against Israel—the Palestine Liberation Organization (PLO). The PLO was an organization encompassing a number of Palestinian groups. The largest was Fatah, led by Yasser Arafat and actively engaged in the armed struggle. Fatah and Arafat gained considerable international recognition and notoriety for their airplane hijackings and other violent acts to gain support and publicity for their cause.

Without an agreeable framework for moving forward to resolve the impasse peacefully, Palestinians and Israelis became embroiled in a protracted conflict that was complicated even further by broader issues that destabilized the region as a whole. In 1973, another major war erupted that had significant global

Camp David Accords
the 1979 peace agreement between Egypt and Israel.

intifada
the Palestinian uprising against Israel.

Oslo Accords
the 1993 Israeli/Palestinian agreement that was designed to set the stage for a comprehensive and permanent peace.

implications due to its effect on oil supplies and prices. Arab oil-producing states that held a considerable share of the world's available oil chose to suspend sales to countries supporting Israel. The price of oil skyrocketed, and the world economy contracted severely.

The United States was mindful of the substantial political and economic consequences of continuing turmoil in the Middle East and became proactive in seeking a diplomatic solution. US involvement would become a regular feature of the Middle East saga as it continued to unfold. In 1978, US president Jimmy Carter convinced the leaders of Egypt and Israel, Anwar Sadat and Menachem Begin, to join him for an intensive effort to find common ground to address the underlying conflict. The meetings took place at the official US presidential retreat in Camp David, Maryland, and the agreements that were signed in 1979 became known as the **Camp David Accords**.[3]

The Camp David Accords were a major breakthrough. Egypt became the first Arab state to formally recognize Israel's right to exist, while Israel agreed to return substantial portions of Egyptian land captured in 1967. The United States also pledged considerable economic and military aid to Egypt, beginning a long relationship that would help to sustain the peace between Egypt and Israel. Resolving the issues relating to the status of Palestinians living in Gaza (and elsewhere) proved illusory. Anwar Sadat, the leading spokesman for the Arab world at the time, was branded a traitor by many Arabs for making peace with Israel. In 1981, he was assassinated in Egypt while reviewing a military parade.

The failure to make headway on the Palestinian issue escalated tensions. Palestinian resistance to Israel's occupation of the West Bank and Gaza intensified, resulting in a more coordinated **intifada** (the Arabic word for uprising) that would last from 1987 to 1993 and included terrorist attacks inside Israel. The situation deteriorated considerably, as Israel responded with increasing military force.

The human, financial, and political costs of the conflict were taking their toll. With the assistance of an experienced Norwegian diplomat, Palestinian and Israeli negotiators met secretly to tackle the impasse under the watchful eye of the United States. In 1993, PLO chairman Yasser Arafat and Israeli Prime Minister Yitzhak Rabin came to the White House to sign the **Oslo Accords**. The agreement provided for the withdrawal of Israel from parts of the occupied territories and the creation of a transitional Palestinian governing authority. It also called on both sides to begin working on a comprehensive and permanent agreement. Arafat recognized Israel's right to exist in peace, while Rabin recognized the PLO as the legitimate representative of the Palestinian people.[4] The handshake between these long-term rivals suggested better days to come. It was followed by the signing of a formal treaty between Jordan and Israel in October 1994. Throughout the history of this conflict, however, agreeing on the details was always problematic. Negotiations stalled, enthusiasm for a conclusive deal waned, and Yitzhak Rabin was assassinated by an Israeli citizen opposed to relinquishing any land to the Palestinians in 1995.

Attempting to salvage the deal as he approached the end of his presidency, Bill Clinton summoned Arafat and Israeli prime minister Ehud Barak to Camp David in July 2000. Optimism quickly faded, as both Arafat and Barak balked as Clinton escorted them to the initial meetings. Neither one wanted to be the first to enter the building; neither one wanted to be viewed as too eager for an agreement or too willing to make concessions to achieve it. By many accounts, Barak offered territorial concessions well beyond any that had been on the table previously or that were likely to garner majority support back home. It did not matter, as the talks adjourned after approximately two weeks without an agreement in place.[5] Shortly thereafter, a second intifada erupted.

Clinton with Arafat and Rabin. Taken on September 13, 1993, this photo captures the historic handshake between PLO leader Yasser Arafat and Israeli prime minister Yitzhak Rabin, which took place at the White House in Washington, D.C.

With violence continuing to escalate, UN secretary general Kofi Annan brought together representatives from the United States, the European Union, and Russia to find a way out of the deadlock. The group, which came to be known as the Quartet, produced a **Road Map for Peace** in 2003 that established a framework for a two-state solution to the Israeli-Palestinian conflict with very explicit goals and a timeline to reach them. The Road Map directly addressed the core issues that framed the conflict and endorsed the principle of a two-state solution. This was the first time the United States publicly supported full Palestinian sovereignty.[6]

The US invasion of Iraq in 2003 was opposed by many Arabs and disrupted the Israeli-Palestinian peace process. Arafat became less inclined to negotiate. Israel responded more forcefully to the violence in the territories but became increasingly frustrated with its inability to gain control over the situation. Arafat's death in 2004 and Israel's military withdrawal from Gaza in 2005, however, seemed to set the stage for a breakthrough.

Road Map for Peace
the 2003 plan that established the framework for a two-state solution to the Israeli/Palestinian conflict.

Internal Palestinian politics made it difficult to capitalize on this opportunity. Mahmoud Abbas, the head of Fatah, was elected president of the administrative body governing the Palestinian territories, the Palestinian Authority. But he had little luck in moving discussions with Israel forward. His popularity among Palestinians quickly faded, even as he held on to power in the West Bank. When Palestinians went to the polls in Gaza in 2006, they voted overwhelmingly for Hamas, an organization opposed to any negotiations and committed to the destruction of Israel. A violent struggle broke out, and

Hamas drove the Fatah forces loyal to Abbas out of Gaza. Palestinian leadership was now divided, making the prospects for peace with Israel more remote.

Meanwhile, matters became even more complicated when war broke out between Israel and Lebanon in 2006. The Israeli military was pitted against Hezbollah, an Islamic party supported by Syria and Iran. To the surprise of many, Hezbollah forces proved highly formidable on the battlefield and demonstrated Israel's vulnerability with their missile attacks on a number of Israeli cities. Palestinians welcomed this turn of events, and the resistance gained momentum. Hezbollah proceeded to expand its political leverage inside Lebanon. Hezbollah and its political allies garnered enough electoral support in 2011 to gain control of the Lebanese government, thereby adding to the uncertainties of the region.

After decades of violence, the Israeli-Palestinian conflict continues to defy resolution. In 2008, a violent confrontation between Israel and Hamas in Gaza further eroded the possibility for a negotiated settlement. Since then, the United States has sought to bring the parties together but has had very limited success. Israel has continued to focus on fortifying its security by expanding Jewish settlements on land that would presumably be part of a future Palestinian state and by building an expansive security wall to stave off terrorist attacks. Palestinians continue to press their case for statehood in the UN and other international organizations and look to isolate Israel politically. They have also moved to reconcile internal differences to add to their diplomatic leverage.

Soldiers line up along the security wall separating Israel and the West Bank.

While the particular circumstances have changed over the years, the core issues have not. The Palestinian-Israeli conflict is about the right to sovereignty and security. It is a dispute over land and political boundaries that involves access to water and other basic resources. It is also about access to holy religious sites. Perhaps most important, the conflict represents a history of two peoples locked in a profound and enduring struggle to control their own destinies. As such, it is a microcosm of the types of conflicts that that have played a critical role in shaping our political world and represents an ongoing challenge with little hope for resolution in the immediate future.

SOWhat? CONFLICT IN THE MIDDLE EAST

By Mor Green, Israel Community Emissary

An Israeli childhood is very different from an American one. When I was four years old, I lived 2 miles from Gaza and experienced my first war. I remember sitting in the bomb shelter with my family for days hearing rocket fire and waiting for the war to end. As a four year old, I was too small to put on a gas mask and instead had to wear a special suit to protect me from the unknown attack. It was terrifying not knowing what the future holds.

The most recent war was in 2009 while I was in business school in Beer Sheva. From the moment an alarm sounds, you have 15 seconds to reach safety in a bomb shelter. The university did not have enough protected classrooms so school was cancelled so we could remain in our "safe areas." Unfortunately, I had no bomb shelter near my apartment and was forced to move in with my parents.

I am now 26 years old and had 3 wars so far in my life time. This is the harsh reality we live with every day. To protect ourselves, all Israelis are drafted in the army. Because of my experiences and the loss of an uncle, I worked hard to become a commander there.

Growing up, my parents always told me that they hope when I turn 18 we will have no need for an army and the draft will stop. One day I will be just like my parents—hoping and promising my kids a better future living in peace with our neighbors. I believe, along with many Israelis and the Israeli Government, that real peace means everyone enjoying a safe and protected future in a Jewish state of Israel alongside a Palestinian state. We recognize this need and hope that one day the other side will also recognize our right to exist.

WEAPONS OF MASS DESTRUCTION

Critical to the instability in the world today are **weapons of mass destruction**, which may be nuclear, chemical, or biological. Progress in curtailing the development and spread of deadly weapons has been limited, even as we have moved beyond the constant nuclear threat that darkened the Cold War era. Many governments and groups still seek to secure the most advanced weapons available. Avoiding the unthinkable may rest largely on the ability of the international community to effectively apply the lessons of the past.

From the earliest days of the nuclear age, governments have recognized the need to restrict the global weapons infrastructure. The array of agreements and

weapons of mass destruction

nuclear, chemical, and biological weapons.

treaties is impressive—at least on paper. A few of these are particularly note-worthy. In 1968, the members of the nuclear club designed the Non-Proliferation Treaty (NPT) to limit the production of such weapons, while the 1972 Anti–Ballistic Missile Treaty (ABM) sought to ban the development of defensive systems that might encourage the first use of nuclear weapons. The nuclear powers also moved forward with the Limited (1963) and then more Comprehensive (1996) Test Ban treaties to discourage further research and development activities. In the early 1970s, the Soviet Union and the United States began discussions that lasted more than two decades to restrict the number and types of weapons composing their respective strategic arsenals. The result was a series of Strategic Arms Limitations Talks (SALT) and Strategic Arms Reduction Talks (START) treaties. The 1987 Intermediate Range Nuclear Forces (INF) accord, moreover, ended the deployment of US and Soviet medium-range missiles across Europe.

In 2010, the US and Russia sealed the first major nuclear weapons treaty in nearly two decades, agreeing to slash their strategic warhead arsenals. Diplomats modeled the treaty, which took effect in January 2011, on the original START agreement. It required both the Americans and the Russians to reduce the stock-piles of their most dangerous weapons—those already deployed and ready to launch at long-range targets—by about 30 percent. While the treaty still allowed each side to retain roughly 1,550 such warheads, this number was 74 percent lower that the limit previously in force. The treaty's duration was set at ten years, with a possible five year extension.[7]

Beyond the nuclear threat, chemical and biological weapons command dip-lomatic attention as weapons of mass destruction. As far back as 1925, the Geneva Protocol banned gas and bacteriological weapons, which had wrought devastation in World War I. The 1972 Biological Weapons Treaty (BWT) and the 1993 Chemical Weapons Convention (CWC) included widespread participation from countries all over the world. These agreements prohibited possession of these dangerous agents while committing all signatories without existing capac-ity to give up their rights to future development.

As it turned out, many of these efforts had limited impacts. Without assur-ance of effective verification or compliance, it proved difficult to move very far along the road to disarmament. The nuclear states understood the seriousness of the threat but not sufficiently to prevent an unnerving arms race fueled by tensions between the superpowers. The early 1980s were particularly delicate, as the United States launched a Strategic Defense Initiative (SDI) to offset growing Soviet strength. The US military designed this so-called Star Wars program with the latest technologies, and President Ronald Reagan touted it as a plan that would render nuclear weapons obsolete. Star Wars raised serious questions about the violation of agreements on the creation of defense-weapons systems and the demilitarization of outer space. While some people credited SDI with getting the Soviets back to the negotiating table, others decried its role in encouraging forays into new areas of weapons development.

Reagan was following the logic of **deterrence**, which involved crafting a credible means to dissuade others from initiating the use of nuclear weapons. For much of the Cold War, experts credited the concept with preventing nuclear war. Precluding a first strike required the development of an effective retaliatory, or second-strike, capability. As a result, during the Cold War, the Soviet Union and the United States felt constantly compelled to one-up each other's new weapons programs with the deployment of air-, land-, and sea-based systems. This very costly and dangerous arms race extended through much of the period. Despite sporadic efforts to curtail these activities, the absence of foolproof monitoring procedures gave way to new waves of development.

Although the thinking behind deterrence was fairly straightforward, different views on how to best actualize the strategy complicated its implementation. In the 1970s and 1980s, for example, the United States flirted with conflicting approaches as it sought to enhance its deterrent capability. One proposal called for the construction of multiple installations over vast distances of American soil to include "dummy" silos devoid of armed missiles. This nuclear shell game was intended to undermine Soviet confidence in their targeting decisions.

Critics called for an opposite approach that concentrated the placement of missiles without much regard for concealing their whereabouts. They argued that if the weapons were densely packed in heavily fortified silos within a few miles of one another, the heat and debris resulting from the impact of the first incoming missile would undermine the capacity of additional incoming missiles to destroy the other silos—thereby preserving the capacity to retaliate. Based on very different assumptions and expectations, these approaches reflected the inherent logic of deterrence—project the certainty of retaliation that will inflict massive and unacceptable levels of damage. Pundits aptly labeled this strategy **MAD**, or **Mutual Assured Destruction**.

The United States remains the only country to have used nuclear weapons, with its bombing of the Japanese cities of Hiroshima and Nagasaki in 1945 during World War II. The rivals' restraint during the Cold War was impressive, since neither the Soviet Union nor the United States relinquished their nuclear options. Some experts have suggested that it was precisely the possibility of mutual destruction that moved the two superpowers to avoid direct confrontation, even when relations were at their lowest points. The lessons of the 1962 Cuban Missile Crisis, when the two countries came perilously close to using their nuclear options, also loomed large. Deterrence has always been an imprecise notion. It assumes rational decision making, the capacity to determine an effective retaliatory capability, and knowledge of when enough retaliatory weapons are in place so that deterrence has been achieved. Deterrence further presupposes that nuclear weapons are reserved as a last resort. However, the risks of miscalculation and misperception during times of tension and crisis call this strategy into question.

Even with these concerns, the record suggests that deterrence has worked, and the effort to control nuclear and other weapons of mass destruction

deterrence
the inhibition of a first strike nuclear attack by an effective retaliatory or second-strike capability.

mutual assured destruction (MAD)
the logic of nuclear deterrence that assumes the certainty of a nuclear retaliation would prevent governments from launching such an attack in the first place.

TABLE 5.1	MEMBERS OF THE NUCLEAR CLUB 2012	
Nuclear Weapon States	Nuclear Weapon Possessors**	States of Proliferation Concern
China	India	Iran
France	Israel	North Korea
Russia*	Pakistan	Syria
United Kingdom		
United States		

*Also controls weapons from Soviet era located in Belarus, Kazakhstan, and Ukraine.

**Known to possess nuclear weapons but not part of Non-Proliferation Treaty.

Source: Arms Control Association, 2012, www.armscontrol.org/factsheets/
Nuclearweaponswhohaswhat.

through treaties and other international agreements has made a difference to this point. But the weapons game has changed considerably since the days of the Cold War. The superpowers guaranteed that they would defend their allies. Without that guarantee, states that previously had no need for nuclear weapons are now crowding the playing field. In addition, nonaligned countries have moved into the nuclear club—most notably India and Pakistan—and many others are eagerly seeking entry. North Korea's and Iran's explorations of their nuclear options are probably the tip of the iceberg, as many governments and groups see nuclear weapons as the path toward increased political leverage and latitude. Their efforts pose a serious challenge to the effective application of the idea of deterrence, which developed at a time when even the thought of deployment remained within the exclusive preserve of the world's superpowers.

The characteristics and political agendas of the new players pose another challenge to deterrence. Authoritarian and unpredictable leaders are particularly enamored of the nuclear route, as are countries with either long-standing or particularly intense rivalries at their doorsteps. Nuclear development feeds on itself by providing inducements to governments or groups with unfinished business. As in the case of India and Pakistan, the results can be unsettling. Prime Minister Zulfikar Ali Bhutto, who committed Pakistan to developing nuclear weapons in 1972, declared that Pakistanis would have nuclear weapons, even if they had to "eat grass."[8]

Advances in technology have raised questions about the ability to maintain an effective deterrent, as it is now far easier than it was during the Cold War to acquire some nuclear capability. Component parts have become far more portable and difficult to track, as they can be easily transported around the world. Furthermore, the rapid growth of the Internet and the increasing sophistication of electronic information transmission systems have significantly enhanced production and assembly capabilities—with respect to both weapons and delivery systems.

The availability of multiple channels to acquire these weapons has also destabilized nuclear security. While conventional arms traders have long worked these routes, they are now also flowing with nonconventional weapons and technology. Ironically, the breakup of the Soviet Union in the early 1990s is what brought such stock to traders. Their quest for personal financial gain, quite apart from political considerations, inspired the sale or transfer of weapons systems housed across a number of former Soviet republics. The suspected sale of sensitive information by individuals in such disparate places as the United States, Iraq, and Pakistan speak to the complexities of controlling the proliferation problem. Today's global arms bazaar is a vibrant one with both organized and ad-hoc private exchanges adding to an already active market fueled by government military assistance and sales programs.

Finally, nonstate actors are increasingly involved in this drama. Chemical and biological weapons pose a particular risk, given the stockpiles available and accessible. Many disgruntled groups and terrorist organizations across the world have explicitly stated their intentions in this area. Incidents involving the suspected or actual use of these devices have brought panic to Tokyo subways, the London transportation system, and the US postal service. These episodes may provide a crucial glimpse into the future.

TERRORISM

To understand the potential destructiveness of modern weapons requires some grasp of the broader challenge of modern **terrorism**. Despite growing recognition of the seriousness of the terrorist threat across the world, there has not been a coherent and coordinated global response. Part of the problem has to do with language. Who is a terrorist, and how is a terrorist organization defined? The answer may vary depending on your point of view.

The organizations and groups employing terrorist tactics resist the label. Instead, they justify their activities in terms of a struggle for high or lofty ideals. It is often said that one person's terrorist is another's freedom fighter. How can a Basque separatist in Spain, a Tamil Tiger in Sri Lanka, an al-Qaeda fighter in Iraq, or a member of the Irish Republican Army be categorized? Generally speaking, terrorism involves the threat or use of violence to instill fear and create uncertainty; this definition rests on broad intents and purposes. A terrorist attack is a premeditated political act that is often directed at civilian targets and designed to change an existing political order.

Anyone who reads or watches the news commonly associates terrorism with nongovernmental groups and networks. However, governments are directly and indirectly complicit in some of these activities. Each year, for example, the US Department of State identifies those governments it categorizes as state sponsors of terrorism.[9] These countries cannot receive US aid in the form of arms, are restricted with respect to the items with military and civilian applications they may purchase from the United States, and are eligible only for very limited types of US aid. The 2012 list included Cuba, Iran, Sudan, and Syria—countries long at odds with the United States and disdainful of its designations and policies. The countries appearing on the list defiantly

terrorism
the threat or use of violence to change an existing political order.

dismiss its validity, citing the United States itself as the chief perpetrator of terrorist activity.

Terrorism is by no means a new phenomenon. The word itself originated during the French Revolution and the Jacobin Reign of Terror in 1792–94. Individual terrorist acts can be traced at least as far back as ancient Greek and Roman times, and group terrorism became more common during the Middle Ages.[10] At times, terrorism has changed the course of history on a large scale, as when the 1914 assassination of Austrian Archduke Franz Ferdinand by a Serb extremist sparked the outbreak of World War I.

Since 9/11, governments and the media have focused on religious, and especially Islamic, fundamentalists who may seek violent means to resist outside influences and to promote the values and customs of traditional Islam. Terrorism is not restricted, however, to a particular ideology or political perspective. It may be born out of frustration and adopted by groups or individuals with unresolved grievances. Terrorism is a calculated political tool that may compensate for otherwise limited resources or leverage. Some terrorists ally with groups that do not share their political agendas but may have other common interests. In Colombia, for example, **narcoterrorism** blends the political ideology of the FARC (Colombian Revolutionary Action Front) with the financial interests of local drug lords.

Terrorism appears in many shapes and forms. Its perpetrators use terrorist acts for a wide range of purposes. Terrorism's victims may be individuals, as in the kidnapping or execution of journalists or transnational corporations' employees, as well as the assassination of political leaders. They may be groups, such as passengers on hijacked airplanes or workers and visitors in embassies or other buildings of political or symbolic importance. Innocent bystanders may be caught up in bombings of hotels and restaurants in areas catering to tourists and other foreign nationals or attacks on public transportation systems.

While the specific methods and objectives of terrorist groups may differ considerably, they share a number of common purposes. First and foremost, they want attention. Their actions may seem random, but this is generally not the case. Unpredictability spreads fear and uncertainty. The more extreme or violent the event, the better the publicity will be.

Such exposure may serve a number of needs. Gaining sympathy for the cause is often a key motive, although particularly deadly attacks can have the opposite effect of galvanizing opposition. The cycle may include equally violent acts of retaliation, however, thereby offering additional opportunity to build momentum for future actions. Terrorist actions themselves are useful recruiting devices. The ability to execute an attack, even if the result is less than completely successful, enhances the legitimacy and credibility of the initiating group. The martyrdom of suicide bombers is compelling to people who feel alienated or hopeless or seek some financial remuneration for their families. A number of Palestinian families received compensation from Libya and other groups for the martyrdom

narcoterrorism
the alliance of drug traffickers and antigovernment revolutionaries, often used in reference to political violence in Colombia.

of family members. The deaths of activists add to the sense of outrage among supporters and often attract replacements.

Since the attacks on the United States in September 2001, many governments have joined in a concerted effort to uncover and destroy terrorist networks operating across much of the world. The global war on terror has become intense and lethal. The United States has assumed leadership and has used all means deemed necessary in pursuing this agenda. It has also attempted to enlist the support of allies and other countries particularly vulnerable to attack.

The US government has realigned and redesigned its intelligence and security operations toward this end. The controversial 2001 **USA Patriot Act** provided for the considerable expansion of government surveillance and expanded the government's law enforcement powers in dealing with terrorism. The creation of the Department of Homeland Security and the post of director of national intelligence represented the largest increase in the US federal bureaucracy since the creation of the Central Intelligence Agency, National Security Council, and Department of Defense through the National Security Act of 1947. Meanwhile, efforts to better secure US borders and draft new legislation governing immigration are a high priority. By many accounts, however, the country remains quite vulnerable.

USA Patriot Act
the controversial 2001 law that expanded the government's law enforcement powers in dealing with terrorism.

The global effort to contain terrorism has produced mixed results and faces a difficult future. First, the covert and secretive nature of terrorist groups makes them difficult to track and expose. Whenever possible, terrorist leaders operate under the cover of rugged terrain that is familiar to them, and they often enjoy the protection of compliant or supportive local populations. Such legitimacy enables them to stay "underground" for long periods of time, surfacing only when absolutely necessary. The elusive Osama bin Laden successfully adhered to this strategy for nearly a decade while maintaining refuge in the region bordering Afghanistan and Pakistan.

Second, a ready reservoir of potential terrorists and an ample supply of leaders are waiting to serve their causes. The United States claimed many victories in its War on Terror launched by the Bush administration in the wake of the 9/11 attacks. Evidence suggested that the campaign had indeed impacted the leadership ranks of al-Qaeda and other terrorist networks. In 2004, for example, the Associated Press (AP) news service identified a dozen young leaders of groups associated with the al-Qaeda network in the Middle East, North Africa, South Asia, and Europe.[11] By mid-2006, almost half had been killed or forced into hiding to avoid detection.[12] But it was difficult to gauge the longer-term effects of these developments.

This is an undated file photo of al-Qaeda leader Osama bin Laden in Afghanistan. While bin Laden is now dead, killed in a US raid on his compound in Pakistan in 2011, other terrorist leaders and groups persist.

The media heralded the June 2006 killing of Abu Musab al-Zarqawi, the leader of al-Qaeda in Iraq, as a potential turning point in that war. He had become the symbol of the insurgency and had been behind many of its most violent episodes. His death came only days after the highly publicized arrest of Islamic activists suspected of plotting assassinations of officials and the bombing of landmarks and government buildings in Canada. Al-Zarqawi was replaced quickly, however, and the war in Iraq dragged on for many additional years. Al-Qaeda persevered, and its unifying figure, Osama bin Laden, eluded his pursuers until the US commando attack on his compound in Pakistan resulted in his death in 2011. The transnational integration of these terrorist networks like al-Qaeda makes them even more difficult to counter. Al-Qaeda Arabian Peninsula, commonly referred to as AQAP and based in Yemen, has been especially aggressive in recruiting across the Persian Gulf and has plotted bombings and other actions aimed at a wide array of targets in various locations.[13]

Third, many of these groups have become quite capable in their use of media and advanced forms of electronic communication. They have capitalized on the development of 24/7 news coverage by the Cable News Network (CNN), among others, and people's access to news from any network in the world. Elaborate news networks have emerged in many parts of the world and provide opportunities for extended coverage. The Qatar-based **al-Jazeera** network, for example, has become very influential with its often sympathetic reports highlighting the conditions that give rise to terrorists and mold their missions. Al-Jazeera also emerged as the vehicle of choice for Osama bin Laden to transmit tapes designed to convey his public thoughts and messages. In March 2008, he issued a statement condemning European involvement in Afghanistan, and denouncing the Pope as a responsible party for the publication of political cartoons in Denmark that al-Qaeda saw as disparaging of the prophet Muhammad.

Access to the Internet has contributed further to raising the profiles of terrorist groups. Not only do sophisticated terrorist websites and social networking sites provide basic information, publicize activities, and recruit new members, but they also serve as a means for communicating plans for upcoming missions. Meanwhile, an increase in cyberterrorism disrupts and penetrates the security of targeted government and corporate websites. The control of information is key in the struggle with terrorism, making cyberspace an important battleground.

Fourth, the global effort to contain terrorism suffers from terrorists intimidating or even blackmailing certain states to limit their counterterrorism efforts. The case of Saudi Arabia is illuminating. For decades, Saudi Arabia and the United States have maintained a close strategic and financial relationship. The threat to the Saudi monarchy posed by Iraq in 1991 was an important consideration prompting the United States to launch Operation Desert Storm. Protecting

al-Jazeera
the broadcast network owned by Qatar.

the royal family and the security of Saudi oil fields remain key US objectives in the Persian Gulf. However, Saudi Arabia was also home to Osama bin Laden and to most individuals implicated in the September 11 attacks. It remains an active and fertile recruiting ground for terrorists. The Saudi government's reluctance to crack down has stemmed, in part, from the fear of increased domestic targeting. More important, some of these groups have received support from sympathetic Saudi officials even as they have launched attacks within the country with the intent of destabilizing the government. This Saudi ambivalence speaks directly to the difficulty of devising effective counterterrorism measures on a broader scale.

Finally, terrorist groups have an ever-growing number of options with respect to establishing bases for their operations. Despite increased surveillance and periodic detection, terrorist cells take advantage of porous borders across much of the world and often function with few constraints in the very countries they seek to target. They find hospitable and welcoming environments elsewhere as conflicts evolve and supportive leaders emerge. In Afghanistan, for example, the government has been unable to break the back of the fundamentalist Taliban movement or to gain full control over parts of the country that harbor opposition forces. From Somalia to Sudan to Iran to Syria, sympathetic and cooperative governments maintain safe havens for terrorist groups. Meanwhile, stubborn insurgencies such as those of Abu Sayyaf—a group with ties to al-Qaeda seeking a separate Islamic state for Muslims in the Philippines—and the Haqqani family—an organization based in Pakistan and Afghanistan looking to undermine US security interests in the region—suggest the continuing efforts of terrorist networks to extend across the globe.[14]

WHAT CAN BE DONE?

In many respects, today's international system is limited in terms of its ability to handle conflicts. While the more powerful states closely monitor events that affect their vital interests and are willing to intervene—politically, diplomatically, and militarily—to protect those interests, they increasingly do not have the capacity to act unilaterally. The United States continues as one of the most powerful actors, but a number of other states wield sufficient influence to thwart US efforts to place its overarching imprint on various regions and their conflicts.

The Palestinian-Israeli conflict exemplifies the challenge of calming tensions that destabilize the global political arena. The United States and other powers both in and outside the region have used varying techniques over the years to bring about a solution, ranging from promises of financial and military assistance to threats of diplomatic and economic sanctions. External mediation has proven useful at times, particularly in terms of defusing crises. But the conflict remains today what it has been throughout—a struggle for security and the ability to control one's own destiny. Continuing efforts by the United States and other influential parties are necessary to keep the peace process alive. A resolution of this enduring conflict will be possible, however, only when the protagonists themselves come to realize that their goals can be attained only through a lasting and comprehensive peace.

International agreements offer another way to bring real cooperation, especially in the area of nuclear weapons. Progress on the Comprehensive Nuclear Test Ban provides hope but also suggests limits to what can be accomplished. The Comprehensive Test Ban Treaty was negotiated through the UN General Assembly in the mid-1990s. By 2011, 182 states had signed the treaty, and 153 had ratified it.[15] It cannot enter into force, however, until 44 nuclear-capable states ratify it and only 35 have done so to date. The United States signed the treaty in 1996, but the US Senate has been unwilling to ratify it. China, Iran, and Israel have also not seen fit to move forward with ratification. India, North Korea, and Pakistan—three countries whose inclusion is indispensable to the effectiveness of this treaty—have chosen to not support it.

The war against terrorism has yielded some important, yet limited success. Terrorism remains a useful tool for those frustrated by the inability to find a full airing of their grievances. It is also particularly alluring for those who are lacking in conventional military strength. A growing body of literature suggests that if more countries embrace a democratic form of government, guided by the rule of law and expanding participation in the political process, there will be less inclination to resort to terror or other forms of conflict to advance particular political interests.

The spread of democracy may not be enough, however, to bring about a world markedly more peaceful than the one we know today. While democracies may not fight one another, they are frequently involved in conflict with authoritarian regimes.[16] Moreover, the process of trying to achieve democracy can be an important source of conflict itself. The attempted transitions to democracy in the Middle East following the Arab spring of 2011 actually fueled tensions, as different groups that had long been denied access to power sought to use elections to impose their own perspectives and agendas.

It is not simply the division of the world by political borders that produces the challenges of war, weapons of mass destruction, and terrorism. There are also economic interests and disparities that have contributed to their development. The ability to transform political relationships is frequently influenced by economic ties and considerations. Chapter 6 examines these economic borders, how they are determined, and where the fault lines may emerge.

KEYConcepts

al-Jazeera 110
Balfour Declaration 98
Camp David Accords 100
deterrence 105
intifada 100
mutual assured destruction (MAD) 105

narcoterrorism 108
Oslo Accords 100
Road Map for Peace 101
terrorism 107
USA Patriot Act 109
weapons of mass destruction (WMD) 103

TO LEARNMore

Books and Other Print Media

Aaron David Miller, *The Much Too Promised Land: America's Elusive Search for Arab-Israeli Peace* (New York: Bantam, 2008).

This is an insider's account of the Palestinian/Israeli peace process from an American diplomat who participated in many of the initiatives launched by the United States. Miller offers a good, objective overview of core issues fueling the conflict and the reasons why peace has been so difficult to achieve.

Bruce Riedel, *Deadly Embrace: Pakistan, America, and the Future of the Global Jihad* (Washington, DC: Brookings Institution Press, 2011).

Riedel explores the historical relationship between Pakistan and the United States and the challenges they face today.

Cindy C. Combs, *Terrorism in the Twenty First Century,* 7th ed. (Upper Saddle River, NJ: Prentice-Hall, 2012).

Combs's volume is a valuable resource for understanding the roots and causes of contemporary terrorism that offers both a historical perspective and several case studies that illustrate the analysis.

Joseph S. Nye, Jr. and David A. Welch, *Understanding Global Conflict and Cooperation: An Introduction to Theory and History,* 7th ed. (Upper Saddle River, NJ: Prentice-Hall, 2012).

This is a definitive work on the role of conflict in shaping international politics.

Richard Rhodes, *The Twilight of the Bombs: Recent Challenges, New Dangers and the Prospects for a World Without Nuclear Weapons* (New York: Vintage Books, 2010).

Rhodes offers a lengthy and illuminating analysis of the evolving nuclear threat in the post–Cold War era.

Websites

International Atomic Energy Agency (IAEA), www.iaea.org/.

The IAEA is an intergovernmental organization within the UN system that is the focal point for nuclear cooperation.

Israel Palestine Center for Research and Information (IPCRI), www.ipcri.org/.

Based in Jerusalem, IPCRI is a joint Palestinian-Israeli public policy organization seeking to develop practical solutions to the conflict.

Middle East Institute, www.mei.edu/.

The Middle East Institute is a Washington, D.C., think tank that promotes research and discussion of Middle East issues.

United Nations Office for Disarmament Affairs (UNODA), www.un.org/disarmament/.

Established in 1998 as a department of the UN Secretariat, UNODA promotes disarmament and the nonproliferation of weapons.

Washington Institute for Near East Policy, www.washingtoninstitute.org/.

The Washington Institute for Near East Policy is an educational foundation, or think tank, that conducts scholarly research and policy analysis relating to the Middle East.

Videos

Avoiding Armageddon: Our Future, Our Choice (2004).

Although a bit dated, this set of programs contains much valuable information and provides important context for understanding the challenges of terrorism and weapons of mass destruction. The package includes four separate discs that cover biological and chemical weapons, nuclear weapons, the globalization of terror, and the effectiveness of security measures in confronting these challenges.

Fighting in the Fifth Dimension (2012).

From Al Jazeera World, this documentary explores what is called the "fifth dimension of warfare" or cyberwar, a phenomenon made possible by technological innovations. www.aljazeera.com/programmes/aljazeeraworld/2011/10/201110191916939402528 .html

The Intricate Economics of Terrorism (2009).

Economist Loretta Napoleoni discusses the Italian terrorist group Red Brigade, arms smuggling, and the hidden economics of terrorism, or "rogue economics." Napoleoni exposes how the structure of rogue economics is parallel to that of the international economic system and describes its growth through three stages: state sponsorship of terrorism, privatization of terrorism, and globalization of terrorism. Finally, Napoleoni uncovers the surprising connection between American legislation and the illegal activities of terrorist groups. www.ted.com/talks/loretta_napoleoni_ the_intricate_economics_of_terrorism.html

Middle East: Challenges in Defining an Israeli-Palestinian Border (2012).

An excellent resource produced by *The New York Times* and accessible online that explains the key issues and the challenges of reconciling Israeli-Palestinian differences. It is divided into five segments and includes a series of short clips that address the complexities of the conflict. Separate *individual voices* clips feature people impacted directly. www.nytimes.com/interactive/2011/09/05/world/middleeast/challenges-in-defining-an-israeli-palestinian-border.html

One Day of War (2005).

While a bit dated, this program was produced by the British Broadcasting Company and offers great insight into the nature and range of conflict across the world by covering 16 separate wars over the same 24-hour period.

Pakistan: Children of the Taliban (2009).

Pakistani journalist Sharmeen Obaid-Chinoy exposes the powerful and dangerous influence of the Taliban throughout Pakistan. Obaid-Chinoy shows how the Taliban has infiltrated Pakistani cities and countryside alike, destroying schools, displacing hundreds of thousands of people, and recruiting youth into their terrorist network. Pakistan and its 80 million children, Obaid-Chinoy concludes, will be lost forever should the militants continue to expand. www.pbs.org/frontlineworld/stories/pakistan802/video/video_index.html

Seeking Prosperity

The Global Economy

The words of noted Peruvian economist Hernando de Soto at the turn of this century remain relevant today. The global economy affects the food we eat, the clothes we wear, the products we use, the cars we drive, the technology at our fingertips, the jobs we work, and the material wealth we can expect to attain. As de Soto suggests, it also generates very different sets of interests and perceptions regarding its successes and failures. States struggle to bring greater order to their financial markets, and companies weigh the merits of operating in relatively unfamiliar locations. Meanwhile, countless individuals cope with the uncertainty of a transforming job market or are in desperate search of their next meal.

As globalization has brought disparate parts of the world closer together, it has also compounded the difficulties of managing economic relationships. Since the early 1990s, a more privatized and deregulated global economy

"For Americans enjoying peace and prosperity, it has been all too easy to ignore the turmoil elsewhere. How can capitalism be in trouble when the Dow Jones Industrial average is higher than Sir Edmund Hillary? Americans look at other nations and see progress, even if it is slow and uneven. Can't you eat a Big Mac in Moscow, rent a video in Shanghai, and reach the Internet in Caracas?"

—economist Hernando de Soto, 2000[1]

has developed that clearly transcends state boundaries. The global market system has become highly integrated and interdependent. Private transnational commercial enterprises, whose activities often render political boundaries obsolete, have progressively expanded. Economic disasters that start in one locale can quickly reverberate to other parts of the globe. As states seek to promote and defend their interests, they may be inclined to act in ways that threaten to disrupt the flow of financial resources or commercial exchanges. Their willingness to empower regional or global organizations with the authority to impose uniform standards or behaviors is also limited.

A significant shift in the relative positioning of a number of pivotal players across the system adds to the uncertainty. The United States, the dominant force throughout much of the twentieth century, is struggling to maintain its global economic leadership. Meanwhile, China has enjoyed an extended period of substantial growth and is poised to emerge as the world's lead economy, even as it has expanded its stake in the United States and elsewhere through investments and debt financing. Poorer countries and those that have recently emerged from decades of isolating themselves from the forces of global **capitalism** are in highly uncertain times. Whereas some proponents view globalization as a way to catch up economically and to offer their people a way out of persistent poverty, detractors caution that they will continue to remain susceptible to forces beyond their control and be forced to adopt policies that undermine the prospects for sustainable development.

As today's global transactions accelerate at unprecedented speed, questions arise as to the world economy's underlying character. Is it poised to work toward the elimination of significant disparities between the rich and the poor? Can it avoid disruptions of trade stemming from the efforts of countries to protect domestic industries threatened by global completion? Is it capable of strengthening institutions that might foster

Though economic borders have grown increasingly porous, in places like Dharavi, one of the world's largest slums, in Mumbai, India (foreground), the gulf separating its inhabitants from the people living and working in the glittering high-rise buildings in the background is vast. This chapter explores the ways that the growth of global capitalism has both separated and joined world citizens.

capitalism

a system of economic organization based on private property and free markets.

better management of crises that arise? Can it provide a measure of financial stability that would promote sustained and sustainable growth? It is difficult to predict the direction of things to come.

This chapter looks inside the global economy and some of the key issues affecting its operation. It begins with a historical overview of global economic development and the emergence of contrasting economic ideas. It then proceeds to review some of the more critical events that have shaped the transformation of the system into what it is today.

DEFINING ECONOMIC BORDERS: A VERY SHORT HISTORY

mercantilism

the economic approach that promotes the aggressive pursuit of export outlets and the simultaneous protection of domestic markets to acquire and expand national wealth and power.

liberalism

the economic approach, commonly traced to the writings of Adam Smith, that emphasizes the role of the free market in promoting economic growth and prosperity.

Historians trace the origins of the modern capitalist world economy to the sixteenth century, with the rise of European expansionism and the development of **mercantilism**. This in turn led to the emergence of economic **liberalism**, the principle that markets are the best path toward improvements in the quality of life. As the Arab-Muslim empire declined and the Ottoman Turks defeated Constantinople, Europeans began to step up their activities to expand the scope of their political, military, and financial influence. Portugal and Spain were particularly adept in their explorations of Africa and the Americas. They were soon eclipsed by Dutch, British, and French explorers, who benefited from the support of their respective monarchies and the active involvement of their growing merchant classes in developing new markets. Merchants were instrumental in shaping a new economic order that moved beyond feudal relationships to one in which capital fueled broader commercial ties.

The establishment of joint stock enterprises owned by their contributing investors, such as the Dutch East India Company in 1602, marked the emergence of private corporate actors in building overseas trading networks. The Dutch East India Company was the first trading company of its kind created to facilitate the spice trade and was the largest European trading company by 1620.[2] With the advent of the modern state in 1648 as a result of the Peace of Westphalia, trade in manufactured goods became a key factor in accumulating national wealth and power. Intense competition prompted states to aggressively pursue export outlets while restricting the access of foreigners to home markets. Such mercantilist policies promoted their interests and extended both the breadth and depth of their influence. But mercantilism was a risky strategy that invited retaliation and threatened to disrupt the flow of commercial activity. As both a trade policy and a more general way of thinking about the forces driving the world economy, it emphasizes intense competition for limited resources and vigilance in protecting national interests, regardless of international consequences. Mercantilism has remained popular, particularly during periods of economic contraction when competition is most intense.

By the late 1700s, Britain was becoming a dominant force within the system. As the birthplace and center of the Industrial Revolution, it had the resources and capability to extend its commercial reach. The development of new technologies provided the incentive to seek additional materials and new markets. Britain's overwhelming political and military power facilitated the development of a vast colonial empire that contributed greatly to its dominance during this period. Although other European nations sought to limit competition by restricting imports of British goods, Britain's exports continued to rise. The British Parliament's 1846 repeal of its Corn Laws, designed to protect national agriculture through tariffs and other measures, signaled an important move to freer trade and was met with similar initiatives by a number of Britain's European partners.

During this period, the drive for expansion and growth encouraged the adoption of progressive policies based upon the principles of economic liberalism. Eighteenth-century thinkers such as Adam Smith and David Ricardo advocated free and open markets as the best means to enhance the lives of people across the world. Adam Smith was a Scottish political economist and philosopher considered by many to be the father of modern economics. While acknowledging the market's often chaotic and uneven nature, his 1776 work, *The Wealth of Nations,* put forward the case for allowing its "invisible hand" to ensure the spread of its benefits.

Like Smith, the British political economist David Ricardo opposed protectionist trade policies. He argued that free trade would extend the availability of goods and services and promote efficiency by encouraging countries to specialize in producing and exporting those goods for which they had a **comparative advantage**. Liberal thinkers recommended importing a product when the relative cost of domestic production exceeded that of buying it elsewhere, taking

> Every individual necessarily labours to render the annual revenue of the society as great as he can. He generally, indeed, neither intends to promote the public interest, nor knows how much he is promoting it. By preferring the support of domestic to that of foreign industry, he intends only his own security; and by directing that industry in such a manner as its produce may be of the greatest value, he intends only his own gain, and he is in this, as in many other cases, led by an invisible hand to promote an end which was no part of his intention. Nor is it always the worse for the society that it was no part of it. By pursuing his own interest he frequently promotes that of the society more effectually than when he really intends to promote it. I have never known much good done by those who affected to trade for the public good.[3]

IN THEIR OWN WORDS | **Adam Smith**

comparative advantage
the idea that countries should produce and export those goods they can produce at a lower cost than others and import those items that others produce at lower cost.

into account the lost revenues resulting from the decreased production of other items. In short, these theorists saw an open economic system as the best option for producing the greatest good for the greatest number of people. These ideas were not universally accepted, however, particularly among people who did not have the political or economic capabilities to compete effectively in the marketplace.

While British colonialism was indispensable to the expansion and integration of the global economy, it also contributed to a growing disparity in the levels of economic prosperity between the colonizers and the colonized. In addition to maintaining open markets and the free movement of goods across oceans, Britain gained considerable advantage by serving as the world's financial center and presiding over an international monetary system based on gold and supported by its national currency (the pound). Its colonial activities and role in opening China and Japan to trade also helped to bring disparate places into a unified system that was controlled by and structured to advance the interests of its more powerful members. The costs and burdens of that leadership, however, eventually took their toll.

Depositors gather outside the shuttered doors of American Union Bank in New York City, 1931, during the Great Depression.

By the latter part of the nineteenth century, Britain was losing is preeminent position. Industrial development was spreading rapidly across Europe and beyond. Japan was emerging as a major industrial power, due to strong government guidance and its large business conglomerates, and launched a series of military adventures to extend its imperial reach. The United States, for its part, was on a path to extend its overseas activities and interests beyond Latin America and would eventually emerge as a global power. Across Europe, economic rivalries intensified as political tensions led to the appearance of two competing alliances that were destined to collide. These conflicts resulted in the outbreak of war in 1914.

World War I was an important turning point in the evolution of the global economy. Beyond the financial and commercial disruptions, the war marked the beginning of the end of European colonial empires and Britain's dominant role in the world's financial and commercial systems. Heavy European war debts and German reparations requirements significantly slowed the pace of economic recovery. Meanwhile, the United States was enjoying a period of economic expansion marked by the growth of manufacturing and consumption. The values of many companies appreciated, fueled in part by speculative stock purchases with borrowed money. As the economy slowed and stock prices began to decline, the system began to unravel. The collapse of the US stock market in 1929 had immediate and profound international ramifications.

By this time, the United States had become a major economic player. The Great Depression following the stock market crash extended well beyond America's borders. To substantially increase the protection of US markets, in 1930 Congress passed the Smoot-Hawley Tariff bill, which reflected the considerable isolationist sentiment across the country and the desire to limit potential vulnerabilities to outside forces. This action produced comparable responses. Competing nations organized trade blocs, further fracturing pre-existing relationships. One after another, countries began defaulting on their loans as they were unable to sustain economic activity. Meanwhile, declining markets in the leading industrial countries resulted in a significant drop in demand for raw materials and primary exports from the developing world.

The growing economic malaise was transforming economic and political life in these areas. In Latin America, a wave of military takeovers empowered repressive regimes who promoted economic nationalism. In Africa, organized resistance to colonial rule was mounting. Populist movements were also gaining momentum across Asia and the Middle East to challenge struggling colonial powers.

With the British unable and the United States unwilling to take the lead, global economic conditions deteriorated. A weakened British pound undermined the stability of the world's monetary system, while trade barriers limited commercial interactions. The 1931 collapse of the German economy dealt a devastating blow. It fueled the rise of Adolph Hitler and his drive to restore German prosperity and pride through aggressive military and political expansion. Japan charted a similar course as it moved into China and other neighboring territories to establish the Greater East Asia Co-Prosperity Sphere. Before long, much of the world was drawn into another encompassing and protracted conflict—World War II.

In part, the absence of leadership or direction had led to such disarray. Throughout its history, the modern world economy has often operated under the wings of its **hegemon**, or dominant power. The hegemon invests many of its resources to keep the system operating in an orderly and predictable fashion. As Yale historian Paul Kennedy has argued, however, hegemons tend to overestimate their capabilities in manipulating economic and political structures to preserve their advantage.[4] The relative decline of these great powers has ushered in periods of uncertainty marked by the absence of effective management. Eventually a new hegemon arises, and the cycle begins again. The events that led up to World War II followed from British hegemonic decline and the unwillingness of the United States to assume that role.

hegemon
the dominant power in the global economy.

THE BRETTON WOODS SYSTEM

As the war was drawing to a close, the United States emerged as the world's lead economy. The physical and financial devastation of Europe stood in contrast to conditions in the United States, which had the resources to spearhead the drive to recovery. In 1944, allied officials met in the New Hampshire resort town of Bretton Woods to discuss postwar reconstruction. They ultimately agreed on a broad set of arrangements for what would become known as the Bretton Woods system, which would guide the operation of the world economy from the end of World War II to the early 1970s. While based on liberal economic principles intended to promote a reopening of commercial and financial channels, the Bretton Woods system also relied heavily on the ability of the United States to shoulder much of the initial burden. Although weary from war, the United States did not have the luxury of turning its back to the emerging political and military challenge of the Soviet Union. To gain its allies' support, the United States tolerated their efforts to protect their fragile economies from unfettered competition by agreeing to move more slowly in pushing for a more open trading system. All sides expected that once economic recovery had gained momentum, the responsibilities for managing and sustaining an open world economy would be shared more equally.

With this in mind, the United States proceeded on a number of fronts. The 1947 Marshall Plan, named for Secretary of State George Marshall, was especially noteworthy. It provided substantial funds to assist European countries in their recovery from the war and to promote the resumption of commercial activity. The United States contributed approximately $13 billion in aid to 16 countries, and by 1951, industrial production in these countries was 37 percent higher than in 1947, and exports had risen at an annual rate of over 20 percent.[5] The Soviet Union refused to participate in the program, seeing it as a US mechanism to further American influence and interests. As it turned out, the Marshall Plan served as an important catalyst in rebuilding the economic strength of countries that proved critical to US efforts to contain Soviet political and military aspirations.

The Bretton Woods system revolved around the operation of a well-defined set of goals and institutions. Established in 1944, the International Monetary Fund (IMF) would oversee the world's financial system and function as its central bank, offering technical assistance and training and acquiring capital from member states to stabilize currency values. It also provided short-term loans for countries with immediate financial needs and particularly difficult economic circumstances. The US dollar stabilized the emerging financial order and came to be considered "as good as gold." This term reflected the long-term strength of the dollar, whose value was set and backed by this precious commodity deemed to have enduring value.

The International Bank for Reconstruction and Development (IBRD), more commonly known as the World Bank, was another key Bretton Woods institution.

The architects of the agreement designed the World Bank initially to further hasten recovery from the war by lending funds for projects to promote longer-term economic development. Finally, the Bretton Woods participants formed the General Agreement on Tariffs and Trade (GATT) to foster greater cooperation in opening global markets by monitoring and promoting trade relationships.

They hoped to establish an International Trade Organization, a body with broad regulatory powers. Unable to forge the consensus necessary to launch the organization, the negotiating countries focused their attention on the series of arrangements they were developing under the umbrella of GATT to reduce tariffs. The GATT agreements were predicated on two basic principles to guide trade policies—**reciprocity** in the dismantling of trade barriers and **nondiscrimination** in the treatment of imported goods. The idea was to get countries to progressively eliminate preferences and protectionist inclinations by extending **most-favored nation (MFN)** status to all of their trading partners.

With these mechanisms in place, the post–World War II global economy began to take shape. It relied extensively on the United States for direction and leadership. The Bretton Woods system stimulated economic recovery and growth, especially in Western Europe and Japan, where the United States had a particularly large stake in assuring sustained economic progress. The success of Bretton Woods became increasingly tied to America's strategy in the developing Cold War, as the United States sought to enhance its allies' political and economic capabilities to gain additional leverage in its struggle with the Soviet Union.

The effectiveness of the United States in managing these affairs actually eroded its dominant position. On the political and strategic front, the need to counter Soviet activities resulted in an array of commitments and actions across the world that were both costly and, at times, rather risky. Meanwhile, excessive US spending to meet its growing financial obligations began to take its toll. By the late 1960s, confidence in the strength and stability of the dollar had fallen, and many countries feared an impending adjustment that would lower the value of the dollar to address the mounting deficit. These developments prompted US President Richard Nixon to prohibit withdrawals of gold from the United States in exchange for dollars. He took this step—known as the "closing of the gold window"—to prevent a further outflow of gold, which would undermine the value of the dollar. This decision marked a fundamental shift in policy and reflected increasing US frustration with its closest partners.

Tensions had mounted as the world became a more dangerous place. The Cold War had heated up considerably during the 1960s, but America's allies did not universally share the US view of the Soviet threat. A number of them began to question US actions, raising concerns over their costs and potential impacts. US weapons development programs and deepening American involvement in Vietnam were particularly controversial and financially draining. For its part, the United States grew resentful of this lack of support and the unwillingness of its allies to assume an additional share of the burden. Furthermore, US efforts

reciprocity
the idea that countries would respond to actions taken by their trade partners to reduce trade barriers with similar reductions of their own.

nondiscrimination
the idea that countries would extend preferential trade status to all their trade partners.

most-favored nation (MFN)
a means to promote equality in trade relationships by guaranteeing that if one country is given better trade terms by another, all other trade partners must receive the same terms.

to convince the European Economic Community and Japan to open their markets further to American products went largely unheeded. This was not surprising, as these countries had benefitted considerably over the years from their relatively free access to the US market without having to reciprocate fully. The broad consensus that had propelled the Bretton Woods system was unraveling.

At the same time, political changes in other parts of the world were affecting the foundation of the global economy. The end of colonialism led to the creation of new countries across Africa and Asia with limited capabilities and considerable needs. The transition to independence was frequently violent and destructive and added further to the tasks at hand. Expectations were high and in stark contrast to the harsh realities of everyday life. Insufficient support from international agencies and more-developed countries raised serious questions as to the future path to development.

In response, less-developed countries (LDCs) from Africa, Asia, and Latin America joined forces in the United Nations (UN) to establish the Group of 77 (G-77), named for the number of states that joined. This organization was designed to air collective concerns and to engage industrial countries in continuing discussions on the need for economic restructuring on a global scale. These countries are often referred to today as the "Global South" to reflect the location of most in the world's southern hemisphere.

The G-77 critique saw the inequities of the Bretton Woods system as part of the historical evolution of a global capitalist economy that empowered and enriched a few core countries at the expense of a far greater number of peripheral ones. The unequal economic relationships between core and periphery, they argued, extended beyond the formal bonds of colonialism and perpetuated the gap in levels of economic development. Influenced by Marxist thought, sociologist Immanuel Wallerstein had been the first to propose this theory, which he called "modern world systems."[6]

Political economist Andre Gunder Frank, among others, further examined the difficulties of moving beyond the constraints of this system, focusing on the structures of dependence embodied in a global economy that continued to disadvantage the countries on the periphery.[7] He noted that LDCs were mostly relegated to the exchange of generally cheaper raw materials or food products, which were frequently subject to considerable price fluctuations, for more expensive manufactured goods. International investment and finance sectors, dominated by large and primarily American companies and banks, wielded their power and leverage to dictate the nature of their engagements with LDCs in need of their capital. In the late 1960s, **dependency theory** provided an intellectual framework for many G-77 members who did not see incremental change as the way to enhance their position. Citing the inability to break the cycle of poverty within established frameworks, in the 1970s they called for the creation of a New International Economic Order (NIEO), a reform program designed to comprehensively restructure global economic relationships. In his 1969 book *Latin America: Underdevelopment or Revolution,* Andre Gunder

dependency theory
the view that the development of countries in the Global South is limited by the unfavorable terms through which they have been integrated into the global capitalist economy.

Frank explains the basic underpinnings of dependency theory.

The G-77 envisioned the NIEO as a comprehensive program of fundamental reform to bolster the LDCs' economic performance and capacity. It included plans to provide preferred access to global markets, to enhance and stabilize the prices of food and raw materials, to offer financial and technical assistance at more favorable terms, to encourage local input in devising development projects, and to monitor the business practices of large transnational corporations. Most developed countries were not willing to make sweeping concessions or respond under pressure, however, noting their continued confidence in a global economy based on the liberal principles of free and open exchange to address the needs of the LDCs as they moved forward with their economic agendas. Some critics of globalization today reflect the underlying concerns of the NIEO program, especially the pressures imposed on developing countries to adjust their policies to accommodate the interests of more powerful economic actors.[9] Despite its widespread support across the developing world, the NIEO program itself made only limited progress in influencing policy outcomes at the time.

> It is generally held that economic development occurs in a succession of capitalist stages and that today's underdeveloped countries are still in a stage of history, sometimes depicted as an original stage, through which the now developed countries passed long ago. It is also widely believed that the contemporary underdevelopment of a country can be understood as the product or reflection solely of its own economic, political, social, and cultural characteristics or structure. Yet historical research demonstrates that contemporary underdevelopment is in large part the historical product of past and continuing economic and other relations between the satellite underdeveloped and the now developed metropolitan countries. Furthermore, these relations are an essential part of the structure and development of the capitalist system on a world scale as a whole.[8]

IN THEIR OWN WORDS | **Andre G. Frank**

BEYOND BRETTON WOODS: THE ROOTS OF CONTEMPORARY GLOBALIZATION

Any hope of resolving these outstanding issues cooperatively faded as the world economy came under enormous pressure during the 1970s. Most Arab members of the Organization of Petroleum Exporting Countries (OPEC) imposed an embargo on oil shipments to countries supporting Israel during the 1973

Oil fields like the one shown here are part of a global industry that today produces many billions of barrels of oil annually. The production and sale of oil and gas spurs development worldwide but also leads to economic and political instability.

petrodollars
US dollars earned through the sale of petroleum.

Middle East war. OPEC was founded in 1960, and its original members were Iran, Iraq, Kuwait, Saudi Arabia, and Venezuela. By 1973, OPEC had expanded, and its members controlled 55.7 percent of the world's crude oil production. Their decision to restrict supply resulted in an unprecedented quadrupling of prices between 1973 and 1974.[10]

No one anticipated the crisis, and with so much of the world's economy dependent on the availability of inexpensive oil, its effects were widespread. Economic output contracted as money became tight and prices soared. Many companies were forced to curtail their operations and cut back their workforces. In the United States alone, economic output declined 6 percent between 1973 and 1975, and the unemployment rate surged to 9 percent.[11] The world was slipping into recession. Ironically, the OPEC countries emerged as the major sources of financing at this time, depositing the sizable earnings from oil sales in international banks. These banks, in turn, lent these **petrodollars** (US dollars acquired through the sale of petroleum) to countries so that they could purchase the oil they needed to keep their economies afloat.

These conditions made it difficult to sustain an open global economy, although its advocates felt some optimism when GATT member countries agreed to move forward with new international trade discussions. The Tokyo Round, the latest in a succession of negotiations under the auspices of GATT to combat trade protectionism, began in 1973. Previous rounds had succeeded in reducing or eliminating tariffs across a broad range of products. As a result, countries were now resorting to an array of other measures not covered by existing arrangements to limit access to their markets. The Tokyo Round developed new codes of conduct covering such barriers to free trade as subsidies of domestic producers, government purchasing practices favoring domestic producers, and excessive customs duties designed to undermine the competitiveness of imported goods. These agreements regarding nontariff barriers (NTBs) proved difficult for the GATT to monitor and enforce, and they provided only modest relief in offsetting the mercantilist trading tendencies that gained footing during these uncertain times.

The gradual easing of oil prices also offered hope. The uncertainty of the global economy posed a unique dilemma for OPEC. Oil producers had a major stake in economic recovery due to their considerable loans and investments. By 1974, OPEC members had sent about a third of their $60 billion surplus revenue to the United States, investing mainly in Treasury bills and other short-term holdings.[12] The 1979 outbreak of war between Iran and Iraq, two of OPEC's largest producers, once again forced many countries to borrow heavily to secure necessary imports. Fearful of massive defaults on outstanding loans, large international banks extended payment schedules and offered additional financing opportunities in a very uncertain environment. Some of these institutions incurred significant costs for their uncharacteristically risky behavior. However, this patchwork did serve to prevent a global economic meltdown.

By the mid-1980s, signs of recovery were emerging. Economic output was expanding, and financial markets were settling down. However, the global economic order was a far cry from that envisioned at Bretton Woods. Transnational connections between states and other actors were expanding, thereby contributing to the emergence of a system of "complex interdependence."[13] While the incentives for cooperation were significant, managing relationships was a more daunting task. This was certainly evident in the international monetary system, where the fixed exchange rate system of the Bretton Woods period had proven incapable of accommodating the shifts in economic conditions that affected the realistic values of the US dollar and other currencies. The values of currencies would now fluctuate or float on an ongoing basis to more accurately reflect daily ebbs and flows in economic conditions. Money markets had become far more fluid and speculative, with private financial institutions, transnational corporations, and even individuals buying and selling currencies.

The global economy had also become intensely competitive. The pressures were particularly acute for many American companies that had seen their positions erode over the previous decade. They found themselves increasingly forced to cut costs and aggressively pursue new markets to keep pace with European and Japanese businesses. LDCs also began to figure prominently in the community of globally minded companies. A number of "newly industrializing countries" such as Taiwan, Singapore, and South Korea (then referred to as NICs and today as emerging markets) became more significant players by virtue of their ability to provide reduced labor costs or other financial enticements to companies in developed countries.

Keeping markets open remained a challenge. The rigors of what economist Lester Thurow labeled "head to head" competition made it difficult to offset the inclinations of many countries to protect their respective companies and interests.[14] In 1986, the GATT organized the Uruguay Round, its next series of multilateral trade discussions, to continue efforts to limit existing and emerging trade restraints. The United States pressed hard to incorporate into the deliberations an initiative to liberalize the fast-growing services sector (e.g., accounting, financial, insurance, legal), as it continued to enjoy a considerable advantage in this area and looked to ensure access to a broad range of markets. This did not sit well with other aspiring providers, however, who sought to maintain some level of protection that might enable them to emerge as viable competitors.

Overall, this round of talks was difficult to sustain and would take nearly a decade to bring to closure.

Its most significant breakthrough was the agreement to create the World Trade Organization (WTO). Established in 1995, the WTO supplanted GATT as the body intended to preserve open markets by developing and overseeing the rules that guide global trade. It was designed to provide officials with enhanced capabilities to settle disputes and to enforce established rules. Both the mandate and the membership of the WTO expanded over the years, but the organization struggled to regulate international trade, since countries had considerable incentive to skirt existing requirements to gain competitive advantage.

Meanwhile, Japan and the United States had to deal with strains in their critical relationship. The economies of the two countries were closely linked by trade and investment activity, while the United States was committed to guard and fund a substantial portion of the military security of Japan as part of the arrangement derived at the close of World War II. Japan's meteoric rise as a global economic power was due, in large part, to its proactive business practices. With limited natural resources, Japan pursued a mercantilist development strategy to promote exports and protect its domestic market. This approach put the country at direct odds with the United States and other partners, who complained about currency manipulations and pricing practices designed to preserve low-cost advantages for Japanese products.

Japan's large industrial groups or *keiretsu,* such as Mitsubishi, had proven quite effective in penetrating the US market with high-quality products. Japan's direct commercial presence in the United States also expanded with the establishment of production facilities, the purchase of some prominent companies, and the acquisition of prime real estate in major American cities. By 1990, about 1,350 Japanese-owned manufacturers employed approximately 290,000 workers in the United States.[15]

Meanwhile, Japan continued to offer preferential treatment to its domestic companies. While the United States protested this policy, Japan countered by contending that the ineffectiveness of US export promotion policies and the ineptitude of American companies accounted for their limited success in the Japanese market. The widening and persistent trade gap, which was running between $40 and $50 billion at the time, was a particular source of friction.[16] Their growing stake in each other's economies did compel the two countries to address some of their more serious grievances through ongoing negotiations. The 1990 Structural Impediments Initiative (SII), with its emphasis on altering some longstanding Japanese market access restrictions, helped to avoid a potentially disastrous all-out trade war.

Concurrently, Western European countries discussed developing a framework for further European integration. In 1957, Italy, France, Belgium, Luxembourg, the Netherlands, and West Germany had created the European Economic Community (EEC or Common Market) to promote closer economic ties and policy coordination among its members. Over time, the organization took a number of steps to extend its membership and its mandate. It was renamed the European Community (EC) in 1967 to reflect its commitment to broader cooperation and gained new momentum with the addition of the United Kingdom, Denmark, and Ireland in 1973. Membership grew to twelve members with the entry of Greece in 1981 and Portugal and Spain in 1986.[17]

This development did not come without challenges. Member countries with weaker economies strained EC resources, and adding them proved divisive. In particular, members argued over the Community's comprehensive agricultural subsidy program financed by member taxes. Great Britain was particularly vexed by what it believed to be a disproportionate share of the cost it was expected to bear in funding the Common Agricultural Policy (CAP). Nevertheless, a broad sense of common interest prevailed. Through the leadership of Jacques Delors, the president of the European Commission, a plan was launched to move toward a fully integrated market and jointly managed monetary system.

The United States, Japan, and Europe were locked in an increasingly competitive struggle as they wrestled with the challenge of recovering from the disruptions of the 1970s. At the same time, some nations were committed to maintaining an open market system. US president Ronald Reagan and British prime minister Margaret Thatcher were at the forefront of this effort. They argued, among other things, for balanced budgets, a more limited government role in the economy, and policies that encouraged private sector initiatives. This renewed support for traditional liberal economic principles came to be known as new or **neoliberalism**. They put forward these ideas as a formula for domestic economic restructuring and for the promotion of a more open global economic environment.

Neoliberal practices caused considerable controversy, especially across the developing world, which immediately felt its effects. Freer trade undermined the ability of weaker companies to compete effectively, and large transnational companies gained considerable leverage in many countries, as they used their capital and superior technological capabilities to overwhelm smaller local firms seeking to maintain their market positions. By the mid-1980s, collective efforts to improve the position of these countries had brought only limited relief. As they struggled to enhance their indigenous capabilities and to tap into world markets, they now faced increasing demands for domestic reform along neoliberal lines. The global economy offered little opportunity for many LDCs to advance. They considered the further opening and deregulation of domestic markets to be yet another example of the undue leverage of the more industrial countries and their continuing ability to advantage themselves at the LDCs' expense.

The International Monetary Fund's **conditionality** policy frustrated many LDCs. Major contributors determined the practices of international financing agencies. To qualify for IMF loans, countries were obliged to adhere to more "responsible" policy principles that often limited spending for programs

neoliberalism

the economic principles that promote free market capitalism and closely reflect the ideals of contemporary globalization.

conditionality

the requirements imposed on prospective borrowers by the IMF or other lending institutions that emphasize economic growth over welfare considerations.

intended to provide for the basic needs of the most vulnerable segments of their populations or to improve overall social welfare. Prospective borrowers generally had little choice but to accept these terms to secure necessary financing. It reinforced broader concerns among many of these countries regarding their disadvantaged position within the global economy and the continued demand of its wealthier and more powerful members to dictate terms of involvement.

The world economy was becoming increasingly difficult to navigate, as countries sought to balance their domestic needs and international obligations. A consensus was emerging, at least among its more advantaged participants, around the need to work toward further integration of the market system through a set of fairly well-defined principles. However, the international institutions designed to develop rules and monitor compliance remained weak, and a number of bilateral and multilateral disputes emerged that threatened this fragile arrangement.

Oddly enough, a series of extraordinary and mostly unanticipated events outside the global capitalist orbit helped to shape and define its direction. The decades of Cold War had severely weakened the economies of the Soviet Union and its satellite countries across Eastern Europe. In the late 1980s, mounting resistance led to the fall of Soviet-backed regimes in such places as Albania, Czechoslovakia, Poland, Romania, Yugoslavia, and East Germany. The dismantling of the Berlin Wall symbolized the end of the Cold War era. The Soviet Union itself did not survive. These developments offered both monumental challenges and opportunities, unleasing a set of forces that shaped the global economic system as we know it today.

EMERGING ECONOMIC CENTERS

The experiences of the countries transitioning from communist rule provide a good snapshot of the changes in the structure of today's global economy. Early efforts to implement political and economic reforms were uneven. In Russia (and a number of former Soviet republics), the introduction of market reforms did not bring about an expected improvement in overall living standards. Instead, a relatively small group of investors with access to government officials gained considerable wealth and influence over the direction of the economy. These new elites, commonly referred to as the *oligarchs,* took advantage of their position to challenge the government's control over economic policy until their activity was eventually curtailed by Russian president Vladimir Putin (2000–2008).

Russia's economy expanded considerably under Putin, owing largely to its flourishing energy industry and rising prices for oil and natural gas on world markets. Rates of economic growth remained relatively healthy and steady—expanding an average 7.3 percent between 2004 and 2007. Although it experienced some drop off to 5.6 percent growth in 2008, the overall state of the Russian economy remained strong until the downturn in global economic conditions took their toll. As Putin handed off political control to his handpicked successor, Dmitri Medvedev, economic output fell a considerable 7.8 percent in 2009. Yet, Russia recovered as the global financial crisis eased, posting 4.3 percent gains in both 2010 and 2011. Although still plagued by a fair share of corruption and inefficiency, Russia's economy was in relatively good shape when Putin reacquired the presidency for another term in 2012.[18]

China's emergence has been steadier. China has become one of the world's leading economies, with an average annual growth rate that has generally exceeded 10 percent and gross domestic product (GDP) of more than $7 trillion. Not even China remained immune from the effects of the global recession, as its annual rate of growth slowed to 9.6 percent in 2008 and 9.2 percent in 2009 after accelerating a full 14.2 percent in 2007.[19] With growth rates of 10.4 percent and 9.2 percent in 2010 and 2011, China's economic dynamism appeared to remain intact. It seems poised to surpass Japan and perhaps even the United States as the world's largest economy before the end of the twenty-first century.

China is deeply enmeshed within the global economy and has become especially linked to the United States through expanding trade ties and the financing of significant amounts of US debt. At the same time, its ruling Communist Party has resisted US pressure to enact political reforms that would undermine its authority. China applies its own unique vision in the pursuit of its broad economic and political agenda. This dates back to the 1970s, when China's leader, Deng Xiaoping enacted major reforms designed to introduce market principles to the country's socialist economy. This model of "socialism with Chinese characteristics" has endured. It is reflected in the development of special administrative regions in Macao and Hong Kong, where there are different sets of rules and regulations to facilitate the coexistence of socialist and capitalist principles. Encouraged by the government, developers have made the island of Macau the world's casino capital, exceeding Las Vegas in revenues from its gambling operations. A leading global financial center, Hong Kong is an important economic asset to China and critical to its future economic planning.

China's success may be traced, in part, to its advantages as a producer of lower cost goods and its vast market potential. International companies have flocked to China to capitalize on its huge and inexpensive workforce. For its part, China has welcomed foreign investment to fuel its ambitious modernization agenda. In 2010, foreign direct investment reached a record $105.7 billion, continuing a pattern of relatively steady and substantial growth. By 2010, China ranked among the top five destinations for foreign investment across the world.[20]

China has amassed additional wealth by parlaying its role as a leading manufacturing center into an aggressive export strategy. In 2010, China's foreign trade totaled nearly $3 trillion, resulting in a significant $183.1 billion surplus. Its lopsided trade relationship with the United States—which led to a surplus of $227 billion in 2009 and $273 billion in 2010—remains a particularly sore point between the two countries.

The United States, for its part, has accused China of keeping its currency (the yuan) undervalued to enhance the pricing advantages of Chinese products. China has denied this claim, suggesting instead that American firms need to become more efficient to compete more effectively.[21] Nevertheless, in June 2010, China did bend to increasing pressures by agreeing in principle to allow for more exchange rate flexibility.

In return for the capital and technology provided by outside investment, China provides consumers elsewhere with an array of inexpensive goods. Meanwhile, China's more than 1.3 billion people are especially attractive to retailers. Chinese consumers may shop at Walmart after dropping by a McDonalds or Kentucky Fried Chicken, whose menus have been tweaked to reflect local tastes. The economic indicators in Table 6.1 reflect China's growth.

In many ways, China's expanding influence speaks to the fundamental transformation of the global economy. Despite the continuing dominance of its Communist Party and differences with the West on many strategic issues, China has embraced core capitalist economic precepts and has become both a critical partner and formidable competitor. As an outlet for investment and a source of

TABLE 6.1   MEASURING CHINA'S GROWTH*

	2006	2007	2008	2009	2010
GDP	2,657.8	3,382.4	4,519.9	4,990.5	5,930.4
Real GDP Growth	11.6	13.0	9.6	8.7	10.5
Foreign Exchange Reserves	1,066.3	1,528.2	1,946.0	2,399.2	2,847.3
Exports	969.0	1,220.5	1,430.7	1,201.6	1,577.9
% Change	27.2	26.0	17.3	−16.0	31.3
Imports	791.5	956.1	1,132.6	1,005.6	1,394.8
% Change	19.9	20.8	18.5	−11.2	38.7
World Trade Balance	177.5	264.3	298.1	195.7	183.1
With US	232.5	256.3	266.3	226.8	273.1
Inward FDI	63.0	74.8	92.4	90.0	105.7
% Change	4.5	13.6	23.5	−2.6	17.4

*Numbers shown are in billions of US dollars.

Sources: US-China Business Council, 2012, www.uschina.org/statistics; IMF World Economic Outlook Database, April 2012, www.imf.org.

finance, China has considerable leverage and latitude to pursue its economic and political interests. Its aggressive policies often provoke tensions with the United States, Japan, and other key partner-competitors. China's labor practices, including the use of prison and child labor and the alleged manipulation of its currency, are especially contentious yet effective ways to undercut trade competition. China's trading partners are also concerned about its expanding demand on global energy resources. The growing stake these partners have in each other's economies provides them an incentive to negotiate solutions to emerging political and economic disputes.

India's emergence as an important player in the twenty-first century also reflects shifting roles in the global economy. With its long-standing democracy and strong educational system, India has experienced significant growth and has attracted the interest of foreign businesses and investors seeking to engage the country's economic and human resources. Although it is one of the world's most populous countries, many of its more than one billion people endure conditions of extreme poverty even as a vibrant English-speaking middle class has developed. Continuing religious tensions between Hindus and Muslims, and other differences that surface in India's multiethnic society, periodically result in bombings and other acts of violence. Modern office parks house some of the world's most sophisticated software firms in areas surrounded by shantytowns that lack any modern conveniences. Although it is a country of paradoxes, India has become one of the world's most dynamic economies and has secured an important niche in the rapidly developing information technology (IT) sector.

India has had considerable success in the global marketplace. Its top IT companies are among the world's leaders. TCS (Tata Consultancy Services) has close to 200,000 employees worldwide and is the largest IT services firm in Asia, and Infosys Technologies, with its 135,000 workers, ranks 28th among IT service providers globally. In addition, India's Tata Motors is poised to become an important global player in the industry. It purchased Jaguar and Land Rover from Ford for $2.3 billion in early 2008 and planned to bring automobile ownership within the reach of millions of Indian families through the production and sale of its Nano model for approximately $2500.[22]

Meanwhile, wealthy Indian entrepreneurs are being courted by foreign firms eager to secure contracts for services previously performed in house. Anyone in the English-speaking world in need of assistance with a malfunctioning computer or booking reservations for an upcoming airline flight has a

---

HOW DO YOU CONNECT? | **CALLING INDIA**

Have you ever had an encounter with a call center located in India?

a. yes

b. no

c. I have connected to a call center located in another country.

Were your questions or concerns addressed effectively?

a. yes

b. no

c. to some extent

In what areas do you think call centers excel?

a. familiarity with the issue

b. technical expertise in terms of devising a solution

c. clarity of communication

Employees at a busy call center in Bangalore, India, provide customer support for callers worldwide. These jobs provide new opportunities for a rising Indian middle class but raise criticism in other countries that jobs are being outsourced.

outsource/offshore

often used interchangeably, these terms refer to the displacement of work activity. Outsourcing involves the transfer of certain specific functions performed within a company to an outside provider. Offshoring entails the relocation of an entire business operation to another country.

good chance of connecting to a call center in India. These facilities are staffed by young, highly educated Indian workers pursuing modern lifestyles that stand in stark contrast to traditional Indian values.

India's engagement with the global economy has raised questions regarding its impact. Soaring economic growth has done little to lessen the gap between India's modern and traditional sectors. The draw of the country's relatively inexpensive, technologically savvy workforce has proven unsettling in other parts of the world. Companies based in the United States and other high-wage countries have transferred hundreds of thousands of white-collar jobs to India. It is far more profitable to them to **outsource** particular jobs to other companies and **offshore** complete business operations to other locales. By 2005, outsourcing generated approximately $16 billion and employed 800,000 people across India. By 2015, a projected 3.4 million US jobs will have been transferred to workers in India and other low-wage countries.[23]

Within a global economy that has had difficulties sustaining growth over recent years, economic output across the developing world has remained relatively healthy. At the height of the global financial crisis in 2009 when global output shrank 2.4 percent, for example, developing countries actually grew 2.4 percent. This could be traced to the fact that the crisis originated in the developed world and that, in a number of developing countries, governments enacted financial stimulus measures to reinforce domestic demand and trade linkages. This pattern continued into 2010 and part of 2011. With the global economy recovering modestly and tenuously (4 percent growth in 2010 and 2.8 percent in 2011), developing countries expanded at a higher rate (7.5 percent in 2010 and 6 percent in 2011). This rate far outpaced the performance of the more developed economies, which continued to struggle with high levels of debt, unemployment, government austerity measures, and a host of other economic difficulties.[24]

These figures contribute to the notion that the world economy has become "upside down," as developing countries have come to account for more of the world's capital investment, trade, and consumption of resources.[25] In 1999, the Group of Seven industrial countries (popularly known as the G-7) accounted for around 50 percent of world output; a decade later its share had declined to around 41 percent. The IMF expects this figure to fall to approximately 36 percent by 2015, as countries such as China, India, Brazil, and Mexico—among others—continue to expand their economies.[26]

While these numbers may suggest a leveling of the global economic playing field, there are considerable disparities. The more dynamic economies in the Global South contribute most significantly to this aggregate picture, but many others have continued to lag seriously behind due to failures to successfully address economic or political challenges. In East Africa, for example, severe drought has devastated crops in Eritrea, Ethiopia, and elsewhere and has resulted in widespread famine. In Somalia, the ability to deal with this situation has been compromised further by a protracted civil war and dysfunctional government. The unsettled nature of the global economy, moreover, has hit developing countries hard. Uncertain employment and income prospects have hampered governmental and nongovernmental efforts to improve living conditions. In 2009 alone, the economic slowdown left an estimated 47 million people across the developing world in extreme poverty. Of these, the largest number (around 29 million) lived in densely populated East and South Asia, with another 14 million in Africa and 3 million in Latin America and the Caribbean.[27]

The difficulty of maintaining steady worldwide demand for commodities in the aftermath of the 2009 recession contributes heavily to the challenges many countries face across the Global South. Lower prices have debilitating effects on the ability to generate funds that might be used to support efforts to reduce poverty and to invest in infrastructure to promote more sustainable production. These countries also remain dependent on continuing public and private capital flows from more developed countries facing their own sets of financial constraints. Economic uncertainties have dampened the enthusiasm for globalization across many parts of the region, where support has resurged for populist leaders who promised to reassert national control over resources and economic policy, such as Venezuela's Hugo Chavez. Support for populist leaders suggests citizens' heightened desire for more leverage over the terms of participation in the global economy, but by no means signals a desire to retreat from that engagement.

HOW DO YOU CONNECT? | **OUTSOURCED!**

Do you know someone who has lost a job due to outsourcing?

a. yes

b. no

If you do, was he or she able to find another job locally at comparable pay?

a. yes

b. no

c. was able to find a job at comparable pay but had to move elsewhere

d. was able to find a job but at considerably lower pay

Has your community had an entire business relocate offshore?

a. yes

b. no

If so, what happened to the facility?

a. A new business moved in.

b. It remains vacant.

c. The facility was torn down and the space is now used for other purposes.

KEY PLAYERS IN TRANSITION

Uncertainties in the global economy affect people around the world. The realignment of some of the more pivotal players in the post–World War II period has added to this dynamic. Countries that played a major role in fueling growth during the latter half of the twentieth century are now attempting to retain their vibrancy in the face of increasing competition and demands for greater sharing of resources from those that are now more prominently positioned to shape the direction of the twenty-first century.

Japan, which enjoyed extraordinary economic performance in the 1970s and 1980s, has floundered in a prolonged recession that calls into question its basic economic orientation and strategy. Japan built its expansion on a fragile foundation of overvalued land and ephemeral stock market prices. The collapse of that financial bubble in the early 1990s sent Japan's economy into a persistent tailspin.

To make matters worse, Japan's political environment, which has been prone to considerable instability, discourages significant restructuring. The governing *iron triangle* of politicians, bureaucrats, and big business that oversaw the economic boom continues to dominate the system but has reconsidered its approach to sustain the country's global competitiveness. Under the leadership of Junichiro Koizumi, elected prime minister in 2001, Japan enacted reforms that included privatizing inefficient government agencies, forcing banks to write off bad loans, and limiting any tax increases in an effort to increase corporate and individual spending. These were seen as critical to the resumption of economic growth. His youthful successor, Shinzo Abe, who was elected prime minister in 2006 on a platform of further reform to restore Japan's economic luster, quickly lost this office, as his tenure was punctuated by a number of political and financial scandals. Japan's political uncertainties have shown few signs of abating. From 2006 to 2012, the country had six prime ministers. None was able to avoid the infighting and improprieties that stymie the political process and limit the ability of successive governments to navigate through turbulent economic times.

From every indication, Japan's economic recovery will be a slow process. Annual growth rates in 2004–07 hovered in the modest 2 percent range, owing largely to relatively limited capital investment and consumer spending. With a severe reduction in global demand for automobiles, information technology, and other exports, Japan's economy contracted 1.1 percent in 2008 and a more significant 5.5 percent in 2009. As the global financial system came back from the crisis of that time, Japan continued to struggle. While its economy rebounded with 4.4 percent growth in 2010, it retracted again (just under 1 percent) in 2011.[28] The extensive damage and disruption stemming from the massive earthquake and tsunami in March 2011 contributed to this decline.

Even such enduring symbols of Japan's global economic prowess as Honda, Sony, and Mitsubishi have fallen on hard times. Meanwhile, Toyota, long known for its quality control and assurance, suffered a dramatic decline in sales as production practices became shoddy and effective managerial oversight and responsibility failed. To adjust to slumping sales and preserve their competitive posture, many Japanese companies have had to rethink such traditional business practices as lifetime employment guarantees, strategic partnerships with non-Japanese companies, and the offshoring of production facilities. For example, in 2007, in order to comply with legislation that mandated the use of domestic components, 70 percent of the parts that went into the Accords manufactured at Honda's plant in Ohio came from within the United States.[29] As a result of this legislation, Honda (and other manufacturers) established American affiliates of many of their suppliers.

Europe, for its part, has proceeded with a broad-based integration strategy. The 1992 Treaty of Maastricht resulted in a set of agreements to promote broader and deeper cooperation. In recognition of this effort, the European Community was renamed the European Union (EU). The building of this union of 27 countries proceeded through the creation of a single European market and a jointly managed monetary system. Through delicate maneuverings and compromises they worked together to strengthen the EU's governing institutions. However, breakthroughs have not come easily.

In 1999, the European Union took a landmark step with the introduction of a single currency, the euro. Initially, 11 of the 15 EU members at the time adopted it, and Greece followed shortly thereafter. (Denmark, Sweden, and the United Kingdom chose to continue using national currencies.) Participants are required to meet targets relating to inflation, interest rates, and debt. They are also subjected to rules and policies of the European Central Bank, a body that limits the sovereign authority of individual governments and seeks to ensure that the euro works to broaden EU trade and investment goals. Between 2007 and 2011, five additional members joined the *eurozone*—the members of the European Union that use the euro as their official currency—as it moved toward even greater economic coordination and political management.

Support for extending the EU's coverage is, in part, a response to the challenges many of its members (and aspiring ones) face in coping with new economic realities. Broader integration promotes levels of cooperation and efficiency required to compete effectively in global markets, although it is sometimes difficult to reconcile divergent interests and perspectives. However, the debt crisis that engulfed a number of European economies in 2010 and 2011 dampened enthusiasm for this strategy considerably.

Some of the EU's more stable and established members, such as Germany and France, have found it increasingly difficult to bail out members facing severe capital shortages, such as Greece and Italy, while continuing to attend to the pressures of preserving traditional entitlements and social welfare policies at home. The relatively weaker economies that are either unwilling or unable to curtail their expenditures have placed an additional strain on the euro and undermined its value. Surging government debts resulted, in large measure, from spending surges intended to stimulate recovery from the global recession. Following annual increases in 2006 and 2007 of around 3.5 percent, EU output stalled in 2008 and dropped 4.2 percent in 2009. While it recovered somewhat in 2010 (2 percent) and 2011 (1.6 percent), Europe continues to face severe challenges, as it copes with financial uncertainty that threatens the stability of the euro and an unemployment rate hovering around 10 percent.[30] The following debate suggests the complexity of reconciling regional and national interests.

PRO/CON
Should the EU control member states' budgets?

PRO	CON

Markus Ferber
Markus Ferber, German Member of the European Parliament and Member, Economic and Monetary Affairs Committee. Written for *CQ Global Researcher*, April 2012

Nikolaos Chountis
Nikolaos Chountis, Greek Member of the European Parliament and Member, Economic and Monetary Affairs Committee. Written for *CQ Global Researcher*, April 2012

Recent debt problems in the eurozone have shown the need for more central European Union (EU) control and influence over national budgets. Eurozone countries cannot continue to pile up deficits and then launch desperate rescue attempts. EU member states that violate the EU's debt criteria have to be punished more quickly than in the past—and with tougher penalties. The recently adopted fiscal pact provides national debt brakes and automatic sanctions. This means a tightening of fiscal controls in the eurozone.

Since the establishment in 1997 of the Stability and Growth Pact, the European Commission has monitored the development of the budgetary situation in eurozone countries. Under the pact, each EU member state must submit an updated stability program annually to the commission, providing information on medium-term budget planning. The commission must also be notified twice per year of the projected deficit and the expected total debt. The Stability and Growth Pact clearly says that member states must limit the amount of their annual budget deficit to 3 percent of their gross domestic product (GDP) and their overall public debt to 60 percent of GDP.

Even before the current financial and economic crisis hit Europe, the institutional weaknesses of the pact became clear. Even major economies such as Germany and

With the outbreak of the debt crisis in the eurozone, the dominant political forces (the social democrats and the conservatives) decided to minimize public spending and impose austerity policies all over Europe. To more closely coordinate fiscal policies and control national budgets, the EU recently adopted an "Austerity Treaty" [known as the fiscal treaty], called for European Commission control of national budgets and strengthened the Stability and Growth Pact through penalties to member states.

Fiscal policy is a very important tool for the implementation of economic and development policy. Especially, after the introduction of the eurozone, fiscal policy is the only macroeconomic instrument that member states have.

The suffocative coordination of fiscal policies under this austerity policy eliminates the capability and the flexibility of EU member states to pursue an effective and countercyclical stabilization policy, geared toward redistribution of wealth, sustainable development and maintaining adequate public services and infrastructure.

Tighter fiscal discipline and closer coordination of fiscal policies along the lines of dominant economic policies will not help member states recover from this crisis or prevent a future one. Instead, this kind of coordination exacerbates

PRO	CON
France did not adhere to its criteria, which led to the weakening of the pact.	the effects of a crisis, increases social inequalities, poverty and unemployment and eventually leads to the impoverishment of Europe.
The new "six-pack" is a legislative package that includes six reports that toughen European borrowing and debt-reduction rules. In the negotiations, the European Parliament fought for a hard line on the measure. Until now, sanctions against an EU member violating Stability and Growth Pact rules had to be decided by a majority of EU member states. Under the six-pack, the sanction process starts automatically and can only be stopped by a majority of EU finance ministers. Thus, in the medium term EU members are forced to keep to a balanced budget, without resorting to new borrowing.	Unfortunately, the EU has decided practically to cancel the role of national parliaments, which are elected by the people, in order to give superpowers to bureaucratic institutions, such as the European Commission and the European Central Bank.
As a next step, the European Parliament is working on the so-called two-pack, which would further improve the control and coordination of national budgets. Euro countries should adopt far-reaching domestic and economic reforms only after the EU Commission and the remaining members of the eurozone have been consulted.	The tightening of the Stability Pact, the institutionalization of austerity and the limitation of democracy and national sovereignty are the new components of the European Union. The results of this change and of EU control of national budgets are more than obvious in Greece. The economic program to be implemented by Greece has nothing to do with the vision of a united Europe. It is incompatible with the European social model, with the ideas of solidarity and economic and social convergence of member states with the values—of democracy and social justice.
Recent history has clearly taught us that allowing member states to go it alone in setting budgetary policy is not sustainable once you have a monetary union.	The experiment conducted in Greece is not confined to Greece. On the contrary, what we live today in my country, Greece, is the future of Europe and the euro.

Source: Brian Beary, "Future of the EU," *CQ Global Researcher 6 (2012):* 181–204.

WHERE Do You Stand?

1. Does the need to balance European budgets take priority over the need for government spending on programs to stimulate growth and employment?
2. Given its financial uncertainties, does the EU have the right to impose more stringent requirements on countries failing to reduce their deficits?

The United States remains the world's largest economy, although its growth has slowed over recent years. While expanding modestly before contracting 3.5 percent in 2009, its recovery was slow (3 percent in 2010 and 1.7 percent in 2011).[31] The United States continues to advance free-market principles and policies in both regional and global forums, although many citizens have come to question this approach. They are particularly concerned about the loss of American jobs. The closing of factories and their relocation to lower-wage countries, such as Mexico, the Dominican Republic, Indonesia, and China, has hit the US manufacturing sector hard. Other sectors have also suffered, as advances in information technology and telecommunications make it easier and easier for companies to turn to India and other countries for cheap labor. Highly trained and relatively inexpensive workforces in these places are now engaged in a wide array of increasingly complex tasks previously performed in the United States. The considerable decline in other employment opportunities only magnifies the impact of these job losses.

The cost of maintaining America's economy is also a source of contention among politicians and citizens as it involves questions regarding the advisability of increasing budget deficits and debt. The US **current account** deficit, which reflects a net outflow of money from the country, was $473.4 billion in 2011.[32] With an annual government budget deficit of around $1.3 trillion and an outstanding national debt of $16.4 trillion, the country has been hard pressed to sustain itself financially.[33] Once the world's leading creditor country, the United States now faces a more vulnerable economic future as it has come to rely on China and other foreign sources of financing. By 2011, foreigners owned approximately $5 trillion of the US national debt held publicly, with a full $1.2 trillion held by China.[34]

The US economic downturn that surfaced in 2008 and reverberated across the global economy magnified uncertainties about the future. An extended period of risky and ill-advised mortgage lending practices precipitated the collapse of the housing market and set in motion a series of events that undermined financial markets at home and abroad. As unemployment grew to 9.3 percent and consumer confidence declined against a backdrop of business failures and personal bankruptcies, the US government implemented a massive economic stimulus package designed to prevent further fallout.[35] While this infusion of money resulted in additional debt, the government hoped that it would invigorate credit markets and promote the resumption of sufficient levels of investment and financing activity to restore economic confidence.

As the impact of the American financial meltdown spread across the globe, the volatility of oil prices compounded economic uncertainty for many countries. Oil drives economic activity across the world, and its ready availability at a reasonable cost is critical to stable markets. This is not easy to guarantee. To begin with, demand for oil has escalated. Table 6.2 suggests, moreover, that the members of OPEC account for an overwhelming 81.3 percent of proven reserves and are in a position to control production decisions. In the United States and numerous other consumer countries, enthusiasm for conservation or the pursuit of alternative energy sources waned after the crises of the 1970s and generally resurfaced only during periods of rising prices.

At the same time, the thirst for oil in China, India, and other emerging economies has rapidly expanded with industrial development. Although tempered a bit by the global recession of 2008–09, the demand for oil increased as the recovery proceeded. This resurgence contributed to the price hikes noted in

current account
the equivalent of a country's check book, reflecting the combined balances on trade in goods, services, income, and net transfers.

TABLE 6.2	OPEC MEMBERS: PROVEN CRUDE OIL RESERVES 2010 (BILLIONS OF BARRELS)

Algeria	12.20	Libya	47.10
Angola	9.50	Nigeria	37.20
Ecuador*	7.21	Qatar	25.38
Iran	151.17	Saudi Arabia	264.52
Iraq	143.10	United Arab Emirates	97.80
Kuwait	101.50	Venezuela	296.50
TOTAL	1,193.17**		

*Ecuador suspended its membership in 1992 and reactivated it in 2007.

**This represents 81.3% of the world's proven oil reserves.

Source: OPEC, *Annual Statistical Bulletin,* 2010/2011 edition, www.opec.org.

Table 6.3. Since oil is purchased around the world with US dollars, the fluctuating value of the currency has added to the pressure on prices. So has the heightened involvement of speculators looking to reap significant financial gain from the flourishing oil market. These speculators, anticipating a rise in prices, sign contracts for future deliveries at the current price. Their purchases are often considerable, thereby impacting available supply and market prices. As noted in Table 6.4, for example, prices surged to around the $100-per-barrel mark in 2011.[36]

Political instability in the Middle East and other major supply areas continues to affect oil markets. In Saudi Arabia and other Persian Gulf oil-producing countries, internal opposition threatens the future of long-standing monarchies. Ongoing political tensions in Iraq, Iran, Nigeria, and Venezuela add to these uncertainties and threaten to interrupt production or otherwise disrupt the flow of oil to its intended destinations. With supplies so vulnerable to shifting political winds, oil markets remain jittery and are often subject to unanticipated spikes. Rising prices may offer windfall profits to oil companies and producer countries; however, they disrupt economic activity and create severe hardships for dependent consumers.

TABLE 6.3	AVERAGE WORLD CRUDE OIL PRICES (US DOLLARS PER BARREL), 2000–11*

Year	Price
2000	$26.72
2001	$21.84
2002	$22.51
2003	$27.56
2004	$36.77
2005	$50.28
2006	$59.69
2007	$66.52
2008	$94.04
2009	$56.35
2010	$74.71
2011	$95.73

*Domestic first purchase price, annual average

Source: Energy Information Administration, US Department of Energy: *Monthly Energy Review,* May 2012, www.eia.gov/totalenergy/data/monthly/archive/00351205.pdf.

TABLE 6.4	WORLD CRUDE OIL PRICES (US DOLLARS PER BARREL), 2011*		
Month	Price	Month	Price
January	$85.66	July	$97.82
February	$86.69	August	$89.00
March	$99.19	September	$90.22
April	$108.80	October	$92.28
May	$102.46	November	$100.18
June	$97.30	December	$98.71

*Prices as of last week of each month.

Source: US Energy Information Administration, US Department of Energy, *Monthly Energy Review,* May 2012, www .eia.gov/totalenergy/data/monthly/archive/00351205.pdf.

CONCLUSION: THE EVOLUTION OF THE WORLD ECONOMY

The world economy is constantly evolving. On the one hand, the spread of globalization has benefited people previously outside the mainstream, who have become deeply engaged and productive participants. In China and other emerging economies, for example, eager governments and bold entrepreneurs have parlayed local advantages into impressive growth and development. A good case in point is Jian Shuo Wang, one of a growing number of young Chinese innovators seeking to capitalize on the country's growing market opportunities. After working for Microsoft, he launched Kijiji—eBay's classified advertising business in China. While enjoying considerable success in expanding these listings to more than 300 cities, he then spun off Baixing.com, an online community with listings for houses, jobs, and second-hand goods.[37]

At the same time, the extension of the free market has destabilized the lives of many others who continue to operate on the periphery without sufficient tools to compete. This has certainly been true for Neah, a young woman from the Philippines whose encounter with globalization brought her into the web of human trafficking—a growing segment of today's global economy that involves recruiting and transporting persons through force or coercion. This sector generates more than $31.7 billion in profits and denies victims more than $21 billion in earnings.[38] Although promised a job as a waitress in Germany, she found herself transported to Nigeria and then to Togo where she was confined to working in brothels under harsh supervision and with insufficient means to alter her situation. She made her way to another brothel in Cyprus and eventually succeeded in earning enough money to buy a ticket home.[39]

This contrast between Jian and Neah epitomizes the complex and often contradictory nature of today's global economy. It affects the fates and fortunes of countries and their people in very different ways. The challenge is magnified by the shifting boundaries of economic activity and the absence of broad consensus as to the policies that are most useful and desirable in tackling issues such as stabilizing financial markets, managing debt, and alleviating poverty that are pivotal to the economic well-being of people across the world.

Important questions remain as to the future resiliency of the world economy and the extent to which it will be poised to meet the basic and sometimes divergent needs of its varied participants. Trade, investment, and finance are three critical areas that will require considerable attention. Chapter 7 looks at the challenges of addressing these issues.

KEYConcepts

capitalism 118
comparative advantage 119
conditionality 129
current account 140
dependency theory 124
hegemon 121
liberalism 118

mercantilism 118
most-favored nation (MFN) 123
neoliberalism 129
nondiscrimination 123
outsource/offshore 134
petrodollars 126
reciprocity 123

TO LEARNMore

Books and Other Print Media

Bruce C. Greenwald and Judd Kahn, *Globalization: The Irrational Fear that Someone in China Will Take Your Job* (Hoboken, NJ: John Wiley & Sons, 2009).

Greenwald and Kahn look at the impact of globalization on people's lives.

Dani Rodrik, *The Globalization Paradox: Democracy and the Future of the World Economy*, (New York: W.W. Norton, 2011).

In this book, Rodrik offers a historical and contemporary analysis of the tension between economic globalization and the spread of democracy.

Jeffrey A. Frieden, *Global Capitalism: Its Fall and Rise in the Twentieth Century* (New York: W. W. Norton, 2006).

This book is a good review of the earlier wave of globalization in the early twentieth century and how it collapsed with the outbreak of World War I in 1914. It is very helpful in understanding contemporary globalization and the idea that it is necessarily inevitable and irreversible.

Joseph P. Quinlan, *The Last Economic Superpower: The Retreat of Globalization, The End of American Dominance, and What We Can Do About It* (New York: McGraw-Hill, 2011).

This book is an intriguing look at the reconfiguring of the global economy following the 2008 financial crisis, with special emphasis on the rise of China and other emerging market economies.

Paul Kennedy, *The Rise and Fall of the Great Powers* (New York: Random House, 1987).

Kennedy's classic and comprehensive history of the development of the global economy focuses on how great powers arise and eventually lose their preeminent status.

Websites

Europa (the European Union), http://europa.eu/.

This official website of the European Union contains a wealth of information on the organization and its member states.

Group of 77 (G-77), www.g77.org/.

This organization represents the interests of developing countries within the UN and beyond.

International Labor Organization (ILO), www.ilo.org/.

The official website for this UN specialized agency contains information about the ILO along with publications, research, labor standards, and a statistical database.

Organization for Economic Cooperation and Development (OECD), www.oecd.org.

This organization's website houses its storehouse of data and statistics and provides access to publications and reports.

Organization of Petroleum Exporting Countries (OPEC), www.opec.org.

OPEC is an intergovernmental organization representing the major oil-producing states, primarily those in the Middle East. The official website hosts information about the organization, including data, publications, and other media.

US–China Business Council (USCBC), www.uschina.org/.

The USCBC is a private, nonprofit organization of US companies that do business with China.

Videos

1-800 India (2006).

Examines the human and cultural impact, especially on women, of the emergence of India as a leader for outsourced white-collar jobs.

Cappuccino Trail: The Global Economy in a Cup (2004).

This documentary addresses issues of equity and profit in international trade by following the trail of two coffee beans grown in Peru—one that takes the route of the open market and the other that becomes part of a gourmet coffee introduced by a British company committed to paying fair prices to farmers.

Commanding Heights: The Battle for the World Economy (2003).

A three-part series tracing the transformation of the global economy from the beginning of the twentieth century to the 1990s, this is an excellent source for understanding the conflicting views on the relationship between governments and markets. The contrasting ideas of economists John Maynard Keynes and Friedrich von Hayek are noted throughout as a means for understanding current disagreements over economic policy. There is also a comprehensive website with many special features hosted by PBS.

Keynesianism: It's All About Spending (2010) and *Fight of the Century* (2011).

These are lighthearted and entertaining, yet informative reviews of the how the ideas of Hayek and Keynes informed the debates over how to respond to the financial crisis of 2008.

The First Red Multinational (2007).

This documentary presents a case study of China's first multinational corporation, TCL—the parent company of Thomson Color TV.

Challenges to Prosperity

The World Economic Forum (WEF), an independent nonprofit foundation that annually brings together political, financial, and corporate leaders to promote networking among them and to address an array of global issues, met in Davos, Switzerland for its 42nd annual meeting in January of 2012 under the general theme of "The Great Transformation: Shaping New Models." As founder and chief executive officer of the WEF, Klaus Schwab observes—in this quote from the closing plenary session—that transformation is needed, as economic success will require greater attention to the real problems facing society today. This has been an evolving position for the WEF, long considered elitist and pro-business in nature. To counter criticism, the group has taken to inviting celebrities such as Bono and Angelina Jolie to its annual meetings to raise awareness of and funding for debt relief, AIDS research, and other humanitarian causes.

For opponents of the WEF, this has not been enough. They have organized their own annual forum, The World Social Forum, which offers individuals and representatives of groups and organizations that are part of the antiglobalization movement an opportunity to voice their

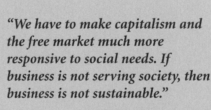

> *"We have to make capitalism and the free market much more responsive to social needs. If business is not serving society, then business is not sustainable."*
>
> —Klaus Schwab, Founder and Chief Executive Officer of the World Economic Forum, 2012.[1]

concerns. Meeting annu-
ally at the same time as
the WEF, the World
Social Forum seeks to
advance alternative mod-
els of economic and social
development. Participants
see themselves as economically
disadvantaged and likely to fall
further behind within a free-market
system. Meeting in Brazil in January of
2012, they reiterated their position that
the current system is inherently unfair by
design, and only significant change will provide a
more equal distribution of wealth.

Much of their skepticism stems from the neoliberal
"rules of the game" that are administered largely by governments
and businesses with the greatest leverage within the global economy. Economist
Joseph Stiglitz, who has written widely on the challenges and limitations of globalization, believes that these rules undermine the sovereignty of developing countries by
restricting their ability to control decisions affecting their well-being.[2] Despite their
broader access to world markets, many of the countries of the Global South remain
highly critical of the system. They want to see the world's economic powerhouses more
directly address such challenges as pervasive poverty, trade fairness, transnational corporate behavior, unregulated capital flows, and debt relief.

The rancorous debate over globalization and its impacts suggests a somewhat
unpredictable future. Very different perspectives fuel the disagreements that play out
when international agencies such as the WTO meet to consider ways to address complaints about the trade policies of certain members and when leaders gather to develop
plans to prevent the collapse of global credit markets. Supporters of globalization point
to the alleged benefits flowing from the opening of global markets, which spreads
capital and other resources to areas in need. Opponents focus on the hardships and
costs to workers without the requisite skills or wherewithal to survive free-market
uncertainties. They complain that the imposition of globalization's neoliberal principles
and policies does not account sufficiently for unique local needs or circumstances.

Sacks of coffee are offloaded from a ship at a dock in Hamburg, Germany. The global trade in commodities like coffee is a sign of potential increases in prosperity worldwide, and yet the world's citizens do not share the rewards equally.

Decisions made today about trade, investment, and finance will shape the future of the world economy. The willingness of governments to address their differences over proposals to open markets more fully will determine whether the WTO can succeed in resuming formal international trade negotiations. Where Korea's Hyundai Motor or some other transnational company locates its next assembly plant will impact employment prospects across its production network. The lending practices of Germany's Deutsche Bank and other leading financial institutions will affect the stability and potential expansion of global capital markets.

TRADE

The volume of trade has expanded considerably since the end of World War II. The progressive reduction of tariffs and other barriers that countries use to protect their domestic markets has facilitated a broader exchange of goods and services. Total trade in 2000, for example, was 22 times the level in 1950.[3] There are incentives to keep trade lines open. Exports are an important source of income and employment, while imports offer opportunities to enhance the quality of life by providing consumers a broader array of products. For the world's poorer countries in particular, trade is a means to engage with the global economy and to gain access to critical items such as food and medicines that might not be available otherwise.

Maintaining stable and cooperative trade relationships can be challenging. Countries often find it difficult to withstand the temptation to seek any possible advantage in their dealings with others, especially if they are having difficulties competing effectively in global markets or under pressure at home to focus more exclusively on building domestic capacity and creating more jobs. This can lead to the use of policy tools that may be questionable in terms of their fairness or legality. The WTO has handled well over 400 complaints through its Dispute Settlement process since 1995. These cases have covered an array of subjects, ranging from Antigua's claim that the United States unlawfully closes it market to Antiguan remote gambling services to Japan's concerns over China's use of quotas and questionable licensing requirements to restrict the export of rare earth metals that are critical to the development of new technologies. The WTO has had a mixed record in terms of reconciling differences and defusing tensions that arise from these conflicts.[4]

The trade system itself is impacted heavily by the ups and downs of the global economy (Table 7.1). After rising 8.5 percent in 2006 and 5.5 percent in 2007, for example, the volume of trade contracted more than 12 percent in 2009 as the effects of the financial meltdown spread across the world. This was the steepest decline in more than 70 years. While it rebounded 13.8 percent in 2010, growth

TABLE 7.1 **MERCHANDISE TRADE 2011 (IN BILLIONS OF US DOLLARS)**

	Exports				Imports			
		Annual % Change				Annual % Change		
	Value	2009	2010	2011	Value	2009	2010	2011
World	17,779	−12.0	13.8	5.0	18,000	−12.9	13.7	4.9
North America	2,283	−14.8	14.9	6.2	3,090	−16.6	15.7	4.7
Europe	6,601	−14.1	10.9	5.0	6,854	−14.1	9.7	2.4
Latin America	749	−8.1	5.6	5.3	727	−16.5	22.9	10.4
CIS*	788	−4.8	6.0	1.8	540	−28.0	18.6	16.7
Africa	597	−3.7	3.0	−8.3	555	−5.1	7.3	5.0
Middle East	1,228	−4.6	6.5	5.4	665	−7.7	7.5	5.3
Asia	5.534	11.4	22.7	6.6	5,568	−7.7	18.2	6.4

*Commonwealth of Independent States (Russia and former Soviet republics: Armenia, Azerbaijan, Belarus, Georgia, Kazakhstan, Kyrgyz Republic, Moldova, Tajikistan, Turkmenistan, Ukraine, Uzbekistan).

Source: World Trade Organization Secretariat, Press Release, April 12, 2012.

slowed to 3.7 percent in 2011 as world demand receded. The sovereign debt crisis in Europe, supply chain disruptions from natural disasters in Japan and Thailand, and political turmoil across the Middle East contributed significantly to a slow-down in the overall rate of global economic growth (2.4 percent).[5]

While trade is affected by the overall state of the global economy at any given time, it is also impacted by the trade policies of individual countries. Government officials across the world frequently endorse free trade in principle, but an actual commitment to the practice of free trade does not always follow. Trade policies tend to be quite contentious and highly sensitive to political pressures and maneuverings, especially when world economic output is contracting and jobs are at risk. Citizens expect governments to protect their interests, particularly if they see themselves threatened by excessive or unfair competition. As a result, trade strategies are often a mix of approaches that reflect multiple agendas and perspectives.

The world's diverse economies have difficulty striking a balance acceptable to all. In 2001, the World Trade Organization kicked off the **Doha Round**, its first negotiations of the twenty-first century, in Qatar. The Doha Round's proclaimed "development agenda" had been designed to pay close attention to the needs and concerns of poorer countries. Serious discord plagued the meetings almost from the outset. In 2006, negotiations broke off over questions relating to the willingness of countries to take definitive steps to further open their markets.

Doha Round
the most recent international trade negotiations conducted under the auspices of the World Trade Organization.

protectionism
government policies to restrict imports to shield local businesses from global completion.

intellectual property rights (IPRs)
patents, copyrights, and trademarks extended to individuals and organizations to protect their ownership of products or other creative works generated through their original ideas.

Both before and since the suspension of the Doha talks, **protectionism** in agriculture has been a particularly delicate issue. The countries of the Global South have pushed hard for the timely elimination of American, European, and Japanese subsidies. At the same time, they have argued the need to retain their right to preserve their own subsidies to offset competitive disadvantages and to gain preferential access to lucrative markets in the Global North. The response of the developed countries has not been enthusiastic. In their efforts to placate powerful farming interests at home, they have called instead for a gradual and reciprocal process that corresponds more closely to WTO principles and accounts for the politically sensitive nature of these matters.

Developed countries and developing countries also debate a number of other world-trade matters. The issue of **intellectual property rights (IPRs)**—the patent, copyright, and trademark protections extended to individuals and organizations whose original ideas have led to the design of particular products or other types of creative works—have been especially contentious. The developers of intellectual property (disproportionally located in more advanced countries) argue in favor of retaining these exclusive rights as a means of encouraging further innovation. Those who are critical of these IPR protections, on the other hand, point to their role in limiting the diffusion of knowledge to the Global South. This is particularly problematic with respect to extending access to critical medicines at affordable cost in the poorest countries.[6]

While the disagreement over IPRs continues, counterfeiters and copyists commonly infringe on these protections. They may circumvent the rules by selling an unauthorized DVD of a newly released Hollywood film on a Beijing corner, a knockoff pocketbook from a New York street vendor, a pair of "designer" jeans from a budding entrepreneur in Moscow, or an "exclusive" watch in a back alley in Cairo. Markets for these types of goods are robust, as prices are a fraction of what they would be if purchasing the authentic item. China and other developing countries have benefited handsomely from these practices and are resistant to greater enforcement of protections for the owners of intellectual property.

The breakdown of the Doha Round negotiations illustrates the unwillingness of many countries to open themselves fully to the global market. It also suggests their continuing reluctance to extend the regulatory and enforcement capabilities of the WTO. Such ambivalence has contributed to the emergence of an alternate strategy—regional trade pacts. Some economists recommend this approach as an initial building block for developing trust and establishing guidelines that would ultimately lead to broader global cooperation. Others argue that the elimination of trade barriers and expansion of transactions within these regional compacts will actually cause trade between regions to diminish.

The European Union has led the way in promoting regional integration. The development of a single market has been intended to maximize trade among members by promoting the free movement of goods within the bloc. Regional free trade arrangements have gained considerable popularity elsewhere. Across Asia, for example, the Association of Southeast Asian Nations (ASEAN) and the Asia-Pacific

Economic Cooperation (APEC) body have worked to enhance trade and investment linkages in the region. Additional initiatives are anticipated as China moves to extend its trade with Japan, South Korea, and other countries across the area.

Similar interests have taken root in the Americas. Since the 1990s, governments have used regional trade agreements to build export-oriented development strategies. Argentina, Brazil, Paraguay, and Uruguay came together in 1991 to form the Common Market of the South or Mercosur. Like other groupings already in place, Mercosur was symptomatic of a growing recognition of the need to promote cooperation based on common interests within geographic regions in the face of heightened global competition. In the case of the Americas, moreover, the historically dominant role of the United States has prompted some other countries to devise new arrangements to advance their independence. At the same time, the United States has continued to exercise considerable influence in shaping the regional trade picture.

In 1994, the United States, Canada, and Mexico signed the **North American Free Trade Agreement (NAFTA)**, which extended a free trade arrangement and sought to broaden commercial ties among the three partners. Opposition arose in many quarters. In the United States, many workers feared a significant transfer of jobs across the Mexican border. A staunch NAFTA critic, US businessman and third-party presidential candidate Ross Perot injected this issue into the 1992 presidential election. Although Perot captured only a small fraction of the vote, he galvanized concerns about the potential impact of NAFTA on US employment and trade prospects. American environmental and labor rights groups also weighed in on the discussion, arguing for stricter workplace standards. Ultimately, there were separate protocols attached to the agreement to guard against potential environmental and labor abuses. In Mexico and other parts of Latin America, NAFTA once again raised the specter of US dominance and control.

The controversies surrounding NAFTA have continued to this day. Much of the debate surrounds the agreement's purported impact on employment. Although NAFTA has helped create more than a million export-related jobs in the United States, some critics have argued that NAFTA's displacement of domestic production has cut more than two million positions. Similarly, Mexico has lost an estimated 1.3 million farm jobs by lowering tariffs that had previously enabled the country to compete more effectively with heavily subsidized US agribusinesses. There are also lingering concerns over the effectiveness of the rules put in place to protect the environment and to govern working conditions in the manufacturing and assembly plants near the United States–Mexico border.

Since NAFTA has been in place, trade and investment flows across the region have expanded considerably. From 1993 to 2007, for example, trade among the partners more than tripled—from $297 billion to $930 billion. The value of Mexican exports to the United States more than quadrupled, increasing from $60 billion to $280 billion per year, while US exports to Mexico tripled. Meanwhile, Canada emerged as the leading market for American agricultural products, with sales increasing from $4.2 billion in 1990 to $11.9 billion in 2006.

North American Free Trade Agreement (NAFTA)

an arrangement designed to expand cross-border trade and investment signed by Canada, Mexico, and the United States in 1994.

Overall, NAFTA constitutes the world's largest free trade area linking some 454 million people producing $17.2 trillion in goods and services.[7]

Other efforts to develop trade agreements across the Americas have produced their own controversies. Highly charged debates over the 2005 Central American Free Trade Area (CAFTA-DR) focused on questions over the agreement's potential impact on workers' rights and protections, the competitive balance between US and Central American farmers, and a host of other political and economic issues related to the overall advisability of the arrangement. Many groups lined up to lobby lawmakers prior to the ultimate passage of the accord.

One of the more vocal opponents, the consumer advocacy group Public Citizen (www.citizen.org), argued that "passage would serve to push ahead the corporate globalization model that has caused the race to the bottom in labor and environmental standards and would promote privatization and deregulation of key public services." The Business Roundtable, an association of chief executive officers of leading US companies, countered by noting that

> Central America has undergone a spectacular transition from a place where dictatorships were the norm to a democratically-based region where freedom predominates . . . CAFTA-DR will help foster the continuation of the political enlightenment that has taken hold by modernizing Central American economies.[8]

NAFTA and CAFTA-DR signaled steps toward the deepening economic integration of the Americas. The next piece was the Free Trade Area of the Americas (FTAA) linking 34 countries, scheduled for implementation in 2005. The effort stalled, however, as issues similar to those that framed the debates over NAFTA and CAFTA-DR surfaced. Negotiators could not reconcile differing perspectives as to how the FTAA would affect job growth, labor rights, and the survival of small farmers and local businesses.[9] The comprehensive coverage, both in terms of countries and sectors incorporated, raised the stakes of moving forward in the absence of broad consensus. While the FTAA is still on the table, there has been no concerted effort to reopen formal discussions. Instead, governments have proceeded to negotiate agreements with individual trade partners in the region to expand their commercial dealings.

The rhetoric of free trade continues to fuel the efforts of governments to negotiate additional market opening measures both regionally and internationally. According to the WTO, opening national markets to international trade "will encourage and contribute to sustainable development, raise people's welfare, reduce poverty, and foster peace and stability."[10] At the same time, countries that may be among the most vocal supporters of freer markets often engage in protectionist policies to further their national interests. Despite their long-standing commitment to open trade, for example, the United States and Canada continue to extend preferential treatment to domestic companies when awarding contracts for defense-related projects and have employed restrictions in energy and other sectors to promote local business.[11]

The sluggish recovery from the 2008–09 global financial crisis further dampened support for free trade across many parts of the world. This was the case in the United States, where groups representing workers and domestic producers lobbied hard, yet unsuccessfully, to derail the free trade pact with South Korea. Although supporters touted the agreement as a vehicle to significantly open the Korean market to US goods, opponents argued that it would lead to higher trade deficits, lost jobs, and the continuation of unfair Korean trade practices.[12] Opposition to further market opening measures also surfaced in Malaysia. Activists protested the country's proposed free trade agreement with the United States, arguing that the arrangement would further undermine the ability of local businesses to compete with US firms and would imperil the survival of Malaysian farmers unable to keep pace with stronger US farmers who flood the Malaysian market with cheap rice (a staple of the local diet).[13]

While the United States, Germany, and other advanced industrial economies continue to rank among the most active traders, the structure of the world trade system is changing. Emerging market economies are playing an increasingly larger role. China has become the largest exporter, accounting for 10.4 percent of the world's total in 2011. This has been largely due to China's ability to produce low-cost goods and an economic development policy that has emphasized the importance of maximizing the country's export potential. Mexico, India, and Brazil have also come to acquire respectable shares of the market. These same countries are also significant importers, further reflecting their growing presence on the global economic stage (Table 7.2).

TABLE 7.2 | MERCHANDISE TRADE 2011: SELECT EXPORTERS AND IMPORTERS

	Exports			Imports		
	Value*	% Share	Rank	Value*	% Share	Rank
China	1,899	10.4	1	1,743	9.5	2
US	1,481	8.1	2	2,265	12.3	1
Germany	1,474	8.1	3	1,254	6.8	3
Japan	823	4.5	4	854	4.6	4
France	597	3.3	6	715	3.9	5
Rep. Korea	555	3.0	7	524	2.9	9
Russia	522	2.9	9	323	1.8	17
Mexico	350	1.9	16	361	2.0	16
India	297	1.6	19	451	2.5	13
Brazil	256	1.4	22	237	1.3	21

*In billions of US dollars.

Source: World Trade Organization Secretariat, Press Release, April 12, 2012.

Women check the final detail on Reebok athletic shoes as they roll by on a conveyor belt in Zhongshan, Guangdong Province, China.

A wider group of countries have the opportunity to participate fully in today's trading system. At the same time, however, many countries of the Global South decry what they see as an inherent unfairness that leaves them vulnerable and marginalized. They continue to press the Global North for preferential treatment to level the playing field and to improve their competitiveness. These concerns ring out at meetings of the WTO and other trade forums and limit efforts to build broader policy consensus.

When Ford and General Motors decide to relocate auto assembly plants to save on production costs, Americans lose job opportunities, while Mexican workers acquire them. When hospitals and physicians in Europe or Japan seek use of the latest technology to assist in diagnosing patient illnesses, they may turn to Trivitron Healthcare in India, where highly trained technicians are able to perform the task at a relatively reasonable cost. When China assembles and exports inexpensive cell phones and other electronic items, consumers in the importing countries benefit. The basic challenge facing today's trade system is to accommodate the needs of countries to address their national interests while securing their commitment to an approach that does not threaten the flow of goods and services across the world. This will require a delicate balancing of policies and perspectives.

INVESTMENT

portfolio investment
the purchase of stocks, bonds, or other financial assets that does not result in direct management or control over an enterprise.

Cross-border investment is a key factor fueling the development of the global economy. Between 1991 and 2000, trade among industrial countries expanded an impressive 63 percent. But capital flows topped that, growing by a whopping 300 percent.[14] Advances in transportation and telecommunications have made it easier for companies to manage operations abroad. The emergence of new market-oriented economies and the liberalization of financial markets have also contributed to this expansion.

Foreign investment generally comes in two forms. **Portfolio investment** includes the purchase of stock or bonds. This type of investment tends to be mobile and sensitive to shifts in financial conditions that affect its profitability and might prompt its transfer to another, more lucrative locale. Countries that rely on this money must pay particular attention to maintaining interest rates that offer an acceptable rate of return and other incentives that assure an attractive investment climate. The United States is certainly no exception, as it has grown increasingly dependent on investment from China and other countries to cover its burgeoning deficits. If the government cannot bring its spending under control, it must borrow from foreign nations in ever increasing amounts.[15]

Direct investment occurs when a foreign entity acquires a stake in an enterprise through the purchase of property, a plant, or equipment. This makes direct investment more visible than portfolio investment. Much direct investment originates with the world's largest **transnational corporations (TNCs)**, which operate on a global scale with integrated operations across any number of regions and countries. Some TNCs have more assets than many countries have. In 2011, for example, Walmart's (United States) revenues exceeded the GDP of all but 27 countries, oil and gas multinational BP's (Britain) revenues outstripped Egypt's GDP, Toyota's (Japan) revenues topped the GDP of Ireland, and Singapore's GDP was lower than petrochemical giant Sinopec's (China) revenues (Table 7.3).

direct investment
the acquisition of corporate assets through the purchase of property, a plant, or equipment.

transnational corporations
companies that operate on a global scale with integrated operations across regions and countries.

TABLE 7.3   COUNTRY/TNC REVENUES 2011

Rank	Country/Corporation	GDP/Revenue (in billions of US dollars)	Rank	Country/Corporation	GDP/Revenue (in billions of US dollars)
1	United States	15,094.0	17	Netherlands	840.4
2	China	7,298.1	18	Turkey	778.1
3	Japan	5,869.5	19	Switzerland	636.1
4	Germany	3,577.0	20	Saudi Arabia	577.6
5	France	2,776.3	21	Sweden	538.2
6	Brazil	2,492.9	22	Poland	513.8
7	United Kingdom	2,417.6	23	Belgium	513.4
8	Italy	2,198.7	24	Norway	483.7
9	Russia	1,850.4	25	Iran	482.4
10	Canada	1,736.9	26	Taiwan	466.8
11	India	1,676.1	27	Argentina	447.6
12	Spain	1,493.5	28*	Walmart (US)	421.8
13	Australia	1,488.2	29	Austria	419.2
14	Mexico	1,154.8	30	South Africa	408.1
15	Korea, Rep.	1,116.2	31*	Royal Dutch Shell (Netherlands)	378.2
16	Indonesia	845.7			

(Continued)

TABLE 7.3 (CONTINUED)

Rank	Country/Corporation	GDP/Revenue (in billions of US dollars)
32	United Arab Emirates	360.1
33*	Exxon Mobil (US)	354.7
34	Thailand	345.6
35	Denmark	333.2
36	Colombia	328.4
37	Venezuela	315.8
38*	BP (Britain)	308.9
39	Greece	303.1
40	Malaysia	278.7
41*	Sinopec (China)	273.4
42	Finland	266.6
43	Singapore	259.8
44	Chile	248.4
45	Hong Kong, China	243.3
46	Israel	242.9
47*	China National Petroleum (China)	240.2
48	Nigeria	238.9
49	Egypt	235.7
50*	State Grid (China)	226.3
51*	Toyota (Japan)	221.8
52	Ireland	217.7
53	Czech Republic	215.3
54	Philippines	213.1
55	Pakistan	210.6

Rank	Country/Corporation	GDP/Revenue (in billions of US dollars)
56*	Japan Post Holdings (Japan)	203.9
57*	Chevron (US)	196.3
58	Algeria	190.7
59	Romania	189.8
60*	Total (France)	186.1
61*	Conoco Phillips (US)	184.9
62	Kazakhstan	178.3
63	Kuwait	176.7
64	Qatar	173.8
65	Peru	173.5
66*	Volkswagen (Germany)	168.0
67	Ukraine	165.0
68*	AXA (France)	162.2
69	New Zealand	161.9
70*	Fannie Mae (US)	153.8
71*	General Electric (US)	151.6
72*	ING Group (Netherlands)	147.1
73*	Glencore International (Switzerland)	144.9
74	Hungary	140.3
75*	Berkshire Hathaway (US)	136.2

*Transnational corporation.

Sources: "Global 500, Our Annual Ranking of the World's Largest Corporations," *Fortune Magazine,* http://money.cnn.com/magazines/fortune/global500/2011/full_list/; IMF, World Economic Outlook Database, April 2012, www.imf.org/external/pubs/ft/2012.

It may well be that private corporate networks and alliances are more central to the future world economy than more traditional interactions among nation-states. Of the world's 50 largest economic entities, 7 (14 percent) are TNCs. However, this figure does not provide the complete picture. While 18 of these companies (24 percent) rank among the world's top 75 economic units, 40 (40 percent) of them are on the list of the 100 largest.[16] It is interesting to note that 7 of the 10 largest TNCs are petroleum and energy-related companies.

In many respects, TNCs lie at the heart of the globalization debate. Supporters tout their role in expanding production and trade. They generate employment and integrate developing countries into the global economy by infusing capital, supplying jobs, and transferring modern technology. TNC investment in new and emerging markets helps them to build infrastructure and to enhance their capacity for economic growth.

Critics are far more suspicious of TNCs' motives and wary of their clout. Working conditions in some of their factories and plants have prompted charges that these facilities are modern-day sweatshops, where employees are subjected to unsafe and unhealthy environments. Kathy Lee Gifford, the morning TV talk show personality, shut down the manufacture of her signature clothing line following disclosures that its factory in Indonesia employed child laborers. Nike altered its production of athletic footwear after similar revelations regarding conditions in its plants in Indonesia, Mexico, and elsewhere. In response to a campaign launched by the United Students Against Sweatshops, a grassroots organization lobbying on behalf of worker rights, some universities have altered their arrangements with suppliers of licensed apparel found to tolerate labor abuses in their production facilities.[17] Even Apple, a company admired for its innovation and marketing prowess, has been the subject of numerous investigative reports relating to safety and other workplace conditions at its plant in China.[18]

Complaints against TNCs have also surfaced with respect to a host of other issues, ranging from their undermining of environmental protection efforts to their alleged role in perpetuating extreme income disparities and poverty across the Global South. In early 2006, Internet giants Google, Yahoo, and Microsoft faced strong criticism from human rights activists around the world for their role in assisting China's government to curb political opposition. The companies were restricting Internet searches to sites acceptable to the government and providing it with personal tracking data.

The challenge for Internet providers in China is considerable. China seeks access to the most advanced technology and uses that technology to pursue its core political interests. Google has had its share of controversy stemming from its efforts to satisfy the demands of the Chinese government in order to maintain its lucrative business. It has endured cyber attacks allegedly aimed at stealing technology and Gmail account information of suspected Chinese human rights activists and has been forced to compromise on some of its principles. The July 2010 decision of China's government to extend Google's contract in the country, for example, came only after months of intense negotiations and the company's willingness to modify its method of processing searches that were objectionable to the Chinese government. Although Google did not eliminate these searches entirely, they became far more difficult to execute.[19]

The emergence of TNCs headquartered in developing countries suggests the increasing integration and progressive leveling of the global economy. In 2011,

TABLE 7.4 | GLOBAL 500 COMPANIES 2011

Country	Number of Companies
United States	133
Japan	68
China	61
France	35
Germany	34
Britain	30
Switzerland	15
Canada	11
South Korea	14
Netherlands	12
Italy	10
Spain	9
Australia	8
India	8
Taiwan	8
Brazil	7
Russia	7
Belgium	5
Mexico	3
Sweden	3
Others*	19

*Countries with one or two companies.

Source: "Global 500: Our Annual Ranking of the World's Largest Corporations," Fortune Magazine, July 25, 2011, money.cnn.com/magazines/fortune/global500/2011/full_list/.

117 (23.4 percent) of the leading 500 firms were located in emerging or developing countries (Table 7.4).[20] South Korea's Hyundai (autos), Mexico's Cemex (cement), and China's Haier (appliances and electronics) reflect this new wave in what used to be an exclusively American phenomenon. China is marketing distinctively Chinese-branded products worldwide. Lenovo, the world's third-largest PC maker, took its brand beyond China with a line of low-priced machines following its purchase of IBM's PC business in 2005.[21] Concluding that PC companies could not flourish or even survive by simply producing computers, Lenovo moved forward by entering the expanding tablet and smartphone markets. In 2012, the company launched its first smart TV as part of its strategy of offering a full range of Internet consumer devices.

China's auto industry has also been on the move. Geely, one of its leading automakers, purchased Sweden's Volvo Cars for $1.8 billion from Ford Motor Company in 2010. Ford had sold its Jaguar and Land Rover brands to India's Tata Motors for $1.7 billion in 2008. Great Wall Motors opened an assembly plant in Bulgaria in 2012 with plans to eventually sell a wide range of models across Europe. Some analysts predict that China could capture as much as 10 percent of the European market by 2020. China's success in Europe and the United States will depend on its ability to continue to enhance the quality of its vehicles so that they meet product safety standards in Western countries.[22]

Dealing with TNCs is difficult for many countries. On the one hand, they offer capital and jobs. They also foster contact and integration into the global economy. For these reasons, governments in developing countries may find themselves obliged to offer overly generous tax incentives or other financial concessions to secure TNC business. This "race to the bottom," as it has come to be known, can severely limit the economic benefits that the host country sought by opening the doors to this investment in the first place.

In addition, it can be quite difficult for the host country to curtail the autonomy of these companies or to regulate their impacts. But it is not impossible. In South Africa, for example, foreign companies such as Anglo American and BHP Billiton in mining and Coca-Cola and Nestle in food and beverages have worked cooperatively with government authorities to promote adherence to strict environmental standards. The active engagement of nongovernmental organizations and local agencies to monitor compliance has been instrumental in the success of this arrangement.[23] Conditions are not always so favorable, however, to reigning in the activities of TNCs. In the Niger Delta of Nigeria, an estimated nine million barrels of oil have spilled over the years. This has contaminated swamps, rivers, and farmlands and has seriously affected the health of people in the region. The oil companies ignore their spills, for the most part, and continue to operate their businesses with little regard for the environmental or health effects of their activities. In this particular case, moreover, the Nigerian government has done little in holding these companies accountable.[24]

Broader efforts by the United Nations (UN) and other international bodies to address the activities of TNCs have met with mixed results. One of the more ambitious was the Multilateral Agreement on Investment (MAI), launched in 1995 under the auspices of the Organization for Economic Cooperation and Development (OECD). While the OECD now includes a fairly diverse group of advanced and emerging market economies, it was composed almost exclusively of more advanced countries at the time. The MAI negotiations sought to develop a treaty, open to both OECD members and nonmembers alike, that assured foreign investors fair and uniform treatment while granting host countries greater authority to mandate responsible behavior within their borders. Discussions broke off in 1998, however, with opponents charging that the proposed accord was weighted heavily in favor of the TNCs.[25] In 2000, the UN concluded a global compact addressing child labor, environmental protection, and other matters relating to corporate behavior. However, the agreement was voluntary and was opposed by Greenpeace and other environmental advocacy groups seeking binding and enforceable codes of conduct.

As markets become more interconnected, regulating TNCs is more problematic. The formation of cross-border business alliances and joint ventures complicates matters. The automobile industry is a good case in point. Although some partnerships—such as General Motors/Toyota and Daimler/Chrysler—did not survive the 2008 economic downturn, others continue. Ford (US) maintains its ties to Mazda (Japan) and Aston Martin (UK), Chrysler (US) has an arrangement with Fiat (Italy), and General Motors (US) has a deal in place with China's SAIC Motor Corporation.

The story does not stop there. Countries that seek to promote their own companies or patriotic consumers who want to buy domestic products may find it difficult to execute those plans. Half of the top selling 2010 "domestic" models of cars in the United States—as measured by the origin of their parts and assembly— came from Japanese automakers Toyota and Honda (Table 7.5). In addition, numerous models produced by United States–based companies do not qualify

BUYING AN AMERICAN CAR?

Thinking about a new car any time soon? There are many things to consider. How much will it cost, and is it affordable? How fuel efficient is it? Is it reliable? Is the styling suitable? Does it have desired options?

Some Americans feel that it is important to support the national economy by purchasing an American car. Indeed, a few decades ago, it was not all that uncommon to hear the slogan repeated on commercials and advertisements that "what's good for General Motors is good for America." But the globalization of the auto industry makes it increasingly difficult to identify the makes and models that might fit this mold.

Automobile American-Made Index 2010

Rank	Make/Model	%US Content	Assembly
1	Toyota Camry	80	Kentucky, Indiana
2	Honda Accord	75	Ohio, Alabama
3	Ford Escape	90	Missouri
4	Ford Focus	90	Michigan
5	Chevrolet Malibu	75	Kansas
6	Honda Odyssey	75	Alabama
7	Dodge Ram 1500	76	Michigan
8	Toyota Tundra	80	Texas
9	Jeep Wrangler	79	Ohio
10	Toyota Sienna	85	Indiana

Source: Kelsey Mays, "The Cars.com American-Made Index," November 23, 2010, www.cars.com/go/advice/Story.jsp?section=top&subject=ami&story=amMade0710.

as "domestic," since they are assembled abroad with limited American-made parts. Next time you are sitting at a traffic light, think about the Honda Accord idling next to your Volkswagen assembled in Mexico. Chances are it was put together by American workers in Ohio with at least some of its parts made in China by Honda's Japanese suppliers.[26]

Even as TNCs may offer countries opportunities to enhance their economic growth, these firms remain the targets of critics who question their considerable economic and political influence. While a case can be made for measures to curtail their autonomy, TNCs will require sufficient inducements to encourage their further investment and production. An established set of multilateral rules regulating TNC behavior would help relieve the stress on the host countries. But TNCs are not inclined to submit to any significant restraints, so finding the right balance will be a challenge.

FINANCE AND DEVELOPMENT

Today's financial system is noted for its unpredictability. In May 2012, for example, two events within a single week shook financial markets that had been relatively calm the preceding months. Coping with a stagnant economy and high unemployment brought on by severe government spending cutbacks, Greek voters went to the polls and voiced their opposition to the austerity measures that were in place to tackle the country's large debt. Financial markets contracted due to concerns that Greece could default on its outstanding loans and forfeit its eligibility as a member of the eurozone. At around the same time, JPMorgan Chase, one of the world's leading banks, disclosed that it had lost more than $2 billion on risky investments that were strikingly similar to those that contributed to the worldwide financial crisis just a few years earlier. The specter of another round of uncertainty undermined confidence in the financial system.

A frenzied trader at the Chicago Board of Options Exchange reacts as the Dow takes a nose dive of over 500 points.

Financial markets are truly global, difficult to regulate, and marked by extraordinary transfers on a daily basis. More than $1.5 trillion changes hands each day in foreign currency transactions. The security of these markets is critical to the efforts of countries to manage their accounts, retain access to capital and investment, preserve the values of their currencies, and remain competitive in international trade.

The International Monetary Fund (IMF) continues to play an important role in steadying markets. With 187 members, the IMF works to promote cooperation on monetary policy and to stabilize currency exchange rates. Its primary activity is to assist countries attempting to balance their accounts and meet their outstanding obligations. It does so through an extensive network of lending programs supported by more than $300 billion raised through member payments (known as quotas). The IMF has made a special effort to assist low-income countries and, in 2009, doubled borrowing limits and committed up to $17 billion under very favorable terms.[27]

Despite these seemingly good works, the IMF has been buffeted by blistering criticism. Antiglobalization protestors usually target its general meetings, like those of the WTO, and view the IMF as an extension of its largest and most influential member, the United States. They charge it with advancing US policies and prescriptions through what has become known as the **Washington Consensus**, a set of economic policy reforms imposed on prospective borrowers

Washington Consensus
the set of economic policy reforms imposed by the IMF and other Washington, D.C., based financial institutions on potential borrowers.

Demonstrators protesting the International Monetary Fund carry signs as they march from the White House to the IMF building. The protesters were calling for the World Bank and IMF to accelerate their debt reduction efforts for the world's poorest countries.

by the IMF and other Washington, D.C., based financial institutions that require borrowers to take certain steps as a condition of receiving funds. These requirements may include liberalizing trade and financial markets, privatizing state enterprises, deregulation of markets, and reducing government spending. The IMF defends these policies as essential to break the cycle of indebtedness.

Critics charge that these policies add to the vulnerabilities of recipient countries and place disproportionate burdens on their poorest inhabitants. In Mozambique, for example, the IMF mandated the ending of government subsidies for urban transport and other basic services in return for its 2008 support. Subsequent price increases sparked considerable protests that were put down forcefully by the government. In 2009, the IMF required Jamaica to eliminate tax exemptions on basic foodstuffs such as bread, vegetables, and fish meal as a precondition for its $1.2 billion loan.[28]

The World Bank is another key node in the global financial network. Its lending activities are more project oriented than the IMF's and may include assistance to build roads as well as communications, energy, and other infrastructure to improve a country's prospects for long-term development. In fiscal 2010, the Bank had commitments for 875 projects totaling $72.2 billion, up from $58.8 billion in 2009. These included $14.5 billion in interest-free loans and grants to the world's poorest countries under the auspices of the organization's International Development Association.[29] While it is particularly interested in promoting grassroots and private sector initiatives, the Bank also encourages governmental reform to strengthen public policy. To supplement the funding supplied by its members, the Bank raises money through private financial markets to support its work.

Originally, the World Bank followed a top-down approach and emphasized broad principles that were applied to almost all of its funded projects. Recently, the Bank has encouraged more widespread input into the framing of its initiatives and has attempted to ensure that its activities are consistent with local needs and conditions. In Liberia, for example, the Bank has worked with the government to create a national development plan that is both country led and results oriented. This development is in contrast to previous plans that lacked coherence and did not include strategies to monitor progress or measure outcomes. With input and support from World Bank personnel, the Liberian government adopted an approach that included a concerted effort to involve local stakeholders. Some 50 representatives across 24 sectors participated in the process and were trained in results-focused planning.[30]

Since 2000, the World Bank has also been heavily involved in promoting a UN program to enlist additional support to substantially improve education, health, and material well-being in poorer countries by 2015. The Bank has incorporated specific targets and performance indicators to frame its activities in meeting the Millennium Development Goals (MDGs). The extraordinary needs and amounts of money required, estimated at $40 to $60 billion a year in additional support, makes it difficult to realize these objectives.[31]

Regional bodies such as the African Development Bank, Asian Development Bank, and Inter-American Development Bank have contributed to these efforts to enhance the quality of life. Despite having more limited resources than the World Bank, they often focus on supporting projects likely to make the greatest difference to individual lives and to promote environmentally sustainable development. The African Development Bank's water-harvesting project in South Africa is a good case in point. The 2011 initiative aimed to improve output from communal food gardens in a particular province through more efficient collection and management of surface runoff from precipitation.[32]

Developments in private financial markets will influence the future security of the world's financial order (and the fate of its poorer countries) more than the activities of public international or regional lending institutions. These markets faced significant pressures as the global economy struggled to recover its vibrancy. In 2011, for example, net capital flows to emerging markets totaled $910 billion. This was a decline from the $1,040 billion in 2010, yet considerably above the $530.8 billion in 2009 and $588.2 billion in 2008, when the fragile state of financial institutions across the world limited the amount of credit available.[33] Subject to short-term ebbs and flows, these private markets account for an increasing share of capital flows across the global economy and contribute significantly to its risky and uncertain nature.

The events of 2008 and 2009 spoke directly to these vulnerabilities. Problems in the US mortgage market spread quickly, as they revealed some fundamental weaknesses in a global financial system that was operating, in part, beyond effective control. The progressive deregulation of financial markets over previous years had encouraged the creation of new instruments that enabled banks to engage in highly profitable and excessively risky lending practices. One of these instruments was **securitization**, the pooling of various loans (including those with considerable risk) into **securities** and selling them to other institutions.[34]

The increasing use of these types of devices added to the exposure of banks and investment houses and led to the unraveling of the system. Even as financial institutions sought to spread the risk of questionable investments, they could not avoid the consequences. Lenders drastically curtailed their financing activities and scrambled to protect their assets. However, for many it was too late.

securitization

the pooling of various loans (including those with considerable risk) into securities and selling them to other institutions.

securities

bond or stock certificates.

sovereign debt
a government's outstanding financial liabilities and obligations.

Some of the largest investment banks (Bear Stearns, Lehman Brothers), which played a vital role in financing the global economy, collapsed, and major banks around the world found themselves perilously close to failing as well. Ultimately, a number of governments spent considerable sums of money to bail out the banks, thereby adding to their **sovereign debt**.[35]

While there was much debate over the advisability of these rescues, they did contribute to the survival of the world's financial system—albeit in a more fragile state. The lack of credit and the weakened financial conditions of banks and governments resulted in a significant contraction of economic activity worldwide. As the global economy struggled to recover, important issues remained unresolved as to how governments might best proceed to restore the confidence of prospective investors while avoiding excessive government spending and deficits that would undermine the sustainability of the process.[36]

Nobel laureate economist Paul Krugman noted that these developments bore striking similarity to the Asian financial crisis of the late 1990s. The 1997 collapse of Thailand's currency (the baht) set in motion a chain of events that threatened the economic security of numerous countries in the region and well beyond. Up to that point, Thailand had been a magnet for investment with its relatively secure and expanding economy. Problems began with the withdrawal of some $9 billion of foreign funds in 1997 after a series of bad loans by local banks and excessive government spending resulted in the use of $33 billion of the country's reserve assets. As a result, the baht lost approximately half its value, and many Thai citizens found their dreams of wealth turn literally overnight into the nightmare of bankruptcy. Investors were also affected by the depreciation in the value of their holdings. Panic spread quickly across the region to Indonesia, Malaysia, and South Korea, as investors removed over $100 billion. Before long, the drama extended to disparate places such as Brazil and Russia, as jittery investors searched in vain for opportunities that entailed limited financial risk.[37]

These events underscore the challenges of today's financial system. With an emphasis on mobility and maximum return on investments, global finance is a fast-paced and volatile game. On any given day, trillions of dollars exchange hands electronically in a relatively seamless fashion. Professional money traders, investors, lenders, and borrowers have much to gain as they access and place the funds that determine the health of the global economy and its constituent parts. While sound financial management calls for prudent and reasoned behavior, it also places a premium on risk taking and speculative activity. The expansion and deregulation of financial markets has contributed significantly to the potential for growth by providing countries with additional funding options and opportunities. This money may disappear as quickly as it materializes if investors lose confidence or interest—for either real or imagined reasons.

soWhat? INTERNATIONAL ECONOMICS AND DEVELOPMENT

By Puneet Gupta, International Studies Graduate Student in New Delhi, India

For me, all economic issues like trade, investment and finance are important, not only professionally but also personally. Professionally, developing countries like my home, India, depend a lot on donor funding from abroad. If there are trade imbalances that induce the government of either the home country or the foreign country to change its trade policies, both the countries will be impacted not only in terms of trade, but also in terms of capital flows.

On a personal front, investment and finances are very important in my life. As someone has said: "If you want to save your money, then save the taxes and the money will automatically be saved." If you invest rightly and save the maximum possible tax you can, you can create a fortune for yourself in a very short duration of time. One very good example of this can be a tax saving systematic investment plan. These small strategies not only benefit the person, but also the government, as the economy gets a continuous supply of the household savings in terms of investment and assistance in keeping its growth up. I have found that I unintentionally tend to compare the demand and supply of anything I am talking about or even while thinking, but this is primarily because that's the kind of orientation I have got.

I believe international finance and trade play a very important role in addressing the development challenges like poverty, especially in a developing country like India. Globalization has been the biggest contributory factor. With world economies being so interconnected and dependent on each other, even a person sneezing in one part of the world can impact another entirely different part of the world! International finance becomes all the more complex with the so-interconnected development issues like poverty, malnutrition, lack of sanitation, gender inequality and environmental degradation.

Recently, I came across a case study of Aravind Eye Care, an Indian specialized eye care institution focusing on protecting people's eyesight with the help of cataract surgeries. They have a very nice business model of catering to the people at the bottom of the pyramid while also generating profits at the same time. They charge market price from the rich people and cross-subsidize poor. International trade and support has been an important factor in their success. The intra-ocular lenses (the costliest thing in the cataract surgery) they use previously had to be imported, but Aravind has set up a manufacturing unit in India itself, which has reduced its cost dramatically. The reason they have been able to do so is through technology transfer from the US. This would not have been possible without the technology support and the interconnectedness of the global economies.

WHAT CAN BE DONE?

The global economy is dynamic, yet unpredictable. It is difficult to manage the complex relationships of its participants, especially as they have become more interconnected through trade, investment, and financial networks. Keeping trade lines open and expanding in the face of often unsettled markets is essential. Jumpstarting the WTO's Doha negotiations would be useful, particularly in terms of addressing the particular needs of emerging and developing countries.

The fragile state of the world's financial markets continues to cause concern. Investor confidence is shaky and many banks face uncertain futures. Since the mid-1990s, the system has confronted a series of crises brought on by risky and, at times, irresponsible behavior. Numerous governments must come to terms with the realities of cutting back on expenditures to address excessive debt, while also responding to the demands of their citizens for services and the opportunity to maintain an acceptable quality of life. As the United States and others moved toward greater oversight of financial institutions in the aftermath of the crisis in 2008—reversing a pattern of progressive deregulation—some economists questioned the potential impact of these measures on the willingness and ability of prospective investors to fortify capital markets.[38] Meanwhile, banks across the world resist governmental efforts to control their activities and continue to execute complex and sometimes questionable transactions.

There is broad consensus on the need to reduce the volatility of financial markets. Identifying the specific steps that might be taken—and their advisability—remains a significant challenge. The efforts of the European Union to address the spiraling deficits of Greece and some of its other troubled members in 2012 illustrated the difficulty of striking the right balance of approaches. The need to reign in the spending of these governments stood in stark contrast to the demands of their citizens for additional public expenditures to create jobs and stimulate economic growth. The EU's delicate maneuvering in this instance would go a long way toward determining feasible and appropriate remedies for similar crises that may emerge.

As the global economy moves through the twenty-first century, more effective multilateral leadership could help manage the challenges and uncertainties that lie ahead. The Group of Twenty Finance Ministers and Central Bank Governors representing leading industrial and emerging market countries (**G-20**) has assumed an active role. Established in 1999, the G-20 has emerged as an important international forum looking to build support for common approaches in meeting the world's financial challenges.[39] It is seeking to find the appropriate mix of policies that allows markets to operate without overbearing government intrusion, while having sufficient protections in place to curb excesses and abuses.

G-20
the Group of Twenty Finance Ministers and Central Bank Governors representing leading industrial and emerging market countries.

It is the *global* economy that will determine future job and income prospects across the world. A national economy's ability to succeed will depend largely on an understanding of the global economy's rigors and demands. For most countries (and their people), the challenge will be to extend and upgrade the skills needed to secure a creative and competitive edge. Given the pace of technological change and development, this will be an ongoing process. Considerable flexibility will also be required to take advantage of the opportunities and to counter the threats that arise in this increasingly borderless and integrated economic system.

KEY Concepts

direct investment 155
Doha Round 149
G-20 166
intellectual property rights (IPRs) 150
North American Free
Trade Agreement (NAFTA) 151
portfolio investment 154

protectionism 150
securities 163
securitization 163
sovereign debt 164
transnational corporations (TNCs) 155
Washington Consensus 161

TO LEARN More

Books and Other Print Media

Dambisa Moyo, *Dead Aid: Why Aid Is Not Working and How There Is a Better Way for Africa* (New York: Farrar, Straus, and Giroux, 2009).

Zambian economist Moyo discusses how the current aid paradigm harms developing countries in sub-Saharan Africa, and maps out country-led economic solutions to foster growth and erase dependency.

Jeffrey D. Sachs, *The End of Poverty: Economic Possibilities for Our Time* (New York: Penguin, 2005).

Economist Sachs lays the groundwork for how we should respond to global poverty in this book.

Jennifer Clark, *Mondo Agnelli; Fiat, Chrysler and the Power of a Dynasty* (Hoboken, NJ: John Wiley & Sons, 2012).

A fascinating glimpse into the realm of global business, this case study of Italian automaker Fiat (founded by the Agnelli family) traces its development and how it acquired control of a bankrupt Chrysler in 2009.

Joseph E. Stiglitz, *Making Globalization Work* (New York: W. W. Norton, 2007).

> This book offers a comprehensive discussion of the ways globalization has transformed trade, investment, and finance. Focusing on the ways globalization has contributed to greater disparities in wealth and opportunity across the world, Stiglitz recommends a wide range of reforms to address these issues.

Paul Krugman, *The Return of Depression Economics and the Crisis of 2008* (New York: W. W. Norton, 2009).

> This sequel to Krugman's account of the Asian financial crisis of the late 1990s traces the factors that contributed to the unraveling of global financial markets in 2008. This thoughtful and sobering analysis suggests striking similarities between current economic conditions and those of the 1930s.

Raghuram G. Rajan, *Fault Lines: How Hidden Fractures Still Threaten the World Economy* (Princeton, NJ: Princeton University Press, 2010).

> Rajan takes a broad look at the foundations of the global financial system and particularly the encouragement of excessive risk taking. He offers a set of recommendations for restoring stability to the world economy and for promoting long-term prosperity.

Websites

The Conscience of a Liberal, http://krugman.blogs.nytimes.com/.

> Economist Paul Krugman's Op-Ed column for the *New York Times* is also a blog, featuring insight on domestic and global economic issues.

International Monetary Fund (IMF), www.imf.org.

> The International Monetary Fund was established in 1944. It oversees the world's financial system, provides loans to countries facing immediate and particularly difficult economic circumstances, and offers technical assistance and training.

World Bank, www.worldbank.org.

> The International Bank for Reconstruction and Development (IBRD), more commonly referred to as the World Bank, was established in 1944 to provide loans and grants for projects that reduce poverty and promote sustainable, long-term economic development.

World Economic Forum, www.weforum.org.

> The World Economic Forum is the independent nonprofit foundation that hosts an annual meeting in Davos, Switzerland, attended by political, financial, and corporate leaders to promote interpersonal networking and to address an array of global issues.

World Social Forum, www.forumsocialmundial.org.br/.

> The World Social Forum is the annual meeting attended by individuals and representatives of groups and organizations that are part of the antiglobalization movement and that seek to advance alternative models of economic and social development.

World Trade Organization, www.wto.org.

> The World Trade Organization (WTO) is an international organization established in 1995 to develop and oversee the rules that guide global trade.

Videos

*Bananas!** (2009).

> This documentary focuses on the conflict between Nicaraguan banana plantation workers and Dole Food Company over alleged cases of sterility caused by a banned pesticide.

Comrade Kamprad: IKEA Goes to Russia (2005).

> This film is an entertaining and informative account of the efforts of Ingvar Kamprad—the founder of the Swedish retailer IKEA—to establish his business in Russia. The program follows Kamprad on a trip to Russia, where he confronts a series of logistical and political challenges (including the demands of a local official to be compensated for his support in navigating bureaucratic hurdles).

Global Car: Who Really Builds the American Automobile (2009).

> Focused around the production of a Dodge Ram pickup truck, the program highlights the truly global nature of a process that incorporates the use of hundreds of manufactured parts circulating across 40 countries.

Globalization at a Crossroads (2010).

> This production provides a good, concise overview of the core principles guiding globalization and offers a glimpse into how it has transformed the role of different groups of countries in the world economy. Includes segments on China, Russia, and the United States.

The Warning (2009).

> This is an excellent account of the events and conditions that resulted in the global financial meltdown in 2008. www.pbs.org/wgbh/pages/frontline/warning/

The Whole World Was Watching (2009)

> This short documentary reflects on the Battle in Seattle, a large protest against the World Trade Organization negotiations in Seattle in 1999. http://video.kcts9.org/video/1493266255/

Protecting Identity

The People of the World

In traveling to different places, we frequently encounter objects, foods, and social practices that are new to us. Unfamiliar American sights and smells were overwhelming to Valentino Achak Deng when he first arrived in the United States from Sudan. One of the "lost boys" who fled their native homeland in the midst of civil war, Valentino had spent many years as a refugee in Ethiopia and Kenya before seeking asylum in the United States. Many foods that Americans commonly eat, such as fresh fruit, vegetables, and cow's milk, were so different that they made him sick. But such physical discomfort was only part of what he suffered as he tried to adjust to a new culture.

The other sickness Valentino felt was from a jarring shift away from Sudanese social and cultural expectations. This response is commonly referred to as **culture shock**, a psychological and sometimes physical response to the

> *"We tried to be polite about our eating, but there were many new foods on the Mays's table, and we could not know what was a danger and what was not."*
>
> —Dave Eggers, quoting Lost Boy Valentino Achak Deng in *What Is the What*, 2006[1]

challenges of traveling to or living in another country or different culture. Culture shock can occur when you are in a new realm where customs, practices, eating, and living arrangements are different. Culture shock occurs when people are removed from their comfort zone. While some people are fascinated by differences, others are overwhelmed by them and can even be repulsed, and still others experience all these emotions at the same time. Food was not the only thing Valentino found overwhelming as he entered his new life in the United States. He physically suffered from headaches and had to deal with new things he had never seen. For example, when they first moved into an apartment in Atlanta, Valentino and his fellow Sudanese roommate did not know they could cut the air conditioner off, and, in Dave Eggers fictionalized memoir based on Valentino's experience, they "slept with all of our clothes on, covered in blankets and towels, every linen we owned."[2]

In a ritual familiar to many young people across the globe, a group of boys enjoys a fast food meal at a shopping mall in Doha, Qatar. Worldwide, many of our cultural practices are increasingly overlapping, yet our varying cultural and social practices also differ in important ways.

It is very hard to know what life is *really* like in a country or region when you have never directly experienced it. It is very easy, however, to have the illusion of knowing what it will be like—from images furnished by popular communications media, from reading, or perhaps from having met a few people from there. Reconciling the differences between what you expect and how things really are can be very challenging.

Simply knowing about another culture is not the same as living in it. Every culture has distinct characteristics. Some differences are obvious, such as language, religion, and political organization. Others can be so subtle that they are unsettling to foreign visitors, such as how to greet someone (the Japanese bow, for instance) or when dinner is served (very late in Spain). Visitors may be vaguely aware of such cultural differences, but making adjustments is a complex process. They may feel uncomfortable and

culture shock
a physical and psychological response to cultural differences when traveling away from home.

The "W" Curve

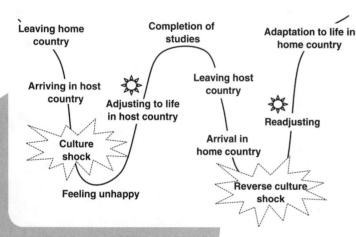

Leaving home country

Completion of studies

Adaptation to life in home country

Arriving in host country

Adjusting to life in host country

Leaving host country

Readjusting

Culture shock

Arrival in home country

Feeling unhappy

Reverse culture shock

Shown here is what is called the W curve, which represents the ups and downs of cultural adjustment, from the time of leaving one's home to that of returning.

culture
"the set of distinctive spiritual, material, intellectual and emotional features of society or a social group, that encompasses, not only art and literature, but lifestyles, ways of living together, value systems, traditions and beliefs," as defined by UNESCO.

off balance for quite some time. Adaptation comes in waves, including a readjustment on reentry into one's home country, as illustrated in this culture shock curve of a foreign student's emotions in a new host country.

People's actions are a result of their social and cultural surroundings—where they live, where they went to school, their parents' beliefs, their ethnicity, their race, their religion, and their gender. These variables not only color how individuals experience their own cultural identity but can also affect how they relate to other cultures. Sociocultural variables influence human behavior.[3] When these defining characteristics are challenged, individuals might believe that others are trying to change their fundamental identity and may move beyond uneasy feelings to a backlash against those who are challenging them. The tightening of religious beliefs along fundamentalist lines, the ethnic conflict that emerges, and even the failure of states that did not respect differences in the first place are all examples of these types of responses.

Social divisions are another border that determines how people perceive themselves and their relationship to others. In addition to such features as language, religion, and ethnicity, people also define themselves on the basis of their social standing—distinguished by birthright, relative power, and wealth. How much money people have, the value of their homes, or their status in the community can further delineate their identity.

Together, cultural and social borders significantly influence identity and the steps people will take to preserve it. They are what define us—our common practices and how we respond to different ones that disorient us. Ethnicity, race, gender, and religion further delineate our identity. All of these characteristics create the cultural framework in which we place ourselves. Reflecting these distinctions, the United Nations Educational, Scientific and Cultural Organization (UNESCO), a specialized agency of the United Nations devoted to the fostering of peace through intercultural dialogue defines **culture** as "the set of distinctive spiritual, material, intellectual and emotional features of society or a social group, that encompasses, not only art and literature, but lifestyles, ways of living together, value systems, traditions and beliefs."[4] We can build upon this definition to understand who we are and our relationship to others in terms of the world's cultural and social borders.

CULTURAL AND SOCIAL BORDERS: UNDERSTANDING IDENTITY

Historically, people gathered into distinct groups based on common practices and the need for survival. The naturally occurring geographic boundaries that brought people together were the primary markers of identity. The basic needs for water, food, and shelter unified them. Means of communication, religion, and societal practices further solidified their relationships. Tradition or physical strength determined leadership within the group. For each unit, a sense of identity also emerged from its shared experiences and indigenous traits.

As particular groups of people began to encounter other groups—the "other" became a defining factor in their identity. Trade routes developed, and accounts of early long-distance journeys reflected how people saw themselves as different or superior. Cultural anthropologist Ida Magli notes that the first published "anthropological" description of Native Americans as a result of these early journeys appeared in 1512.[5] These observations relied both on the physical characteristics of the peoples they encountered and on these people's clothing, weapons, and customs. Englishman John White would bring these images to life with his watercolor drawings of the Algonquian Indians he encountered when he sailed with an early expedition to Virginia in 1585. His images offered Europe some of its first visual representation of this new land and its inhabitants.

Many students of culture argue that the emergence of the modern state system crossed many naturally occurring borders and became a primary source of conflict among peoples beginning in the 1600s. Anthropologist Manning Nash goes so far as to suggest that the nation-state is responsible for "the rise and definition of social entities that are currently called 'ethnic groups.'"[6] While cultural diversity and political differences existed prior to the emergence of the state system, its development and the diversity of people within state borders facilitated the differentiation of ethnicity. In many cases, this led to ethnic conflict. The delineation of borders in the African subcontinent provides an excellent example.

As illustrated in Map 8.1, over 300 distinct cultures can be drawn on the same piece of land where only 54 states exist. Colonial powers frequently

HOW DO YOU CONNECT? | **WHAT IS YOUR CULTURE?**

What is your native state or country?

Where did you grow up?

Where do you live now?

What religion or traditions do you or your family practice?

What languages do you speak?

What are you the first person in your family to do?

This illustration, a watercolor by Englishman John White, dates back to 1585 and depicts an Algonquian Indian fire ceremony. White's images helped shaped European conceptions of American Indian groups.

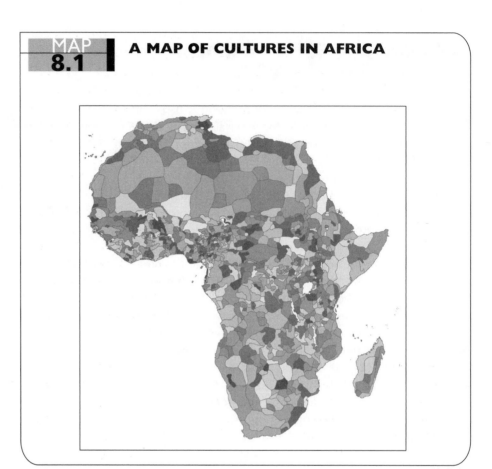

MAP 8.1   A MAP OF CULTURES IN AFRICA

drew these political borders to enhance their own political and economic interests. By splitting indigenous groups across these newly created borders, colonizers were able to divide and conquer. At the same time, previously independent
indigenous groups were forced into closer contact with others, increasing the
potential for conflict.

THE AGE OF ENLIGHTENMENT

While the delineation of the nation-state often had negative effects on distinct
cultures, an understanding of the concept of culture evolved concurrently with
its development. As trade routes expanded and settled into patterns of interaction, thinkers and scholars began to consider their identity. The emergence of a
system of states and the self-inspection that was inspired by the Enlightenment
from the mid-1600s to the 1800s helped formulate the concept. European and

American scholars advocated a society based on personal choice, guided by reason. Scholars of the day, called the *philosophes* (Enlightenment thinkers), included British (David Hume and John Locke), French (Francois-Marie Arouet de Voltaire and Jean-Jacques Rousseau), German (Immanuel Kant), and even some early American authors (Benjamin Franklin, Thomas Jefferson, and Thomas Paine). Their general argument sought to move away from a worldview dominated by religion and suggested a more scientific approach to understanding the realities of the day. This self-conscious view of society gave rise to efforts to better understand identity.

Cultural anthropologist Adam Kuper identifies three schools of thought among the intellectual trends that emerged during this time to understand culture generally and justify the territorial expansion that was taking place—the enlightened view of the French, the romantic or counter-Enlightenment view of the Germans, and the traditional views held by the English.[7] The French were greatly influenced by the Enlightenment and viewed culture as a progressive, cumulative, and distinctly human achievement. Everyone could evolve to be civilized as the French defined it: having a cosmopolitan view of the world. As such, territorial expansion would provide opportunity to those they encountered by giving them the option to embrace "civilization."

In contrast, the German view held that cultures were distinguished by natural and spiritual sources. This perspective was greatly influenced by the Reformation of the Christian church, which sought a more direct relationship between the people and religion. The splintering of the church led to a major political realignment in Europe. The promotion of a more egalitarian view of Christianity held that people should not be required to aspire to others' notions of "civilization." The authenticity of their culture should be preserved.

The English relied on the classical view of the world, focusing on history, as described by English poet Matthew Arnold as "the best that has been known and said."[8] Their world was steeped in traditions that offered a way to live. Like the French, the British believed their practices were superior and should be adopted by all they encountered. The colonial empire they built during this time flows from these views, and many of the practices they promoted endure today.

For example, while no longer expansionist in their political objectives, British traditions continue not only in the United Kingdom but throughout many of the countries that consider themselves part of the Commonwealth—an association of 54 states listed in Table 8.1 that grew out of the British Empire and was formally established in 1931 to promote "democracy, freedom, peace, the rule of law and opportunity for all."[9] Decades after the end of colonialism, this diverse group still recognizes the Head of the Commonwealth as Her Majesty, Queen Elizabeth II of England. The elaborate practices surrounding the marriage of Prince William and Princess Kate in 2011 are another example of how this adherence to custom and ritualized behavior has been perpetuated.

Enlightenment views evolved in conjunction with a changing economic reality. The search for riches, new markets, natural resources, and slaves had fueled

TABLE 8.1   COMMONWEALTH MEMBER COUNTRIES

Antigua and Barbuda	India	St. Lucia
Australia	Kenya	St. Vincent and the Grenadines
The Bahamas	Kiribati	Samoa
Bangladesh	Lesotho	Seychelles
Barbados	Malawi	Sierra Leone
Belize	Maldives	Singapore
Botswana	Malaysia	Solomon Islands
Brunei Darussalam	Malta	South Africa
Cameroon	Mauritius	Sri Lanka
Canada	Mozambique	Swaziland
Cyprus	Namibia	Tanzania
Dominica	Nauru	Tonga
Fiji	New Zealand	Trinidad & Tobago
The Gambia	Nigeria	Tuvalu
Ghana	Pakistan	Uganda
Grenada	Papua New Guinea	United Kingdom
Guyana	Rwanda	Vanuatu
Jamaica	St. Kitts and Nevis	Zambia

exploration. Through this process, cultural understanding was refined but incomplete. Identity was understood, to a great extent, relative to others. As the Enlightenment gave way to the Industrial Revolution, social divisions became more complex with the emergence of new classes of workers and entrepreneurs. Social status became an additional factor in the definition of identity.

SOCIAL BORDERS

There always have been social divisions, whether they are defined by birth or privilege of wealth. In some societies, this class structure is quite rigid, such that those who are of the "highest" classes are born into it. The inheritance lines of the monarchies in Morocco and Saudi Arabia are two examples. Frequently, financial riches come with this hereditary stature. The caste system found in South Asia is another instance of birthright determining social identity. There is little room to change your fate in life when it is dictated by birth. For example, caste distinctions in remote areas of Nepal perpetuate ancient practices, where women are married as children and sent to live in outbuildings during menstruation to prevent bringing "bad luck" to their families and animals.[10] Members of lower castes are required to wash their dishes before using them to share a meal with people from another caste, and even then, their dishes may be used only after "purifier" has been sprinkled on them.

Where you are born can dictate your opportunities as well. In China, this distinction is applied to rural and urban birthrights. People born in rural areas have very limited opportunities, even if they move to an urban area. China has a registration system—*hukou*—that is based on one's parents' birthplace.[11] City dwellers are entitled to public education if they have inherited an urban registration. The vast numbers of rural migrants now moving to urban areas in China, however, retain their rural registration, and the only education they can get for their children must be obtained privately and is frequently substandard. As a result, children are frequently left with relatives in their home villages—an estimated 58 million in 2010. While 19 million other children accompanied their parents, they were treated as second-class citizens. Leslie Chang chronicles the story of many of the women and men who come from rural areas to China's bustling cities for work in her book, *Factory Girls.* These mostly young women find themselves creating a new cultural identity as they are no longer from the rural area but do not really qualify for the privileges of urban residency.

Social identity can also be defined by the job that you perform, a concept that found new meaning with the creation of a worker class and a wealthy class of factory owners during industrialization. The wealthy upper class wielded political power. The lower or working classes were those who toiled in the factories, confined to poorly paying jobs with little hope for advancement. The promise of industrialization, however, was that it would bring about a redistribution of wealth that would allow individuals to move from one class to another.

The tensions that existed between people during these great periods of change were voiced by those who believed the underlying social stratification was not equal and could not be overcome without significant action. The writings of German-born philosophers Karl Marx and Frederick Engels sought to explain why the workers in society would not benefit from the economic developments that were occurring during industrialization. In their classic work, *Manifesto of the Communist Party,* first published in 1848, they took a historical perspective to argue that industrialization was developing in a fundamentally unequal fashion and created further social borders within societies.

Class divisions that had separated people by birth now hinged on new wealth and the jobs people performed. The **bourgeoisie**, the owners of the means of production, had little respect for the **proletariat**, the workers, except to the extent to which the workers would enhance their wealth. Marx and Engels believed the only way to address these inequities was a restructuring of the social order. They sought the creation of a new social movement—**communism**—that

bourgeoisie
the owners of the means of production.

proletariat
the industrial workers.

communism
a social movement that promoted the communal values of the worker class.

> In short, the Communists everywhere support every revolutionary movement against the existing social and political order of things.
>
> In all these movements, they bring to the front, as the leading question in each, the property question, no matter what its degree of development at the time.
>
> Finally, they labor everywhere for the union and agreement of the democratic parties of all countries.
>
> The Communists disdain to conceal their views and aims. They openly declare that their ends can be attained only by the forcible overthrow of all existing social conditions. Let the ruling classes tremble at a communist revolution. The proletarians have nothing to lose but their chains. They have a world to win.
>
> Proletarians of all countries, unite![12]

IN THEIR OWN WORDS   **Karl Marx and Frederick Engels**

would champion the communal values of the worker class. It was up to those who embraced this perspective, the communists, to unite to overthrow the oppressive bourgeoisie. Moreover, they believed the inequities of wealth would lead to a spontaneous uprising among the workers. Marx and Engels concluded their *Communist Manifesto* with an exhortation to the world's workers to rise up in a revolution against the bourgeoisie.

The problem was that Marx's and Engels's expectations that the workers would spontaneously unite did not happen, and subsequent efforts to bring communism to bear fell on deaf ears. The efforts of Vladimir I. Lenin to establish communism in Russia upon the overthrow of the tsar in the beginning of the twentieth century required a very different approach. When the workers did not rise up on their own, Lenin realized they would need to be led. He created the Communist Party to be the "vanguard of the people" and lead the revolution. The result was far from an egalitarian society but much more in line with a totalitarian state, in which members of the Communist Party became the leaders, despite their lip service to equality.

THE STUDY OF SOCIAL AND CULTURAL BORDERS

sociology
a field of study that focuses on people and their relationships to the societies in which they live.

Efforts to intellectually understand society, culture, and identity have led to several methods of examination, most notably the disciplines of **sociology**, **anthropology**, and **psychology**. These fields of inquiry seek to understand human behavior—what are the influencing factors? Anthropology examines the physical attributes of human beings as well as their social and cultural characteristics. Sociology focuses on people and their relationships to the societies in which they live, and psychology seeks to understand the motivations behind the decisions they make.[13] The writings of Charles Darwin and his theory of evolution in the 1860s played heavily in early conceptualizations of these fields.[14] The notions of evolution and survival of the fittest were groundbreaking ways to consider the plight of humankind.

In the 1940s and 1950s, some sociologists attempted to turn anthropological understanding of cultural differences into broad scientific theories of human behavior. Anthropologists, however, believed that culture was learned behavior and as such needed to be studied in context. In response, they turned to **ethnography** in the 1960s, the observation and description of people in their environment through in-depth analysis and interaction, focusing on tribal units, their linguistic patterns, and their cultural practices in remote areas to understand pure cultures.

What these anthropologists wanted to capture was a better understanding of cultural learning, recognizing that it occurs in a number of different ways. Most commonly a group's beliefs and shared practices are passed down from one generation to another. A person's rites of passage within a group mark successful transitions in this learning process, known as **enculturation**.[15] These practices, such as rituals surrounding the transition from childhood to adulthood and the acceptance of polygamy as way of life, may be unique to cultural groups and not generally accepted outside of them. The idea that cultural meaning is relative to the environment in which it exists is called **cultural relativism**. The notion here is that culture is situational and should be respected as such.

Writing in the early twentieth century, American anthropologist Margaret Mead believed a better understanding of others could come from openness to examining their cultural differences without intellectual bias. In her observations about the tribal people of three islands in the western Pacific, she wrote:

> If we are to achieve a richer culture, rich in contrasting values, we must recognize the whole gamut of human potentialities, and so weave a less arbitrary social fabric, one in which each diverse human gift will find a fitting place.[16]

Mead examined gender roles in other societies, as well as how children learned social patterns. Her contribution was significant in its effect on scholarly exploration of perception and cultural identification.[17]

Later authors, such as Clifford Geertz, came to understand that individuals ascribe many identities to themselves. He examined not just the ways that people learn culture but also how their political and economic situations, what he called the "hard surfaces of life," color how culture is defined

anthropology

a field of study that examines the physical attributes of human beings as well as their social and cultural characteristics.

psychology

a field of study that seeks to understand the motivations behind the decisions people make in terms of their cognitive orientation.

ethnography

the observation and description of people in their environment through in-depth analysis and interaction.

enculturation

the process by which a society learns its culture.

cultural relativism

cultural understanding in terms of the environment in which it exists.

cultural diffusion
the spreading of culture beyond a specific group to be embraced by a wider audience.

assimilation
the submerging of cultural differences into a broader, dominant culture.

cultural imperialism
when one culture is dominated by another culture to the point that the victimized culture is forced to change its cultural practices.

and understood.[18] Cultures adapt over time to their "hard surfaces." When people outside the immediate circle of a group embrace the group's manners, ideas, or identity, this is known as **cultural diffusion**. Cultural diffusion occurs when characteristics of one culture, such as Chinese food or Levi's jeans, become part of another. This adaptation is not universally welcomed. Indigenous identity is particularly sensitive to these changes, as languages are lost and cultural practices give way to different patterns of behavior.

For many years, the perceived purpose of many societies was to create a common culture such that immigrants to a new place would restructure their identity or "melt" into a common pot. The emphasis on **assimilation** submerged cultural differences into a broader, dominant culture. Sometimes assimilation was taken to an extreme, driven by inherent biases against those who were different. For example, many first-generation immigrants to the United States in the early twentieth century forbid their children to learn their native languages and insisted on "English only" to succeed in America. Similarly, British colonizers restructured Indian society to adopt British customs, food, and dress.

Assimilation is not always a voluntary process undertaken to gain acceptance. Colonized natives often had little or no choice but to adopt the cultural practices and lifestyles of the colonial powers. Dominating cultures routinely victimized smaller cultures in a process of **cultural imperialism**. People were frequently forced to abandon time-honored traditions in favor of a more "civilized" course. Nigerian writer Chinua Achebe describes the colonization of his country to the great detriment of the culture of the indigenous people in his 1958 novel, *Things Fall Apart*:

> Does the white man understand our custom about land? How can he when he does not even speak our tongue? But he says that our customs are bad; and our own brothers who have taken up his religion also say that our customs are bad. How do you think we can fight when our own brothers have turned against us?[19]

Many groups have worked to preserve their cultural identity in the face of pressure to integrate into broader societies. Instead of melting into the predominant culture, they maintain their unique attributes. Difficulties remain in crossing cultural borders, given the reality of multiple identities that may exist at any particular time. Respect for these differences is critical, but there are also broader concerns that may bring people together. The following debate on whether indigenous peoples should be educated in their own languages or that of the dominant cultures examines the fine line that must be maintained to provide successful outcomes while being cognizant of cultural realities.

PRO/CON

Should indigenous peoples be educated in their own languages?

PRO	CON

Jon Todal
Jon Todal, Professor of Sociolinguistics, Sami University College, Guovdageaidnu, Norway. Written for *CQ Global Researcher*, September 2011

Helen Hughes
Helen Hughes, Emeritus Professor and Fellow, Research School of Asia and the Pacific, Australian National University, Canberra, and Senior Fellow, Centre for Independent Studies Sydney, Australia. Written for *CQ Global Researcher*, September 2011

PRO

The living conditions of indigenous peoples vary across the world. In some countries they are integrated into society, while in others they are marginalized. Despite these differences, indigenous peoples share many experiences, including the attempt by nation-states to eradicate indigenous languages.

Since the 19th century countries have used schools to achieve monolingualism, or "one state—one language," and all teaching in compulsory education was in the majority language.

As a result, indigenous children struggle more at school than children from the majority population, because they must learn not only their subjects but also a new language. The policy has signaled that indigenous languages are not valued, and such negative school experiences account in part for why indigenous peoples have a lower level of education than majority peoples.

One response among indigenous peoples has been to reject schooling as irrelevant, leading to low levels of education. Another strategy has been to adjust to the schools' values. For example, parents may stop speaking the indigenous language with their children at home so that by the time the children start school they are more on a par with majority children. But this strategy halts the intergenerational transmission of indigenous languages, and the languages become endangered. In other words, both these strategies (rejection and adjustment) have a negative impact on indigenous societies.

A third strategy—to make schools in indigenous areas adjust to the children's language and culture—has produced

(Continued on next page)

CON

Open ended, this is a nonsensical question. However desirable for children to learn to read and write in their mother tongues, in many situations it is impractical. In Papua New Guinea, for example, a developing country with just under 7 million people, it has not been possible to train teachers and develop reading materials in the more than 800 indigenous languages spoken there.

Pretending to do so has contributed significantly to the country's failure of education. After nearly 40 years of independence, education is in crisis, with only about 20 percent of the population literate.

Some languages are dying out—not only in Oceania, but also in the Americas, India, China and many other parts of Asia and Africa—while new ones, such as Bahasa Indonesia, have been evolving. Countries must decide on language teaching that is best for their inhabitants, and this usually means compromises between resources and ideals.

Children must become articulate and literate in the principal language or languages of their country so they can function in its economy and society. They have to be able to qualify for jobs, participate in democratic decision-making and contribute to civil society. In countries made up of disparate groups, a national language or languages can make a contribution to stability, equity and economic and social development.

Fortunately, research on the human brain has demonstrated that children can absorb new languages at very early ages and can absorb several languages simultaneously when very young. Research also shows that linguistic development makes a special contribution to the

(Continued on next page)

PRO/CON (Continued)
Should indigenous peoples be educated in their own languages?

PRO	CON
good results. It is now supported in Scandinavia, for example, where the indigenous Sámi people can receive primary education in Sámi as a separate subject, and they may choose to have Sámi as the language of instruction in other subjects. The level of education among the Sámi is no longer lower than among the majority peoples in Scandinavia, and the Sami language has been strengthened.	development of children's brains. Teaching several languages simultaneously in pre-schools that take in children at 3 years of age and (even earlier) has made a multilingual approach to teaching languages possible.
Those advocating indigenous peoples receiving education in their own language can find support for their view in international conventions. However, these formal rights are not the main issue. They key points are that education in indigenous languages gives children a positive experience of their own culture and also strengthens the traditional indigenous languages. In this way children are better prepared for life both in the wider society and in the indigenous society.	Equality of opportunity demands quality education from very early years so that children are fully articulate and literate by the end of their primary education in a country's principal language or languages. The extent to which it is sensible to teach mother or traditional tongues in practice depends on a range of factors, including the extent to which such languages are developed and used, a country's resources and parents' wishes. There is no one-size-fits-all model.
For this reason education in their own language must be an important right for all indigenous peoples.	

Source: Brian Beary, "Saving Indigenous Peoples." *CQ Global Researcher 5* (2011): 447–472.

WHERE Do You Stand?

1. Do you think indigenous people should receive instruction in their native language?
2. Does instruction in their native language offer protection for their cultural identity?
3. Does a society have the right to demand that all people speak the dominant language?

GLOBALIZATION: HOMOGENIZATION OR HYBRIDIZATION?

Over thousands of years, group identities evolved with little influence from the outside world. Anthropologist John H. Bodley observes that "as recently as 200 years ago, 50 million people continued to live in politically autonomous domestic-scale tribal societies."[20] Different groups controlled large areas of the globe, and external forces such as commercial enterprise did not affect them. Bodley argues that while these tribal groups (more commonly referred to as indigenous peoples) still exist, the commercial world has penetrated and altered their realities.

The impact of globalization on culture and identity has been significant. As sociologist and cultural communications expert John Tomlinson suggests, greater mobility results in a progressive **deterritorialization** of the world that weakens the connection between culture and a particular place.[21] The ability to communicate instantly around the world has rendered the attachment to place less potent. Moreover, many of the issues that affect the peoples of the world are not limited by its borders, such as technological innovation, environmental degradation, terrorism, and financial interactions. As a result, a common cultural experience emerges.

Some people are concerned that globalization results in a **homogenization** of culture. A range of cultural forms has been incorporated into a more uniform set of values and practices, primarily Western and specifically American in nature, that threatens cultural diversity and people's ability to maintain their distinctive identities. The pressures to conform and adapt are plentiful and difficult to resist. Shopping centers around the world are populated by the same stores, clothes, and services. Kentucky Fried Chicken and other fast food establishments can be found on main streets from New York to Paris to Doha, as seen in the opening picture to this chapter.

Not everyone shares this concern. In contrast to those who caution against the homogenizing impacts of globalization are those analysts who emphasize the resilience of existing cultural forms and their ability to endure the effects of external pressures. Instead, they point to the countervailing influence of local customs and cultural practices on these outside forces that has produced a **hybridization** of cultures—a blending that incorporates aspects of different cultures. While the concept of hybridity comes from agrarian roots, where new varieties of plants are created by grafting one plant to another, sociologist Jan Nederveen Pieterse, in his book *Globalization and Culture*, argues that hybridity occurs today due to the mobility of people, their ability to migrate, and the multicultural identities they have developed.[22] This extensive migration, coupled with new forms of communication that provide broader transmission of information and the creation of transnational social networking sites such as Facebook, has an impact on identity. Rather than threatening identity, this exposure simply results in a modification or adaptation as new identities may emerge. US president Barack Obama is a prime example—his multicultural roots challenge traditional definitions of race, ethnicity, and even homeland. Golf champion Tiger Woods characterizes his identity as "Cablinasian"—a blend of Caucasian, Black, Indian, and Asian.[23]

Whether globalization is contributing to the homogenization or hybridization of culture, it is clear that it is having a profound impact. A number of leading analysts see globalization as the source of significant cultural conflict, due to its complex and often contradictory components. In his 1999 bestseller, *The*

deterritorialization
the weakening of cultural ties to specific locations.

homogenization
the incorporation of a range of cultural forms into a uniform set of values and practices.

hybridization
a blending of cultures that incorporates different aspects of each culture to create a new entity.

Lexus and the Olive Tree, Pulitzer Prize–winning columnist Thomas Friedman has argued that through the development and rapid spread of technology, embodied in the state-of-the-art facility manufacturing Toyota's luxury Lexus automobile, globalization can improve the quality of life for workers who have historically been left behind. At the same time, however, he realizes that the intense desire to protect and preserve individual cultures and identities—symbolized by the ongoing struggle and often violent clashes between Israelis and Palestinians over the ownership of particular olive trees—will persist.

In a more dramatic scenario than Friedman's, political scientist Samuel Huntington projects a future marked by what he terms a "clash of civilizations" (or cultures). In his groundbreaking 1996 work, *The Clash of Civilizations and the Remaking of World Order,* Huntington envisioned global interactions among seven or eight major civilizations—Western, Japanese, Confucian, Islamic, Hindu, Slavic-Orthodox, Latin American, and possibly African.[24] Future conflicts, he argued, were most likely to fall along cultural lines, with the most significant potential for discord between Islam and the West. If not addressed and contained, this conflict could even result in a highly contentious global environment where the West would find itself aligned against all other major civilizations.

MAP 8.2   CLASH OF CIVILIZATIONS

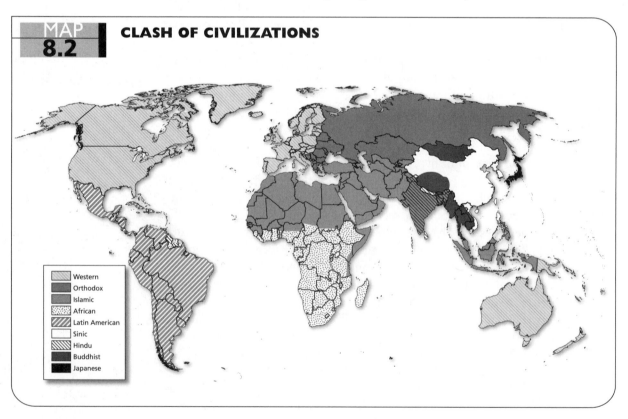

Legend:
- Western
- Orthodox
- Islamic
- African
- Latin American
- Sinic
- Hindu
- Buddhist
- Japanese

Huntington's thesis provoked considerable criticism among thinkers who questioned the premise of his argument and the implications of his projections. For some, Huntington went too far in emphasizing the hostility generated by intercultural contact. Still others were concerned that he had not underestimated the differences and distinctions among civilizations, yet had put forward a far too simplistic scenario that was likely to provoke such policies as restricting immigration or imposing restraints on minorities. Such actions would only reinforce existing or latent hostilities. Some went on to suggest that Huntington's ideas might even be used as a rationale to justify extreme forms of ethnic violence. Nevertheless, Huntington's clash of civilizations argument continues to be an important part of the debate that highlights globalization's evolving and multiple impacts.

McDonalds

Globalization's critics love to take aim at McDonalds restaurant, whose global reach extends to 123 countries and sovereign territories around the world. They see it as the embodiment of America's dominant cultural presence and market position across the world—not to mention as a prime culprit in spreading the consumption of food of questionable nutritional value. However, the ubiquitous McDonalds may bring about more than just hamburgers or the homogenization of culture. Thomas Friedman introduced the idea of a "golden arches theory of conflict prevention," for example, in suggesting that countries with McDonalds restaurants (whose presence indicates that these countries are open to global capitalism) are less likely to go to war with one another so as to avoid the risk of economic disruption.[25]

McDonalds "golden arches" are shown here juxtaposed against the traditional roofline of the Drum Tower in Xian, Shaanxi Province, China. As McDonalds goes global, it has become the symbol for the spread of a homogenized Western consumerism, but at the same time, it also highlights the possibility of the peaceful relations that can be achieved via a stable global trading system.

In his 1996 book on this topic, *Jihad vs. McWorld*, political theorist Benjamin Barber describes two different scenarios to illustrate the integrative and the polarizing tendencies of globalization. *McWorld* symbolizes the connectivity of globalization and its capacity for bringing diverse communities into contact with one another. While this connectivity presents an opportunity for increasing mutual understanding, it is also indicative of globalization's homogenizing tendencies.

In contrast, *jihad* is an Arabic word that is often identified with the notion of the "holy war" that has motivated al-Qaeda and other Islamic groups seeking to thwart what they perceive as the threatening dominance of Western values and ideology. As Barber uses the concept, it refers to the resistance of these groups to the perceived cultural uniformity that has come with globalization.[26]

Sociologist George Ritzer uses the term *McDonaldization* to describe processes that have come to dominate the organization of more and more sectors of production around the world and to impose pressure to adhere to homogenous standards and values. These principles include efficiency, calculability, predictability, and control. McDonalds has been a model of efficiency in its movement of goods from one place to another as well as its ability to capture market share. It has also been a leader in calculability, an emphasis on time and money that delivers a product quickly and cheaply to its customers. One of the hallmarks of McDonalds is its predictability—its products and service are generally the same all over with the exception of local market adaptation. Finally, McDonalds exerts significant control over how goods are distributed in its restaurants, from drive-up windows and line service to the appearance of its employees.[27]

Other academics argue that the McDonalds effect noted by Ritzer and other commentators may be somewhat overblown, as it assumes cultural impact to be a one-way street. Political scientist Michael Veseth calls this overemphasis on the homogenizing nature of globalization *globaloney*.[28] In fact, he says, McDonalds must tailor its menus to local tastes and cultural practices in order to retain its competitive position. In India, where eating beef is sacrilege, the Maharaja Mac is a Big Mac made of chicken; in Chile, avocado paste is a standard fixing, with a side of cheese empanadas; and in Japan, you can order a Teriyaki McBurger made of ground pork and teriyaki sauce. McDonalds also serves different purposes in different countries—coffee shop, community gathering location, study hall, or just a place to take the kids. The adaptation of local forms of expression and identity to exposure from outside influences is a process known as **glocalization**.[29]

Anthropologist Arjun Appadurai has coined the phrase *global scapes* to describe the increasing flows that globalization has released. Global scapes are redefining people's identities.[30] They include the following scapes:

> mediascapes: flows of information through the mass media
>
> financescapes: flows of capital
>
> technoscapes: flows of technology
>
> ethnoscapes: flows of people
>
> ideoscapes: flows of ideas

Rather than imposing Western culture and values on others, Appadurai argues, these flows may help to invigorate local culture by infusing a broader range of perspectives.

Music and Sport

Music and sport, two elements that often contribute significantly to defining who we are and our relationship to others, are large parts of the global scape that

glocalization
the adaptation of local forms of expression and identity to outside influences.

is redefining cultures. Technology has made local sounds global. New recording and sound production technologies have broken down old barriers to transmitting music. While digitization expands opportunities for reproduction and dissemination, the Internet offers a far wider network for exposure than the radio ever did. The ease of downloading music of all types and genres and the extraordinary growth in the use of iPods and other similar devices for storing and playing have been critical. Musicians are able to travel more easily actually and virtually than ever before, bringing new sounds to peoples in different places.

As is the case with other cultural forms, however, music has been a source of concern for people who fear globalization's homogenizing effect. The international nonprofit organization Global Music Project aims to preserve the uniqueness of different forms of music. Its mission is to promote collaboration and peace through music and cultural awareness.[31] It seeks not only to preserve musical traditions around the world but to share those traditions as well. Its website includes recommended songs from across the globe and provides free downloads. Through artist donations of songs, sponsors, and merchandise sales, the Global Music Project promotes cross-cultural appreciation for music and the unique cultures it represents.

There is actually little evidence to suggest that greater standardization in production has had a homogenizing effect on music. Instead, it has contributed to a greater degree of diversity. As particular types of music originating in one locale spread to other places, musicians modify their sounds as a result of their contact with those of other cultures. These modifications enhance the meaning of the music in a way that fits more easily with existing values and experiences.

The introduction and consumption of Afro-Caribbean music in Japan is a case in point. Due to limited contact and communication between Latin America and Japan, Afro-Caribbean music was transmitted largely through the United States and Europe. While some forms such as tango and bolero were favorably received in the 1920s, others such as rumba gained little following. The differences had much to do with the extent to which these different genres resembled Japanese popular music in terms of their beat and tone and how they fit into Japan's value system.[32]

A significant turning point came in 1984 with the creation of the Orquesta de la Luz, a salsa band of Japanese musicians with experience in playing Afro-Caribbean music. Its popularity, both inside Japan and internationally, stemmed largely from its ability to maintain the authenticity of its sound as a distinctively Japanese group. This unique collaboration demonstrated how a local culture can be enriched through its exposure to other cultural forms while simultaneously influencing the composition of those forms.[33]

HOW DO YOU CONNECT? | **WHAT MUSIC MOVES YOU?**

What kinds of music do you listen to?

a. pop
b. rock
c. reggae
d. hip hop
e. soul
f. country
g. classical

Do you listen to music in other languages?

a. yes
b. no

This interplay of the global and local is also reflected in the development of hip hop, a musical form with global appeal. Originating in the 1970s in the Bronx borough of New York City, hip hop was based on themes of urban life and evolved into a broader form of expression for young people. In addition to its music, hip hop incorporates dance, art, and fashion in reflecting a particular outlook and lifestyle. As hip hop gained in popularity and spread to different parts of the world, it came to take on additional meaning and more varied forms of expression. Hip hop's themes relating to personal liberation, rebellion, and social justice appealed to masses of youths in far corners of the world.[34] Now a global movement, hip hop is even considered by some to have grown to the point where it has become a culture in and of itself.

As hip hop spread across the globe, the genre itself underwent considerable transformation. While the message spoke to the experiences of disenfranchised or alienated youth worldwide, each community incorporated its own unique elements to reflect local conditions and circumstances. Different mixes of language and beat give hip hop in Brazil a different feel from hip hop in Tanzania. As local attributes distinguish and differentiate the identities of these respective varieties, they also influence the genre in turn.[35] In the case of hip hop, globalization has yielded glocal hybrids, not Western purebreds.

Similar impacts have flowed from the increasing globalization of sport, another agent of culture whose popularity across borders brings people together. Where and how particular games are played can be traced to broader historical patterns. South Asian countries adopted cricket as their national sports pastime from their British colonial occupiers. The Scottish games that originated as a celebration of a hunt with measures of strength and agility, such as "tossing the caber" (throwing a 14-foot pole similar to a log end over end) and "throwing the hammer," are now celebrated in "Highland Games" in distant places. The largest gathering of the Scottish clans globally to participate in such games takes place annually in a small town in the mountains of North Carolina, far from Scotland's shores.

The expanding global reach of premier American professional sport leagues goes beyond the traditional diffusion of sports through colonization or immigration. Through the leadership of its commissioner, the National Basketball Association (NBA) has made a concerted effort to penetrate new markets in Europe and beyond to enhance the profitability of the enterprise. This global strategy has paid handsome dividends, as games are broadcast to over 750 million households in more than 40 languages in 212 countries. By 2008, international players held 80 of the 430 roster spots on NBA teams.[36]

Marketing techniques contributed significantly to the growing popularity of this game. They focused largely on promoting key players whose appeal elevated them to the status of cultural icons and placed an emphasis on interpersonal rivalries (as opposed to team rivalries). The epic Larry Bird–Magic Johnson duels and the Michael Jordan phenomenon were instrumental in moving the process forward. The role of advertisers was critical. The Michael Jordan brand promoted by Nike was especially effective and has retained its appeal long after his retirement.[37] It even prompted one observer to note the emergence of Jordanscapes (using the Appadurai terminology) in explaining the source of the NBA's growing global appeal.[38] This marketing strategy has continued with the latest generation of stars such as LeBron James and Kobe Bryant.

China's Yao Ming considerably helped to broaden the NBA's worldwide appeal during his tenure with the Houston Rockets. Although plagued by injuries throughout his career and ultimately forced to retire prematurely in 2011, Yao became a popular hero and an important symbol of China's full-scale emergence on the world stage.[39] The development of Taiwan-born and Harvard-educated Jeremy Lin, a marginal player who had a succession of electrifying performances with the New York Knicks during the 2012 season, contributed further to the NBA's expanding Asian connection.

Major League Baseball (MLB) has also gone global. At the start of the 2011 season, non-American players filled 27.7 percent of team rosters.[40] Often touted as an American game, professional baseball has undergone some significant changes. The World Baseball Classic, established in 2009, brings together national teams from across the world and has contributed to the sport's growing popularity in a variety of markets.

Despite its American roots, professional baseball has long been a part of Japan's sports scene. Americans who have played for Japanese teams have often expressed their difficulties in adjusting to a different style of play that emphasizes such Japanese values as group identity, cooperation, and harmony. Tom Davey, who pitched in the Japanese majors, observes,

> You need to keep an open mind, nod your head and do what they ask. Maybe I'm not going to do a 300-pitch bullpen, but I'll do the crazy agility drills they have. It's the Japanese Samurai mentality. They can't say, "No, I'm done." You respect it like you respect everything else here.[41]

Similarly, Japan's teams have exhibited some discomfort with their US players—seeking to take advantage of their contributions while not necessarily being interested in having them upstage their local counterparts. This may be understood in terms of the country's homogeneous character and antipathy toward foreigners. Japanese players, on the other hand, are beginning to make their way into the MLB. While a few have enjoyed considerable success (most notably, Ichiro Suzuki and Hideki Matsui), many others who starred in Japan found the transition difficult and failed to live up to expectations.[42]

The most significant development with respect to the internationalization of the MLB itself has been the infusion of Latin players. While this is not necessarily a new phenomenon, given baseball's longstanding presence in parts of the Caribbean and Central and South America, it has reached impressive proportions. Unlike the NBA, the MLB does not appear to have much interest in establishing franchises overseas. Rather, it has capitalized on and sought to enhance the availability of Latin talent as a means to expand into those markets.[43]

The player "pipeline" between the Dominican Republic and the United States is especially notable. Many major league clubs run training camps for the purpose of spotting and developing local talent. By 2011, close to 500 Dominican players had reached the MLB, with thousands more having played in the minor leagues. With top prospects commanding hefty signing bonuses and having the potential to land multimillion dollar contracts, baseball has become an important path out of poverty.[44]

As would be expected, the entry of large numbers of foreign-born players (and even a handful of managers and team executives) is transforming the character and culture of major league baseball. Playing styles are more varied, while the managing of intercultural relationships and communications has become an important factor in maintaining team chemistry. This diversity is readily apparent not only in terms of the composition of teams but in the makeup of their fan bases. Ballparks now cater to a wider degree of tastes in terms of the foods they offer and the apparel and other items they market both at home and internationally. For example, churros, a fried dough treat that originated in Spain, may be found at many major league stadiums.

The globalization of sport is not a phenomenon exclusive to American efforts. In fact, soccer is the most universal sport, even as it has been slow to catch on in the United States. Soccer's progressive spread has been a lengthy and complex process that can be traced all the way back to the time of the Roman Empire. Its governing body—the Federation Internationale de Football Association (FIFA)—oversees its operation and development and has over 200 national members. FIFA has very successfully promoted the commercialization of the sport, capitalizing on interest in the World Cup, which engages and mobilizes people all over the world as they root for their respective national teams. Premier teams such as Manchester United, Real Madrid, and FC Barcelona have fanatical global fan bases and are readily distinguishable by their jerseys, symbols, and styles of play. The biggest stars, similar to those of the NBA, are elevated to iconic or cult status.

During the match between Mexico and South Africa at the 2010 FIFA World Cup in South Africa, a fan blows his vuvuzela horn while decked out in the colors of South Africa.

The same interplay of global and local forces in other global scapes is at work in soccer. Whereas the world's top professional soccer leagues and the center of FIFA's power are located in Europe, top players come from all over. This process has had some important and intriguing effects. To begin with, teams in the Global South have suffered from the loss of some of their very best local players to elite teams across Europe in the premier leagues. These players have been lured by high salaries, the promise of broad exposure, and other benefits.[45] National teams competing in the World Cup and other championship events have worked to facilitate the relocation of talented players as a means of recruitment.

The globalization of the game has enabled certain players to attain levels of mobility and wealth that would not be possible otherwise. Yet, globalization has also produced its share of challenges. Soccer has traditionally been an important source of local and national identity. The styles of play of particular clubs may often mirror the cultures of their particular communities, while locals may come to the point where their sense of self is tied closely to the ups and downs of their favorite teams and players. The familiar sight of enthusiastic fans wrapping themselves in the national flag or covering their bodies with paint in their national colors is as important a part of the overall ritual as the incessant sound of the vuvuzela horns.

While potentially a key force in unifying local communities, soccer team loyalty can also serve as a source of conflict when fans of competing teams react in violent ways to the ups and downs of the game. Globalization of the rosters of these teams can also have a significant effect. The increasing racial diversity of many European teams, for example, has resulted in any number of racially tinged taunts and incidents by fans and players alike. In a few cases, it has even led some to question the representative nature and national character of their very own teams.

HOW DO YOU CONNECT? | **HOW DO YOU PLAY?**

Do you play any team sports?
a. basketball
b. baseball
c. soccer
d. football
e. cricket

Do you watch any sports on television?
a. basketball
b. baseball
c. football
d. soccer
e. cricket
f. tennis
g. golf

Have you ever been to an international sports event?
a. yes
b. no

CONCLUSION: IDENTITY AT THE CROSSROADS

Social and cultural borders can sit on top of and across geographic, political, and economic borders. In any given day, we navigate multiple identities as students, teachers, sons, daughters, workers, and players, but we still find ourselves sharing many commonalities. The world has been drawn closer together in terms of political and economic cooperation as similar interests develop. Cultural integration has created new ground for people to work together. In response to concern over the spread of a common world culture, however, many people across the globe are revisiting their traditional and historical identities. A fear of integration and a perceived need to protect identity raise the potential for conflict. As we will see in the next chapter, the challenges that face individuals across social and cultural borders emerge from these tensions.

KEYConcepts

anthropology 179
assimilation 180
bourgeoisie 177
communists 177
cultural diffusion 180
cultural imperialism 180
cultural relativism 179
culture 172
culture shock 172

deterritorialization 183
enculturation 179
ethnography 179
glocalization 186
homogenization 183
hybridization 183
proletariat 177
psychology 179
sociology 178

TO LEARNMore

Books and Other Print Media

Allan Bairner, *Sport, Nationalism and Globalization: European and North American Perspectives* (Albany: State University of New York Press, 2001).

Bairner takes stock of the state of sports around the world and how it is affected by the forces of globalization.

Benjamin R. Barber, *Jihad vs. McWorld: Terrorism's Challenge to Democracy* (New York: Ballantine Books, 2001).

In this volume, Barber asserts that there are two interdependent forces shaping today's world: religious fundamentalism represented by Jihad, which breaks people apart; and consumer capitalism represented by McWorld, which brings people together.

Dave Eggers, *What Is the What: The Autobiography of Valentino Achak Deng* (San Francisco: McSweeney's, 2006).

This book details Valentino Achak Deng's struggles as a refugee, Lost Boy, and finally resident of the United States, as told to novelist Eggers.

Jan Nederveen Pieterse, *Globalization and Culture: Global Melange* (Lanham MD: Rowman & Littlefield, 2004).

In this book, Pieterse looks forward to the post-McDonaldization era, where a culture of hybridization has new implications for global challenges and cooperation.

Margaret Mead, *Coming of Age in Samoa: A Psychological Study of Primitive Youth for Western Civilization* (Gloucester, MA: Peter Smith, 1961).

Mead's psychological study of what it was like in the 1920s for girls growing up in the primitive culture of the Samoan Islands is a classic in scholarly exploration of perception and cultural identification.

Samuel Huntington, *The Clash of Civilizations and the Remaking of World Order* (New York: Simon & Schuster, 1997).

This widely received and highly controversial book asserts that the greatest threat to peace is the friction between cultural groups.

Websites

Center for World Indigenous Studies (CWIS), www.cwis.org/.

CWIS is an American-based research and education nonprofit focused on the political, social, and economic issues of indigenous peoples worldwide.

Ethnologue: Languages of the World, www.ethnologue.com/web.asp.

Ethnologue is a web-based catalogue of the world's 6,909 known languages.

Global Memory Net (GMNet), www.memorynet.org/.

Supported by the National Science Foundation's International Digital Library program, GMNet is a global digital library aimed to preserve global history, culture, and heritage through its image collections, ranging from antique maps to photos of ethnic groups and places.

United Nations Educational, Scientific and Cultural Organization (UNESCO), www .unesco.org/new/en/.

UNESCO is a specialized agency of the UN that promotes global cooperation through the sharing of education, science, and culture. Its objectives are to strengthen human rights and mutual respect, and to alleviate poverty.

The Valentino Achak Deng Foundation, www.valentinoachakdeng.org/.

The Valentino Achak Deng Foundation is a nonprofit organization dedicated to improving education in South Sudan. Its founder and namesake, Valentino Achak Deng, is the focus of Dave Eggers's semiautobiographical novel, *What Is the What*.

Videos

China Blue (2005).

China Blue is a groundbreaking documentary following the life of 17-year-old Jasmine, a worker in a blue jeans factory in Guangdong, China. It exposes the conditions of laborers in Chinese sweatshops and China's growth as a chief exporter. www .pbs.org/independentlens/chinablue/

Ecuador: Dreamtown—Soccer's Ticket Out (2010).

Produced by Frontline/World, this video tells the story of young Ecuadorian soccer players who see the game as their ticket out of poverty.

The Gods Must Be Crazy (1980).

A classic film from South Africa, *The Gods Must Be Crazy* is an allegory about a Bushman and his first experiences with modern civilization and culture.

Sabah: A Love Story (2005).

This movie is about a Syrian Muslim woman living in Toronto who falls in love with a Canadian man and must come to terms with the clash of cultures.

Thomas L. Friedman Reporting: The Other Side of Outsourcing (2004).

Thomas Friedman, of *The World Is Flat* fame, travels to India to see first-hand the clash between Western and Indian cultures.

Challenges to Identity

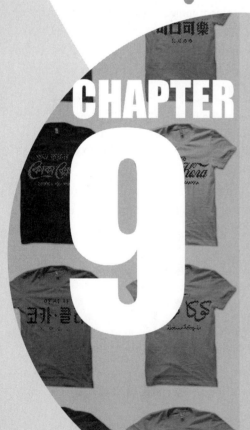

CHAPTER 9

"*People need to see that, far from being an obstacle, the world's diversity of languages, religions and traditions is a great treasure, affording us precious opportunities to recognize ourselves in others.*"

—Youssou N'Dour, Senegalese musician and 2012 presidential candidate[1]

As the ability to cross borders becomes a greater part of our everyday lives, the differences that characterize us have become more pronounced. Both physically and technologically, we are increasingly able to know more about one another, sharing cultures and creating new ones. Youssou N'Dour, a popular world musician from Senegal who was named one of the 100 Most Influential People in the World by *Time Magazine* in 2007 for his activities in the fight against malaria and HIV/AIDS in Africa, supports the positive role that cultural differences can play in bringing peoples of the world together.[2] In a documentary about his life in 2009, he observes that there is a perception that this diversity can divide us as well and is an obstacle that we must overcome. A Starbucks coffee cup series, "The way I see it," has made N'Dour's quote popular. Modernity and technology are *both* bringing people together *and* simultaneously challenging their collective identities to the point that it divides them as well.

These trends of integration and disintegration can be seen in several areas. People who feel threatened by cultural integration frequently try to protect their identities by returning to their religious or ethnic roots. The rise of religious fundamentalism is a

response to this threat. Integration may accentuate ethnic differences as well. Competition for scarce resources can increase tensions between groups. The desire to eliminate the "other" can lead to conflict, civil war, and even ethnic cleansing, where one group seeks to eradicate those who are different, such as the German effort to eradicate Jews during World War II, the Serbian effort in Bosnia to eliminate Muslims in the early 1990s, the Hutu genocide of Tutsis in Rwanda in 1994, and Iraqi attacks against the Kurdish minority under Saddam Hussein that lasted several decades.

When the artificial boundaries that frequently delineate nation-states disintegrate under pressure, states can fail. Unable to meet the basic needs of their people, shaky governments lose their hold on power and ultimately dissolve into chaos. It is a vicious pattern, as state failure exacerbates the conflict, and rather than strengthening identity, further erodes it.

Contributing to these failures is the movement of people across borders. To escape conflict, environmental crises, poverty, and social upheavals, groups of people are forced to leave their homelands. **Migration**, whether in times of war or peace, famine or prosperity, creates opportunities for both the dissemination of culture and its breakdown. As people learn of the cultural practices of the new groups they encounter, they begin to forget the old ways; languages are lost, and a cultural heritage dies.

Overcoming differences and working together requires the ability to see integration in a positive light. Religion, ethnic conflict, and failed states are major forces that can divide people and create clashes over identity. But there are ways to overcome these challenges. Civil society can respect religious laws by recognizing their significance to those who are guided by them. The emergence of truth commissions to reconcile lingering emotions about ethnic conflict and genocide can also provide closure for those who have been most affected by these atrocities. As a result, the ability to move forward for all parties concerned can be greatly facilitated by these simple acts.

A convoy of trucks carry Ethiopian refugees home from Walde, in northern Kenya, in 1993. Elections held the previous year had sharpened divisions among groups from rival political parties and ethnic groups, leading to widespread harassment and violence and causing many to flee the country. Conflicts like these often lead to civil conflict and war, and shape migration patterns worldwide.

THE ROLE OF RELIGION

Throughout history, religion has played a large role in many conflicts. It has been a key factor in people's relationships to one another and their homelands. Some of the earliest known divisions emerged in the fifth century BCE from the philosophical views of Confucius, Confucianism, and Lao-tzu, whose writings formed the basis of Taoism. Early Christians were pitted against Jews as Christianity was founded in the first and second centuries. Religious divisions in India between Hindus and Muslims date to the early 700s and continue today. During the Crusades of the Middle Ages (1095–1291) Christians fought against Muslims for control of lands that both groups considered holy, particularly Jerusalem. In 1920, differences between Protestants and Catholics split Northern Ireland from the rest of the country. Today the focus is on how religion has driven a backlash against globalization, as different groups seek ways to clearly reiterate their identity through the expression of their beliefs.

How religion is understood and applied to daily life is key to how the potential for conflict has developed. For example, there are different interpretations of Islam that have divided Muslim followers. Islam is based on the teaching of the Prophet Muhammad who, in the early seventh century, received several revelations that instructed him to be a messenger of God.[3] These messages urged him to teach that there is only one God to whom all people must commit. Subsequent interpretations of Muhammad's message and disagreements over who should succeed him resulted in a split among Muslims. Two Islamic groups formed—**Sunni** and **Shi'a**. Sunni Muslims believe the rightful successor to the Prophet was Abu Bakr, one of his close companions. A smaller group, the Shi'a, supported the Prophet's son-in-law and cousin, Ali, as the true successor, and their name in Arabic means "partisans of Ali."[4] Both Sunni and Shi'a Muslims adhere to the same holy book, the Quran, for their guiding principles, however, the Shi'a follow a much more literal interpretation of it.

Until the twentieth century, these differences were not a major issue. The intricacies of political conflict within the Islamic world since the 1980s and how it has shaped ruling parties has made the differences between Sunni and Shi'a more pronounced.[5] The vast majority of Muslims identify themselves as Sunni, almost 90 percent, and they have frequently been in conflict with Shi'a authorities. The Shi'a view of Islam is reflected in their political administration. The Iranian revolution in 1979 resulted in Iran being ruled by a Shi'a majority. They have pursued conservative social policies and interpreted globalization as undermining these religious values. In contrast, a Sunni minority ruled Iraq under Saddam Hussein, while the majority of the population considered themselves Shi'a. When the United States overthrew Saddam, the Shi'a saw an opportunity to regain control

migration
the movement of people across borders that reshapes identities, both within states and nations, and between them.

Sunni
Muslims who accept Abu Bakr as the rightful successor to the prophet Muhammad.

Shi'a
Muslims who support the prophet's son-in-law and cousin, Ali, as the true successor.

of the country. Shi'a Muslims now lead the government in Iraq and as a result, Iran and Iraq have more in common politically, a situation that could lead to additional political instability in the region.

Similarly, religious differences in the pursuit of political power have driven unrest in Syria. Syria's leader, Bashar al-Assad, is an Alawite—a member of a Shi'a Muslim sect that represents a small fraction of the country's population. This accounts, in part, for Iran's continuing support for the regime. Syria's Sunni Muslim majority has long felt marginalized politically and looks to enhance its position and power.

Despite their varying interpretations of Islam, many are united in their opposition to Western influence. They believe that reliance should be on Islam as a way of life and to provide a legal system for punishment. Based on the writings of the Prophet Muhammad, **sharia law** applies broadly to how devout Muslims should live their lives. Thirty-five nations, primarily in the Middle East and sub-Saharan Africa, embrace some form of this religious legal system.[6]

Some of these states have based their constitutions on sharia law, including Egypt, Saudi Arabia, Sudan, Afghanistan, Iran, and Pakistan.[7] Others have found themselves internally divided, like Nigeria, where Muslims hold the majority in the northern part of the country and Christians dominate the south. Nigeria's extreme form of sharia law calls for punishments that include stoning

sharia law
a legal system that relies on Islam and applies broadly to how Muslims should live their lives. It includes punishments for crimes that may not be acceptable universally.

MAP 9.1   ISLAMIC LAW

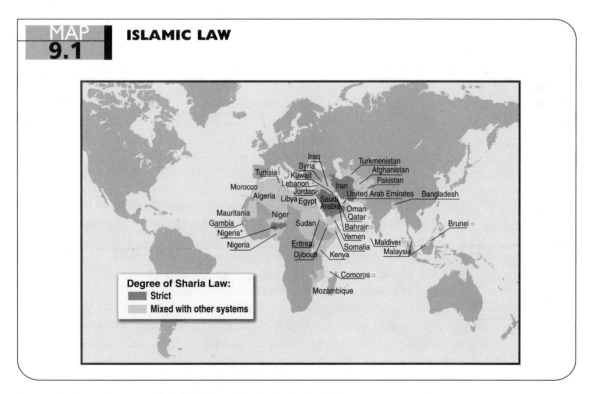

Source: Sarah Glazer, "Sharia Controversy," *CQ Global Researcher* 6, no. 1 (2012): 1–28.

HADD PUNISHMENTS IN 12 MUSLIM COUNTRIES

Stoning, amputation are rarely used.

A handful of predominantly Muslim countries — such as Saudi Arabia, Iran and Pakistan — allow *hadd* punishments (such as stoning or amputation) for serious crimes, but such punishments are rarely carried out.

Hadd punishments in 12 muslim countries

Country	Allowed by Law	Are Used Today
Egypt	No	n/a
Morocco	No	n/a
Saudi Arabia	Yes	No recent stonings, but amputations continue
Sudan	Yes	Has declined significantly
Turkey	No	n/a
Afghanistan	Yes, but with disputed legality	No
Iran	Yes	Irregularly
Pakistan	Yes	No
Indonesia	No	n/a
Malaysia	No, except in certain states	No
Mali	No	No
Nigeria	Yes, in northern states	No stoning; amputations have declined significantly

Source: Sarah Glazer, "Sharia Controversy," *CQ Global Researcher* 6, no. 1 (2012): 1–28.

and amputation, but Nigeria's Christians do not embrace this system.[8] Such *hadd* punishments are rarely carried out due to international scrutiny.

When religious groups use their faith to fuel their nationalistic desires, serious security issues arise. The terrorist organization al-Qaeda finds its roots in the Sunni tradition of Islam. Founded by Osama bin Laden in the late 1980s from the remnants of the Muslim resistance to the Soviet takeover of Afghanistan in 1979, al-Qaeda was formed to directly combat the increasing role of Western influences on Muslim countries and return those nations to more fundamental Islamic regimes.[9] While the death of Osama bin Laden in 2011 weakened the organization, many other groups remain committed to Islamic rule. The Taliban in Afghanistan, Lashkar-e-Taiba in Pakistan, the Abu Sayyaf group in Malaysia and the Philippines, and the Armed Islamic Group in Algeria persist. Since the mid-1990s, al-Qaeda has also reached out to groups loyal to the Shi'a view of Islam, most notably Hezbollah, an Iranian backed Lebanese militia that has exerted influence across the Middle East.

The return to religion as a governing concept is not limited to Islam. While Israel is a secular, democratic state, it is also constituted as a Jewish state based on general acceptance of Judaism. As Israel has evolved, religious tensions have arisen between secular Jews and those who favor more religious views and practices in state policy. These differing perspectives have created conflict within the Israeli population. For example, in Israel there is compulsory military service, but since the beginnings of the state, ultra-Orthodox, very religious Israeli citizens have been exempted. Some Israelis question this practice, given Israel's ongoing security needs in the troubled region.

Israelis also have different attitudes about territories occupied during the 1967 war with neighboring Arab states. Support for continuing occupation is much greater among more orthodox Jews, who see these territories as rightfully theirs from Biblical times. This demand is proffered by the majority of Israelis living in these areas who are Orthodox and see their occupation as a religious mandate.

The role of Christianity in governing across Africa, Europe, and the United States has also been a point of contention. Political parties frequently invoke Christianity as a defining concept, as in the Christian parties that can be found across Europe and the emphasis on Christian values in US political discourse. In the lead-up to the 2012 US presidential race, Republican contenders for their party's nomination divided over Christian issues and the extent to which they should lead political interests. Rick Santorum, a devout Catholic, held conservative positions that were pro-life and anti–gay marriage. Mitt Romney held similar views, but his candidacy brought the Christian debate into a new realm, given Romney's Mormon roots. Mormons identify themselves as Christians but follow their leader John Smith's distinct interpretation of the Bible. Both men sought support from Christian, faith-based voters.

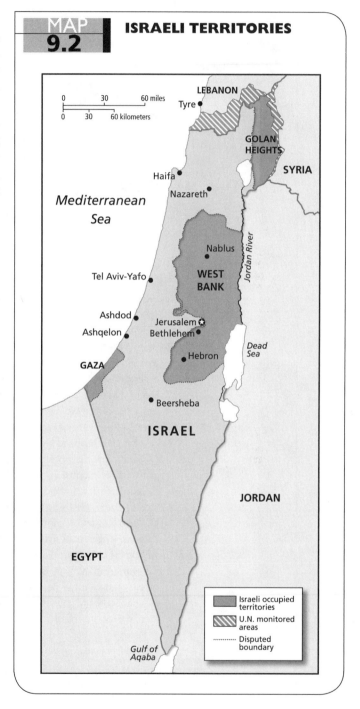

MAP 9.2   ISRAELI TERRITORIES

- Israeli occupied territories
- U.N. monitored areas
- Disputed boundary

SOWhat? RELIGIOUS FREEDOM AND THE HEADSCARF CONTROVERSY

By Asli Akbas, International Studies Master's Graduate, Istanbul, Turkey

As a Turkish woman who wears a headscarf, I think wearing a headscarf is not a detached issue from the freedom of belief or religion. It is one of the religious responsibilities of not only Muslim women but also many women from the traditions of Judaism and Christianity.

According to Islam, religious deeds, including wearing a headscarf, should be done as a person's choice with the intent of pleasing God. To me, any "religious" state institutions should not have the right to force women to wear a headscarf on behalf of God or any secular state should not deprive women from the right to wear a headscarf, thereby interfering in the relationship between religion and people. I think the only way to solve the headscarf issue is to establish or strengthen genuine democratic state institutions that do not use the headscarf issue as a tool of power or repression.

Westerners' negative feeling towards the headscarf is very understandable since many women are forced to wear it in many "Islamic" countries. The Islamic headscarf also brings to mind many events, like the Iranian Revolution and 9/11. But, Islamic clothing or the headscarf should be considered separately from these contexts. Westerners need to accept that there are many different motivations for Muslim women to wear headscarves and most of the women with headscarves wear them by their free will. Moreover, the Western democracies require the kind of thinking that respects all religions and free will.

I had the chance to live in the United States before and after the 9/11 terrorist attacks. Of course, the reactions to my headscarf were different during those two periods. I lived almost three months in New York City before 9/11 and I was practically invisible in the streets. Then, I remember, when I got on the subway two days after 9/11, people were looking at me like I was a danger to them. But this reaction did not last very long. The United States and American people overall have had a culture of genuine democracy for decades, longer than many countries or communities have. Also, this country is more welcoming of foreigners and different religions and cultures than most of the countries in the world, including my country, Turkey. But it is obvious that the American public relies on the media a lot while they make up their thinking about Islam and other cultures.

Specifically, my country, Turkey, is an exceptional Muslim country with its 99 percent Muslim population and being a secular state. In Turkey, the Islamic headscarf in public life has been a very controversial issue for decades. For example, Muslim women in Turkey are banned from wearing the headscarf while they work in state institutions and they cannot work as doctors, lawyers, or teachers in state buildings. Although more than half of the women wear headscarves, we do not have any women representatives wearing headscarves in the Turkish Parliament. In this respect, I felt freer in the United States while I was going to school. Sometimes I feel like an unwanted child of an authoritative parent in Turkey. But I also know that it is my country and people in the street love and respect me although my state does not want to accept me as I am. Turkey is more democratic now than it was a decade ago and I believe that Turkey will be a true democratic country sooner or later.

In some countries, extremist parties have developed as a backlash to the immigration of minorities. They frequently invoke religion as a cover for their opposition to those who are different. This increase is particularly noticeable where large Muslim immigrant populations are changing the face of communities, most recently in European countries. For example, researchers have found that opposition to Muslim immigration in Great Britain has outweighed all other factors in bringing some political groups like the British National Party (BNP) together. Moreover, some of these groups have not ruled out violence as a way of addressing the issue.[10]

ETHNIC CONFLICT

Religious differences have frequently given rise to further divisions along ethnic lines. Ethnicity is a defining principle in identity as determined not only by common linguistic and cultural practices but reinforced by religious adherence as well. The lengths to which cultural groups will go to assure their identity may be considerable. The result can be **ethnic conflict** over disputed territories, which can lead to **ethnic cleansing**, where groups are forcibly removed from an area by violence or deportation. The extreme application of this behavior can result in **genocide**—where one group seeks to deliberately kill members of another group based solely on their national or ethnic differences. The breakup of Yugoslavia in the post–Cold War period and the ethnic conflict that ensued between Serbia and Bosnia illustrates how devastating these conflicts can be.

For decades the strong political leadership of communist war hero Josep Broz, also known as Tito, kept together the various ethnic groups that had been brought together under the Yugoslavian flag after World War II. After he died in 1981, the various states began to secede from the country along ethnic lines. The first two of the six states that had been part of Yugoslavia—Slovenia and Croatia—declared their independence in June 1991. Macedonia followed in January of 1992, and in April of 1992, Bosnia and Herzegovina declared their independence. Montenegro then entered into a federation with Serbia. Serbian nationals claimed a historic relationship to Bosnia and responded to the declaration of independence by its largely Muslim population with attacks that killed an estimated 200,000 people.[11] The leader of Serbia, Slobodan Milosevic, later faced international criminal charges for his part in calling for the genocide, as did military commanders Radovan Karadzic and Ratko Mladic.

Often the blame for ethnic conflict is attributed to the colonial experience and how states were formed. Colonizers bound traditional groups together by artificial geographical delineations that did not correspond to how these communities lived and worked. While some states, such as India and Indonesia, have been able to overcome their differences and survive with a multitude of ethnic

ethnic conflict
when differences in identity are too great to reconcile within state boundaries.

ethnic cleansing
when one group forcibly removes another by violence or deportation.

genocide
the extreme form of ethnic cleansing, where one group seeks to deliberately kill members of another group based solely on their national or ethnic differences.

During the mid-1990s, Yugoslavia witnessed a terrible civil war. Here, Bosnian refugees from Srebrenica arrive at the Tuzla refugee camp in July 1995.

identities, others have not fared as well. This is particularly evident in sub-Saharan Africa, where ethnic differences are exacerbated by other factors, such as the severe lack of basic necessities that pushes groups to rebel against one another.

Tensions have driven violent behavior in the Democratic Republic of the Congo and its neighbor, Rwanda, in central Africa. These countries demonstrate the disasters of the colonial experience and the challenges exacerbated by cultural differences in the effort to unite them under one flag. One of the first places in sub-Saharan Africa to be visited from the Western world, the Congo area was ruled by tribal leaders who led kingdoms in low-lying, mineral-rich lands. The Europeans would use this fertile ground, not only for the minerals but the human potential it represented in the form of slaves. In 1885, European powers met and divided their holdings in Africa, giving a major portion of the land to Belgium and specifically, King Leopold II.[12] Leopold went on to use the land as his personal fiefdom and imposed brutal law upon the native people to achieve his economic ends. He divided the country and posted European officials throughout to assure compliance with his demands.

In literature, the depravity of the crimes committed under Leopold's reign was captured by Joseph Conrad's classic novel, *The Heart of Darkness*. Written in the early part of the twentieth century, it was based on the brutal actions of Europeans in the Congo. Director Francis Ford Coppola adapted the book to reflect the violence of the Vietnam War in his 1979 blockbuster, *Apocalypse Now*. The film's central character, renegade US military officer Walter E. Kurtz, was styled after one of the most notorious European officials in the Congo, Leon Rom, who made the villagers his personal slaves, cutting off the heads of those who did not obey and displaying them on his property.

The atrocities were so great that Belgium offered to buy the Congo back from Leopold in 1908. It reverted to a Belgian colony, and for the next several years, the Congo enjoyed an uneasy peace and successful economic development. Long-simmering ethnic divisions began to boil after the Congo declared independence from Belgium in 1960. Within a few years, these divisions would spill over into a series of conflicts that persist today.

Complicating the situation were both Hutu and Tutsi Rwandans brought into the Congo by the Belgians to meet labor needs and ease demographic pressure in their home country. They changed the face of the Congo while exacerbating longstanding tensions among the various ethnic groups. The minority Tutsis were favored by the Belgians who considered them genetically superior due to their larger skull size and lighter skin, relying on the "science" of eugenics—a now discredited practice that stemmed from the Darwinian notion of survival of the fittest. They were given preferential treatment and dominated the government. In the early 1960s, both countries gained independence from Belgium, but ethnic tensions remained. In Rwanda, decades of delicate political balancing fell apart in 1994 as the Hutus rose up against the minority Tutsis. It is estimated that up to 800,000 people were murdered in just four months. Almost 1.5 million more fled into the Congo, creating large refugee camps that still exist today.[13]

Even today, the tensions from both ethnic unrest and a rising refugee population continue to jeopardize the future of the Democratic Republic of the Congo. Many groups have come into the country (see Map 9.3) as a result of other conflicts. One group of those fleeing includes refugees from the Lord's Resistance Army of Uganda. The virally popular video *KONY 2012* made by the nonprofit Invisible Children organization depicts the violence of the Lord's Resistance Army and its recruitment of child soldiers. The leader of this army, Joseph Kony, has claimed he has a spiritual mission to "purify" the people of Uganda. For the most part, his mission is simply to perpetuate his group and as a result, his activities have crossed into several regions in central Africa, including the Democratic Republic of the Congo.

Child soldiers of the Union des Patriotes Congolais wait for their orders in Bule, Ituri District, Democratic Republic of the Congo (DRC), in December 2007. The DRC contains one of the highest numbers of child soldiers in the world. Many are abducted or recruited by force, and they are often compelled to follow orders under threat of death. Others join armed groups out of desperation. Denied a childhood and often subjected to horrific violence, child soldiers endure one the most appalling of human rights abuses.

FAILED STATES

Under extreme pressure both politically and economically, nation-states have frequently been destroyed by the turmoil of ethnic conflict. While global conflict on a grand scale has diminished since the Cold War ended, ethnic conflict has become so prevalent that the Fund for Peace, a nonprofit organization based in Washington, D.C., that works to prevent violent conflict, estimates two billion people live in countries that cannot survive these tensions.[14] The Democratic Republic of the Congo is one of 10 nation-states on a list of **failed states** and states likely to fail. Failed states are nation-states whose governments can no longer provide political, economic, and social stability.

Two former US government officials, Gerald Helman and Steven Ratner, were the first to use this term. They argue that the commitment to self-determination that was an important part of the United Nations (UN) charter,

failed state
a nation-state whose government can no longer provide political, economic, and social stability.

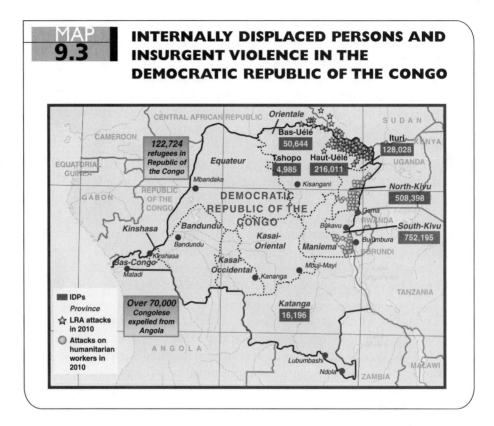

MAP 9.3   INTERNALLY DISPLACED PERSONS AND INSURGENT VIOLENCE IN THE DEMOCRATIC REPUBLIC OF THE CONGO

Source: Josh Kron, "Conflict in Congo," *CQ Global Researcher, 5,* 157–182. (April 5, 2011). Retrieved from http://library.cqpress .com/globalresearcher/document.php?id=cqrglobal2011040513&type=hitlist&PHPSESSID=51l0mqs7trudkqafpoo2j20ks1.

adopted at the end of World War II, as well as the effort to move beyond colonial relationships contributed to this proliferation of states.[15] Many states achieved independence without the requisite infrastructure to support it. While some of these states survived on Cold War infusions of cash from the United States and the Soviet Union as a way to preserve their respective spheres of influence, money was not enough. For example, oil-rich Angola found itself in the crosshairs in the mid-1970s as both East and West sought access to its resources. In the post–Cold War era, as the Soviet Union broke up and the United States cut back on international support, these states were particularly challenged to survive.

The Failed States Index, developed by the Fund for Peace in cooperation with the journal *Foreign Policy,* ranks states on 12 indicators required for stability. The 2012 Index includes 177 states. Table 9.2 delineates the indicators and the 10 most fragile states. The closer the score is to 10, the less stable the state on that indicator. Somalia and Democratic Republic of the Congo

TABLE 9.2 FAILED STATES INDEX DATA 2012

		Total	Demographic Pressures	Refugees and IDPs	Group Grievance	Human Flight	Uneven Development	Poverty and Economic Decline	Legitimacy of the State	Public Services	Human Rights	Security Apparatus	Factionalized Elites	External Intervention
1	Somalia	**114.9**	9.8	10.0	9.6	8.6	8.1	9.7	9.9	9.8	9.9	10.0	9.8	9.8
2	Congo (D. R.)	**111.2**	9.9	9.7	9.3	7.4	8.9	8.8	9.5	9.2	9.7	9.7	9.5	9.6
3	Sudan	**109.4**	8.4	9.9	10.0	8.3	8.8	7.3	9.5	8.5	9.4	9.7	9.9	9.5
N/R	South Sudan	**108.4**	8.4	9.9	10.0	6.4	8.8	7.3	9.1	9.5	9.2	9.7	10.0	10.0
4	Chad	**107.6**	9.3	9.5	9.1	7.7	8.6	8.3	9.8	9.5	9.3	8.9	9.8	7.8
5	Zimbabwe	**106.3**	9.0	8.4	8.7	9.0	8.9	8.9	9.4	9.1	8.9	8.7	9.8	7.5
6	Afghanistan	**106.0**	8.9	9.0	9.4	7.4	8.1	7.7	9.5	8.5	8.5	9.7	9.4	10.0
7	Haiti	**104.9**	9.5	8.1	7.0	8.8	8.6	9.5	9.3	9.3	7.7	8.2	9.0	9.7
8	Yemen	**104.8**	8.8	8.7	9.0	7.0	8.4	8.7	9.1	9.0	8.4	9.7	9.8	8.3
9	Iraq	**104.3**	8.0	8.5	9.7	8.6	8.7	7.7	8.4	7.8	8.3	9.9	9.6	9.0
10	Central African Republic	**103.8**	8.8	9.7	8.5	5.6	8.7	8.0	8.9	9.1	8.5	9.6	9.1	9.3

Notes: *IDP* refers to internally displaced persons—those people who must leave their homes but are still in the country. *Group grievance* refers to those groups who feel they have suffered as victims of ethnic persecution or from political exclusion and whose concerns have not been addressed. *Human flight* refers to those people who choose to leave voluntarily.[16]

Source: The Fund for Peace, Failed States Index, 2012, www.fundforpeace.org/global/?q=fsi-grid2012.

are at the top of the list, followed by Sudan, South Sudan, Chad, and Zimbabwe. Despite ongoing US intervention, Iraq and Afghanistan remain in the top ten, with Central African Republic, Haiti, and Yemen rounding out the group.

As the Index indicates, population pressures, both from migrations into the country and from those fleeing uncertainty, contribute to the instability of these states. Uneven economic development and the general social decline that accompanies it are also factors. The result is that the governing bodies have no legitimacy; they are not able to provide public services or safety to their people. Human rights abuses abound, external intervention is more likely, and those who have the potential to govern—the elites—cannot agree.

The pursuit of political power has frequently intensified ethnic, clan, and tribal differences. In Zimbabwe, for example, there remain deep divisions between the dominant Shona tribe and the minority Ndebele. The two groups united in their pursuit of independence, but when faced with sharing power, their differences became more important. Moreover, those who were able to secure power were more concerned with their own personal interests than stability for all. As a result, the state has spun into a downward spiral that has left it as one of the poorest countries in Africa today.

Formerly part of the larger British colony of Rhodesia, Zimbabwe's move for independence was motivated by both racial and ethnic factors. Initially ruled by a white minority who declared themselves independent from Great Britain in 1965, they were pressured to hold free elections in 1979 by the indigenous majority, and in 1980, current leader Robert Mugabe was elected.[17] Mugabe,

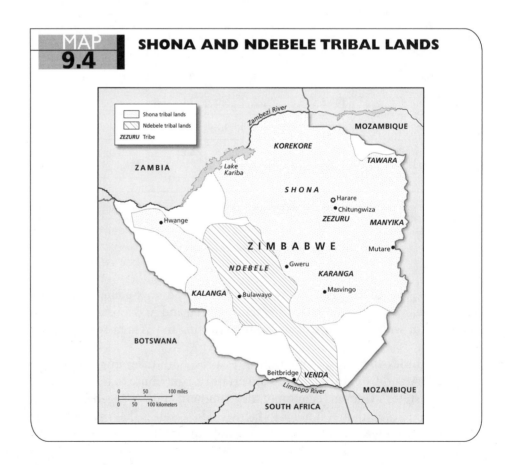

MAP 9.4 SHONA AND NDEBELE TRIBAL LANDS

from the majority Shona tribe, redistributed the lands previously owned by the white farmers, suppressed the other major ethnic group, the Ndebele, and generally destroyed the country. Corruption, economic mismanagement, and his continued instigation of racial antagonism marred his leadership. Despite efforts to share power with opposition leader Morgan Tsvangirai, who comes from the Ndebele tribe and serves as prime minister, the country remains in chaos as Mugabe continues to hold tightly to power through violence and intimidation by forces loyal to him.

At the extreme, other countries have responded to these tensions by simply dividing into separate states. For example, Sudan moved to split into two parts completely, driven by religious differences between the dominant Muslim population to the north and the non-Muslim groups in the south, despite peacekeeping efforts by the UN. Following many years of conflict, South Sudan was recognized as an independent state in July 2011 by the UN. The leader of northern Sudan, Omar al-Bashir, an accused war criminal for the years in which his government engaged in the massacre in the Darfur region, did not accept this division. Some question whether a similar solution will be inevitable in Iraq as it also remains divided by religious and ethnic differences. When the United States leaves, will the various groups strive for peaceful coexistence or break into separate states? This is a particularly sensitive case for the Sunni Muslims and Kurdish ethnic group that have been caught in the crossfire.

WHAT CAN BE DONE?

The challenges created when cultures clash are not easily solved. An initial step toward ending conflict is to recognize that culture and human identity underlie both the problems and their solutions. The early development of languages, practices, and other aspects of the world's diverse cultures was a product of the isolation of groups of people from one another. It is not surprising, then, that a degree of cultural fusion has occurred as transportation and communications have improved, bringing people of various societies into ever more frequent contact. Global cultural differences have decreased substantially since the 1960s in many meaningful ways. Globalization is contributing to these connections, but the coexistence of different groups is still very much an issue.

While religious differences are more readily understood in today's interconnected world, a key question is whether they can coexist. In the United Kingdom, the government allows local Sharia councils to rule on Muslim family issues. For example, a Muslim woman may be one of several wives not legally recognized by British law who therefore cannot get a civil divorce in England. The Sharia council can grant her a religious divorce, providing for some type of financial restitution and the freedom to marry again.[18] The number of these councils has grown significantly in Great Britain, to more than 80 by some estimates, and they provide a much-needed service for new immigrants who find themselves and their relationships outside the realm of the official courts. Though there has been some concern that these practices are creating a parallel legal system, proponents argue they perform an important function.

An informal way that ethnic conflicts are moving toward resolution is the development of **truth and reconciliation commissions**. These groups bring together those who have committed the most heinous crimes against one another and seek to develop an understanding that will allow them to let go of their hatred. The effort began in Latin America in the 1980s to address the crimes of military dictators and move beyond them. These commissions have since moved on to South Africa and Rwanda. The Truth and Reconciliation Commission of South Africa formed in 1995 was the first such commission to include the concept of reconciliation in its mandate.

In Rwanda, these efforts have been very active through a process called *gacaca* or "justice on the grass."[19] Built upon practices that predate the colonial experience, gacaca trials have frequently allowed people to know more about what really happened to their relatives and provide a framework for healing. This short excerpt from a gacaca trial gives a flavor of the proceedings, as a Hutu deputy minister of the former governing party is accused of conspiracy in the killing of Tutsis. He claims that despite his high position in the party's organization, he could not support its Committee de Crise, as that would have meant killing his wife!

> He was called to testify about the Committee de Crise and its work. "The actions of the Committee de Crise were to discriminate against non-Hutu tribes." He tells of his job as deputy minister. "I was not among those who worked with the Committee de Crise, but they would call me to advise them as a minister. People supreme to me would send letters telling me to encourage Hutus to kill. Because I avoided encouraging the Interhama, I was removed from my job, forced out of my position as deputy minister."
>
> "My superiors would write letters telling me to order killings—but I didn't do it. By not doing so, I was no longer a minister." "I was not among the Committee de Crise, except the day I got fired. I went to Gisenya (a town in the west, on Lake Kiva, near the Congo border) to find food for my children until I heard that the army of the RPF had reached Kigali, so I returned. I was not among those responsible."

truth and reconciliation commissions
groups formed to bring together those who have suffered under ethnic conflict to resolve their differences and move forward.

gacaca
an effort in Rwanda dating back to pre-colonial times when differences were addressed informally through "justice on the grass" to bring healing.

Judge: "Didn't you support the Committee de Crise financially?"

"No"

"Why not?"

"I knew they supported the ex-President and Interhama. My wife is Tutsi tribe. They wanted to kill Tutsis, and my wife would have been killed. I didn't want to join and I didn't support them." [20]

In March 2005, a Rwandan genocide suspect stands trial before a community court, also known as a gacaca, in Zivu, southern Rwanda. In 1994, Rwanda set up the community courts in an effort to speed up trials for 63,000 people in detention on charges of taking part in the slaughter of more than 500,000 minority Tutsis and political moderates from the Hutu majority.

The significance of this excerpt lies in the real people who fight one another when ethnic conflict occurs. It can pit family members against one another, resulting in tragedy beyond measure.

The fact remains that people are crossing new borders every day and constantly refining their individual and collective identity. Where your ancestors came from meant something in the past and still matters today. However, the diffusion of cultural practices and accelerated migration are affecting how people define themselves. This definition is becoming less tied to a particular physical space. New ways of interacting are needed that recognize our similarities while appreciating our differences. As former UN secretary general Kofi Annan observed in his 2001 Nobel Prize lecture,

> People of different religions and cultures live side by side in almost every part of the world, and most of us have overlapping identities which unite us with very different groups. We can love what we are, without hating what—and who—we are not. We can thrive in our own tradition, even as we learn from others, and come to respect their teachings.[21]

The ability to work together may require new forms of cooperation that transcend traditional borders.

KEY Concepts

ethnic cleansing 201
ethnic conflict 201
failed state 203
gacaca 208
genocide 201

migration 196
sharia law 197
Shi'a 196
Sunni 196
truth and reconciliation commissions 208

TO LEARN More

Books and Other Print Media

Adam Hochschild, *King Leopold's Ghost: A Story of Greed, Terror, and Heroism in Colonial Africa* (Boston: Mariner Books, 1999).

This volume details the pursuit of colonial lands by King Leopold II of Belgium, his reign of terror over what are now the Democratic Republic of the Congo and the Republic of the Congo, and its lasting aftermath.

Chinua Achebe, *Things Fall Apart* (Portsmouth, NH: Heinemann Educational, 1996).

This classic by Achebe explores life in a Nigerian village as European colonialists arrive, come to power, and ultimately forever change social order. Achebe paints a troubled picture of precolonial Nigerian culture on the cusp of its destruction.

John Esposito, *Unholy War: Terror in the Name of Islam* (New York: Oxford University Press, 2003).

Written in the wake of the 9/11 terrorist attacks, this book offers a solid historical and philosophical account of Islam, jihad, and terrorism.

Joseph Conrad, *Heart of Darkness* (Mineola, NY: Dover, 1990).

Conrad's most famous work, first published in 1899, this novella exposes the darker side of colonization and the cruelty with which the Europeans treated native Africans.

Latifa, *My Forbidden Face: Growing Up Under the Taliban: A Young Woman's Story* (New York: Miramax Books, 2003).

Latifa recounts her experiences as a young woman growing up in Afghanistan when the Taliban took over, denying the people of Afghanistan basic rights and freedoms and spreading fear.

Paul Hopper, *Understanding Cultural Globalization* (Cambridge, UK: Polity Press, 2007).

Hopper explores the various cultural issues brought on by globalization and introduces new critical ways of examining culture.

Websites

Failed States Index, www.fundforpeace.org/global/?q=fsi-grid2012.

The Fund for Peace, a sustainable security nonprofit, publishes the Failed States Index annually. On the interactive website version, users can explore the world's states and the fund's indicators.

International Rescue Committee (IRC), www.rescue.org/

The IRC is an international relief organization that aids people impacted by humanitarian crises across the world.

Religions, www.bbc.co.uk/religion/religions/.

This website, produced by the British Broadcasting Corporation, provides an overview of major religions in the world today.

United Nations High Commissioner for Refugees (UNHCR), www.unhcr.org.

The UNHCR was established by the UN General Assembly in 1950 to assist refugees around the world.

Women's Refugee Committee (WRC), http://womensrefugeecommission.org/about.

A branch of the IRC, the WRC advocates for refugees and internally displaced women and children.

Videos

Apocalypse Now (1979).

This Vietnam War–era movie, based loosely on Joseph Conrad's *Heart of Darkness,* illustrates the psychological damage that can be inflicted by war.

The Devil Came on Horseback (2007).

Based on the book by Brian Steidle, this documentary tells the story of Steidle and his time working for the African Union as a photographer in Darfur.

Hotel Rwanda (2004).

This is the true story of a hotel manager who offered shelter to refugees during the massacre that occurred in 1994.

KONY 2012 (2012).

A short film created by the group Invisible Children, *KONY 2012* aims to inform the public of the war crimes perpetuated by Uganda's Joseph Kony and the Lord's Resistance Army.

Seoul Train (2005).

Seoul Train is a critically acclaimed documentary about North Korean defectors seeking freedom by escaping into China. www.pbs.org/independentlens/seoultrain/

UNHCR Videos, www.youtube.com/user/unhcr.

The UNHCR YouTube channel features hundreds of videos covering just as many topics.

Managing the World

Cooperation at the Global Level

CHAPTER 10

"We have heard clear warnings from Nature that humanity is arrogantly pushing her boundaries, just as we have heard societies demanding human rights and justice, opportunities and decent jobs, affordable health care and energy access. Responding successfully will require decision-makers from across the environmental, social and economic divides coming together to create the future we all want."

—Olav Kjørven, UN Assistant Secretary-General and UNDP Bureau of Development Policy Director, 2012[1]

In 1992, the UN Conference on Environment and Development (UNCED), or Earth Summit, provided a working blueprint for dealing with an array of economic and environmental issues. In 2012, the Rio+20 conference marked the Earth Summit's twentieth anniversary. That same year, leaders from government and civil society, development experts, and UN officials gathered for the first Human Development Forum in Istanbul to identify global policies that would guide the Rio+20 UN Conference on Sustainable Development. Norwegian UN officer Olav Kjørven's remarks at the meeting emphasized that cooperation remains critical to addressing the issues confronting us in the global arena today. The most serious contemporary problems—poverty, disease, human rights, and environmental concerns—are global in nature and cannot be solved by individual countries alone.

The barriers to cooperation, however, are the very same borders these issues cross. National borders protect states' interests first and foremost. Economic relationships may frequently dictate behavior, when the bottom line is emphasized over public good. Social and cultural barriers may prevent groups and people from working together when protection of their identity clashes with the need for cooperation. As a result, the world remains divided on many of the critical issues it must face, and its people must identify new ways to manage their relationships.

Historically, the management of states' behavior toward one another has been addressed through international law and the creation of international organizations. As the modern state system emerged in the seventeenth century, there was a need to regulate relationships among countries and identify ways to collaborate. International law developed to formalize operating rules among states that had been based on customary practices. Organizations were formed through written agreements, as treaties were negotiated, to serve the greater good. Philosophically, these organizations grew out of the liberal intellectual tradition we explored in regard to political borders in Chapter 4, but they were bound by the nation-states that constituted their membership. As a result, nonstate actors have emerged to provide other ways to work across borders.

Today, international organizations (IOs) have become influential actors on the world stage. There are two basic types of international organizations: **intergovernmental organizations (IGOs)**, like the United Nations (UN), whose members are governments or states, and **nongovernmental organizations (NGOs)**, whose members are individuals. IGOs revolve around three common objectives: (1) to provide a means of cooperation for states, (2) to provide a forum in which decisions on cooperation can be reached and the administrative machinery to carry them out, and (3) to provide multiple channels of communication among governments by offering areas of accommodation and easy access when problems arise.[2] In contrast, nongovernmental organizations (NGOs) provide a means for cooperation among individuals on issues of

Here, rainforests burn in the Amazon, representing the growing threat of deforestation and climate change. This is not only a local environmental problem—something to be solved in Brazil—but one that affects the entire globe and requires coordination and cooperation at all levels.

intergovernmental organizations (IGOs)

formal, international public bodies whose members are nation-states.

nongovernmental organizations (NGOs)

formal, nonprofit, voluntary organizations whose memberships are composed of individuals organized around specific issues or common concerns.

supranational entities

international organizations that operate beyond the national boundaries of their member states.

international law

the regulation of relations among sovereign states emerging from customary practices.

common concern. Their strength lies in their ability to communicate their interests without being bound by governmental constraints. The creation of these new **supranational entities**—that is, organizations that exist beyond member state boundaries—has grown exponentially since the end of World War II.

This chapter explores the role of international law and organizations in promoting cooperation and providing effective management at the global level. As the world becomes more interdependent, there is a greater role that IGOs and NGOs can play in addressing the problems facing the international system. The need for regulation of many issues across borders and beyond states' interests requires institutional structures that can both address the problems and represent all interests. IGOs and NGOs may well be better suited to this job than are nations-states alone. They can provide important structures and forums for essential research and information about global problems.

DEFINING THE GLOBAL ORDER: INTERNATIONAL LAW AND ORGANIZATIONS

The evolution of international organizations is directly related to the development of international law, as it established the framework within which international organizations operate. Prior to the seventeenth century, customary practices defined the relations between states. They extended from rules of engagement on the battlefield that respected noncombatants to accepted practices for ships passing on the high seas. At the beginning of the 1600s, however, changes in the European political system prompted the development of **international law** in tandem with the sovereign state system to create a framework for cooperation. Concurrent with the Thirty Years War (1618–1648), European thinkers attempted to address the legal responsibilities among states—what principles should guide behavior and how they would be measured. Of critical importance were the writings of Hugo Grotius.

Hugo Grotius was a Dutchman, born in 1583, who by the age of 16 had become the lawyer for the Dutch East India Trading Company—the largest trading company of its time. When Grotius was about 15, an Italian-born professor of civil law at Oxford named Gentilus published a groundbreaking work called *De Jure Belli* (*Laws of War)* that separated international law from ethics and theology—defining international law as a distinct new branch of law. Intrigued by Gentilus's writings, in 1625 Grotius penned his own monumental piece, *De Jure Belli Ac Pacis—On the Law of War and Peace.*

Grotius rejected the notion that the principles of the law of nature came directly from divine authority; instead, he argued these principles should come from universal reason. He believed the customary practices of nations (*jus gentium,* also called *jus voluntarium*) as they related to one another must guide the law. His distinctions would go on to form the basis of **positivism**—the theory and development of international law based on the practice of states and conduct of international relations as evidenced by custom or treaties. But it would take until the nineteenth century for the concepts to really guide behavior. In the following excerpt from his *On the Law of War and Peace,* Grotius details his understanding of this critical distinction between natural and manmade law.

positivism

the theory and development of international law based on the practice of states and conduct of international relations as evidenced by custom or treaties.

Grotius's book was an important contribution to the evolution of the political order that was emerging. Its successful reception was driven by Grotius's prestigious legal background combined with renown from his position with the Dutch East India Trading Company. Over time, his work would be regarded as the first comprehensive basic treatise on international law. The important distinctions he had made and the extent to which they would inform the future have resulted in Grotius being considered the father of modern international law.

The Creation of International Organizations

Not long after Grotius's writings, in 1648, a system of independent states developed that depended on a balance of power to keep the peace. At the outset, these new states relied on the relationships that had provided kingdoms with protection for generations—alliances. States were able to maintain a balance of power by the use of force in conjunction with their allies against their enemies. But there was a broader desire for peace to be maintained through a more formal cooperative struc-

Natural right is the dictate of right reason, shewing the moral turpitude, or moral necessity, of any act from its agreement or disagreement with a rational nature, and consequently that such an act is either forbidden or commanded by God, the author of nature. The actions, upon which such a dictate is given, are either binding or unlawful in themselves, and therefore necessarily understood to be commanded or forbidden by God. This mark distinguishes natural right, not only from human law, but from the law, which God himself has been pleased to reveal, called, by some, the voluntary divine right, which does not command or forbid things in themselves either binding or unlawful, but makes them unlawful by its prohibition, and binding by its command.[3]

IN THEIR OWN WORDS | **Hugo Grotius**

ture, and the **Concert of Europe** was formed in 1815. This collaborative group was created to enforce decisions that had been reached at the Congress of Vienna, where the European powers who had defeated Napoleon—Russia, Prussia, Britain, and Austria—gathered to negotiate the peace. The Concert formalized the alliances that emerged from the Congress, served as an enforcement mechanism for the agreements that had been made, and sought to

Concert of Europe
a formal collaborative group formed in 1815 to enforce the decisions reached at the Congress of Vienna.

promote a cooperative international environment. It hobbled along until the 1870s, undermined early on by the nationalistic tendencies of the member parties.

A second effort at international cooperation came with the International Peace Conferences of 1899 and 1907. Convened by Russia at the request of Tsar Nicholas II, 26 governments gathered to meet in the political capital of the Netherlands, The Hague, to develop a series of agreements to enforce a broader peace and reduce armaments.[4] Most notably, the First Hague Peace Conference, as it came to be known, created a Permanent Court of Arbitration for resolution of conflict among states. The United States sought to push this body to a world court system at the Second Hague Conference but failed. A third conference was scheduled for 1915 but never met due to the outbreak of World War I.

The Peace Palace, shown above, is the seat of the International Court of Justice (ICJ) in The Hague, the Netherlands. The ICJ is one of many international organizations designed to facilitate global cooperation.

While the conferences may have failed in their broad objectives, they were successful in the creation of public international unions, the first permanent intergovernmental organizations (IGOs) that addressed practical areas of exchange—communication, transportation, international trade regulation, standards of weight and measure, and so on.[5] World War I made it evident that greater international cooperation was needed for global peace as well. Politically, the origins of modern IGOs came from US president Woodrow Wilson's idealism, the negotiated peace in the Treaty of Versailles, and the creation of the League of Nations. President Wilson recognized the need for a new global order as World War I was coming to an end. He elaborated on this vision in his Fourteen Point Speech to Congress on January 9, 1918: "A general association of nations must be formed under specific covenants for the purpose of affording mutual guarantees of political independence and territorial integrity to great and small states alike."[6] Wilson sought the creation of a platform for international cooperation.

The Treaty of Versailles of 1919 that negotiated the peace for World War I included the creation of the League of Nations. From the outset, however, its success was limited by the lack of US participation. Though the idea had come from the American president and was included in the peace pact, the US Senate refused to ratify the treaty, favoring an isolationist stance. The League went forward, without the United States, as the first formal international organization to foster the goals of promoting peace and preventing war. It consisted of a Council, Assembly, and Secretariat. An international court, known as the

Permanent Court, was separate from the organization. Membership was by invitation, and headquarters were established in Geneva, Switzerland, in November 1920. The first general assembly of the League held that month had representatives from 41 nations.

Continued global conflict and the United States' failure to join the organization weakened the League. The United States subsequently tried to lend its support to the League through its backing of the **Kellogg Briand Pact**. Introduced to the United States in 1927 by Aristide Briand, the French foreign minister, as a proposed treaty between the two countries, US president Calvin Coolidge and Secretary of State Frank B. Kellogg wanted to expand its scope as a general pact against war. The final document was signed by 15 countries in 1928 and subsequently ratified by 62 states to outlaw war as a means of conflict resolution.[7] Such assistance was too little, too late for the League of Nations. With no way to enforce Kellogg Briand, its signatories saw armed aggression by the Japanese in Manchuria and the Italians in Ethiopia, followed by Hitler and the Nazi party's emergence in Germany in the early 1930s. The actions of these belligerent states ultimately undermined both the League of Nations and the Kellogg Briand Pact.

The outbreak of World War II and the early cooperation between the United States and Great Britain with the creation of the **Atlantic Charter**, a joint declaration that detailed the position of the two countries in regard to the growing conflict and a desire for peace, laid the foundation for the conception of the UN following the end of the war. The United States realized that its strategy of disengagement had failed it between the world wars and that the evolving world order after World War II would require it to take an active role. A series of meetings among the Allies, beginning in 1942 and culminating in San Francisco in 1945, led to the creation of the UN.

Kellogg Briand Pact
a multinational pact that outlawed war as a means of conflict resolution.

Atlantic Charter
a joint declaration by the United States and Great Britain that detailed the position of the two countries relative to World War II and their goals for postwar peace.

THE UNITED NATIONS

The political nature of the international system after World War II limited the UN and frustrated the efforts of founding UN secretary general Tryvge Lie of Norway (1946–1952). In response to the political order that emerged after World War II, as well as compromises made in the finalization of the founding UN Charter, five states—the United States, United Kingdom, France, China, and Russia—received special status as permanent members of the Security Council, the policy making body of the UN (Figure 10.1). Ten additional seats were allocated for nonpermanent members that represent geographical diversity and rotate every two years. The permanent members of the Security Council have a veto power that ensures any policy considered by the group that is not in their

Published by the United Nations Department of Public Information DPI/2470 rev.2—11-36429—October 2011

FIGURE 10.1 UNITED NATIONS ORGANIZATIONAL CHART

The United Nations System

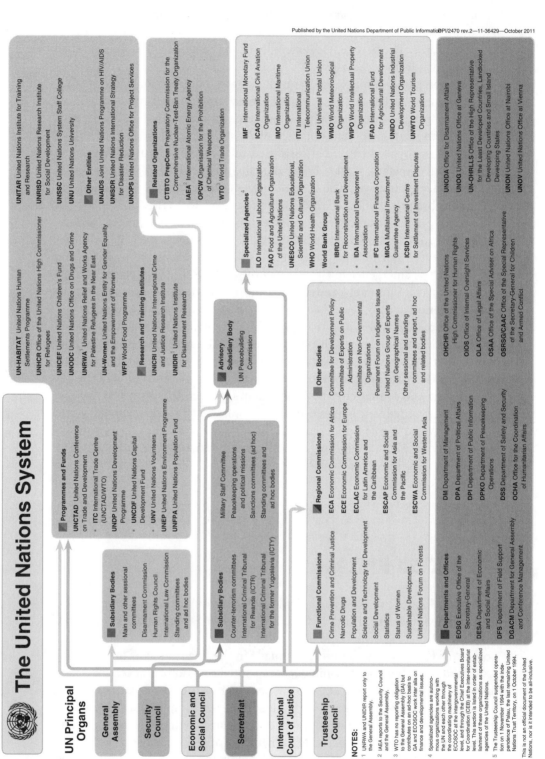

UN Principal Organs

General Assembly

Security Council

Economic and Social Council

Secretariat

International Court of Justice

Trusteeship Council[5]

Subsidiary Bodies
Main and other sessional committees
Disarmament Commission
Human Rights Council
International Law Commission
Standing committees and ad hoc bodies

Subsidiary Bodies
Counter-terrorism committees
International Criminal Tribunal for Rwanda (ICTR)
International Criminal Tribunal for the former Yugoslavia (ICTY)
Military Staff Committee
Peacekeeping operations and political missions
Sanctions committees (ad hoc)
Standing committees and ad hoc bodies

Functional Commissions
Crime Prevention and Criminal Justice
Narcotic Drugs
Population and Development
Science and Technology for Development
Social Development
Statistics
Status of Women
Sustainable Development
United Nations Forum on Forests

Regional Commissions
ECA Economic Commission for Africa
ECE Economic Commission for Europe
ECLAC Economic Commission for Latin America and the Caribbean
ESCAP Economic and Social Commission for Asia and the Pacific
ESCWA Economic and Social Commission for Western Asia

Other Bodies
Committee for Development Policy
Committee of Experts on Public Administration
Committee on Non-Governmental Organizations
Permanent Forum on Indigenous Issues
United Nations Group of Experts on Geographical Names
Other sessional and standing committees and expert, ad hoc and related bodies

Departments and Offices
EOSG Executive Office of the Secretary-General
DESA Department of Economic and Social Affairs
DFS Department of Field Support
DGACM Department for General Assembly and Conference Management
DM Department of Management
DPA Department of Political Affairs
DPI Department of Public Information
DPKO Department of Peacekeeping Operations
DSS Department of Safety and Security
OCHA Office for the Coordination of Humanitarian Affairs
OHCHR Office of the United Nations High Commissioner for Human Rights
OIOS Office of Internal Oversight Services
OLA Office of Legal Affairs
OSAA Office of the Special Adviser on Africa
OSRSG/CAAC Office of the Special Representative of the Secretary-General for Children and Armed Conflict

Programmes and Funds
UNCTAD United Nations Conference on Trade and Development
• ITC International Trade Centre (UNCTAD/WTO)
UNDP United Nations Development Programme
• UNCDF United Nations Capital Development Fund
• UNV United Nations Volunteers
UNEP United Nations Environment Programme
UNFPA United Nations Population Fund

UN-HABITAT United Nations Human Settlements Programme
UNHCR Office of the United Nations High Commissioner for Refugees
UNICEF United Nations Children's Fund
UNODC United Nations Office on Drugs and Crime
UNRWA United Nations Relief and Works Agency for Palestine Refugees in the Near East
UN-Women United Nations Entity for Gender Equality and the Empowerment of Women
WFP World Food Programme

Research and Training Institutes
UNICRI United Nations Interregional Crime and Justice Research Institute
UNIDIR United Nations Institute for Disarmament Research

UNITAR United Nations Institute for Training and Research
UNRISD United Nations Research Institute for Social Development
UNSSC United Nations System Staff College
UNU United Nations University

Other Entities
UNAIDS Joint United Nations Programme on HIV/AIDS
UNISDR United Nations International Strategy for Disaster Reduction
UNOPS United Nations Office for Project Services

Advisory Subsidiary Body
UN Peacebuilding Commission

Related Organizations
CTBTO PrepCom Preparatory Commission for the Comprehensive Nuclear-Test-Ban Treaty Organization
IAEA[2] International Atomic Energy Agency
OPCW Organisation for the Prohibition of Chemical Weapons
WTO[3] World Trade Organization

Specialized Agencies[4]
ILO International Labour Organization
FAO Food and Agriculture Organization of the United Nations
UNESCO United Nations Educational, Scientific and Cultural Organization
WHO World Health Organization
World Bank Group
• IBRD International Bank for Reconstruction and Development
• IDA International Development Association
• IFC International Finance Corporation
• MIGA Multilateral Investment Guarantee Agency
• ICSID International Centre for Settlement of Investment Disputes

IMF International Monetary Fund
ICAO International Civil Aviation Organization
IMO International Maritime Organization
ITU International Telecommunication Union
UPU Universal Postal Union
WMO World Meteorological Organization
WIPO World Intellectual Property Organization
IFAD International Fund for Agricultural Development
UNIDO United Nations Industrial Development Organization
UNWTO World Tourism Organization

UNODA Office for Disarmament Affairs
UNOG United Nations Office at Geneva
UN-OHRLLS Office of the High Representative for the Least Developed Countries, Landlocked Developing Countries and Small Island Developing States
UNON United Nations Office at Nairobi
UNOV United Nations Office at Vienna

NOTES:
[1] UNRWA and UNIDIR report only to the General Assembly.
[2] IAEA reports to the Security Council and the General Assembly.
[3] WTO has no reporting obligation to the General Assembly (GA) but contributes on an ad-hoc basis to GA and ECOSOC work inter alia on finance and developmental issues.
[4] Specialized agencies are autonomous organizations working with the UN and each other through the coordinating machinery of ECOSOC at the intergovernmental level, and through the Chief Executives Board for Coordination (CEB) at the inter-secretariat level. This section is listed in order of establishment of these organizations as specialized agencies of the United Nations.
[5] The Trusteeship Council suspended operation on 1 November 1994 with the independence of Palau, the last remaining United Nations Trust Territory, on 1 October 1994.

This is not an official document of the United Nations, nor is it intended to be all-inclusive.

Source: The United Nations Department of Information.

country's interest can be overridden by a permanent member's negative vote. The Security Council requires nine affirmative votes to take action, and the "Big Five" permanent members frequently used their veto power, especially the Soviet Union as the Cold War evolved. It used its veto power 79 times in the first 10 years of the UN's existence, compared to France who used it twice and China who used it only once.[8]

Secretary General Dag Hammarskjold of Sweden (1953–1961) established the character of the organization by professionalizing the Secretariat—the body that runs the UN's day-to-day business under the secretary general's stewardship—and moving the UN forward as an institution of peace. Known for his "quiet diplomacy," Hammarskjold fostered the idea of UN presence as a method of preventing conflict. During his second five-year term, to which the General Assembly had appointed him unanimously, he died in a plane crash while on a diplomatic mission in Africa. He was posthumously awarded the Nobel Peace Prize in 1961 for his contributions.

The General Assembly is the representative body of the UN. All states that have ratified the UN Convention are members of this body. The General Assembly supervises UN activities, can decide on financial matters, and elects the nonpermanent members of the Security Council and the secretary general, with the recommendation of the Security Council. It may also play a role in amending or revising the Charter of the UN. Despite its broad membership, the General Assembly lacks policymaking power. Only the Security Council has this authority. Nevertheless, the UN remains the most universal forum for the consideration of critical issues confronting the global system today.

Other organs of the UN include the Economic and Social Council (ECOSOC) which prepares studies and reports on economic and social concerns. ECOSOC consists of 54 members, elected by the General Assembly for three-year terms with 18 national members elected each year. Their influence is broadly felt through their administration of the majority of human and financial resources of the UN, which include fourteen specialized agencies, nine functional commissions, and five regional commissions.[9] The list of the commissions illustrates their breadth and depth:[10]

ECOSOC Functional Commissions

- Statistical Commission
- Commission on Population and Development
- Commission for Social Development
- Commission on the Status of Women
- Commission on Narcotic Drugs
- Commission on Crime Prevention and Criminal Justice
- Commission on Science and Technology for Development

- Commission on Sustainable Development
- Forum on Forests

ECOSOC Regional Commissions

- Economic Commission for Africa (ECA)
- Economic and Social Commission for Asia and the Pacific (ESCAP)
- Economic Commission for Europe (ECE)
- Economic Commission for Latin America and the Caribbean (ECLAC)
- Economic and Social Commission for Western Asia (ESCWA)

The International Court of Justice (ICJ) is the legal branch of the UN and is composed of 15 judges, who are elected by the General Assembly and Security Council for nine-year terms. There cannot be more than one judge from any country. Member states involved in a case must agree to the court's authority before it hears the case. It is also limited in its judgments, as it has no coercive power, such as fines or jail sentences, to enforce its decisions. As a result, it depends on nation-states to voluntarily comply with its rulings. The ICJ pronouncement in the case of Nicaragua vs. the United States is considered a critical landmark in this regard.[11]

In 1984, Nicaragua brought a case before the ICJ charging the United States with interfering in its internal affairs. Nicaragua's ruling party—the Marxist Sandinistas—estimated the United States had provided supplies to an opposition force of more than 10,000 troops—the Contras—along Nicaragua's border with Honduras. The Contras were deemed responsible for laying mines in Nicaragua's harbors using materials supplied by the United States. The United States would not agree to the case being heard by the court, but the court went ahead anyway—extending its compulsory jurisdiction, a right the United States had supported since the creation of the ICJ in 1946. The case was considered, and in 1986, the United States was found guilty of violating the sovereignty of Nicaragua. The court ordered that the United States pay reparations of $300 million to Nicaragua. The United States refused to abide by the decision, however, arguing it did not accept the court's jurisdiction in this case because of its historical relationship with Latin America and Nicaragua specifically.

Finally, in terms of the organs of the UN, the Trusteeship Council was established to administer trust territories that existed when the UN was created to facilitate their transition to independence. The council's members were the five permanent members of the Security Council. The work of this body from its original charge was completed in 1994. It remains available to meet should a need arise.

Since its origins in the post–World War II period, the UN has grown considerably—from 51 founding members to 193 today. However, the permanent members of the Security Council have resisted expanding their membership. Given their growing influence in the international system politically and economically, Germany and Japan have actively sought this distinction. Brazil and India have also argued for inclusion based on their increasing global status and geographic location as part of the Global South. Another approach for changing the membership has been to simply expand the number of nonpermanent members of this group. Any of these actions would require amending the UN Charter, which is a very onerous process. Two-thirds of all members of the General Assembly must adopt and ratify the amendment, and all permanent members of the Security Council must be on board. Attaining such a level of comprehensive agreement is highly unlikely.

> **HOW DO YOU CONNECT?** | **HAVE YOU EVER BEEN TO THE UN?**
>
> Have you ever visited the UN Headquarters in New York City or any other UN offices abroad?
>
> a. yes
>
> b. no
>
> Have you ever interned for the UN?
>
> a. yes
>
> b. no

INTERDEPENDENCE AND REGIONAL INTERGOVERNMENTAL ORGANIZATIONS

As the UN emerged from the trials and tribulations of the World War II, its most critical objective was peace. Other international organizations that developed were influenced by functional considerations—the need to cooperate on many different levels. These organizations have become more critical as countries find themselves increasingly interdependent. Their reliance upon one another, particularly in economic terms, has created new structures to facilitate cooperation. International relations scholars Robert Keohane and Joseph Nye describe this relationship as one of **complex interdependence**, where states have come to realize how sensitive and vulnerable they are in relation to others.[12] In this context, *sensitivity* refers to how quickly changes in one country may affect another, while *vulnerability* explores the range of options available for response and their cost. To strengthen state relationships in this regard, one response has been the creation of regional organizations.

Regional organizations are composed of nation-states based on their geographical proximity and common interests. Some of the more broad-based associations that have followed from the UN example include the Organization of American States (OAS), the Arab League, the African Union (AU), and the Association of Southeast Asian Nations (ASEAN). The Charter of the OAS, the

complex interdependence

the interdependent relationship that exists between states such that variation in one state's behavior significantly affects the other.

world's oldest regional organization (dating from the First International Conference of American States in 1889 and formalized in 1948), is reflective of the broad objectives of these organizations. Article 2 of the OAS charter identifies the following "essential purposes:"

a) To strengthen the peace and security of the continent;

b) To promote and consolidate representative democracy, with due respect for the principle of nonintervention;

c) To prevent possible causes of difficulties and to ensure the pacific settlement of disputes that may arise among the Member States;

d) To provide for common action on the part of those States in the event of aggression;

e) To seek the solution of political, juridical, and economic problems that may arise among them;

f) To promote, by cooperative action, their economic, social, and cultural development;

g) To eradicate extreme poverty, which constitutes an obstacle to the full democratic development of the peoples of the hemisphere; and

h) To achieve an effective limitation of conventional weapons that will make it possible to devote the largest amount of resources to the economic and social development of the Member States.[13]

Similar language can be found in the operating principles of the other organizations.

Regional organizations have also been created for very specific purposes. These include modern-day alliances, like the North Atlantic Treaty Organization, which formed for security purposes after World War II and today includes a broad range of states from both Eastern and Western Europe and the United States. Similarly, economic needs have brought states together; perhaps the best-known organization in this regard is the European Union (EU) introduced in Chapter 6.

Through a series of multilateral treaties, the EU has expanded to become a major regional power. It is integrated on multiple levels, including a common passport and currency—the euro. Today, more than 25 of Europe's 49 countries are members of the EU (Table 10.1), an association of states that has developed its own parliament, laws, and coordinated trade policies. Six countries are candidate members: Croatia, Macedonia, Iceland, Montenegro, Serbia, and Turkey. Their candidacy has forced the EU to look more closely at itself and the practices of its member states. A critical issue has been the extent to which the membership can be more broadly defined. The EU requires member states to adhere to a set of economic policies. There is some concern that these measures are so strict as to deny membership to states that may be fundamentally different culturally from long-standing members of the EU. Even current member states have questioned the capacity of the organization to sustain necessary levels of cooperation, in light of the difficulties of reconciling the interests of its stronger and weaker states. Despite these challenges, the European Union remains the model for economic integration and one not easily duplicated by other regional bodies.

TABLE 10.1	EUROPEAN UNION MEMBERS (2012)		
Country	Entry	Country	Entry
Austria	1995	Latvia	2004
Belgium	1957	Lithuania	2004
Bulgaria	2007	Luxembourg	1957
Cyprus	2004	Malta	2004
Czech Rep.	2004	Netherlands	1957
Denmark	1973	Poland	2004
Estonia	2004	Portugal	1986
Finland	1995	Romania	2007
France	1957	Slovakia	2004
Germany	1957	Slovenia	2004
Greece	1981	Spain	1986
Hungary	2004	Sweden	1995
Ireland	1973	United Kingdom	1973
Italy	1957		

Source: "Countries," official website of the European Union, http://europa.eu/about-eu/countries/index_en.htm.

NONGOVERNMENTAL ORGANIZATIONS

When Lost Boy Valentino Achak, who we met at the outset of Chapter 8, fled civil war–torn Sudan in the late 1980s, he was helped along the way in his journey to the United States by nongovernmental organizations (NGOs). Organizations like the International Committee of the Red Cross provided basic necessities for the boys and girls who found their way to refugee camps in Kenya. The International Rescue Committee facilitated the relocation of many of these young people to safe havens, with many of them ending up in the United States. Both organizations continue to work closely with refugees of war, famine, and environmental disasters all over the world. Their operations are funded by voluntary contributions from both individuals and countries.

Such NGOs, the other broad type of international organizations, are the fastest-growing entities in the world today. Their ability to bring together people driven by common interests on specific issues gives them great flexibility. Frequently, they are best situated to perform some of the functions of IGOs when the IGOs' member states are stymied by their own interests, lack the necessary expertise, or are unable or unwilling to cooperate. Increasingly, the spread of information about events around the world, such as the Sudan crisis, has brought the plight of distant nations into the collective psyche, and it is NGOs that have responded.

A Red Cross plane and truck deliver supplies in Afghanistan, May 14, 2010.

civil society

nongovernmental organizations that are active in public life through the expression of their members' values and interests.

The history of NGOs is tied to the development of individual activism on critical issues. Today, we use the term **civil society** to describe these actors. The World Bank offers a good definition of civil society that is commonly accepted: "the wide array of non-governmental and not-for-profit organizations that have a presence in public life, expressing the interests and values of their members or others, based on ethical, cultural, political, scientific, religious or philanthropic considerations."[14] One of the first international NGOs was the Anti-Slavery Society, which had its origins in England but came to America in 1833 with the founding of the American Anti-Slavery Society in Philadelphia.[15] Their ranks expanded rapidly in the United States, supported by the abolitionist movement, as their membership grew to more than 250,000 in just five years.[16] By 1874, there were 32 similar organizations with international linkages. Over the next 40 years, NGOs grew steadily, with 1,083 reported in 1914 at the outset of World War I.

NGOs developed rapidly in the post–World War II period, as the UN Charter explicitly recognized them as contributing bodies to the work of ECOSOC. As a result, the World Bank observes that by the mid-1970s, NGOs were significant actors in the field of international development. This trend has continued as the participation by NGOs and, specifically, civil society organizations (CSOs) in World Bank–funded projects increased from 21 percent in fiscal year 1990 to an estimated 81 percent in fiscal year 2009.[17]

Today, the UN recognizes more than 3,500 NGOs as having consultative status to ECOSOC. This status gives NGOs the ability to participate in UN international conferences on a broad range of issues, such as gender, sustainable development, small arms, and human rights.[18] The United Nations Education, Scientific, and Cultural Organization (UNESCO) uses three criteria to distinguish the different types of NGOs in its civil society network: country or region of origin, field of activity, and organizational type. This last can include anything from academic groups, such as the American Anthropological Association, to representatives of indigenous people, such as the Aboriginal and Torres Strait Islander Commission from Australia (Figure 10.2).[19]

We can think about NGOs today in terms of their political advocacy, economic and development activities, environmental activities, and humanitarian affairs. An example of a political-advocacy NGO would be Amnesty International.

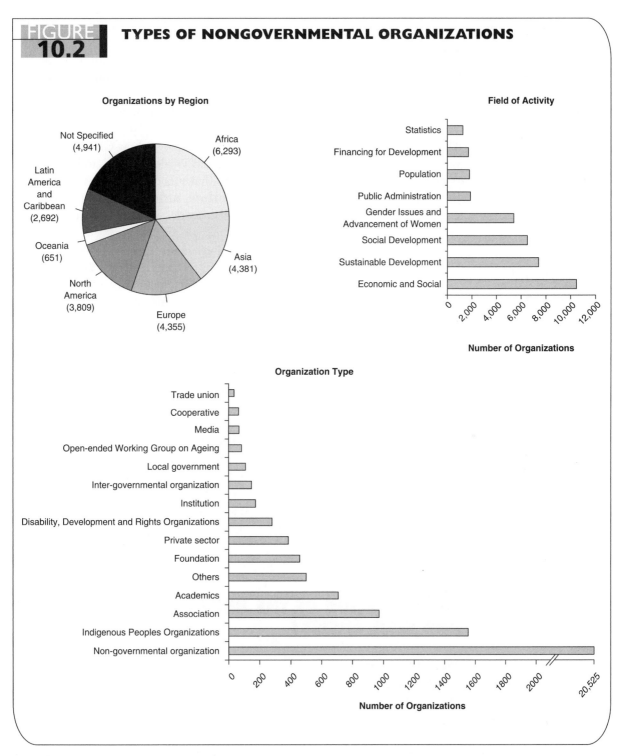

Source: "Integrated Civil Society Organizations System," NGO Branch, United Nations Department of Economic and Social Affairs, http://esango.un.org/civilsociety/login.do.

HOW DO YOU CONNECT?

WHAT IS YOUR EXPERIENCE WITH NGOs?

Do you belong to any NGOs?

a. yes

b. no

What kind of NGOs interest you?

a. political (Amnesty International, etc.)

b. environmental (World Wildlife Fund, etc.)

c. humanitarian (Doctors without Borders, etc.)

Have you ever traveled to another country to work with an NGO?

a. yes

b. no

Where?

a. Africa

b. Asia

c. Middle East

d. Europe

e. North America

f. South America

g. Latin America

h. Australia

Formed in 1961, it advocates for the political freedoms of citizens regardless of their country's orientation. Its annual report has become an important part of the human rights dialogue. Economic development work is carried on by a broad range of NGOs, from religion-based groups, such as Catholic Relief or Lutheran World Services, to large operations that subcontract with national governments, such as CARE International, which works in over 80 countries to address global poverty.[20]

Many environmental NGOs are well known, ranging from the World Wildlife Fund, which promotes conservation of nature, to some of the more politically active organizations like Greenpeace and Sea Shepherd Conservation Society. The Sea Shepherd's mission to preserve marine wildlife and particularly to prevent the harvesting of whales by Japanese whalers has been captured in the popular Animal Planet television series, *Whale Wars*. Humanitarian NGOs seek to provide direct services to those in need. For example, Medecins Sans Frontieres—Doctors without Borders—works in almost 70 countries all over the world in response to health threats from violence, poor medical care, and natural disasters.

THE EVOLUTION OF THE UNITED NATIONS AND CIVIL SOCIETY

Formed in response to the horrific tragedies of World War II, which saw tremendous loss of life and territorial devastation, the UN's founding premise was to promote peace. In keeping with its organizing principles, its objective in intervening in conflict was simply to maintain and enforce agreements among previously warring parties. Forces would be formed with soldiers from member states to act as peacekeepers. The famous blue helmets they would wear and the clear labeling of their support vehicles was to keep them out of harm's way as they provided an important service. In the post–Cold War world, however, the UN has been called upon for a broader mission—to be a peacemaker. In the early 1990s, UN peacekeeping forces frequently found themselves in positions that required armed intervention, a response well outside the mandate of their mission; yet, the circumstances demanded more aggressive action if only for the survival of the troops deployed. For example, with the breakup of the Soviet Union and Yugoslavia, new states sought assistance from the UN to protect their independence. In 2012, the UN had 17 peacekeeping missions throughout the world, as follows:

UN Peace Keeping Missions (2012)

Africa

- UN Mission in the Republic of South Sudan (UNMISS)
- UN Interim Security Force for Abyei (UNISFA)
- UN Organization Stabilization Mission in the Democratic Republic of the Congo (MONUSCO)
- African Union–UN Hybrid Operation in Darfur (UNAMID)
- UN Operation in Côte d'Ivoire (UNOCI)
- UN Mission in Liberia (UNMIL)
- UN Mission for the Referendum in Western Sahara (MINURSO)

Americas

- UN Stabilization Mission in Haiti (MINUSTAH)

Asia and the Pacific

- UN Integrated Mission in Timor-Leste (UNMIT)
- UN Military Observer Group in India and Pakistan (UNMOGIP)
- UN Assistance Mission in Afghanistan (UNAMA)*

Europe

- UN Peacekeeping Force in Cyprus (UNFICYP)
- UN Interim Administration Mission in Kosovo (UNMIK)

Middle East

- UN Supervision Mission in Syria (UNSMIS)
- UN Disengagement Observer Force (UNDOF)
- UN Interim Force in Lebanon (UNIFIL)
- UN Truce Supervision Organization (UNTSO)

* Please note UNAMA is a special political mission, directed and supported by the Department of Peacekeeping Operations (DPKO) of the UN.

Source: "Current Peacekeeping Operations," United Nations Peacekeeping, www.un.org/en/peacekeeping/operations/current.shtml.

French UN troops are shown being deployed in 1992.

peacebuilding
the UN in conjunction with humanitarian NGOs organizes elections, reorganizes police forces, provides relief services, and participates in any other activities that are needed to create a viable state.

In 1992, the UN responded to the need to enhance its organizational capabilities in this area by creating the Department of Political Affairs to coordinate peacemaking and preventive diplomacy. Headed by the under-secretary-general for political affairs, today this organization has over 250 staff at UN headquarters in New York and supervises over 1,700 staff in Africa, Asia, and the Middle East. It has offices in Burundi, Guinea-Bissau, the Central African Republic, and Sierra Leone.[21] As a result, the UN has shifted even further from peacekeeping and peacemaking to **peacebuilding**.[22] In conjunction with humanitarian NGOs, the UN sets up elections, reorganizes police forces, provides relief services, and participates in any other activities that are needed to create a viable state. It tracks global political developments, advises both the UN secretary general and peace envoys in the field on best courses of action to attain peace, and provides service to states directly in the electoral process.

But the UN staff are outsiders to the conflicts they address, and many question their right to intervene as well as their capacity to bring about a lasting peace. NGOs can sometimes bridge the gap between the UN and the local people. They are frequently better situated than the UN to provide many of the services needed. They operate closer to the people, at a grassroots level, and can be more nimble in their response to humanitarian crises. Political unrest in North Africa and the Middle East—the Arab Spring—that has included Tunisia, Morocco, Egypt, Libya, and Syria led UN Secretary General Ban Ki-moon to emphasize the important role NGOs can play for countries in transition.[23] In a meeting with representatives of the NGO community in October 2011, the secretary general cited their efforts in disarmament and sustainable development as examples of successes where partnerships with the UN had been significant. He noted that civil society's engagement with the creation of new governments would be critical:

> There can be no success without a healthy civil society. Please, do your part. Help these women's groups, social media activists, human rights defenders and others to take their rightful place in society—in government, in parliament, in every public institution.[24]

PRO/CON
Can outsiders build lasting peace?

PRO	CON
Vanessa Wyeth Vanessa Wyeth, Research Fellow, Peacebuilding and State Fragility, International Peace Institute. Written for *CQ Global Researcher*, June 2011	**John Caulker** John Caulker, Founder, Fambul Tok*, Sierra Leone Written for *CQ Global Researcher*, June 2011

Since Liberia's civil war ended in 2003, the country has benefited from strong domestic leadership, billions of dollars in international support and the presence of 15,000 U.N. peacekeepers. As Liberia prepares for elections later this year, it is widely hailed as a peacebuilding success story.

Other countries have not been so lucky. In the Democratic Republic of Congo and Haiti, years of peacekeeping and billions of aid dollars have not led to peace and stability. Even cases once hailed as successes warrant a closer look. Recently, international observers warned that Bosnia faces a political crisis that threatens to undo the peace that has lasted there since 1995. The murder rate in Guatemala is now higher than it was at the height of the civil war in the 1980s.

Peacebuilding is a high-stakes political enterprise: It is complex and messy and requires tough compromises. And it takes a long time: The World Bank estimates that it takes at least a generation to move a country from where war-torn Liberia was in 2003 to where peaceful Malawi is today.

That requires domestic political leadership, the restoration of trust between citizens and their institutions and the slow work of transforming political processes so societal conflict can be managed without violence. Peace

(Continued on next page)

Ultimately, peace is sustainable when it is internalized by those who experienced the conflict. They are in a better position to identify lasting solutions to the post-conflict problems of rebuilding state and society. As the saying goes: "He who wears it feels it." Within communities, local people know who can credibly lead a process, for example, and who instills confidence. This is only achieved when those people lead the peacebuilding process. The process and methodology must be designed, owned, led and contextualized by the people.

Effective peacebuilding involves constructive dialogue between all relevant stakeholders with the aim of finding a lasting solution to the underlying problems. Trust and respect are prerequisites for such open dialogue. These values can only be built by the parties themselves, not by outsiders.

Externally designed and led mechanisms can include, for example, truth and reconciliation commissions, special tribunals and support for the police and military in various forms. But these will not likely be sufficient to develop a lasting peace. Looking at Sierra Leone and Liberia as case studies, the ongoing threats to the fragile peace are clear, because people at the grassroots were not consulted in designing transitional justice institutions suitable

(Continued on next page)

PRO/CON (Continued)
Can outsiders build lasting peace?

PRO	CON
cannot be imposed from the outside, as the United States has learned in Afghanistan and Iraq. Lasting peace can be built only from within.	for their contexts. The ownership then becomes questionable. Consequently, even with all the resources put into these countries there is little to show as a result of outside contributions toward lasting peace.
But resources matter. How can a country establish the rule of law if it can't pay its judges, let alone its police and prison guards? How can a government win the confidence of citizens who can't feed their families? International aid alone is not enough, but it can be essential, especially in the short- and medium-term. In 2008, for example, international aid to Liberia was worth 180 percent of the country's gross national income. International actors also provide crucial political support, technical assistance, training and security in the form of peacekeeping. Without international support for mediation efforts, there often would be no peace to build.	But by understanding the importance of the kind of dialogue I have described, and by providing the support needed to make it happen, outsiders can play a valuable facilitative role, if they work alongside local leadership.
	In three-and-a-half years running *Fambul Tok* in Sierra Leone, I've seen ordinary people come up with creative approaches and follow their own route toward lasting peace—a process that comes when both victim and perpetrator acknowledge what went wrong, the dignity of victims is restored and the offenders seize the opportunity to apologize and to explain why they committed atrocities.
We still have much to learn about the impact—good and bad, intended and unintended—of international peacebuilding assistance and the complex political dynamics of war and peace. At the end of the day, peacebuilding contains a catch-22: Peace cannot be built from the outside. But it also might not survive without outside support.	A process that allows this to happen can play an important role in reknitting the fabric of community that is torn by war. My hope is that *Fambul Tok*'s example will open the way for others to work in similar ways.

* Krio for "family talk"

Source: Jina Moore, "Peacebuilding: Can It Stabilize Countries after the Fighting Stops?" *CQ Global Researcher 5* (June 21, 2011): 291–314.

WHERE Do You Stand?

1. Do you think the UN can perform a viable role in the resolution of these types of conflict?
2. Are NGOs better suited to address these issues? Why or why not?

THE EXPANSION OF INTERNATIONAL LAW AND THE INTERNATIONAL CRIMINAL COURT

Concurrent with the growth of UN activities, the post–Cold War period has also been marked by the progressive expansion of international law. The broadening of the concepts of rule of law and the means for enforcement through the creation of more binding statutes has resulted in more cases going to the International Court of Justice than ever before. While case decisions that are made by the court do not constitute precedents in the same way that they do in the US court system, they do inform how the law is applied in the future. Most notably, the development of international criminal law has followed this pattern.

Within just decades of the Nazi atrocities of World War II, the world would learn of Rwandans and Serbians actively committing crimes of genocide. At first, the UN responded with the creation of ad hoc courts to address the crimes on an international basis. By 1994, there was a growing international consensus that the time had come for a permanent international criminal court. Based on the Nuremberg war crime trials of Nazis and the ad hoc courts, the International Law Commission of the UN drafted a statute calling for the creation of the International Criminal Court (ICC).

In 1998, the UN General Assembly adopted the ICC's Rome Statute, which details the governing principles of the court. Citing sovereign national interests, the United States has never ratified the statute. However, international support is widespread, and by 2002, enough states (60) had ratified the statute to make the ICC a fully functioning institution. By 2012, 121 countries had signed on to that statute.[25]

The ICC has been critical to a new level of attention given to violations of the Geneva Convention, which outlines the rule of war and engagement, as well as to the Universal Declaration of Human Rights. Since ratification, the court has considered 16 cases across seven countries: Uganda, the Democratic Republic of the Congo, Sudan, Central African Republic, Kenya, Libya, and Cote d'Ivoire.[26] Despite widespread international support for the court, the United States has chosen not to participate in its cases, again citing sovereign national interests. This lack of US support as well as the court's limited enforcement capabilities raises the question as to whether it can be truly effective in deterring crimes against humanity.

CONCLUSION: COMPLIANCE AND ENFORCEMENT

Despite the reluctance of states to formally commit to some far-reaching agreements, like the formation of the ICC, there are broad areas of agreement on the laws governing the seas, outer space, and the Arctic. Treaties are the instruments of global cooperation and may be bilateral or multilateral. Since World War II, agreement and compliance have been found in major multilateral international treaties that involve the global commons and seek to protect the "common heritage of man." The following list includes some of the most important and their functions:

1959: Antarctic Treaty System—governs the protection of the Antarctic

1968: Nuclear Nonproliferation Treaty—prevents the spread of nuclear weapons and promotes the goal of nuclear disarmament

1979: Moon Treaty—governs the activities of states on the moon

1992: UN Framework on Convention on Climate Change—seeks cooperation on the prevention of climate change

1994: UN Convention on the Law of the Sea—governs territorial claims to the oceans and rules on the high seas

1994: UN Convention to Combat Desertification—seeks agreement to assist those in dry areas and prevent further destruction

1996: Comprehensive Nuclear Test Ban Treaty—bans nuclear testing on earth for both military and civilian purposes

It may take member states of IGOs years to negotiate treaties and accords like these that govern specific areas. Then these treaties still require ratification from the signatories to go into force. For any IGO, the greatest limiting factor can in fact be its member states. The United States is noteworthy in this regard. For example, in the treaties that have been negotiated to cover the Law of the Sea and to enact a Comprehensive Nuclear Test-Ban Treaty, the United States has signed the relevant treaties but the US Senate has not ratified them, citing "national interests." In these cases, international decisions become driven by domestic issues, and states put their own perceived national self-interest ahead of the greater global good. These barriers are porous, however, as countries like the United States may still generally abide by the principles of the agreements, even if they do not ratify them.

Clearly, the increasing severity of global issues that defy national boundaries, such as poverty, infectious disease, and human rights, requires cooperation on the global level. The evolution of international law and its role in regulating the international arena, coupled with the activism of IGOs and NGOs, is critical. The extent to which these organizations can help states overcome their differences will have a significant impact on the well-being not only of the planet, but of the people who live here. Their effectiveness in addressing some of the challenges that face the international system is explored in Chapter 11.

KEY Concepts

Atlantic Charter 217
civil society 224
complex interdependence 221
Concert of Europe 216
intergovernmental
organizations (IGOs) 214
international law 214

Kellogg Briand Pact 217
nongovernmental
organizations (NGOs) 214
peacebuilding 228
positivism 215
supranational 214

TO LEARN More

Books and Other Print Media

Carla Del Ponte, *Madame Prosecutor: Confrontations with Humanity's Worst Criminals and the Culture of Impunity* (New York: Other Press, 2009).

In these memoirs, Del Ponte recounts her role as the International Criminal Tribunal's chief prosecutor for former Yugoslavia and Rwanda, bringing justice to those who had committed acts of genocide in those countries.

David Scheffer, *All the Missing Souls: A Personal History of the War Crimes Tribunals* (Princeton, NJ: Princeton University Press, 2011).

Writing from a US-centric view, Scheffer writes about the Rwandan genocide and Srebrenica massacre; his role in establishing criminal tribunals for war crimes in the Balkans, Cambodia, Sierra Leone, and Rwanda; and the subsequent creation of the International Criminal Court.

Leymah Gbowee, *Mighty Be Our Powers: How Sisterhood, Prayer, and Sex Changed a Nation at War* (New York: Beast Books, 2011).

In this harrowing memoir, 2011 Nobel laureate Leymah Gbowee recalls Liberia's civil war and how she led a group of women in healing and reconciliation, protest and peacebuilding. She details the critical role Liberian women played in brokering peace and empowering their sisters in other West African nations.

Paul Diehl and Brian Frederking, eds., *The Politics of Global Governance: International Organizations in an Interdependent World,* 4th ed. (Boulder, CO: Lynne Rienner, 2010).

This edited volume takes a broad look through many different lenses at the activities of international organizations.

Rye Barcott, *It Happened on the Way to War* (New York: Bloomsbury USA, 2011).

This book tells the story of a college student's journeys, which resulted in his creation of the NGO Carolina for Kibera (which helps a slum in Nairobi, Kenya), as well as his experiences as a US Marine.

Wangari Muta Maathai, *Unbowed* (New York: Knopf, 2006).

> Unbowed is the memoir of the late Nobel laureate Wangari Muta Maathai, who established the Green Belt Movement in Kenya. Maathai fought not only for the environment but also for women's rights and democracy.

Websites

Green Belt Movement, www.greenbeltmovement.org/.

> The official website of the Green Belt Movement features information on its tree-planting, advocacy, and community empowerment programs.

International Criminal Court (ICC), www.icc-cpi.int/.

> The official website for the ICC contains information about the court itself as well as its cases, including those in Rwanda, the Democratic Republic of the Congo, and Darfur, Sudan.

International Criminal Tribunal for Rwanda (ICTR), www.unictr.org/.

> The ICTR was created in 1994 by the UN to seek resolution to serious violations of humanitarian law that occurred in Rwanda. The website features a daily journal and proceedings and a database of cases brought to the tribunal.

Union of International Associations (UIA), www.uia.be/.

> The UIA is a Brussels-based institute that documents and researches international organizations and publishes the *Yearbook of International Organizations* and the *Encyclopedia of World Problems and Human Potential*.

United Nations, www.un.org/.

> The main website for the UN features information on peace and security, development, human rights, humanitarian affairs, and international law, as well as publications, databases, maps, and other documents and information on internships and employment.

Videos

I Came to Testify (2011).

> *I Came to Testify* explores the story of 16 women prisoners of the Serbs during the war in the Balkans in the 1990s who testified against their captors in an international court of law. www.pbs.org/wnet/women-war-and-peace/full-episodes/i-came-to-testify/

International Law and Global Governance (2011).

> This series discusses the role of international law in the global system and explores the interaction between domestic and international law. http://ffh.films.com/id/23790/International_Law_and_Global_Governance.htm.

Pray the Devil Back to Hell (2008).

Pray the Devil Back to Hell is a documentary focusing on the role of women in the peacemaking process in Liberia who protested against the war crimes of former dictator Charles Taylor. www.pbs.org/wnet/women-war-and-peace/full-episodes/pray-the-devil-back-to-hell/.

United Nations Association Film Festival (UNAFF), www.unaff.org/.

UNAFF is an international documentary film festival focusing on human rights, the environment, women's issues, health, and other topics. The website contains links to past festivals and its featured films.

United Nations Videos, www.youtube.com/user/unitednations.

The official YouTube channel of the UN features daily videos and messages from the secretary general as well as special videos on a range of topics, including disarmament, the Millennium Development Goals, and peacemaking.

Challenges to Cooperation

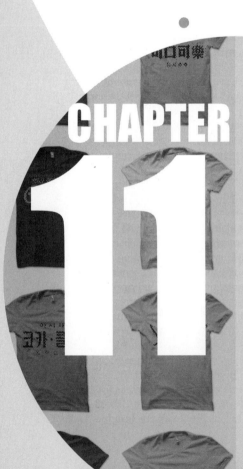

The poverty and despair identified by UN Secretary-General Ban Ki-moon in his opening remarks to the Millennium Development Goals Summit in September 2010 reflect the very personal challenges facing the people of the world today that require global cooperation. They are the most elementary in nature—food, shelter, safe water to drink, and basic medical care. There is great disparity between those whose needs are met and those whose needs are not. If we agree with Jean Jacques Rousseau's eighteenth-century philosophical notion of a social contract, emphasizing the mutual responsibility of people, we must try to work together. Rousseau argued that under this social contract, citizens are "all equal, all can prescribe what all should do, but no one has a right to demand that another shall do what he does not do himself."[2] In today's world, conventions of cooperation help to assure this equality and that people provide for one another.

International organizations have met people's urgent needs, but they are frequently limited by their size and the diversity of members' interests. States are driven by their own self-interests and are often unwilling to cooperate. Nongovernmental organizations

> *"There is more to do for the mother who watches her children go to bed hungry—a scandal played out a billion times each and every night. There is more to do for the young girl weighed down with wood or water when instead she should be in school."*
>
> —Ban Ki-moon, Secretary General of the United Nations, 2010[1]

(NGOs) have stepped in when they can, but their efforts are constrained by resources, and they require greater coordination to be more effective. Some scholars have gone so far as to say that there should be a system of global governance, where international cooperation is regulated on a grand scale using both existing organizations, like the United Nations (UN), and new regulatory mechanisms. There may also be new ways for individuals to act together to make a difference globally.

When UN Secretary General Kofi Annan came into office in 1997, he vowed to revitalize the UN to make it more responsive to the world that had evolved since its inception. Toward the end of his first term, in April 2000, he issued a Millennium Report, entitled "We the Peoples: The Role of the United Nations in the 21st Century," calling on member states to commit themselves to an action plan for ending poverty and inequality, improving education, reducing the number of people suffering from HIV/AIDS, safeguarding the environment, and protecting people from deadly conflict and violence.[3] Introducing the report at a press conference, Annan noted, "If the United Nations does not attempt to chart a course for the world's peoples in the first decades of the new millennium, who will?"[4]

The Millennium Report formed the basis of the Millennium Declaration adopted by heads of state at the Millennium Summit, held at UN headquarters in September 2000. The document identified eight **millennium development goals (MDGs)** that seek to improve the lives of people all over the globe by 2015, as follows:[5]

1. Eradicate extreme hunger and poverty.

2. Achieve universal primary education.

3. Promote gender equality and empower women.

4. Reduce child mortality.

5. Improve maternal health.

In 1991, refugees wait in a food and water distribution line during a famine at Kebri Beyeh, a refugee camp for Ethiopians and Somalis in Ethiopia. A bag marked "wheat," a donation from the United States, sits nearby. The civil war and overthrow of the government in May 1991 caused a disruption in famine relief aid to Ethiopia, causing many to go hungry.

millennium development goals (MDGs)

eight goals adopted by the UN to address inequity in the international system with the objective to improve people's lives globally by 2015.

6. Combat HIV/AIDS, malaria, and other diseases.

7. Ensure environmental sustainability.

8. Develop a global partnership for development.

The UN Department of Economic and Social Affairs has evaluated these goals annually since their inception. The reports assess the progress to date using information from international organizations both within and outside the UN system.[6] By their account, some regions have done better meeting the goals than others. Specifically, the countries of North Africa and Asia are on track to cutting extreme poverty in half in their countries by the year 2015 and achieving many of the social goals. A second group of countries in West Asia, Latin America, and the Caribbean has made good headway toward some individual goals, such as universal primary education, but remains behind in poverty reduction. The third group of countries, found mostly in sub-Saharan Africa, has shown little, if any, substantive improvement on most of the goals. A closer look at the progress made thus far in relation to three broad areas addressed by the goals—poverty, disease, and human rights—demonstrates the critical needs as well as the difficulties that limit cooperation.

POVERTY

One of the most important objectives of the millennium development goals is the eradication of hunger and poverty. **Poverty** refers to the want of food, access to clean water, shelter, health care, education, employment, and general well-being. A critical factor underlying political conflict and economic disparity, it defines social distinctions and can undermine cultures, as members of particular groups may be forced to spread across vast distances in response to conflict, natural disasters, and the most basic needs of food and water. The World Bank estimates that 1.4 billion people globally live on less than $1.25 a day.[7] Chronic hunger is experienced by 27 percent of the population in sub-Saharan Africa and 20 percent in Asia.[8] Over 780 million people lack access to clean water sources. This limitation is coupled with insufficient sanitation facilities, toilets, and bathrooms, with 37 percent of the developing world or 2.5 billion people are affected.[9] Map 0.4 at the front of the book shows the disproportionate distribution of this inequality, as it lies primarily south of the equator.

Poverty prevents many people from being able to appreciate the broader issues of the world in which they live. Writing in 1943, psychologist Abraham Maslow argued that individuals experience five levels of need that affect their motivation and participation in society (Figure 11.1).[10] The first level consists of

poverty

want of food, clean water, shelter, health care, education, employment, and general well-being.

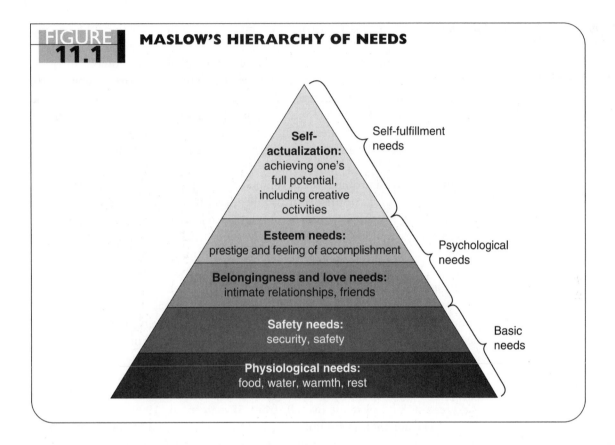

FIGURE 11.1 | **MASLOW'S HIERARCHY OF NEEDS**

physiological needs—the need for food and water. Once these most basic needs are met, the second level can be considered—safety needs, ranging from the creation of shelter to be protected from the elements to more complex notions of security from conflict and crime. The third level expands the individual's relationship to others, as love and belongingness become important. At the fourth level, individuals become conscious of their place in society and relationship to others—esteem needs. Only once these levels have been reached can the final level, the need for self-actualization, be realized. As many of the people of the world are still struggling at the first levels of Maslow's hierarchy, they are unable to achieve their full potential.

The activities associated with achieving the MDGs seek to move people up this pyramid. The most recent report on the MDGs (2012) notes there has been some improvement to date in realizing the goals and the challenges that will continue to impact meeting the 2015 targets.[11] Specifically, progress has been made on the reduction of poverty generally, and it is expected that the MDG goal of cutting extreme poverty in half will be reached by 2015, with the fastest reductions occurring in China. Even with setbacks from the 2008 global financial crisis, the proportion of working people worldwide living on

vulnerable employment
work done by unpaid family workers or by those who keep their own accounts, that is, the self-employed.

less than $1.25 per day has dropped from 26.4 percent in 2000 to 14.8 percent in 2011.[12]

Problems remain, however, in relation to employment growth, adequate nutrition, and educational opportunities. The number of workers engaged in **vulnerable employment**, defined as work done by unpaid family workers and workers who keep their own accounts, has decreased more slowly. Women are particularly affected by these more informal working arrangements. In sub-Saharan Africa, for example, 85 percent of women compared to 69 percent of men are impacted.[13]

Hunger is still a problem for developing countries as well, with 15 percent of the population undernourished. In some areas, such as sub-Saharan Africa and southern Asia outside of India, these figures reach as high as 27 percent and 22 percent respectively. The lack of adequate nourishment is particularly detrimental to children. The poorest households continue to be the most affected, most notably in southern Asia, where 32 percent of children were underweight in 2010, compared to sub-Saharan Africa at 22 percent, and Southeast Asia at 17 percent. Some progress has been made in this area, as the percentage of underweight children under the age of five in developing countries overall declined from 29 percent in 1990 to 18 percent in 2010. This improvement is insufficient, however, to meet the MDG targets by 2015.[14]

There also has been slow growth in the percentage of children from the developing world who are enrolled in primary education. Sub-Saharan Africa has had the greatest improvement overall, from 58 percent in 1999 to 76 percent in 2010.[15] The advantages are not shared equally by men and women, however, as girls do not receive the same access to education as boys. Still, the number of girls in the out-of-school population has declined slightly, dropping from 58 percent to 53 percent between 1999 and 2010.[16]

Given these inequities, how are the world's most powerful political and economic entities responding to meet the challenges of global poverty? What are the implications of these policies for the United States? The European Union? How well are they doing in regard to the millennium development goals?

In 2004, the US Congress created the Millennium Challenge Account to address some of these concerns. Administered by the **Millennium Challenge Corporation (MCC)**, this organization provides economic assistance to countries based on their ability to meet political, economic, and social performance standards. A matrix of measures identifies 22 different indicators used to determine eligibility for US assistance (Table 11.1).

A list of countries that have met targets on these issues is generated annually, and funds are appropriated to them through one of two types of grants: compact and threshold. The compact grants are relatively large and are given to countries that clearly meet the eligibility criteria. Threshold grants are smaller and are awarded to those nearing the standards but needing a bit more time.

Millennium Challenge Corporation (MCC)
created by the US Congress to administer economic assistance to developing countries in response to the MDGs.

TABLE 11.1 | MILLENNIUM CHALLENGE CORPORATION COUNTRY ELIGIBILITY CRITERIA

Selection Indicators		
Indicator	*Category*	*Source*
Access to Credit Indicator	Economic Freedom	International Finance Corporation
Business Start-Up Indicator	Economic Freedom	International Finance Corporation
Child Health Indicator	Investing in People	Columbia/Yale
Civil Liberties Indicator	Ruling Justly	Freedom House
Control of Corruption Indicator	Ruling Justly	World Bank/Brookings Institution
Fiscal Policy Indicator	Economic Freedom	International Monetary Fund
Freedom of Information Indicator	Ruling Justly	Freedom House Fringe
Gender in the Economy Indicator	Economic Freedom	World Bank
Girls' Primary Education Completion Rate Indicator	Investing in People	UNESCO
Girls' Secondary Education Enrollment Ratio Indicator	Investing in People	UNESCO
Government Effectiveness Indicator	Ruling Justly	World Bank/Brookings Institution
Health Expenditures Indicator	Investing in People	World Health Organization
Immunization Rates Indicator	Investing in People	WHO/UNICEF
Inflation Indicator	Economic Freedom	International Monetary Fund
Land Rights and Access Indicator	Economic Freedom	International Fund for Agricultural Development International Finance Corporation
Natural Resource Protection	Investing in People	Columbia/Yale
Political Rights Indicator	Ruling Justly	Freedom House
Primary Education Expenditures Indicator	Investing in People	UNESCO
Regulatory Quality Indicator	Economic Freedom	World Bank/Brookings Institution
Rule of Law Indicator	Ruling Justly	World Bank/Brookings Institution
Trade Policy Indicator	Economic Freedom	The Heritage Foundation
Voice and Accountability Indicator	Ruling Justly	World Bank/Brookings Institution

Source: "Selection Indicators," Millennium Challenge Corporation, www.mcc.gov/pages/selection/indicators.

To date, the MCC has approved over $8.4 billion in compact and threshold programs that support projects all over the world in a broad range of areas:

- agriculture and irrigation
- transportation
- water supply and sanitation
- access to health
- finance and enterprise development

- anticorruption initiatives
- land rights and access
- access to education[17]

Compact Grant Recipients	Threshold Grant Recipients
Armenia	Albania
Benin	Burkina Faso
Burkina Faso	Guyana
Cape Verde	Indonesia
El Salvador	Jordan
Georgia	Kenya
Ghana	Kyrgyz Republic
Honduras	Liberia
Indonesia	Malawi
Jordan	Moldova
Lesotho	Niger
Madagascar	Paraguay
Malawi	Peru
Mali	Philippines
Moldova	Rwanda
Mongolia	Sao Tome and Principe
Morocco	Tanzania
Mozambique	Timor-Leste
Namibia	Uganda
Nicaragua	Ukraine
Philippines	Zambia
Senegal	
Tanzania	
Vanuatu	

The list of compact and threshold recipients shows the breadth of this program:[18]

For example, Ghana received a $547,009,000 compact grant in August 2006, which entered into force in February 2007, aimed at reducing poverty through the improvement of agriculture. As of September 2011, nearing the end of the grant time period, the country had used $460,052,883, or 84 percent of the grant. Projects included improving transportation infrastructure, rural development, and agricultural endeavors.[19]

Zambia, on the other hand, was categorized as a threshold country in May 2006 and received a $22,735,000 grant. In order to receive a compact grant at a later date, Zambia was required to improve indicator measurements in the categories of Ruling Justly and Economic Freedom through deflating administrative corruption and administrative barriers to trade. By 2009, these changes had been successfully implemented, and Zambia is now eligible to receive a compact grant.[20]

The European Union has a strong commitment to the MDGs but did not meet its 2010 interim target of 0.56 percent of gross national income given for aid. It has pledged to reach 0.70 percent by 2015. The European Parliament has urged its member countries to increase their support for this effort, focusing on relieving debt burdens and improving health care and education.[21] While member states retain control over their respective allocation strategies, the European Commission has initiated a program that calls for annual individual action plans and peer reviews, coordinated EU policies for development, targeted aid to the poorest countries, and partnerships with the poorest countries.[22] Despite considerable variation in individual countries' contributions, the EU as a whole is the most generous global aid donor, with €53.8 billion (almost $70 billion in US dollars) given in 2010.[23]

GLOBAL HEALTH AND THE THREAT OF DISEASE

The MDGs give a great deal of attention to the global health crisis and particularly the spread of infectious disease. Global health is a critical concern of three of the goals—the fourth seeks to reduce child mortality, the fifth aims to improve maternal health, and the sixth focuses on diseases. Women are the most affected in the poorest countries, having very limited access to health care. The gap between rich and poor is most profound in the area of maternal health care. Almost all women in developed countries receive skilled health care when delivering a child, while such care is far from universal in developing countries. Maternal death in childbirth remains high in the developing world at 240 per 100,000 live births, although it is down from 440 in 1990 and 370 in 2000.[24]

The global transmission of diseases across borders has never been greater, and many of the issues we have examined up to this point have contributed to these paths. From environmental challenges to technological innovation that facilitates travel, political unrest that forces migration, and the economic imperative for trade, all have moved peoples and diseases rapidly around the world. There is a global fear of **pandemics**, the spread of diseases across a wide geographical area and to a large population. These kinds of concerns are not new and go back at least as far as the Black Death, a result of the bubonic plague in the 1300s thought to have killed over 30 percent of the population in Europe. More recent concerns have revolved around severe acute respiratory syndrome (SARS), which affected 8,000 people and resulted in 750 deaths during the 2003 outbreak.[25] Similar concerns are raised periodically by recurrent outbreaks of the avian and swine flus as well.

Goal 6 directly addresses disease, specifically focused on HIV/AIDS and malaria. The growth rate of the number of people newly infected by HIV/AIDS has declined by 21 percent since 1997, while the number of people living with HIV is rising.[26] The creation of drugs that can alter the course of the disease has been significant, as has the development of drugs that can prevent the transfer of the disease in childbirth. However, the costs associated with the medications, as well as the lack of effective distribution networks, have often kept these drugs from those with the greatest need. The developing world has suffered the most, with sub-Saharan Africa remaining the region most affected. Surprisingly, despite an initial decline, the incidence rate is rising in Eastern Europe and Central Asia. Map 11.1 illustrates the distribution of HIV globally.

While the spread of HIV/AIDS has been given the greatest public attention, it is just one small part of the threat. Of particular concern to many people around the world is malaria, which, unlike AIDS, can be successfully eliminated. According to the US Centers for Disease Control, 3.3 billion people, or almost half of the world's population, live in areas where malaria may be transmitted. This includes parts of Asia, Africa, Latin America, and the Caribbean. In 2008, an estimated 708,000 to 1,003,000 deaths resulted from malaria, with young children and pregnant women in the developing world most affected.[27]

One of the most visible responses has been the provision of mosquito nets to people living in malaria areas. The Bill & Melinda Gates Foundation has partnered with a broad range of organizations around the world that includes the National Basketball Association's NBA Cares, The People of The United Methodist Church, VH1, Major League Soccer's MLS W.O.R.K.S, the Women's National Basketball Association, the Union for Reform Judaism, Usher's New

pandemics
the widespread outbreak of diseases.

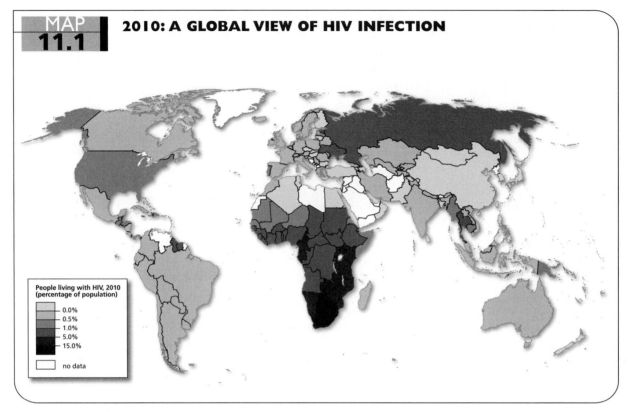

MAP 11.1   2010: A GLOBAL VIEW OF HIV INFECTION

People living with HIV, 2010
(percentage of population)

- 0.0%
- 0.5%
- 1.0%
- 5.0%
- 15.0%

no data

Source: World Health Organization, "2010: A Global View of HIV Infection," www.unaids.org/documents/20101123_2010_HIV_Prevalence_Map_em.pdf.

Look Foundation, Junior Chamber International, and Orkin, Incorporated in the "Nothing But Nets" campaign to solicit $10 donations to purchase a bed net, transport it to Africa, and educate people on how to use it.[28] They work in conjunction with several UN partners to reach the affected areas and hope their efforts will help meet UN MDG goals to end malaria deaths by 2015.

The World Health Organization (WHO) has exercised leadership on issues of global health concerns.[29] The WHO is a specialized agency of the UN, created in 1948, to improve the health of people globally. For a large entity governed by 193 member states, it can be difficult to service the diversity of global health needs. As a result, NGOs have been critical of much of the hands-on assistance rendered for global health. Most notable in this regard is the development of the civil society initiative of the WHO that recognizes the necessity of NGOs in the successful delivery of health care. As of January 2011, 182 NGOs had official relations with the WHO. These included a broad range of international associations, federations, societies, and unions, as well as more popularly known groups such as Oxfam, Save the Children, Rotary International, and World Vision International.

SOWhat? ONE NGO'S EXPERIENCE WITH THE MDGs

By Leah McManus, International Studies Graduate Student, Raleigh, North Carolina

Developing countries, such as Liberia and Haiti, are extremely resource poor and often find it challenging to provide services to persons residing within their borders, particularly ones living in rural areas. The governments of these countries simply do not have the human and financial resource power to provide basic and necessary services. It is also often the case that developing countries have very weak private sectors, thus there is a lack of service provision there as well. Aid from developed countries is critical because of the continued transfer of knowledge that occurs through capacity building—meaning training on "how to" and not simply giving.

As a Program Associate for Curamericas, a Raleigh-based international NGO, I see the positive effects of this type of cross-border cooperation every day. Curamericas' work revolves around building the capacity of local institutions, both private and public, to ensure that persons residing within their borders have increased accessibility, affordability, and availability to basic primary health care services and these services are equitably provided. Curamericas seeks to bridge the gap between the community and health facilities by empowering people to take responsibility for their own health outcomes and by training local institutions on effective and efficient means of locally based outreach. This capacity building allows for an increased quality of life for the population within a country's borders. A country will never be able to develop, and subsequently provide a better quality of life for its people, if only a fraction of its new generation can make it to age 5 and/or if mothers are dying during childbirth.

Curamericas contributes to meeting several of the Millennium Development Goals (MDGs): reducing child mortality and improving maternal health in Guatemala and Liberia, and combating HIV/AIDS in Haiti and Liberia. The emphasis is on building the capacity of local institutions to implement community based outreach services that prevent and treat conditions and illnesses related to child mortality, maternal health, HIV/AIDS, malaria and other diseases. Critical indicators of success include overall statistics, such as child mortality rates, systemic policy changes—such as local NGOs implementing malaria prevention programs based on best practices, and behavioral changes, such as a pregnant woman attending all of her checks during pregnancy.

Successful projects are imperative to countries like Liberia. Not only does the country see unnecessary suffering that can and should be relieved, but a healthier Liberia means

(Continued)

(Continued)

rapid development. Rapid development (which can include education and economic growth) in turn usually leads to a more stable and less corrupt nation, allowing for the democratic process to take place in more than just theory, all of which allows for quality of life to improve. The health and stability of Liberia affects West Africa in that if a conflict arises in Liberia, it is the neighbors of Guinea, Cote d'Ivoire and Sierra Leone that will bear the economic burden of caring for the displaced persons. You could also say it affects the world.

To help those abroad climb out of extreme poverty everyone should become educated on various programs/organizations that work to alleviate poverty. I encourage you to participate. Be an intern or volunteer, become educated about various organizations doing such work in your area, inform your friends, or even donate money or goods in kind. You can be of great support to those who are working every day to chip away at not only alleviating poverty but providing sustainable solutions for the future.

HUMAN RIGHTS

Freedom from poverty and disease is essential to the general well-being of the world and is considered to be a fundamental human right. Amnesty International, an NGO that focuses on the protection of **human rights**, defines them as "basic rights and freedoms that all people are entitled to regardless of nationality, sex, national or ethnic origin, race, religion, language, or other status."[30] The effort to address these distinctions on an international basis is found in the 1948 Universal Declaration on Human Rights. This document remains the defining accord for the protection of human rights around the world and covers a broad range of these rights, from the need to guarantee survival to personal, legal, cultural, and educational obligations of humans to one another. It was a special interest of former US first lady, Eleanor Roosevelt, who believed that respect for human rights was fundamental and that everyone must support them. Speaking to the UN in 1958, she noted, "Without concerted citizen action to uphold them close to home, we shall look in vain for progress in the larger world."[31]

The transparency that has come with globalization through the information revolution has resulted in people all over the world having firsthand knowledge of the physical and mental abuses that still occur in some countries. There is greater exposure and better response to human rights internationally, as there

human rights

the fundamental rights and freedoms based on the premise that all people are inherently equal and must be treated as such, regardless of their nationality or ethnic origin, race, religion, language, or other status.

is nowhere to hide. Anyone with access to YouTube can view videos of abuses, such as factory workers toiling in unsafe conditions and violent suppression of political activism. Pictures of American soldiers posing with corpses of Afghani insurgents can go viral in a matter of moments, spurring global outrage. The uprising in Syria and efforts by the regime there to contain the protests also offers a very clear example of the notion that the whole world is watching.

The greatest difficulties arise in how to address human rights from a global perspective. The efforts to develop **universal norms** for behavior as delineated in the Universal Declaration are inhibited by culturally **relative norms** that are unique to various societies, dictated by their religion, traditional practices, level of development, and acceptable criminal punishments. For example, the rights of women are a critical concern for human rights advocates; however, some religious groups define these rights in very different terms than what might be acceptable to others.

Examples of these effects on women include the unwillingness of the Taliban in Afghanistan to allow girls to attend school, and the policies of a number of Islamic regimes that prohibit women from driving. Female genital mutilation, a procedure that stems from traditional cultural practices and intentionally alters female genital organs, is a common occurrence in many parts of Africa and some countries in Asia and the Middle East. It is a violation not only of women, but children as well, as the practice is generally carried out on minors. By some estimates, 92 million girls age 10 and older have undergone this procedure in Africa.[32] Legal protection against rape is also inadequate in countries as diverse as the Democratic Republic of the Congo, Pakistan, and South Korea. This issue is not restricted to any particular country or part of the world.

The continuing controversies over dress requirements and practices of Muslim women in Europe illustrate the tensions between religious practices and supposed universal norms. The French government has passed legislation that bans the wearing of the burka—a traditional full body cover worn by Muslim women—in public. Similar laws are being considered by Belgium, Spain, and some parts of Italy.[33] This action comes after the French formally banned head-scarves in schools in 2004. The argument the French have used to justify their action is that the headscarf is a religious symbol and has no place in a secular classroom. The French minister of justice, Michele Alliot-Marie, has hailed the burka ban as a "success for French republican values of liberty, equality, fraternity and secularism."[34]

Some question, however, whether the French constitution is in conflict with this ban. Moreover, there are doubts as to whether it is consistent with the broader European Convention on Human Rights, which follows the spirit of the Universal Declaration and was entered into force in 1953. There is also a concern that the actions of the French government are politically motivated and designed to limit the growing Muslim population. A potential punishment

universal norms

human rights as delineated in the Universal Declaration that most countries can agree upon.

relative norms

rights that are unique to an individual society, dictated by its religion, cultural practices, level of development, and acceptable criminal punishments.

This woman is one of the millions worldwide who wears a burka in observance of her Muslim faith.

for being fully veiled is to attend a "French citizenship course" to learn about the "values of the French republic."[35] In fact, only about 2,000 women in France actually wear the burka, but they contend they have that right as part of their cultural and religious values. Since the ban went into effect, 6 women have been fined and 237 cited.[36]

Criminal punishments also vary greatly. In 1993, the caning of an American student in Singapore for writing graffiti in a public place garnered considerable international attention. Similarly, in 2002, there was international outrage at the planned stoning of two Nigerian women for adultery as an exercise of sharia, the Muslim code of law practices in the northern districts of Nigeria. Both were later released under international pressure. More recently, Uganda has resurrected a piece of legislation that could impose the death penalty for a "serial offender" of the "offense of homosexuality."[37] The United States and other Western nations have stridently opposed this act because of its discriminatory nature. Meanwhile, for many countries, the acceptance in the United States of the death penalty as an appropriate criminal punishment is seen as a gross violation of human rights.

Finally, less developed countries are particularly concerned with the way human rights standards have been applied to them. They have argued that the wealthier countries of the world faced circumstances similar to theirs 100 years ago or more. As a result, they often utilized sweatshops and child labor and violated safety standards in their industrialization efforts, just as developing countries sometimes do now. Today, these areas are regulated internationally, and there is a cost associated with compliance. Demands in many developing countries for labor, and the willingness of workers to tolerate these inequities, have exacerbated these tensions.

The plight of a 13-year-old Indian girl who was locked in an apartment by her employers while they went on vacation in March of 2012 illustrates the depth of this issue. The young girl had been sold to a job placement agency by her uncle, and the agency in turn sold her to her employers. She received no compensation for her work and was monitored by closed-circuit cameras to be sure she did not take any extra food.[38] How could this happen? A growing middle class in India has increased demands for domestic helpers. As a result, legislation to regulate child labor allows children between the ages of 14 and 18 to work up to six hours per day in "nonhazardous" conditions. Lax enforcement and extreme poverty have resulted in many children serving as household help without compensation, being frequently beaten and living in almost slave-like conditions. When legal action is taken against their employers, there is no more than a perfunctory penalty.

The specific institution that regulates these concerns is the International Labor Organization (ILO), which sets the standards for the global workplace. Founded in 1919 after World War I in an effort to create greater equality for working people, the ILO became a specialized agency of the UN in 1946.[39] It is the only "tripartite" organization of the UN, bringing together government representatives, employers, and workers in an effort to provide labor standards around the world. Not all states agree with these principles, however, and compliance can be difficult to assure.

The controversy surrounding the production of Apple products in China illustrates this problem. Foxconn, a Taiwan-based manufacturing giant, assembles many of Apple's electronic products. A survey of 35,000 Foxconn workers by a monitoring group found that 43 percent said they had been involved in accidents or witnessed them. An even larger number, almost two-thirds, said their wages were not adequate to "meet their basic needs."[40] Further, it was found that work hours were not regulated, and many employees were working over 60 hours per week and often more than 11 days in a row. As a result of this public investigation, both Apple and Foxconn have vowed to correct the situation.

Such public outcry is not always possible. As a result, the role of NGOs has grown in protecting the rights of individuals. Many NGOs seek to monitor the progress of states in protecting the human rights of their citizens. Human Rights Watch works to give voice to those who are oppressed and by doing so, seeks to enable them to bring about change.[41] Freedom House is another NGO that advocates for human rights and serves as an international watchdog to assure democratic freedoms.[42] Their *Freedom in the World* annual report offers comparative data on global political rights and civil liberties for 193 countries and 15 territories. It is widely used around the world to monitor freedom and human rights generally, including by the Millennium Challenge Corporation detailed previously.

Chinese Foxconn workers labor in a workshop at the company's Shenzhen plant in south China's Guangdong province, May 2010. Controversies surrounding substandard labor practices, as well as a string of suicides at Foxconn, have highlighted the urgent need for China to adjust working conditions in its factories.

WHAT CAN BE DONE?

There is a real and immediate need for effective leadership that can guide governments, corporations, international organizations, and other institutions to work jointly to promote international cooperation. All too frequently, national leaders focus on their own short-term interests and not on broader, global, long-term concerns. IGOs have also struggled to keep pace with the rapid changes transforming the world. They have failed to redefine their core competencies vis-à-vis the emerging capacities of the private sector and NGOs. IGOs are frequently limited by their structure and the interests of their member states. The extent to which they are able to work together to address the really critical issues confronting the world today may well require some system of international cooperation that goes beyond national boundaries.

global governance

voluntary international cooperation to manage transnational issues through a system of governance agreed upon by all interested parties.

While the term **global governance** may sound like global government, in fact, it refers to the "management of transnational issues through voluntary international cooperation," according to Hakan Altinay, senior fellow at the Brookings Institution and the founding director of the Open Society Foundation in Turkey.[43] It has been a successful strategy for the administration of many functional areas in the international system, from simple travel accords and practices to more complicated arenas, such as the environment. Nevertheless, the concept can be problematic for different groups around the world.

Global Governance Watch, a joint project of the American Enterprise Institute (AEI, a conservative public policy think tank in Washington, D.C.) and the Federalist Society for Law and Public Policy Studies (also a conservative organization for legal reformers), argues that the movement toward global governance is a threat to national sovereignty. They focus on monitoring the transparency and accountability of both IGOs and NGOs and the extent to which these organizations are influencing domestic political outcomes.[44] They are particularly concerned with the interface between global action and national interests in four areas: economics, environment and health, human rights, and security. They believe fundamental changes must take place within countries if those countries are to operate successfully in the international arena, and that such change will not result from broader global actions.

For example, AEI scholar and former president of the World Bank Paul Wolfowitz, with coauthors Mark Palmer and Patrick Glenn, argues that the MDGs cannot be successfully met without focusing on governance and the rule of law in developing countries. Specifically, they suggest that "countries that are governed poorly are not reducing poverty, no matter how much foreign assistance they receive."[45]

Global Governance 2025, a study by the US National Intelligence Council (a center within the US government for strategic thinking) and the European Union's Institute for Security Studies (an agency of the European Union for security issues), examines changes in the international system that require global governance, as well as the factors limiting that cooperation.[46] The study outlines four possible scenarios for meeting these challenges. In the first scenario, which is the one the authors believe to be most likely to occur, the international system muddles through without a significant singular event that poses a crisis so great that it cannot be absorbed. Western states bear the brunt of the burden in this scenario. This is not a sustainable model in the long run, however, based on its fundamental assumption that no crisis is so great that it will rock the system.

Their second scenario suggests that powerful states and regional powers may try to severely limit their engagement in the international arena and seek greater self-reliance. In this fragmented system, global connections remain but without the intensity of interaction that characterizes the present system. However, this model does not account for the interdependence of international fiscal problems, and it is questionable if such a scenario is viable in the interconnected world in which we live.

The third scenario envisions the consequences of a globally encompassing conflict or environmental disaster that has the potential to affect everyone on the planet. If this happens, there could be a movement to cooperate, as the issues would be similar to those that brought the Concert of Europe together in the nineteenth century (see Chapter 10). The level of cooperation necessary to address the problem would require states to put their national interests on hold for the greater good, but Global Governance Watch is worried that this level of cooperation would be very difficult to achieve.

Finally, the least likely scenario, but the potentially most dangerous one, is set in a game analogy format, where the domestic demands of states are so great that they carry beyond each state's borders, and all-out conflict occurs. Here "conflict trumps cooperation" as the nuclear arms race continues in the Middle East and competition for scarce resources pits states against one another. Collaboration to solve mutual problems falls by the wayside in this scenario.

Given the potential limitations to global governance, what other approaches can be used to address global issues? The concept of **international regimes** describes one way that groups have worked together outside traditional frameworks.[47] International regimes refer to cooperation among states based on custom and practice, without formal agreement. They represent other avenues that can be pursued when states are unable to reach agreement on steps to address particular issues or situations through formal procedures that exist, and international organizations are not capable of generating acceptable solutions.

international regimes
cooperation among states based on custom and practice, without formal agreement.

In early May, 2012, Occupy Wall Street protesters marched in Manhattan calling for nationwide May Day strikes to protest economic inequality and corporate greed and many other issues.

International regimes have been particularly prominent in relationship to the environment, frequently establishing lines of cooperation that later translate into formal agreements. The Convention on International Trade in Endangered Species of Wild Fauna and Flora, entered into force in 1975, is one example where common concerns about wildlife around the world brought interested parties together for conservation. Today, 175 countries voluntarily agree to comply with the framework of this convention to provide protection to 30,000 animal species and plant specimens.[48]

Individuals can also play a role as they exercise their rights as global citizens. The interdependence of the international system and the way technology has transformed the connectedness between people across the planet requires new institutions that can respond to these challenges. The knowledge people have of others around the globe and the conditions in which they exist creates a global human empathy that returns to Rousseau's concept of social contract. In the age of Twitter and YouTube, people will put pressure upon their own governmental institutions to act in response to human rights abuses.

Margaret Keck and Kathryn Sikkink refer to the new associations of like-minded people who come together on global issues as **transnational advocacy networks (TANs)**.[49] These networks provide opportunities for cooperation and collaboration for people across borders to channel their influence in the international arena. They take some of the issues of greatest concern, such as human rights and the environment, back to the people who are most affected to bring about change beyond national limitations. The Occupy Wall Street movement is an example of a TAN. It originated in the United States and spread to over 100 US cities and 1,500 cities around the world to protest the current structure of the international economy, which it sees as disproportionally favoring the richest 1 percent of the world's population.[50]

Managing the world and the many issues confronting it will require cooperation. Global issues cross international borders, and it will be incumbent on people of different nationalities to work together to solve them. The MDGs offer goals to strive for, and there has been some success. Innovative and dynamic partnerships between and among governments, NGOs, the private sector, and IGOs will be necessary to address the challenges ahead. You will also need to consider your own contributions to this process. Chapter 12 offers you a guide as to how you can participate.

transnational advocacy networks (TANs)

networks that provide opportunities for cooperation and collaboration for people across borders to channel their influence in the international arena.

KEYConcepts

global governance 250
human rights 246
international regimes 251
Millennium Challenge
Corporation (MCC) 240
millennium development
goals (MDGs) 238

pandemics 243
poverty 238
relative norms 247
transnational advocacy
networks (TANs) 252
universal norms 247
vulnerable employment 240

TO LEARNMore

Books and Other Print Media

Laurie Garrett, *Betrayal of Trust: The Collapse of Global Public Health* (New York: Hyperion, 2001).

Best-selling author Laurie Garrett exposes global public health issues that could give rise to a potential disaster, including the outbreak of Ebola in the Democratic Republic of the Congo (then Zaire) and the deterioration of health care in the former Soviet Union.

Nicholas D. Kristof and Sheryl WuDunn, *Half the Sky: Turning Oppression into Opportunity for Women Worldwide* (New York: Knopf, 2009).

This book takes a critical look at the continued disparities and oppression faced by women around the world.

Peter Manzel, Charles C. Mann, and Paul Kennedy, *Material World: A Global Family Portrait* (New York: Sierra Club Books, 1994).

This book unwraps the contents of peoples' homes from around the world to uncover what they value and cherish most.

Rordan Wilkinson and Jennifer Clapp, *Global Institutions: Global Governance Poverty and Inequality* (New York: Routledge, 2010).

This book looks at the role global governance can play in addressing poverty.

Somaly Mam, *The Road of Lost Innocence: The True Story of a Cambodian Heroine* (New York: Spiegel & Grau, 2009).

Sold into sexual slavery at age 12, Mam uncovers the dark world of human trafficking in Southeast Asia and her transformation into a leader in the fight against it.

Websites

Food and Agriculture Organization of the United Nations (FAO), www.fao.org/.

> The FAO is a specialized agency of the UN focusing on food security in developed and developing countries alike. Its website contains a wealth of information including the FAO Food Price Index, descriptions of its key programs, and statistical databases.

Human Rights Watch, www.hrw.org/.

> Human Rights Watch is an independent, nongovernmental organization dedicated to defending human rights and reporting on violations.

Médecins sans Frontières (Doctors Without Borders) (MSF), www.doctorswithout borders.org/.

> The official website of MSF features information about their work, including press releases, blog posts, and videos.

On The Ground, http://kristof.blogs.nytimes.com/.

> The online version of Nicholas Kristof's *New York Times* op ed column discusses an array of global policy issues.

World Food Programme (WFP), www.wfp.org/.

> The WFP is the agency of the UN that deals with matters related to food aid and assistance. Its website features information about hunger and countries with chronic hunger problems.

Videos

Born into Brothels (2004).

> This documentary explores the world of Sonagchi, the red light district of Kolkata, India, and the children who live there.

Emily Oster Flips our Thinking on AIDS in Africa (2007).

> Through an economics lens, Oster reexamines our knowledge about HIV/AIDS in Africa and reorients our strategy in battling the disease. www.ted.com/talks/emily_oster_flips_our_thinking_on_aids_in_africa.html

How Mr. Condom Made Thailand a Better Place (2010).

> Mechai Viravaidya discusses the successes of family planning and child mortality reduction programs in Thailand and the role of condoms in raising Thailand's standard of living. www.ted.com/talks/mechai_viravaidya_how_mr_condom_made_thailand_a_better_place.html

The Perfect Famine (2003).

This short documentary focuses on the conditions that caused famine in Malawi. www.bullfrogfilms.com/catalog/l3tpf.html

Unlock the Intelligence, Passion, Greatness of Girls (2012).

Nobel laureate Leymah Gbowee speaks about how we can transform the world by empowering girls. www.ted.com/talks/leymah_gbowee_unlock_the_intelligence_passion_greatness_of_girls.html

"The Worst Place on Earth to Be a Woman": Healing the Eastern Congo (2012).

A short report on HEAL Africa, an organization that aids women healing from injuries sustained from rape and assault in the Democratic Republic of the Congo. www.pbs.org/newshour/bb/globalhealth/jan-june12/healafrica_03-07.html

Connecting to the World

Where Do You Go from Here?

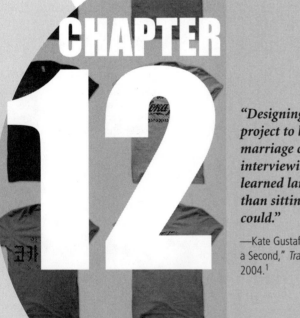

CHAPTER

12

Not that long ago, only the wealthy and powerful had the means to become citizens of the world. The technological revolutions in travel and communications have opened up this possibility to more and more people. Interacting with others whose backgrounds and customs are different from our own is not an easy task. It can lead to embarrassing or uncomfortable moments. If you found yourself sitting down to a meal in another country staring at an undesirable looking local delicacy you are expected to consume, would you risk insulting your hosts by refusing to taste it? Remember Sudanese Lost Boy Valentino Achak Deng's discomfort in the opening to Chapter 8 as he sat down to an unfamiliar meal. If visiting a country where modest types of clothing are the custom, will you wear shorts? Before traveling to another country, are you likely to familiarize yourself with the gestures that are considered disrespectful or profane? These questions relate directly to the challenge

"Designing my own research project to learn about Nepali marriage customs by interviewing women in a newly learned language taught me more than sitting in a lecture hall ever could."

—Kate Gustafson, "I Would Do It All Again in a Second," *Transitions Abroad Magazine*, 2004.[1]

of going beyond our comfort zones to engage more directly with the world in which we live.

To work and operate effectively in a global environment, you will be called upon to demonstrate levels of political, economic, and cultural sophistication. Critical thinking, communication, language, collaboration, and technology skills will be indispensable.[2] International studies programs and courses can help provide you with the requisite tools. To be more fully prepared, however, it is best to experience the world even as you are learning about it. This was clearly evident in the journey of Kate Gustafson, whose study abroad program in Nepal gave her opportunities to encounter unfamiliar circumstances and practices over the course of her travels.[3]

This chapter lays out the practical elements that should accompany your academic studies for a fuller understanding. It identifies some of the hands-on experiences that are at your disposal as you move through your undergraduate studies, such as work and study abroad, service learning, and internships. It also addresses how you might think about and prepare for a career in international service.

Arien Atterberry, African-American college student at Claflin University, South Carolina, shown here during a study-abroad experience in Spain.

INTERNATIONAL STUDIES BEYOND THE CLASSROOM

Study abroad offers students opportunities to expand their horizons and appreciations. Many of our students have reported that the **study abroad** experience was the highlight of their undergraduate education, and some have gone so far as to suggest that it was truly life altering, in terms of thinking about future plans and careers. These experiences expose students to a particular foreign culture, while giving them the opportunity to make important contacts and

study abroad
to attend an educational institution in another country.

forge lasting relationships with people they encounter along the way. They may also provide a base for additional travel during periods when classes are not in session. It is important to select a program that fits with both your interests and academic needs. Living arrangements (apartment, dorm, or host family), instructional language, curriculum or course options available to foreign students, and thematic focus vary. A desirable and safe location is often a high priority.

Study abroad programs and exchanges are the most common ways to study the world beyond the classroom. The 2011 annual report of the Institute of International Education, *Open Doors 2011,* showed that the total number of American students studying abroad has tripled over the past two decades. While European countries remain the most popular destinations, China and a number of other developing and emerging economies now rank among the top 25 sites. But while more Americans are studying abroad, the trend is for shorter stays. The majority (approximately 57 percent) choose programs offered either in the summer session or during midwinter break, rather than a full semester abroad.[4]

These numbers represent a very small percentage of students enrolled on US campuses; only 270,604 studied abroad in 2009–10.[5] Students choose not to go abroad for many different reasons: Their program of study does not allow time for or require an international experience, they lack resources, they do not see its advantages, or their parents do not see the need or will not allow it. Together, these factors keep the overall numbers relatively low. At the same time, America's overseas connections continue to be enhanced by the considerable number of international students on US campuses. In 2010–11, the total reached 723,277 students, up 4.7 percent from the previous year. Since 2000, international students have accounted for around 3.5 percent of total enrollments at US colleges and universities.[6]

For students enrolled in international studies programs, study abroad or some alternative international experience is essential in gaining an appreciation of the world's complexity and the challenges of operating effectively within it. Unfortunately, even some of the most committed students may not have the time or resources to participate beyond a few weeks. But the impact of short-term programs can be enhanced by intensive immersion into another culture as well as thoughtful preparation for and examination of the experience. This is usually provided by the several pre- and postdeparture class sessions that are a part of most of these programs, where students complete readings and assignments (as they would in a more traditional class) and have the opportunity to engage in a thorough debriefing upon their return where they can consider what they have actually gained and learned from the course.

Many employers have come to look favorably on the study abroad experience in terms of the knowledge and skills that it may foster in prospective employees.

It might even tip the balance in a hiring decision. Hiring managers often see experience living and studying abroad as an indicator of such traits as initiative and adaptability.[7]

Most universities offer many options in study abroad programs and have a study abroad office or designated adviser to assist with the selection process. In many cases, programs originate from the school itself, and students are usually eligible to enroll in those offered by other accredited institutions. There are also some highly regarded private companies that organize and administer programs for academic credit. These tend to be rather expensive. A study abroad adviser can ensure that such an experience is reputable and that its academic credits are transferable.

Exchange agreements are the most cost-effective alternatives. These formal arrangements enable students to enroll at foreign universities for the same tuition as they would pay at home. Given the price advantage and the fact that the flow of incoming and outgoing students between the partner institutions must be relatively balanced, spaces in these programs are often limited. Familiarity with the options sufficiently in advance of your planned journey and a prompt application can help to secure an available slot.

While not all study abroad programs center around learning another language, many students use the experience to enhance their language skills. The ability to communicate effectively in a foreign language is a critical requirement for many international careers. Employers view foreign language competency very favorably, and it could well prove the key skill in securing a position. By sequencing your study abroad experience with your advanced language training, you can hone your skills through ongoing communication with native speakers. Given critical shifts in the global political and economic arenas, languages such as Arabic and Chinese are in particularly high demand. While these languages may be challenging to master, time spent on becoming proficient may pay off in terms of expanding employment prospects.

If you cannot participate in a formal study program, there are other ways to sample the world. There are companies that advertise on campus offering relatively inexpensive international airfares to students. Check with the study abroad or student affairs office to help determine the reputation and reliability of these firms. Once abroad, you can usually find reasonable accommodations at youth hostels or other budget rooming houses. Foreign travel of any sort is useful in learning to adjust to unfamiliar circumstances and to interact in a setting where the language is different and local customs seem strange. It might also prove valuable in assisting with decisions regarding the languages you study, the courses you take, or even the career you choose to pursue.

Even if you cannot go abroad, you can increase your international awareness right at home by visiting a local international grocery store, attending an ethnic festival, enjoying food from another country, or viewing a foreign film. These experiences are certainly not the same as traveling or studying abroad, but they

exchange agreements
arrangements that enable students to study abroad at foreign universities for the same tuition that they would pay to the home institution.

service learning
programs that combine classroom education with opportunities that engage students directly in service activities.

can be enlightening. The challenge is greater in less cosmopolitan areas, but today a foreign country is just a click away with a laptop or smartphone at hand.

Globalization has brought the world closer to home. Opportunities have expanded to communicate with international communities, work with agencies or nongovernmental organizations (NGOs) with an international agenda, volunteer to assist immigrant groups, or join in international projects and activities either locally or abroad. These are commonly referred to as **service learning** opportunities, as they engage students in situations that they have become aware of through their classroom studies. Acquiring "real life" experiences is a critical part of any undergraduate education. They have also become increasingly important to employers in evaluating job applicants.

In addition to increasing marketability, service learning and **internship** experiences offer the chance to develop important job-related skills. Although they often do not pay, internships provide practical training in a professional setting and the opportunity to observe actual workplace processes and practices. Interns perform clerical tasks—they run errands, make copies of documents, file papers, and answer the phones. In return, companies or agencies train them to become involved in more meaningful activities. For any internship to be worthwhile, it must offer a reasonable degree of professional engagement. Thus, students need to check to ensure that they will have some opportunity to partake in nonclerical activities related directly to the mission of the organization before accepting a position. The relationships forged with supervisors, clients, and customers may also open doors to future employment.

An internship can be time consuming, but it can also be very rewarding and illuminating. Here is one student's view of her work with a local non-profit that hosted international visitors on formal exchange visits.

HOW DO YOU CONNECT?

HOW CAN YOU GAIN INTERNATIONAL EXPERIENCE?

a. travel independently

b. participate in a formal study abroad program

c. volunteer or work in another country

d. interact with students on my campus from other countries

internship
a position that offers practical training in a workplace setting.

A Nonprofit Experience

My internship at International House has been one of my best career moves yet. I gained insight into the professional realm of non-profits, experience in event coordination and planning, and knowledge about a variety of cultures from all over the world . . . It helped to develop my professional persona . . . and helped renew my passion for culture and showed me that being able to relate to the world from different cultural perspectives will always be an asset.[8]

—Kristina Bergan, May 2009

Kristina would go on to observe that the internship was the highlight of her undergraduate experience as she gained insights about a variety of cultures and peoples from her encounters with visiting officials from Brazil, Tajikistan, Taiwan, and elsewhere.

Since many academic institutions have only limited resources to support internships, students are often responsible for identifying their own opportunities. Planning should begin well in advance. You might start by meeting with your academic adviser and visiting the university career center. The study abroad office or adviser should have information on overseas programs. Be sure to exhaust every potential resource to identify opportunities, including faculty, family members, and even friends and acquaintances. Do not forget your own backyard. Larger communities, especially those located in or near major metropolitan centers, have numerous organizations and enterprises with international connections and interests. Many schools allow students to receive academic credit for their internships. In these cases, a set number of hours will need to be completed, and interns are likely to be responsible for keeping a journal of their activities or completing some other type of written assignment.

INTERNATIONAL CAREER OPPORTUNITIES

Your coursework in international studies and experience with the international community will give you more in-depth knowledge of particular issue areas and a fuller appreciation of the diversity of perceptions and interests across the world. What are you likely to do with this information? How are you going to put your interest in international studies to work? Perhaps most important, what can you do with a degree in international studies? A range of options and numerous resources can help you to answer these questions and to further enhance your global skills and competencies.

A job in the global workplace could take you anywhere in the world that needs your talents. At the same time, rapid advances in technology will lead to the creation of new types of jobs that will demand new or enhanced knowledge and skills. While most students enter international studies programs knowing that they wish to pursue some sort of international career, not many know exactly what that means in practical terms or have a sense of how to go about it, and periods of global recession add to the uncertainty. Despite the ups and downs of the job market, the number of positions in the international field is likely to grow, and there will be opportunities to apply your training in a variety of ways.

Students considering an international studies major (and their parents) frequently express concern about its **employability quotient**—its ability to prepare them for

---

HOW DO YOU CONNECT? | **HOW WILL YOU LEARN ABOUT CAREER OPTIONS?**

a. visit the campus career center
b. attend career-related workshops
c. talk to my professors
d. talk to my parents

employability quotient

the extent to which a course of study provides sufficient preparation for gainful employment.

work in the real world. Questions relating to jobs and careers are both advisable and appropriate. International studies curricula generally incorporate many of the liberal arts and offer training that may open any number of paths to employment. The pursuit of an international studies degree in conjunction with study of a particular academic discipline (e.g., anthropology, economics, geography, history, political science)—either as a second major, minor or track—can be a good way to go to enhance your marketability in a specific area.

Nevertheless, most international studies programs offer strong intellectual preparation in their own right and prepare students for careers that transcend traditional borders. For the most part, these programs have a rigorous set of academic requirements that include direct international experience or exposure and intermediate or advanced foreign language competency. This package can go a long way in providing students with an important competitive edge. Despite only limited prior training related directly to the position she was offered, one of our recent graduates reported that she secured a job with a large French oil company due to her research skills and language fluency as well as the significant on-the-ground experience she acquired while studying abroad.

transferable skills

talents and abilities that may be applied to a range of settings and job environments.

Most international studies curricula also promote the development of effective written and oral communication skills. A major in international studies helps students develop **transferable skills** that they may apply broadly and that a range of prospective employers value. These include writing and research and the ability to communicate across languages and cultures. Together, such skills make international studies graduates attractive job candidates with a set of core competencies that are useful in a variety of settings.

International studies majors may find employment in government, non-profits, business, law, media, education, international program administration, or the military—depending on their interests, skills, and experiences. Our graduates have gone on to work with refugee resettlement agencies, and other humanitarian organizations. They have found positions in public relations, health, teaching, law, student services, and translation services. Some have sharpened their skills to pursue careers in journalism, filmmaking, and photography. Graduates who have entered the business world have worked for airlines, automobile companies, banks, and textile manufacturers in their international divisions. Others have taught English in Japan and South Korea and English as a second language to immigrants at US high schools and community colleges. Still others have secured employment with the US government in diplomatic, military, and intelligence capacities. Our students from abroad have returned home to work for their governments or nonprofit organizations.

US Department of State

Many students are attracted to international studies with an eye toward a career in diplomacy. For American students, this may mean a position with the Foreign Service of the US Department of State. Aspiring **Foreign Service Officers (FSOs)** may choose from among five career paths—political, economic, management, consular, and public diplomacy. Foreign Service officers engage in interesting and rewarding careers, but the selection process is extremely rigorous. It begins with a written Foreign Service examination and continues with a series of other interviews and screenings for those who excel on the exam. It is estimated that no more than 20 to 25 percent of those taking the exam pass during any given year, with far fewer finally receiving an offer of employment.[9] Candidates must be prepared to serve in any capacity anywhere in the world representing and defending all existing policies of the United States.

Many other jobs besides FSO advance the diplomatic mission. The Department of State offers a comprehensive online guide to career opportunities, including information on the application process.[10] Successful candidates generally possess a broad base of knowledge and specialized expertise in some aspect of international affairs. Foreign language fluency is not required at entry, but coming in with a high level of proficiency can lead to a more desirable posting.

Foreign Service Officers (FSOs)

diplomats employed by the US Department of State.

US secretary of state Hillary Clinton and Saudi Arabian defense minister Prince Salman bin Abdul-Aziz Al Saud speak to the press just before their meeting at the State Department in Washington D.C., April 2012.

Other US Government Positions

Many federal departments and agencies—even those with primarily domestic agendas—are likely to have goals that are best served by employees with international sensitivities and perspectives. There are all sorts of options. For students focusing on international business and finance, the Departments of Commerce and Treasury have positions dealing with trade, investment, and other economic policy matters. Through its Foreign Agricultural Service, the Department of Agriculture has a network of offices across the world to promote export opportunities and global food security. The Departments of Education, Energy, Justice, and Labor also have internationally oriented jobs. Any number of executive agencies and commissions may also be worthy of pursuing. These include the Agency for International Development, Drug Enforcement Administration, Environmental Protection Agency, Export-Import Bank, Federal Communications Commission, General Services Administration, and Office of the US Trade Representative. Each of these organizations has its own procedures for recruiting and hiring.

International studies students also look to careers related to defense and security. For some, the path may be through the military. The Department of Defense offers a wide variety of job opportunities of both a military and civilian nature. In addition, many federal departments and agencies have their own intelligence units and personnel. The Central Intelligence Agency, Federal Bureau of Investigation, and National Security Agency are particularly desirable possibilities for those with interest in this field. The Department of Homeland Security is also worth serious consideration. Best known as the guardian of airline security through its Transportation Security Administration, the department is actually a large and complex organization that pursues an overall task of strengthening the country's defense against terrorism. As in the case of the Foreign Service, these intelligence-based positions are highly competitive and rather difficult to attain. Candidates with prior experience, substantive background, and foreign language skills (especially in those languages that are considered of critical strategic importance) will have an advantage.[11]

Job seekers interested in the legislative branch of government may be encouraged to know that the number of employees with international expertise on Capitol Hill has greatly increased since 2001. More and more members of the US Congress find themselves engaged in foreign and defense policy and look to round out their staffs with experts. In addition, dozens of the approximately 250 committees and subcommittees in the US Senate and the House of Representatives seek staff with expertise in international affairs. There is no single recruiting or hiring process for these jobs, and they are difficult to secure. Personal contacts from previous partisan political involvement or prior internships may be particularly important to making these types of connections.[12]

Moreover, state governments (and even some local ones) have needs for people with expertise with respect to immigration, trade, and other sorts of international issues that are of increasing importance to them. Some state governments even have offices abroad to promote economic development opportunities. Washington State is a particularly good case in point, with more than $64 billion in exports and some 90,000 residents working for foreign-owned firms. The state employs a number of foreign trade representatives to further local business interests in European, Asian, and Latin American markets. It also operates offices in China, Mexico, Japan, and the United Kingdom. In addition, periodic overseas business missions by state officials and business executives are sponsored to encourage investment by foreign companies.[13]

For many positions, volunteering with the **Peace Corps** is good preparation. Many of our students have taken this route, completing a two-year commitment to service abroad on behalf of the US government. Established in 1961, the Peace Corps dispatches volunteers to work at the grass roots level in such areas as education, community development, health, agriculture, and

Peace Corps
a US government agency that sends volunteers to assist other countries in order to promote friendship and mutual understanding.

engineering. Some of these positions require specialized skills. For the most part, however, the organization casts a wide net in terms of its recruitment. Today, more than 8,500 volunteers operate in 76 countries, with the greatest concentration in Africa, Latin America, and Eastern Europe/Central Asia.[14] Living conditions for volunteers are often quite basic, and the financial arrangements are modest.

The opportunities described here require US citizenship, but international studies programs in the United States also prepare foreign students for government careers back home. The paths to these jobs are unique to each country. Quite often, these students come from families that have been involved in government service or political activity. For some of our African students in particular, these experiences have resulted in significant personal dramas and uncertainties as political circumstances in their countries have changed. For example, we have hosted students from the Congo, Liberia, and Sudan whose nations and families have endured considerable instability and conflict. Of course, prevailing sociopolitical conditions will influence their prospects for government service or political activism. For one of our former students, a "lost boy" from Sudan whose village was ravaged by war, the easing of violence (along with the financial support he secured from contacts he made in the United States) enabled him to travel home to begin planning for the building of a school to replace the one that had been destroyed.

Community health volunteer Michelle Joffe with her primary school students at an orphanage in Uganda as they celebrate the installation of a new water well. Michelle received both her undergraduate and graduate degrees from Tulane University.

International Organizations

International organizations engaged in a range of activities across the globe number in the thousands. Students with interests in economics and finance should take a look at intergovernmental organizations (IGOs) such as the International Monetary Fund, the World Bank, or similar organizations operating at the regional level. An advanced degree is often a prerequisite, in which case an entry-level position at another, more general organization may be a better place to start.

We occasionally hear from international studies students that their dream job would be one with the United Nations (UN). To be sure, working for the UN is often a particularly good fit, and it offers a variety of options. Entry-level junior professionals working for the Secretariat, the organization's administrative arm, must submit to the National Competitive Recruitment Exam. An Associate Experts program attracts candidates interested in working on projects designed to assist developing countries, and there are other opportunities to work directly for the array of UN agencies, funds, and programs that operate across the world. Jobs are apportioned to ensure representation across all member states. The UN has a comprehensive job portal that advertises career opportunities.[15]

NGOs may offer more options than IGOs. These groups cover the full range of global issues. They frequently operate on a nonprofit basis, so salaries are often modest. Today, there are well over 60,000 international NGOs.[16] While organizations such as Amnesty International and Greenpeace (two particularly well-known NGOs) seek to convey information and bring attention to matters of global significance, it is important to remember that their primary mission is to advocate for change in policies and practices related to their areas of concern. These organizations can be found across a broad political spectrum. The World Association of Non-Governmental Organizations (WANGO) provides considerable information about the work of many groups at www.wango.org and lists NGOs associated with the UN. A good number of NGOs work toward enhancing development across the Global South and provide unique and rewarding, if highly challenging, experiences. The Global Volunteer Network (GVN) Foundation, for example, works to alleviate poverty by partnering with local organizations to complete specific community-based projects. In addition to its staff, the GVN has interns from around the world who volunteer for six-month tours to assist with the implementation of these projects.[17]

Private Sector

For an ever-increasing number of companies, doing business—even if it is primarily in one country—involves global connections. Although international studies majors may lack academic credentials in marketing or finance, employers highly value their broad liberal arts training and sensitivity to the nuances of interacting with clients and partners from other backgrounds and cultures. As one hiring manager has put it, "All major hiring companies need global citizens. Global sensitivities, global perspective, global insight, along with the maturity and a capacity for risk-taking, are exactly the skills every major organization is looking for—in every industry."[18] Quite often, the most important tools required for success in the workplace are acquired on the job itself. Technical training may be provided in house, and the company may support advanced education to promote professional development.

International studies can provide a path to any number of other careers in the private sector, such as banking and other financial services, translating, journalism and other media, travel and tourism, public relations, and law. With so many industries and interest groups actively involved in efforts to influence legislation (many in and around Washington, D.C.), moreover, a position as a political lobbyist is also a possibility. Lobbyists engage in a variety of activities to secure favorable responses from legislators on matters of importance to the organizations they represent.

This brief review of some career options merely scratches the surface. It is never too early, however, to begin thinking about how your choice of a program of study will impact significantly on your future. Finding the path that best meets your needs and suits your talents will probably be a challenge. Given the complex and competitive nature of the job market, it is important to be proactive and to start early in considering the types of positions that might interest you. This process requires time and energy, and you can enhance it considerably by seeking out professors, academic advisers, career services, and other campus resources. As noted earlier, internships can offer real-world experience related to possible fields of interest and add to your credentials. Even if you do not really have a clue at this point, you might spend some time considering your interests and how they might translate into a prospective career path. This would be especially useful in guiding decisions with respect to the courses you take, the types of internships you might pursue, the additional languages you are interested in learning, and the destination for your study abroad experience.

> **HOW DO YOU CONNECT?** | **WHAT TYPE OF INTERNATIONAL CAREER ARE YOU INTERESTED IN?**
>
> a. diplomatic or some other type of government service
> b. nongovernmental organizations
> c. military
> d. education

EDUCATIONAL OPTIONS

A liberal arts education is an approach to learning that is intended to prepare students to deal with the complexity and diversity of the world in which they live. In addition to offering broad knowledge across an array of subjects and academic disciplines, it also provides the opportunity to gain in-depth knowledge in a specific area of interest.[19] Like other liberal arts majors, international studies may not necessarily provide a direct route to a career in the field without training beyond the undergraduate level. A liberal arts degree prepares you for graduate school, business school, law school, journalism school, or other professional degrees.

Graduate Programs in International Affairs

A considerable number of students entering international studies programs express an interest in pursuing a career in teaching and research. The path to becoming a faculty member at a four-year college or university can be a lengthy one. In most cases, a doctorate (usually a PhD) is required for a full-time position. This takes approximately four to six years of study beyond the undergraduate level and includes the writing of a dissertation, a book-length original research project on a particular issue or problem. Your professors can provide you with details as to the nature of the process. A growing number of part-time faculty are teaching classes at many institutions, and these jobs, as well as those at community colleges, may be open to candidates with a master's degree (generally attainable within a two-year period). Teaching languages, history, or social studies at the secondary or even primary level is also a possibility. Certification is usually required and may be secured in combination with many undergraduate majors by taking the appropriate education courses. While an advanced degree is generally not mandatory for teaching secondary or primary school, it is highly recommended and is often necessary to progress professionally and to command higher salaries.

In addition to providing the necessary credential to secure a faculty position at a college or university, a PhD (doctor of philosophy) also qualifies you to work as a researcher or analyst for the government or some privately funded policy institutes (often referred to as **think tanks**). PhD programs are generally organized by discipline, such as anthropology, geography, foreign language, history, or political science. There are also a few interdisciplinary doctoral programs in international/global studies.[20]

In some cases, students may be admitted directly to a PhD program when they finish their undergraduate studies. They earn the master's degree (MA) once they complete the requisite number of classes and requirements along the way. In other instances, students may choose to enroll in a particular institution to acquire the MA and then seek entrance to a PhD program elsewhere to continue with their studies. The standardized Graduate Record Examination (GRE) is often required as part of the admissions process. As you evaluate prospective programs, pay particular attention to financial support for both first-year and continuing students and the procedures for assisting graduates in their search for employment.

Most agencies, and even some companies, looking for employees with international knowledge and awareness will welcome individuals with master's-level training. A discipline-based program offering internationally oriented coursework and training will generally provide preparation of an academic nature. It is designed to further understanding of the theories, concepts, and issues that form the basis of the respective disciplines.

At the same time, the number of master's-level programs that focus on preparing you for a professional career in the field of international affairs is growing. These tend to be interdisciplinary in character and may closely

think tanks
privately funded research- and policy-oriented institutes.

| HOW DO YOU CONNECT? | **WHAT TYPE OF ADVANCED STUDY WOULD YOU CONSIDER AFTER GRADUATION?** |

a. graduate school related to international studies

b. law school

c. business school

d. will take a break from school and then consider at a later time resemble the structure of your undergraduate international studies program. They focus more on training that can be applied directly to work situations and may often include requirements, tracks, or courses relating to policy analysis, program administration, and foreign language proficiency. In the past, these types of programs were geared mainly to students seeking diplomatic or other types of government careers. More recently, many programs have extended their curricula to accommodate students with more diverse career interests and aspirations.

| TABLE 12.1 | ASSOCIATION OF PROFESSIONAL SCHOOLS OF INTERNATIONAL AFFAIRS: MEMBER SCHOOLS |

Institution	Degree Offered or School
American University	School of International Service
Carleton University	Norman Paterson School of International Affairs
Columbia University	School of International and Public Affairs
Duke University	Sanford School of Public Policy
George Washington University	Elliott School of International Affairs
Georgetown University	Edmund A. Walsh School of Foreign Service
Georgia Institute of Technology	Sam Nunn School of International Affairs
Graduate Institute of International and Development Studies	The Graduate Institute, Geneva
Harvard University	John F. Kennedy School of Government
Johns Hopkins University	Paul H. Nitze School of Advanced International Studies
Korea University	Graduate School of International Studies
MGIMO University	Moscow State Institute of International Relations
National University of Singapore	Lee Kuan Yew School of Public Policy
Princeton University	Woodrow Wilson School of Public and International Affairs
Ritsumeikan University	Graduate School of International Relations
Sciences Po (Paris)	Masters in International Affairs
Seoul National University	Graduate School of International Studies

(Continued)

| TABLE 12.1 | (CONTINUED) |

Institution	Degree Offered or School
St. Petersburg State University	School of International Relations
Stockholm School of Economics	Stockholm School of Economics
Syracuse University	The Maxwell School
Texas A & M University	Bush School of Government & Public Service
Tufts University	The Fletcher School of Law and Diplomacy
University of California, San Diego	Graduate School of International Relations and Pacific Studies
University of Denver	Josef Korbel School of International Studies
University of Maryland	School of Public Policy
University of Michigan	Gerald R. Ford School of Public Policy
University of Minnesota	Hubert H. Humphrey Institute of Public Affairs
University of Pittsburgh	Graduate School of Public And International Affairs
University of Queensland, Australia	The School of Political Science & International Studies
University of Southern California	Master of Public Diplomacy
University of St. Gallen	Master of Arts in International Affairs and Governance
University of Texas at Austin	Lyndon B. Johnson School of Public Affairs
University of Washington	Henry M. Jackson School of International Studies
Yale University	The Whitney and Betty MacMillan Center
Yonsei University	Graduate School of International Studies

Source: "Member Schools," Association of Professional Schools of International Affairs, 2012, www.apsia.org/apsia/members/allMembers.php?section=member.

A good place to begin learning about these possibilities is the Association of Professional Schools of International Affairs (APSIA). Its 35 members and some 35 affiliates are among the more interesting and highly regarded programs from around the world.[21] In addition to standard classroom work, many also offer opportunities to acquire practical experience along the way. Although it is certainly no guarantee, a broadly constructed and professionally oriented master's degree in international or public affairs could go a very long way toward enhancing your employability in the field.

By Leah Gardner, Graduate Student, International Studies, United States

I am passionate about design. As a high school student I honed my skills in painting, entering my work in competitions and for display at galleries. Wanting to put my skills to practical use, I applied and was accepted to a five year Interior Architecture program. I learned how to draft and use AutoCAD, render images with traditional and digital media, and apply the elements and principles of design. In my fourth year, I studied abroad at Yonsei University in Seoul, South Korea.

I had traveled to other countries before, but South Korea was unlike any other place that I had visited. By the end of my four months there I was in love with the city of Seoul, and it was absolutely heart-wrenching for me to leave. A year later, I graduated with my degree in Interior Architecture, but instead of finding a job in my field, I took up a teaching position at a private academy in Seoul. I was thrilled to be back in this wonderful city!

I immersed myself as much as possible into Korean life. I picked up a bit of the language, experimented with the food, and started following their music, movies, and television media. Most of all, I found myself paying more and more attention to politics. A short distance from this cosmopolitan city is North Korea. Civilian protection drills became a part of my life. The military and police were ever-present, honing their skills and conducting training exercises. I even visited the Demilitarized Zone (DMZ) to learn more about it. The Korean people put great time and energy into local and national politics, and I guess that energy rubbed off on me.

Most of all, I was heavily influenced by interacting with my students. Never before had I felt so connected to myself and other people than the time I spent with them. I was proud of them for being such demanding students, and proud of myself for contributing to their education. Over time, it became clear to me that I was not destined for a career in design, and I needed to redefine my focus to International Studies.

I returned to the United States for the express reason of entering a graduate program. I chose a Masters of International Studies because it is a designed to give students the skills needed for a successful career. I was also attracted to the fact that a student could specialize in practically any aspect of International Studies—international education, regional or global politics, economics, and more. When I first started I had a loose idea of what I wanted to do, but after getting my feet wet I knew I wanted to specialize in sustainable development. Studying international studies has been exhilarating for me, and I feel that same connected feeling that I did during my time in Seoul. I know I made the right choice.

I now have many career prospects in front of me, but what I really want is to work with an international non-profit, designing and implementing development programs to improve people's lives. I look forward to my future and I am glad I started my journey.

Business School

Given the ever-increasing networks that connect the global marketplace, it is certainly appropriate for international studies graduates to consider careers in management, marketing, finance, or accounting via the business school route. Hiring managers in both the private and public sector may see a master of business administration (MBA) degree as a particularly desirable, if not required, credential. Business school curricula include a heavy dose of quantitatively based courses, and this prompts some undergraduate international studies programs to include required courses in economics or math and statistics as preparation. If you find yourself considering business school, some undergraduate courses in economics and business-related fields will allow you to determine your interest level and the likely suitability of this type of graduate degree. Some graduate programs may require the completion of a few prerequisite undergraduate courses, while others do not. Many schools use the standardized Graduate Management Admissions Test (GMAT) as part of the application process, and an MBA degree generally requires two years of full time study.

As globalization has transformed the fundamental nature and character of business across the world, a considerable number of graduate business schools have internationalized their curricula. In addition to new courses, they are providing opportunities for overseas experiences. Some programs devoted exclusively to international business offer interdisciplinary degrees that are separate from the MBA. The Master of International Business (MIB) program at the University of South Carolina and the Arizona-based Thunderbird School of Global Management are the most noteworthy. These programs offer broader if less technical curricula and emphasize proficiency in foreign language and cross-cultural communication.

Law School

A good number of our students over the years have chosen to attend law school and to pursue careers in international law. Whether you are drawn to the business and commercial side, or immigration issues and political or humanitarian problems, a law degree (JD or juris doctor) may serve you well in seeking a position related to international affairs in government or the private sector. Although international studies may not necessarily provide direct preparation through coursework, it does develop the kinds of reasoning and problem-solving skills you need to be successful in the legal field.

Law schools consider applicants from all majors and tend to favor those with broad interests and experiences. A key factor in the admissions decision will be your score on the LSAT, the Law School Admission Test, which assesses reading and reasoning skills. It generally takes three years of full-time study to complete most programs. If possible, sample a law course or two at the undergraduate level to get a sense of the type of study and work that is involved, both in law school and beyond. While most standard law school curricula include few if any courses devoted exclusively to international law, a growing number of joint or dual programs with an international orientation will grant you both a law degree and a master's degree in public affairs.

CONCLUSION: WHERE DO YOU GO FROM HERE?

As globalization transforms how we live, it forces each of us to consider our relationship to the world and our responsibility for sustaining it. International studies courses and programs can help you to think more clearly as borders shift.[22] First, they foster an appreciation of the multiple perspectives that guide perceptions and visions across the world. Recognition of this diversity of approaches can build understanding of the wide array of political, economic, and cultural systems that dot the planet, while suggesting commonalities of interests both within and across them. Second, international studies puts forward a view of the world as an increasingly interconnected set of systems while emphasizing the interdependence of people living within them. This view serves to advance a truly global perspective.[23] Finally, international studies offers the opportunity to study transsovereign issues that transcend state jurisdictions. These issues cross traditional borders and require joint responses.[24]

The pursuit of international studies helps students to develop **intercultural competence**, that is, an ability to understand other customs and practices and to communicate effectively and appropriately with people whose backgrounds and interests are different from their own. Intercultural competence is critical to developing the perspectives that are necessary to tackle the problems affecting our planet. As international educator Darla Deardorff cautions, however, there is not a quick fix that can be accomplished in one semester or over the course of an undergraduate education. Rather, it is a lifelong process.[25]

Everything local is global, and everything global is local. This simple statement belies the challenges of confronting a changing world, where borders are shifting and interests are often difficult to define. We hope this book has helped you to consider your place in the world and chart a path for where you will go from here.

intercultural competence
the ability to communicate effectively with people from different backgrounds and with different interests.

KEYConcepts

TO LEARN More

Books and Other Print Media

Derick W. Brinkerhoff and Jennifer M. Brinkerhoff, *Working for Change: Making a Career in International Public Service* (Bloomfield, CT, Kumarian Press, 2005).

The Brinkerhoffs discuss career paths in international public service, with particular emphasis on positions in development administration. They include profiles of individuals who have pursued careers in the field and appendices that list related professional associations, degree programs, and job and internship resources.

Jeffrey S. Lantis and Jessica DuPlaga, *The Global Classroom: An Essential Guide to Study Abroad* (Boulder, CO, Paradigm, 2010).

Lantis and DuPlaga's book is particularly useful reading prior to selecting a particular study abroad program. It offers insight on how to choose the right program and suggests steps that can be taken to get the most out of the experience. Worksheets are included to assist the reader in addressing the recommendations included in the text.

Maria Pinto Carland and Candace Faber, *Careers in International Affairs,* 8th ed. (Washington, DC, Georgetown University Press, 2008).

This is a comprehensive review of the array of jobs and career paths for those interested in international affairs. It includes chapters on opportunities available through the federal government, international organizations, banking, business, consulting, nonprofits, and research institutes. Useful information relating to strategies that might be employed in navigating the international affairs job market is also included.

Richard Slimbach, *Becoming World Wise: A Guide to Global Learning* (Sterling, VA: Stylus, 2010.)

Slimbach's focused and informative guidebook offers tips for those considering the many paths to acquiring firsthand global experience, ranging from participation in formal study abroad programs to individually organized travel tours. Particularly useful are the recommendations as to how to maximize the intellectual and personal benefits of an international experience.

Sherry L. Mueller and Mark Overmann, *Working World: Careers in International Education, Exchange and Development* (Washington, DC: Georgetown University Press, 2008).

This is a valuable reference for job seekers. Much of the book is devoted to a listing of resources that may be of use in identifying potential employers and employment opportunities and learning more about different career paths that are available.

Stacie Nevadomski Berdan, *Go Global: Launching an International Career Here or Abroad* (SNB Media, 2011).

This innovative resource, published by an international careers author and consultant, also comes in digital format and is available for downloading. It contains recommendations for acquiring the skills and experiences that will help in launching an international career and incorporates suggestions and anecdotes from practitioners. It also offers opportunities to interact personally with the author, who has other resource materials related to the subject available through her website, http://stacieberdan.com/.

Websites

There are many web-based search engines that are available to assist with internship, study abroad, advanced education, employment, and career opportunities.

For internships, www.internabroad.com and www.internships.com are useful sources of information for programs that are available. For more specialized searches, www.idealist.com identifies opportunities with nonprofit organizations. The Washington Center, www.twc.edu, is a well regarded organization that offers internship and academic seminars in the Washington, D.C., area.

Students interested in exploring a broad range of options in gaining international experience may access www.goabroad.com and its related sites www.interabroad.com, www.volunteerabroad.com, www.teachabroad.com, and www.jobsabroad.com. These have been developed by international educators and focus on linking students with international opportunities. In addition, the International Volunteer Programs Association, an alliance of NGOs that sponsor international volunteer and internship exchanges, provides listings of programs through www.volunteer international.org, and the nonprofit International Partnership for Service Learning and Leadership offers information on earning academic credit for volunteer service abroad through its programs at www.volunteeringinternationa.org.

For students looking to become familiar with schools offering advanced professional training related to careers in international affairs, the Association of Professional Schools of International Affairs (APSIA) at www.apsia.org/apsia/members/allMembers .php?section=member is the gateway to this information. Links to each of its member and affiliate institutions are incorporated.

While academic departments and programs routinely offer career information on their websites, a particularly useful and comprehensive review of career options in international affairs has been prepared by Roy Licklider and Edward Rhodes of the Department of Political Science at Rutgers University and is available at http://polisci .rutgers.edu/index.php?option=com_content&task=view&id=180&Itemid=5.

Those with a particular interest in working for nongovernmental organizations will find considerable information through the World Association of Non-Governmental Organizations, www.wango.com. For groups associated with the UN, see www.ngo .org.

Most agencies, organizations, government offices, and companies offering international career opportunities usually provide online information regarding application qualifications and procedures and prospective jobs that are available. Among those that tend to attract considerable student interest are the US Department of State at www.careers.state.gov and the UN at www.un.org/en/employment.

Videos

Recruitment at the United Nations Secretariat (April 2012) and *Recruitment at the United Nations System (Inter-Agency)* (May, 2010).

These recruitment videos showcase career opportunities with the UN Secretariat and UN system, respectively. www.youtube.com/watch?v=xyRN-rcSjDk http://www.youtube.com/watch?v=k-MEIkzPMmE

YouTube Channel: Council on International Educational Exchange (CIEE) Teach Abroad.

The official YouTube channel for CIEE Teach Abroad hosts videos about getting teaching jobs worldwide and experiences of previous employees. www.youtube.com/user/cieeteachabroad

YouTube Channel: Idealist.

The official YouTube channel for Idealist.org showcases career profiles in a variety of fields, including policy, social work, volunteering, advocacy, and the environment. www.youtube.com/user/idealist

YouTube Channel: Peace Corps.

The official YouTube channel for the Peace Corps features videos about becoming a volunteer. www.youtube.com/user/peacecorps

Notes

CHAPTER 1
GETTING YOUR GLOBAL BEARINGS
1. Douglas Adams, *The Hitchhikers' Guide to the Galaxy* (New York: Harmony Books, 1979).
2. Theodore Levitt, "The Globalization of Markets," *Harvard Business Review,* May-June 1983: 92–102.
3. Colin Hay and David Marsh, eds., *Demystifying Globalization* (London: Macmillan, 2002);
   David Held and Anthony McGrew, eds., *Governing Globalization: Power, Authority, and Global Governance* (Basingstoke, UK: Palgrave, 2002), quoted in Luke Martell, "The Third Wave in Globalization Theory," *International Studies Review 9,* no. 2 (2007): 173–196.
4. International Monetary Fund, *Staff Studies for the World Economic Outlook* (Washington, DC: author, 1997), 79.
5. Brink Lindsey. *Against the Dead Hand: The Uncertain Struggle for Global Capitalism.* (New York: John Wiley & Sons, 2002), 63.
6. Luke Martell, "The Third Wave in Globalization Theory," *International Studies Review* 9, no. 2 (2007): 173–196.
7. Pietra Rivoli, *The Travels of a T-Shirt in the Global Economy* (Hoboken, NJ: John Wiley & Sons, 2005).
8. Colin Hay and David Marsh, eds., *Demystifying Globalization* (Basingstoke, UK: Palgrave, 2002), quoted in Martell, "The Third Wave."
9. Martell, "The Third Wave," 186.
10. Thomas Friedman, *The Lexus and the Olive Tree* (New York: Farrar, Straus, and Giroux, 1999).
11. Offshore IT Outsourcing.com, 2007, offshoreitout sourcing.com/Pages/outsourcing_statistics.asp.
12. Patrick Thibodeau, "IT Hiring in India Outpaces U.S.," *Computerworld,* January 21, 2010, www.computer world.com/s/article/9147258/IT_hiring_in_India_ outpaces_U.S.
13. "China's Trade Performance," The U.S.–China Business Council, accessed July 7, 2012, www.uschina.org/info/ analysis/2007/june-trade-performance.html.
14. Lester R. Brown, *The Twenty-Ninth Day* (New York: Norton, 1978).
15. Mihaly Csikszentmihalyi, *Finding Flow: The Psychology of Engagement in Everyday Life* (New York: Basic Books, 1997).
16. "Rainforest Facts," Raintree Nutrition Inc., accessed July 7, 2012, www.rain-tree.com/facts.htm.
17. Geoffrey Stokes, "Global Citizenship," *Ethos* 12, no. 1 (2004): 20.

18. Marcelo M. Suarez-Orozxo, "Wanted: Global Citizens," *Educational Leadership* 64, no. 7 (2007): 58.
19. Seyla Benhabib, "Borders, Boundaries, and Citizenship," *PS: Political Science & Politics* 38, no. 4 (2005): 673.
20. Megha Satyanarayana, "Site Enables Anyone to Use Small Loans to Change Lives a World Away," *The Charlotte Observer,* July 22, 2007, 1D.
21. Nigel Dower, *An Introduction to Global Citizenship* (Edinburgh: Edinburgh University Press, 2003), 35–49.
22. Oxfam, *Education for Global Citizenship: a Guide for Schools* (London, Oxfam, 2006), 3, www.oxfam .org.uk/education/gc/files/education_for_global_ citizenship_a_guide_for_schools.pdf.
23. Stokes, "Global Citizenship," 21–22.
24. Dower, *An Introduction to Global Citizenship,* 31–32.
25. Ibid., 127–128.
26. Chris Armstrong, "Global Civil Society and the Question of Global Citizenship," *Voluntas: International Journal of Voluntary and Nonprofit Organizations* 17, no. 4 (2006): 348–356, www.springerlink.com.
27. Quoted in Dower, *An Introduction to Global Citizenship,* 81.

CHAPTER 2
POINT OF DEPARTURE
1. Jeffrey D. Sachs, "Weapons of Mass Salvation," *The Economist* (October 24, 2002), www.economist.com/ node/1403544.
2. Garrett Hardin, "The Tragedy of the Commons," *Science* 62, no. 3859 (1968): 1243–1248.
3. Ibid.
4. Quoted in John C. Derbach, *Agenda for a Sustainable America* (Washington, DC: Environmental Law Institute, 2009), 6.
5. "Our Common Future, Chapter 2: Towards Sustainable Development," *Our Common Future: Report of the World Commission on Environment and Develop*ment, accessed July 9, 2012, www.un-documents.net/ocf-02. htm#I.
6. Ellen Bailey, "Eratosthenes of Cyrene," EBSCOhost, 2006, available from Middle Search Plus, Ipswich, MA.
7. Amy Witherbee, "Ptolemy," EBSCOhost, 2006, available from Middle Search Plus, Ipswich, MA.
8. E. Badertscher, "Baron Alexander von Humboldt," EBSCOhost, 2007, available from Middle Search Plus, Ipswich, MA.

9. Alexander Von Humboldt, *Cosmos: A Sketch of the A Physical Description of the Universe,* vol. 2, trans. E. O. Otte (New York: Harper and Brothers, 1850), 351–352.

10. US Geological Survey, "Geographic Information Systems," last modified February 22, 2007, egsc.usgs.gov/isb/pubs/gis_poster/.

11. National Snow and Ice Data Center, "View NSIDC Data on Virtual Globes: Google Earth," accessed July 9, 2012, nsidc.org/data/virtual_globes/.

12. David Smith, "Humanitarian Crisis as World's Largest Refugee Camp Declared Full," *The Guardian,* 2011, www.guardian.co.uk/world/2011/jun/10/humanitarian-crisis-refugee-camp-declared-full.

13. US Census Bureau, "International Programs," last revised June 8, 2012, www.census.gov/population/international/.

14. United Nations Development Programme, "Human Development Report 2007–08", in Richard Payne, *Global Issues: Politics, Economics and Culture,* 3rd ed. (London: Longman, 2011), 253.

15. "India's Still-Growing Population Threatens 'Ungovernable Mess,'" *The National,* UNDP Human Development Reports, 2010, hdr.undp.org/en/reports/global/hdr2010/news/mpi/title,20594,en.html.

16. Ibid.

17. Alan Greenblatt, "The Graying Planet: Will Aging Populations Cause Economic Upheaval?" *CQ Global Researcher* 5, no. 6 (2012), library.cqpress.com/globalresearcher/document.php?id=cqrgloba12011031500.

18. US Census Bureau, "International Programs," last revised June 8, 2012, www.census.gov/ipc/www/idb/groups.php.

19. "Maslow's Hierarchy," Changing Minds, 2012, changingminds.org/explanations/needs/maslow.htm.

20. Yves Charbit, *Economic, Social and Demographic Thought in the XIXth Century: The Population Debate from Malthus to Marx* (Dordrecht, London: Springer, 2009), *13.*

21. David Biello, "Another Inconvenient Truth: World's Growing Population Poses a Malthusian Dilemma," *Scientific American,* 2009, www.scientificamerican.com/article.cfm?id=growing-population-poses-malthusian-dilemma.

22. Food and Agriculture Organization of the United Nations, *The State of Food Insecurity in the World* 2011, www.fao.org/docrep/014/i2330e/i2330e06.pdf.

23. "Crop Prospects and Food Situation," Food and Agriculture Organization of the United Nations (June, 2011), www.fao.org/docrep/014/a1979e/a1979e00.pdf.

24. "SOMALIA Food Security Outlook," Famine Early Warning Systems Network, USAID, 2011, www.fews.net/docs/Publications/Somalia_OL_2011_04.pdf.

25. "Hunger Portal," Food and Agriculture Organization of the United Nations, 2012, www.fao.org/hunger/en/.

26. "Crop Prospects and Food Situation," Food and Agriculture Organization of the United Nations (June, 2011), www.fao.org/docrep/014/a1979e/a1979e00.pdf.

27. "The November FAO Food Price Index Nearly Unchanged from October," Food and Agriculture Organization of the United Nations, 2011, www.fao.org/worldfoodsituation/wfs-home/foodpricesindex/en/.

28. "Update Phase 2: Food Security," *Agriculture Negotiations: Backgrounder,* World Trade Organization, last updated October 10, 2002, www.wto.org/english/tratop_e/agric_e/negs_bkgrnd18_ph2foodsecurity_e.htm.

29. "Weighing the GMO Arguments: Against," Food and Agriculture Organization of the United Nations, 2003, www.fao.org/english/newsroom/focus/2003/gm08.htm.

30. "The Incident, Response, and Settlement," Union Carbide Corporation, Bhopal Information Center, 2012, www.bhopal.com/incident-response-and-settlement.

31. "Facts and Figures about Desertification," Clean Water Space, 2009, www.cawater-info.net/all_about_water/en/?p=114.

32. Ibid.

33. water.org, accessed July 30, 2012, water.org/water-crisis/water-facts/water/

34. "Greenhouse Gas Emissions," US Environmental Protection Agency, accessed July 9, 2012, www.epa.gov/climatechange/emissions/index.html.

35. Reed Karaim, "Climate Change: Will the Copenhagen Accord Slow Global Warming?" *CQ Global Researcher* 4, no. 2 (2010), library.cqpress.com/globalresearcher/document.php?id=cqrgloba12010020000&type=hitlist&num=0.

36. Ibid.

37. "Reduce & Reuse," US Environmental Protection Agency, last updated June 13, 2012, www.epa.gov/epawaste/conserve/rrr/reduce.htm.

38. "Urgent Need to Prepare Developing Countries for Surge in E-Wastes," United Nations Environment Programme, 2010, www.unep.org/Documents.Multilingual/Default.asp?DocumentID=612&ArticleID=6471&1 =en&t=long.

39. "ReStore Resale Outlets," Habitat for Humanity, 2012, www.habitat.org/restores/default.aspx?tgs=Ni85LzIwMTEgMTE6NDU6MjUgQU0%3d.

40. Martin Medina, "The Informal Recycling Sector in Developing Countries: Organizing Waste Pickers to Enhance Their Impact," *GridLines,* October 2008, www.3rkh.net/3rkh/files/44informal_recycling_sectors.pdf.

41. Ibid.

CHAPTER 3
JUMP STARTING THE TRIP

1. Thomas L. Friedman, *The World Is Flat* (New York: Farrar, Straus, and Giroux, 2007), 5.
2. Ibid., 50–200.
3. *Internet World Stats, World Internet Usage and Population Statistics,* accessed December 31, 2011, www.internetworldstats.com/stats.htm.
4. Ibid.
5. Clara Moskowitz, "Earth's Beauty From Space: Q&A With 'Space Clown' Guy Laliberte," Space.com (June 28, 2011), www.space.com/12088-photos-earth-space-gaia-guy-laliberte.html.
6. Virgin Galactic, accessed July 11, 2012, www.virgingalactic.com/.
7. Susan Montoya Bryan, "Virgin Galactic's Branson Says Kutcher is 500th customer to Put Down Deposit for Space Ride," Associated Press (March 20, 2012), news.yahoo.com/virgin-galactics-branson-says-kutcher-500th-customer-put-122015438.html.
8. Norihiko Shirouzu, "Train Makers Rail Against China's High Speed Designs," *The Wall Street Journal* (November 17, 2010), online.wsj.com/article/SB10001424052748704814204575507353221141616.html#ixzz16i7pfQjy.
9. "U.S. International Air Passenger and Freight Statistics," Office of the Assistant Secretary for Aviation and International Affairs, US Department of Transportation, September 2011, ostpxweb.dot.gov/aviation/international-al-series/sept2011.pdf.
10. "The Mystery of the Chinese Consumer," *The Economist* (July 7, 2011), www.economist.com/node/18928514.
11. James Burke, in J. Michael Adams and Angelo Carfagna, *Coming of Age in a Globalized World: The Next Generation* (Sterling, Virginia: Kumarian Press, 2006), 19.
12. Lee Rainie, Kathryn Zickuhr, Kristen Purcell, Mary Madden, and Joanna Brenner, "The Rise of E-Reading," Pew Internet & American Life Project (April 4, 2012), libraries.pewinternet.org/2012/04/04/the-rise-of-e-reading/.
13. Paul Biba, "Mobile Phones in China Increase Reading—120 Million Readers," *TeleRead,* January 10, 2011, www.teleread.com/paul-biba/mobile-phones-in-china-increase-reading-120-million-readers/.
14. Charles More, *Understanding the Industrial Revolution* (London, New York: Routledge, 2000), 98.
15. "Power and Horsepower in Electrical Motors," The Engineering Toolbox, accessed July 16, 2012, www.engineeringtoolbox.com/electrical-motor-horsepower-d_653.html.
16. Thomas Savery, *The Miner's Friend; or, an Engine to Raise Water by Fire, Described: and of the Manner of Fixing it in Mines . . .* (London: S. Crouch, 1827), 26.
17. Research and Innovative Technology Administration, US Department of Transportation, *Freight Transportation: Global Highlights,* 2010, 4, www.bts.gov/publications/freight_transportation/pdf/entire.pdf.
18. Thomas H. White, "Electric Telegraph Development and Morse Code," United States Early Radio History, accessed July 16, 2012, earlyradiohistory.us/sec002.htm.
19. Anna Robertson, Steve Garfinkel, and Elizabeth Eckstein, "Radio in the 1920s," Chicago Radio Show 1924, accessed July 16, 2012, xroads.virginia.edu/~ug00/3on1/radioshow/1920radio.htm.
20. Michael R. Ward, "Rural Telecommunications Subsidies Do Not Work," University of Texas at Arlington, accessed July 12, 2012, www.uta.edu/faculty/mikeward/JRAP.pdf.
21. Kevin Belhumeur, "Landline Telephone Facts," salon.com, accessed July 12, 2012, techtips.salon.com/landline-telephone-20646.html.
22. "Mobile Cellular Subscriptions," ICT Data and Statistics, International Telecommunications Union, last updated July 10, 2012, www.itu.int/ITU-D/ict/statistics/.
23. Martin Campbell-Kelly and William Aspray, *Computer: A History of the Information Machine,* 2nd ed. (Boulder, CO: Westview Press, 2004), 84–85.
24. "UNIVAC," ComputerHope, 2012, www.computerhope.com/jargon/u/univac.htm.
25. "1958," Computer History Museum, 2006, www.computerhistory.org/timeline/?year=1958; "IC," Computer Hope, 2012, www.computerhope.com/jargon/i/ic.htm; "Jack Kilby," biography.com, 2012, www.biography.com/people/jack-kilby-40499.
26. Roy A. Allan, *A History of the Personal Computer: The People and the Technology* (London, ON, Canada: Allan Publishing, 2001), Chapter 3, p. 6.
27. "You Have 15 Tons of Data Inside Your Hard Drive," Disk Depot, accessed July 16, 2012, www.diskdepot.co.uk/blog/index.php/you-have-15-tons-of-data-inside-your-hard-drive/; "1971," Computer History Museum, 2006, www.computerhistory.org/timeline/?year=1971.
28. "1981," Computer History Museum, 2006, www.computerhistory.org/timeline/?year=1981.
29. "Bill Gates," biography.com, 2012, www.biography.com/people/bill-gates-9307520.
30. "Transcript: Vice President Gore on CNN's 'Late Edition,'" CNN, March 9, 1999, www.cnn.com/ALLPOLITICS/stories/1999/03/09/president.2000/transcript.gore/index.html.
31. Raul Rojas, ed., *Encyclopedia of Computers and Computer History,* vol. 2, M–Z, (New York: The Moschovitis Group, 2001), 751–753.
32. Campbell-Kelly and Aspray, *Computer,* 268–270.

33. "1990," Computer History Museum, 2006, www
    .computerhistory.org/timeline/?year=1990.
34. "1990," ComputerHope, 2012, www.computerhope
    .com/history/1990.htm.
35. "Yahoo," ComputerHope, 2012, www.computerhope
    .com/jargon/y/yahoo.htm.
36. "Computer History – 1980 – 1990," ComputerHope, 2012,
    www.computerhope.com/history/198090.htm.
37. Gary Wolf, "Steve Jobs: The Next Insanely Great Thing,"
    Wired Magazine, 1996, www.wired.com/wired/
    archive/4.02/jobs_pr.html
38. Chris Ziegler, "The Apple iPhone," Engadget, January 9,
    2007, www.engadget.com/2007/01/09/the-apple-iphone/.
39. "The State of Mobile Apps," NielsenWire, June 1, 2010,
    blog.nielsen.com/nielsenwire/online_mobile/the-state-of-
    mobile-apps.
40. Melanie Lee, "Analysis: A Year after China Retreat,
    Google Plots New Growth," Reuters, January 13, 2011,
    www.reuters.com/article/2011/01/13/us-google-china-
    idUSTRE70C1X820110113.
41. Sarah Gordon and Richard Ford, *Cyberterrorism?* white
    paper, Symantec, 2003, www.symantec.com/avcenter/
    reference/cyberterrorism.pdf.
42. "What is Wikileaks?" Wikileaks, accessed July 12, 2012,
    wikileaks.org/About.html.
43. "SAP Customer, All for One, Keeps Projects Rolling
    Around the Clock, Around the Globe," SAP StreamWork,
    November 8, 2011, sapstreamwork.com/news-blog/
    sap-customer-all-one-keeps-projects-rolling-around-clock-
    around-globe.
44. "About Us – Overview – History," Infosys, accessed July
    16, 2012, www.infosys.com/about/Pages/history.aspx.
45. "Software Companies in Bangalore," MapsofIndia.com,
    accessed July 12, 2012, www.mapsofindia.com/banga-
    lore/software-companies-in-bangalore.html.
46. "Industries," Infosys, accessed July 16, 2012, www
    .infosys.com/industries/Pages/index.aspx.
47. "Contact Center Technology Solutions," Infosys, August
    2008, www.infosys.com/engineering-services/product-
    engineering/Documents/contact-center-data
    sheet.pdf.
48. "Connected Customer Experience," Infosys, 2011, www
    .infosys.com/microsoft/resource-center/Documents/con-
    nected-customer-experience.pdf.
49. Marisa Urgo, *Al-Shabaab's Exploitation of Alternative
    Remittance Systems (ARS) in Kenya*, June 11, 2009,
    www.orgsites.com/va/asis151/JIEDDO_J2_OSAAC_
    Al-Shabaabs_Exploitation_of_Alternative_Remittance_
    Systems_in_Kenya.pdf
50. Helene Cooper, "U.S. Freezes a Record $30 Billion in
    Libyan Assets," *New York Times*, February 28, 2011,
    www.nytimes.com/2011/03/01/world/africa/01
    assets.html.
51. Ben Parr, "Google Launches Google+ To Battle Facebook
    [PICS]," Mashable.com, June 28, 2011, mashable
    .com/2011/06/28/google-plus/.
52. Ian Black, "A Devastating Defeat for Iran's Green
    Revolution," *The Guardian* (June 13, 2009), www
    .guardian.co.uk/world/2009/jun/14/iran-tehran-election-
    results-riots.
53. "Translations," TED, accessed July 12, 2012, www
    .ted.com/OpenTranslationProject.
54. "Haiti Earthquake Prompts Global Response," Voice of
    America (January 14, 2010), www.voanews.com/english/
    news/Haiti-Earthquake-Prompts-Global-
    Response-81536387.html.

CHAPTER 4
POLITICAL BORDERS

1. Parag Khanna, "10 Ideas for the Next 10 Years: A
   Thinker's Guide to the Most Important Trends of the New
   Decade," *Time,* March 11, 2010, www.time.com/time/
   specials/packages/article/0,28804,1971133_
   1971110_1971105,00.html.
2. "Summer Declaration on Defence Capabilities: Toward
   NATO Forces 2020," North Atlantic Treaty Organization,
   May 20, 2012, www.nato.int/cps/en/natolive/official_
   texts_87594.htm?mode=pressrelease.
3. Thucydides, *The History of the Peloponnesian War,* Rex
   Warner, trans. (Baltimore: Penguin Books, 1972), 400-408.
4. Joseph S. Nye, Jr., *Understanding International Conflicts,*
   7th ed. (New York: Longman, 2008), 2–4.
5. Ibid., 3.
6. Niccolo Machiavelli, *The Prince,* 2nd ed. (New York:
   Norton, 1992), 46.
7. Michael Duffy, "The Causes of World War One," firstworld
   war.com, August 22, 2009, www.firstworldwar.com/ori-
   gins/causes.htm.
8. Michael Duffy, "Archduke Franz Ferdinand's Assassination,
   28 June 1914," firstworldwar.com, August 22, 2009,
   www.firstworldwar.com/source/harrachmemoir.htm.
9. Woodrow Wilson, "The Fourteen Points," in *Classics of
   International Relations,* 3rd ed., ed. John A. Vasquez
   (New Jersey: Prentice Hall, 1996), 38.
10. Hans Morgenthau, *Politics Among Nations: The Struggle
    for Power and Peace* (New York: Knopf, 1948).
11. North Atlantic Treaty Organization, "NATO's Role in
    Afghanistan," 2012, www.nato.int/cps/en/natolive/top-
    ics_8189.htm.
12. US Department of the Treasury, "Iran Sanctions," 2012,
    www.treasury.gov/resource-center/sanctions/programs/
    pages/iran.aspx.

13. Nicholas Onuf, *World of Our Making: Rules and Rule in Social Theory and International Relations* (Columbia: University of South Carolina Press, 1989).

14. J. Ann Tickner, *Gendering World Politics: Issues and Approaches in the Post–Cold War Era* (New York: Columbia University Press, 2001).

CHAPTER 5
CHALLENGES TO SECURITY

1. "Statement by Sam Nunn on 2012 Nuclear Security Summit," Nuclear Threat Initiative, March 27, 2012, www.nti.org/newsroom/news/statement-sam-nunn-2012-nuclear-security-summit/.

2. Robert John, "Behind the Balfour Declaration: Britain's Great War Pledge to Lord Rothschild," *The Journal of Historical Review* 6, no. 4 (winter 1985–86), accessed through Institute of Historical Review, www.ihr.org/jhr/v06/v06p389_John.html.

3. "The Camp David Accords," Jimmy Carter Library & Museum, 2012, www.jimmycarterlibrary.gov/documents/campdavid/.

4. "Oslo Accords," Middle East Research and Information Project, 2012, www.merip.org/palestine-israel_primer/oslo-accords-pal-isr-prime.html.

5. "Camp David 2000 until Today: A Review of the Lessons Learned in the Ten Years Since the Camp David Summit," Israel Palestine Center for Research and Information, October, 19, 2010, www.ipcri.org/IPCRI/Videos/Entries/2010/10/19_Camp_David_2000_Until_Today__Pini_Meidan_and_Nabeel_Shaath.html.

6. Sharon Otterman, "Middle East: The Road Map to Peace," Council on Foreign Relations, February 7, 2005, www.cfr.org/middle-east/middle-east-road-map-peace/p7738.

7. "The New START Treaty Signed," The White House Blog, February 2, 2011, www.whitehouse.gov/blog/2011/02/02/new-start-treaty-signed.

8. "For Sale: West's Deadly Nuclear Secrets," *The Sunday Times,* January 5, 2008, www.informationclearinghouse.info/article19006.htm.

9. "State Sponsors of Terrorism," US Department of State, accessed July 13, 2012, www.state.gov/j/ct/c14151.htm.

10. Cindy C. Combs, T*errorism in the Twenty First Century* (Upper Saddle River, NJ: Prentice-Hall, 2012), 20–21.

11. Marc Sageman, "The Next Generation of Terror," *Foreign Policy*, February 19, 2008, www.foreignpolicy.com/articles/2008/02/19/the_next_generation_of_terror.

12. Paul Haven, "Next Generation in Disarray?" *The Charlotte Observer,* June 10, 2006.

13. "White House Advisor: Bomb Plot Highlights AQAP as Cancer," CBS News, May 8, 2012, www.cbsnews.com/8301–505263_162–57429767/wh-adviser-bomb-plot-highlights-aqap-as-cancer/.

14. "Abu Sayyaf Group," Council on Foreign Relations Backgrounder, May 27, 2009, www.cfr.org/philippines/abu-sayyaf-group-philippines-islamist-separatists/p9235; "Haqqani Network," *The New York Times*, last updated April 17, 2012, topics.nytimes.com/top/reference/timestopics/organizations/h/haqqani_network/index.html.

15. Current Treaty Status, Preparatory Commission for the Comprehensive Nuclear Test Ban Treaty Organization, accessed July 13, 2012, www.ctbto.org/.

16. Thomas Risse-Kappen, "Democratic Peace-Warlike Democracies? A Social Constructivist Interpretation of the Liberal Argument," in *Peace Studies: Critical Concepts in Political Science,* ed. Matthew Evangelista (New York: Routledge, 2005), 78.

CHAPTER 6
SEEKING PROSPERITY

1. Hernando de Soto, *The Mystery of Capital: Why Capitalism Triumphs in the West and Fails Everywhere Else* (New York: Basic Books, 2000), 2.

2. David N. Balaam and Bradford Dillman, *Introduction to International Political Economy* (Boston: Longman, 2011), 58–60.

3. Adam Smith, 1776, quoted in Helen Joyce, "Adam Smith and the Invisible Hand," +*plus magazine* 14 (March 1, 2001), plus.maths.org/issue14/features/smith/.

4. Paul Kennedy, *The Rise and Fall of Great Powers* (New York: Random House, 1987).

5. Vince Crawley, "Marshall Plan for Rebuilding Europe Still Echoes after 60 Years," America.gov Archive, accessed July 17, 2012, www.america.gov/st/washfile-english/2007/May/20070521163245MVyelwarC7.548159e-02.html; Barry Eichengreen and Marc Uzan, "The Marshall Plan," *Economic Policy* 7, no. 14 (April 1992): 13–54, 59–75.

6. Immanuel Wallerstein, "The Rise and Demise of the World Capitalist System: Concept for Comparative Analysis," *Comparative Studies in Society and History* 16, no. 4 (September 1974): 387–415.

7. André Gunder Frank, *Capitalism and Development in Latin America* (New York: Monthly Review Press, 1967).

8. André Gunder Frank, *Latin America: Underdevelopment or Revolution* (New York, Monthly Review Press, 1969), 4.

9. Joseph E. Stiglitz, *Making Globalization Work* (New York, W.W. Norton, 2007).

10. "Brief History," OPEC, www.opec.org/opec_web/en/about_us/24.htm; "Crude Oil Production, OPEC, the Persian Gulf, and the United States," Fact #296, US Department of Energy, December 1, 2003, www1

.eere.energy.gov/vehiclesandfuels/facts/2003/fcvt_ fotw296.html

11. Geoffrey Kemp and Robert Harkavy, *Strategic Geography and the Changing Middle East* (Washington, DC: Brookings Institution, 1997).

12. Spencer L. Davidson, "The U.S. Should Soak Up that Shower of Gold," *Time,* December 16, 1974, 41.

13. Robert O. Keohane and Joseph S. Nye, *Power and Interdependence: World Politics in Transition* (Boston: Little, Brown, 1977).

14. Lester Thurow, *Head to Head: The Coming Economic Battle among Japan, Europe, and America* (New York: William Morrow, 1991).

15. US Department of Commerce, *Survey of Current Business* 54, no. 1 (January 1974) and no. 7 (July 1974).

16. "Foreign Trade, Trade in Goods with Japan," accessed July 17. 2012, www.census.gov/foreign-trade/balance/ c5880.html#1990.

17. EUROPA: Gateway to the European Union, accessed July 17, 2012, europa.eu.

18. "World Economic Outlook Database," International Monetary Fund, April 2012, www.imf.org/external/pubs/ ft/weo/2012/01/weodata/index.aspx.

19. "World Economic Outlook Database," International Monetary Fund, April 2012, www.imf.org/external/pubs/ ft/weo/2012/01/weodata/index.aspx.

20. "Foreign Direct Investment in China," US-China Business Council, accessed July 30, 2012, www.uschina .org/statistics/fdi_cumulative.html; Kenneth Rapoza, "Top 3 Countries to Invest in Next 3 Years, According to the U.N.," *Forbes,* July 5, 2012, www.forbes.com/sites/ken- rapoza/2012/07/05/top-3-countries-to-invest-in-next- 3-years-according-to-the-u-n/.

21. "How Much Does China's Exchange Rate Affect the Trade Deficit?" US–China Business Council, accessed July 30, 2012, www.uschina.org/info/trade-agenda/china- exchange-rate.html.

22. "Top 29 IT Companies in India," *Rediff Business,* August 3, 2011, www.rediff.com/business/slide-show/slide-show- 1-top-20-it-companies-in-india/20110803.htm; "Company Profile," Tata Motors, 2012, www.tata motors.com/know-us/company-profile.php.

23. Allen G. Breed, "Tax Dollars Change Outsourcing Debate," *The Charlotte Observer,* June 6, 2004, 3D.

24. United Nations, *World Economic Situation and Prospects 2012,* (New York: United Nations, January 2012), www. un.org/en/development/desa/policy/wesp/wesp_ current/2012wesp.pdf.

25. Roger Cohen, "The World Is Upside Down," *The New York Times,* June 2, 2008, accessed July 17, 2012, www .nytimes.com/2008/06/01/opinion/01iht-edcohen .1.13366689.html.

26. G-7 members include Canada, France, Germany, Italy, Japan, United Kingdom, and the United States. Data from International Monetary Fund, *World Economic Outlook Database,* April 2012, www.imf.org/external/pubs/ft/ weo/2012/01/weodata/index.aspx.

27. United Nations, *World Economic Situation and Prospects 2010* (New York: United Nations, January 2010), www. un.org/en/development/desa/policy/wesp/wesp_ archive/2010wesp.pdf.

28. "World Economic Outlook Database," International Monetary Fund, April 2012, www.imf.org/external/pubs/ ft/weo/2012/01/weodata/index.aspx

29. "Which Companies Make the Best Cars? Global Fight with Intriguing Results," *Consumer Reports* 72, no. 4 (April 2007), 19.

30. "World Economic Outlook Database," International Monetary Fund, April 2012, www.imf.org/external/pubs/ ft/weo/2012/01/weodata/index.aspx.

31. "World Economic Outlook Database," International Monetary Fund, April 2012, www.imf.org/external/pubs/ ft/weo/2012/01/weodata/index.aspx.

32. "U.S. International Transactions: Fourth Quarter and Year 2011," US Department of Commerce, *Survey of Current Business* 92, no. 4 (April 2012), 22, www.bea.gov/scb/ pdf/2012/04%20April/0412_itaq%20text.pdf.

33. "What Is the Deficit?" accessed May 22, 2012, www .usgovernmentspending.com/federal_debt; "What Is the Deficit?" accessed August 9, 2012, www .usgovernmentspending.com/us_deficit.

34. "Major Foreign Holders of Treasury Securities," US Department of the Treasury, Office of International Affairs, accessed July 30, 2012, www.treas.gov/tic/mfh.txt.

35. "World Economic Outlook Database," International Monetary Fund, April 2010, www.imf.org/external/pubs/ ft/weo/2010/01/weodata/index.aspx.

36. US Energy Information Administration, Office of Energy Statistics, US Department of Energy "Monthly Energy Review"; US Energy Information Administration, US Department of Energy: Official Energy Statistics from the US Government, May 2012, www.eia.gov/total energy/data/monthly/archive/00351205.pdf.

37. Hannah Seligson, "Nine Young Chinese Entrepreneurs to Watch," Forbes.com, February 26, 2010, www .forbes.com/2010/02/26/young-chinese-entrepreneurs- to-watch-entrepreneurs-technology-china_2.html.

38. International Labor Organization, "The Cost of Coercion: Global Report on Forced Labour," 2009, 30–32, www.ilo. org/wcmsp5/groups/public/@ed_norm/@relconf/docu- ments/meetingdocument/wcms_106230.pdf.

39. US Department of State, *Trafficking in Persons Report,* 10th ed., June 2010, 18, www.state.gov/documents/ organization/142979.pdf.

CHAPTER 7
CHALLENGES TO PROSPERITY

1. "Jobs Are Top Priority, Business Leaders Say as World Economic Forum Annual Meeting 2012 Closes," accessed August 4, 2012, www.weforum.org/events/world-economic-forum-annual-meeting-2012/.

2. Joseph E. Stiglitz, *Globalization and Its Discontents* (New York: W.W. Norton, 2002).

3. BASIS (Business Access to State Information & Services), "The World Trade Organisation," accessed July 18, 2012, www.basis.ie/home/home.jsp?pcategory=14424&ecategory=14427&doclistid=18395.&sectionpage=10339&language=EN&page=&link=link001&doc=11119&logname=The%20World%20Trade%20Organisation&urlcode=.

4. World Trade Organization, "Dispute Settlement," accessed July 18, 2012, www.wto.org/english/tratop_e/dispu_e/dispu_e.htm.

5. World Trade Organization, Press Release, March 23, 2009, www.wto.org/english/news_e/pres09_e/pr554_e.htm; World Trade Organization, Press Release, March 26, 2010, www.wto.org/english/news_e/pres10_e/pr598_e.htm; World Trade Organization, press Release, April 12, 2012, www.wto.org/english/news_e/pres12_e/pr658_e.htm.

6. Joseph E. Stiglitz, *Making Globalization Work* (New York: W.W. Norton, 2006), 120–124.

7. Lee Hudson Teslik, "NAFTA's Economic Impact," Council on Foreign Relations, July 7, 2009, www.cfr.org/publication/15790; National Export Initiative, "The North American Free Trade Agreement," last updated October 12, 2011, export.gov/FTA/nafta/index.asp.

8. Public Broadcasting Service, "Debating the Central American Free Trade Act," NOW, March 11, 2005,www.pbs.org/now/politics/caftadebate.html.

9. Global Exchange, "FTAA," 2011, www.globalexchange.org/resources/FTAA.

10. World Trade Organization, "About the WTO—A Statement by the Director-General," 2012, www.wto.org/english/thewto_e/whatis_e/wto_dg_stat_e.htm.

11. Russ Kuykendall, "Going Local in a Global World: Principled Free Trade, Mercantilism, and Environmental Protectionism," October 27, 2011, www.cardus.ca/policy/article/2936.

12. Richard McCormack, "Anti-Free Trade Lobby Is Completely Ignored By U.S. Senators," *Manufacturing & Technology News* 18, no. 12, July, 29, 2011, www.manufacturingnews.com/news/11/0729/KoreaFTA.html.

13. PressTV, "Malaysian Anti-Free Trade Activists Protest FTA Deals with the US," December 5, 2011, www.presstv.ir/detail/213930.html.

14. Martin D.D. Evans and Viktoria Hnatkovska, "International Capital Flows, Returns and World Financial Integration," first draft, September 23, 2005, www9.georgetown.edu/faculty/evansm1/wpapers_files/globalv1.pdf.

15. Robert E. Scott, "US Current Account Deficit Improves in 2007 Despite Rising Oil Prices," Economic Policy Institute, March 26, 2008, www.epi.org/publication/indicators_intlpict_20080326/; Peterson Institute for International Economics, "Hot Topics: US Current Account Deficit," accessed July 18, 2012, www.piie.com/research/topics/hottopic.cfm?HotTopicID=9.

16. "Global 500: Our Annual Ranking of the World's Largest Corporations," *Fortune Magazine*, July 25, 2011, money.cnn.com/magazines/fortune/global500/2011/full_list/.

17. Connor Jones, "University to Implement Anti-Sweatshop Regulation," United Students Against Sweatshops, March 22, 2012, usas.org/2012/03/22/georgetown-to-implement-designated-suppliers-program/.

18. Eduardo Porter, "Dividends Emerge in Pressing Apple over Working Conditions in China," *The New York Times,* March 6, 2012, www.nytimes.com/2012/03/07/business/dividends-emerge-in-pressing-apple-over-working-conditions-in-china.html.

19. Loretta Chao and Amir Efrati, "China Renews Google's Operating License," *The Wall Street Journal,* July 11, 2011, online.wsj.com/article/SB10001424052748704075604575356552939507706.html.

20. "Global 500: Our Annual Ranking of the World's Largest Corporations," *Fortune Magazine,* July 25, 2011, money.cnn.com/magazines/fortune/global500/2011/full_list/.

21. "Business Digest: Around the Nation and World," *The Charlotte Observer,* February 24, 2006, 3D.

22. John Ross, "China's Global Companies: Strengths and Weaknesses," June 26, 2011, www.china.org.cn/opinion/2011–06/26/content_22855094.htm; "Chinese Automobile Industry and Sales of Chinese Cars Abroad," Facts and Details, 2008, factsanddetails.com/china.php?itemid=361&catid=9&subcatid=61.

23. Jana Honke, Nicole Kranz, Tanja A. Borzel, and Adrienne Heritier, "Fostering Environmental Regulation? Corporate Social Responsibility in Countries with Weak Regulatory Capacities," Basel Institute of Governance, SFB-Governance Working Paper Series, No. 9, February 2008.

24. Martin Khor, "The Double Standards of Multinationals," *The Guardian,* June 25, 2010, www.guardian.co.uk/commentisfree/cif-green/2010/jun/25/double-standards-multinationals-ecological-disasters.

25. Organization for Economic Cooperation and Development, "Multilateral Agreement on Investment,"

accessed July 18, 2012, www.oecd.org/document/35/0,3
343,en_2649_33783766_1894819_1_1_1_1,00.html.

26. Kelsey Mays, "The Cars.com American-Made Index,"
November 23, 2010, www.cars.com/go/advice/Story
.jsp?section=top&subject=ami&story=amMade0710;
"How American Is That Car?," *USA Today,* March 21,
2007, www.usatoday.com/money/autos/2007–03–21-
car-content-chart_N.htm.

27. International Monetary Fund, "Factsheet—The IMF at a
Glance," June 24, 2010.

28. Oxfam International, "2011 Review of Conditionality and
the Design of Fund-Support Programs," www
.oxfam.org/sites/www.oxfam.org/files/oxfam-imf-
conditionality-submission.pdf.

29. "Demand for World Bank Group Support Tops $72
Billion as Developing Countries Face Continued
Financing Gaps," *The World Bank*, Press Release No.
2011/001/EXT, July 1, 2010 web.worldbank.org/WBSITE/
EXTERNAL/NEWS/0,,contentMDK:22635131~menuPK:
34463~pagePK:34370~piPK:34424~theSite
PK:4607,00.html.

30. "The World Bank and Aid Effectiveness," The World
Bank, accessed July 18, 2012, www1.worldbank.org/
operations/aideffectiveness/Showcase.html#travel.

31. "Millennium Development Goals," United Nations,
accessed July 18, 2012, www.un.org/millen
niumgoals/goals.html; "What They Are," Millennium
Project, 2006, www.unmillenniumproject.org/goals/
index.htm.

32. African Development Bank Group, "Integrated Water
Harvesting Project," 2011, www.afdb.org/en/
projects-and-operations/project-portfolio/project/p-za-
eaz-002/.

33. Institute of International Finance, "Capital Flows to
Emerging Market Economies," January 24, 2012, www
.iif.com/emr/resources+1670.php.

34. Paul Krugman, *The Return of Depression Economics and the
Crisis of 2008* (New York: W. W. Norton, 2009),139–164;
Anup Shah, "Global Financial Crisis 2008," *Global Issues,*
January 15, 2009, www.globalissues.org/print/
article/768.

35. Krugman, *Return of Depression Economics,* 165–180.

36. International Monetary Fund, *Global Financial Stability
Report,* April 2010, www.imf.org/external/pubs/ft/gfsr/
index.htm.

37. Krugman, *Return of Depression Economics,* 77–100;
BBC News, "Thailand: The Crisis Starts," November 26,
1997, BBC Online Network, news.bbc.co.uk/1/hi/
special_report/1997/asian_economic_woes/34487
.stm.

38. "Financial Regulatory Reform: A New Foundation," US
Department of the Treasury, June 17, 2009, www

.treasury.gov/initiatives/Documents/FinalReport_web
.pdfUS.

39. "What Is the G20 and How Did This International Forum
Begin?" The Group of 20, 2012, www.g20.org/index.
php/en/faqs.

CHAPTER 8
PROTECTING IDENTITY

1. Dave Eggers, *What Is the What: The Autobiography of
Valentino Achak Deng* (San Francisco: McSweeney's,
2006), 175.

2. Ibid., 175

3. Marshall Segall, Pierre R. Dassen, John W. Berry, and Ype
H. Poortinga, *Human Behavior in Global Perspective: An
Introduction to`Cross-Cultural Psychology,* 2nd ed.
(Needham Heights, MA: Allyn & Bacon, 1999), 33.

4. UNESCO, "Universal Declaration on Cultural Diversity,"
November 2, 2001, unesdoc.unesco.org/images/
0012/001271/127160m.pdf.

5. Ida Magli, *Cultural Anthropology: An Introduction*
(Jefferson, NC: McFarland, 2001), 21.

6. Manning Nash, *The Cauldron of Ethnicity in the Modern
World* (Chicago: The University of Chicago Press, 1989), 1.

7. Adam Kuper, *Culture: The Anthropologists' Account*
(Cambridge, MA: Harvard University Press, 1999), 5–9.

8. Matthew Arnold, *Culture and Anarchy,* 3rd ed. (New
York: Macmillan,1882), www.library.utoronto.ca/utel/
nonfiction_u/arnoldm_ca/ca_titlepage.html#search.

9. "The Commonwealth," Commonwealth Secretariat,
accessed July 19, 2008, www.thecommonwealth
.org/Internal/191086/191247/the_commonwealth/.

10. Sarah Crowe and Rajat Madhok, "Gaining Ground on the
Millennium Development Goals, with Equity, in Nepal,"
The United Nations Children's Fund, September 24, 2010,
www.unicef.org/mdg/nepal_56213.html.

11. Tania Branigan, "Millions of Chinese Rural Migrants
Denied Education for Their Children," *The Guardian,*
March 14, 2010, www.guardian.co.uk/world/2010/
mar/15/china-migrant-workers-children-education.

12. Karl Marx and Frederick Engels, *The Manifesto of the
Communist Party* (London, 1848), trans. Samuel Moore,
www.anu.edu.au/polsci/marx/classics/manifesto.html.

13. Kuper, *Culture,* 15–16.

14. Chris Jenks, *Culture,* 2nd ed. (London: Routledge, 2005), 30.

15. Marvin Harris, *The Rise of Anthropological Theory: A
History of Theories of Culture* (New York: Thomas Y.
Croswell, 1968), 11.

16. Margaret Mead, *Sex and Temperament in Three Primitive
Societies* (New York: Morrow Quill Paperbacks, 1963), 322.

17. Her psychological study of what it was like in the 1920s
for girls growing up in the primitive culture of the
Samoan Islands remains a classic in this regard. See

Margaret Mead, *Coming of Age in Samoa: A Psychological Study of Primitive Youth for Western Civilization* (Gloucester, MA: Peter Smith, 1961).

18. Clifford Geertz, *The Interpretation of Cultures* (New York: Basic Books, 1973), 30.

19. Chinua Achebe, *Things Fall Apart* (London: Heinemann, 1958), 124.

20. John H. Bodley, *Anthropology and Contemporary Human Problems,* 5th ed. (Lanham, MD: Altamira Press, 2008), 6.

21. John Tomlinson, *Globalization and Culture* (Chicago: University of Chicago Press, 1999), 27–31.

22. Jan Nederveen Pieterse, *Globalization and Culture: Global Melange* (Lanham, MD: Rowman & Littlefield, 2004), 87.

23. Ibid., 95.

24. Samuel P. Huntington, ed., *The Clash of Civilizations? The Debate,* 2nd ed. (New York: Council on Foreign Relations, 2010).

25. Thomas L. Friedman, *The Lexus and the Olive Tree* (New York, Random House, 2000), 248.

26. Benjamin R. Barber, *Jihad v. McWorld: How Globalism and Tribalism are Reshaping the World* (New York: Random House, 1996).

27. George Ritzer, *McDonaldization: The Reader* (London, Sage, 2002), 16–19.

28. Michael Veseth, *Globaloney: Unraveling the Myths of Globalization* (Lanham: Rowman & Littlefield, 2005), 121–143.

29. Roland Robertson, *Globalization: Social Theory and Global Culture* (London: Sage, 1992), 173–174.

30. Arjun Appadurai, *Modernity at Large: Cultural Dimensions of Globalization* (Minneapolis: University of Minnesota Press, 1996), 48.

31. "Global Music Project," globalmusicproject.org.

32. Maria del Carmen de la Peza, "Music and Globalization: The Impact of Latin American Music in Japan," *Intercultural Communication Studies* 15, no. 1 (2006): 168–173.

33. Ibid.

34. Martha Diaz, "The World is Yours: A Brief History of Hip-Hop Education," Steinhardt School of Culture, Education, and Human Development, New York University, 2012, Steinhardt.nyu.edu/metrocenter/hiphopeducation/hiphophistory.

35. H. Samy Alim, "How Hip-Hop Culture is Changing the Wor(1)d," *UCLA Today,* January 22, 2007, www.today.ucla.edu/portal/ut/h-samy-alim_hip-hop.aspx.

36. Jay Wachtel, "Globalization of Basketball," Connexions, last edited April 16, 2009, cnx.org/content/m22061/1.1.

37. Walter LaFeber, *Michael Jordan and the New Global Capitalism* (New York: W. W. Norton, 1999).

38. David L. Andrews et al., "Jordanscapes: A Preliminary Analysis of the Global Popular," *Sociology of Sport Journal* 13 (1996), 428–457, referenced in Wachtel, "Globalization of Basketball."

39. Chih-ming Wang, "Capitalizing the Big Man: Yao Ming, Asian American, and the China Global," *Inter-Asia Cultural Studies* 5, no. 2 (2004), 263–278, referenced in Wachtel, "Globalization of Basketball."

40. Ezra Fieser, "Red Sox–Yankees Series Highlights Globalization of Baseball," *Christian Science Monitor,* April 8, 2011.

41. Quoted in Paul White, "American, Japanese Players Adapt to New Surroundings," *USA Today,* April 11, 2007, www.usatoday.com/sports/baseball/2007-04-11-japan-cultureshock_N.htm.

42. For a broad discussion on this topic, see Michael Lewis and William Londo, *Studies on Asia: An Interdisciplinary Journal of Asian Studies Series III,* 3, no. 2, (fall 2006), special issue baseball and besuboro in Japan and the US.

43. Leonard Koppett, "The Globalization of Baseball: Reflections of a Sports Writer," *Indiana Journal of Global Legal Studies,* 8, no. 1 (2000), 81–84.

44. Fieser, "Red Sox–Yankees Series."

45. Michael Veseth, *Globaloney,* 102.

CHAPTER 9
CHALLENGES TO IDENTITY

1. Frederic and Mary Ann Brussat, review of *Youssou N'Dour: I Bring What I Love,* directed by Elizabeth Chai Vasarhelyi, Spirituality and Practice, accessed July 20, 2012, www.spiritualityandpractice.com/films/films.php?id=19161.

2. Ibid.

3. Willem A. Bijlefeld, "Islam," Philosophy and Religion, accessed July 20, 2012, www.philosophy-religion.org/world/pdfs/Islam2.pdf.

4. "Religions: Sunni and Shi'a," BBC, last updated August 19, 2009, www.bbc.co.uk/religion/religions/islam/subdivisions/sunnishia_1.shtml.

5. "What Is the Difference Between Sunni and Shiite Muslims—and Why Does It Matter?" George Mason University's History News Network, February 22, 2011, hnn.us/articles/934.html.

6. Sarah Glazer, "Sharia Controversy: Is There a Place for Islamic Law in Western Countries?," *CQ Global Researcher,* 6, no. 1 (2012): 1–28.

7. Ibid.

8. "Nigeria: Facts and Figures," BBC News, April 17, 2007, news.bbc.co.uk/2/hi/africa/6508055.stm.

9. Jayshree Bajoria and Greg Bruno, "Backgrounder: al-Qaeda (a.k.a. al-Qaida, al-Qa'ida)," Council on Foreign Relations, August 29, 2011, www.cfr.org/terrorist-organizations/al-qaeda-k-al-qaida-al-qaida/p9126.

10. Matthew Goodwin and Jocelyn Evans, "From Voting to Violence? Far Right Extremism in Britain," Searchlight

Educational Trust, accessed July 20, 2012, www.channel4.com/media/c4-news/images/voting-to-violence%20(7).pdf.

11. Robert Hayden, "Serbian and Croatian Nationalism and the Wars in Yugoslavia," Cultural Survival, March 19, 2010, www.culturalsurvival.org/ourpublications/csq/article/serbian-and-croatian-nationalism-and-wars-in-yugoslavia.

12. Josh Kron, "Conflict in Congo," CQ Global Researcher 5 (April 5, 2011), 157–182.

13. Ibid.

14. "The Failed States Index: Frequently Asked Questions," The Fund for Peace, accessed July 20, 2012, www.fundforpeace.org/global/?q=fsi-faq.

15. Gerald B. Helman and Steven R. Ratner, "Saving Failed States," Foreign Policy, no. 89 (Winter, 1992–1993), 3–20, www.jstor.org/stable/1149070.

16. The Fund for Peace, "Conflict Assessment Indicators: The Fund for Peace Country Analysis Indicators and Their Measures," 2011, www.fundforpeace.org/global/library/cr-10–97-ca-conflictassessmentindicators-1105c.pdf.

17. "Zimbabwe," The World Factbook, Central Intelligence Agency, last updated July 17, 2012, www.cia.gov/library/publications/the-world-factbook/geos/zi.html.

18. Glazer, "Sharia Controversy."

19. Jina Moore, "Truth Commissions: Can Countries Heal after Atrocities?" CQ Global Researcher 4 (January 2010), 1–24.

20. "Gacaca Court Transcript," Tales of Rwanda, August 6, 2005, talesofrwanda.com/journal/sareljournal-5.html.

21. Kofi Annan, "Nobel Lecture," (Oslo, Norway, December 10, 2001), nobelprize.org/nobel_prizes/peace/laureates/2001/annan-lecture.html.

CHAPTER 10
MANAGING THE WORLD

1. Olav Kjørven, "Road to Rio: Greening Human Development," United Nations Development Programme, March 22, 2012, www.undp.org/content/undp/en/home/ourperspective/ourperspectivearticles/2012/03/22/greening-human-development-olav-kj-rven-.html.

2. A. Leroy Bennett and James K. Oliver, International Organizations: Principles and Issues, 7th ed. (New York: Prentice Hall, 2002), 3.

3. Hugo Grotius, "Chapter 1: On War and Right," in On the Law of War and Peace (De Jure Belli ac Pacis), Book I, A. C. Campbell, trans. (London, 1814), www.constitution.org/gro/djbp_101.htm.

4. "Final Act of the International Peace Conference. The Hague, 29 July 1899," International Committee of the Red Cross, www.icrc.org/ihl.nsf/INTRO/145?OpenDocument.

5. Thomas R. Van Dervort, International Law and Organization: An Introduction, (Thousand Oaks, CA: Sage, 1998), 19.

6. Woodrow Wilson, "The Fourteen Points," in Classics of International Relations, 3rd ed., John A. Vasquez, ed. (Upper Saddle River, NJ: Prentice Hall, 1996), 40.

7. "Milestones 1921–1936: The Kellogg-Briand Pact 1928," US Department of State, Office of the Historian, accessed August 6, 2012, history.state.gov/milestones/1921-1936/Kellogg.

8. Tarik Kafala, "The Veto and How to Use It," BBC News, September 17, 2003, news.bbc.co.uk/2/hi/middle_east/2828985.stm.

9. "About ECOSOC," United Nations Economic and Social Council, accessed July 23, 2012, www.un.org/en/ecosoc/about/.

10. "Subsidiary Bodies of ECOSOC," ECOSOC, accessed July 23, 2012, www.un.org/en/ecosoc/about/subsidiary.shtml.

11. "Military and Paramilitary Activities in and against Nicaragua (Nicaragua v. United States of America)," International Court of Justice, Cases, Judgment of 27 June 1986, www.icj-cij.org/docket/index.php?sum=367&code=nus&p1=3&p2=3&case=70&k=66&p3=5.

12. Robert Keohane and Joseph Nye, Power and Interdependence, 2nd ed., (Glenview, IL: Scott, Foresman, 1989), 12–13.

13. "Charter of the Organization of American States: Chapter 1: Nature and Purposes," Organization of American States, 2012, www.oas.org/dil/treaties_A-41_Charter_of_the_Organization_of_American_States.htm#ch1.

14. The World Bank, "Defining Civil Society" last updated August 4, 2010, web.worldbank.org/WBSITE/EXTERNAL/TOPICS/CSO/0,,contentMDK:20101499~menuPK:244752~pagePK:220503~piPK:220476~theSitePK:228717,00.html.

15. "Chapter 5: Deepening Democracy at the Global Level," Human Development Report, 2002, hdr.undp.org/en/media/chapterfive1.pdf; Louis Ruchames, ed., "The American Anti-Slavery Society," The Abolitionists: A Collection of their Writing (New York: Putnam, 1963), 78, eca.state.gov/education/engteaching/pubs/AmLnC/br18.htm.

16. Louis Ruchames, ed., "The American Anti-Slavery Society," 78.

17. "The World Bank and Civil Society/Background," accessed August 6, 2012, web.worldbank.org/WBSITE/EXTERNAL/TOPICS/CSO/0,,contentMDK:20093161~menuPK:220423~pagePK:220503~piPK:220476~theSitePK:228717,00.html.

18. "At Your Service," United Nations NGO Branch, Department of Economic and Social Affairs, accessed August 6, 2012, csonet.org/index.php?menu=14.

19. "Consultative Status with ECOSOC," United Nations NGO Branch: Department of Economic and Social Affairs, accessed August 6, 2012, esango.un.org/civil

society/displayConsultativeStatusSearch.do?method=searchEcoSoc&sessionCheck=false&ngoFlag=1.

20. "Frequently Asked Questions," CARE, accessed July 23, 2012, www.care.org/about/faqs.asp.

21. "Role of the Department of Political Affairs," United Nations Department of Political Affairs, 2012, www.un.org/wcm/content/site/undpa/main/about/overview.

22. Karen Mingst and Margaret P. Karns, *The United Nations in the 21st Century,* 3rd ed. (Boulder, CO: Westview, 2007), 103.

23. "Ban Stresses Role of NGOs in Helping Transitional Countries Build Institutions," UN News Centre, October 26, 2011, www.un.org/apps/news/story.asp?NewsID=40206&Cr=ngos&Cr1.

24. Ibid.

25. "ICC at a Glance," International Criminal Court, accessed July 23, 2012, www.icc-cpi.int/Menus/ICC/About+the+Court/ICC+at+a+glance/.

26. "Situations and Cases," International Criminal Court, accessed August 6, 2012, www.icc-cpi.int/Menus/ICC/Situations+and+Cases/.

CHAPTER 11
CHALLENGES TO COOPERATION

1. UN Secretary-General Ban Ki-moon, "Remarks to High Level Plenary Meeting of the General Assembly on the Millennium Development Goals," September 20, 2010, www.un.org/apps/news/infocus/sgspeeches/statments_full.asp?statID=940

2. Jean-Jacques Rosseau, *Social Contract,* Book III, Section 16, 1762, www.constitution.org/jjr/socon_03.htm.

3. Kofi Annan, "We the Peoples: The Role of the United Nations in the 21st Century," Millennium Report of the Secretary-General of the United Nations, 2000, www.un.org/millennium/sg/report/.

4. "We the Peoples: Press Conference," Press Release SG/SM/7342, Secretary-General of the United Nations, April 3, 2000, www.un.org/millennium/sg/report/conf.htm.

5. "What Are the Millennium Development Goals?" United Nations Development Programme: Millennium Development Goals, accessed July 25, 2012, www.undp.org/mdg/basics.shtml.

6. "Reports," United Nations: Millennium Development Goals, www.un.org/millenniumgoals/reports.shtml.

7. "Strategic Themes," The World Bank, January 31, 2012, go.worldbank.org/3ZPR01N4I0.

8. "The Millennium Development Goals Report 2011: Addendum: Goal 1," United Nations, mdgs.un.org/unsd/mdg/Resources/Static/Products/Progress2011/Addendum_G1.pdf.

9. "Water, Sanitation, and Hygiene," UNICEF, March 2012, www.unicef.org/wash/.

10. A. H. Maslow, "A Theory of Human Motivation," 1943, *Psychological Review* 50 (1943): 370–396, quoted in Christopher D. Green, Classics in the History of Psychology, psychclassics.yorku.ca/Maslow/motivation.htm.

11. "The Millennium Development Goals Report 2012," United Nations, www.un.org/millenniumgoals/pdf/MDG%20Report%202012.pdf.

12. Ibid., 8.

13. Ibid., 10.

14. Ibid., 13.

15. Ibid., 17.

16. Ibid., 18.

17. "About MCC," Millennium Challenge Corporation, accessed July 25, 2012, www.mcc.gov/pages/about.

18. "Countries & Country Tools," Millennium Challenge Corporation, accessed July 12, 2012, www.mcc.gov/pages/countries.

19. "Ghana Compact," Millennium Challenge Corporation, accessed July 12, 2012, www.mcc.gov/pages/countries/program/ghana-compact.

20. "Zambia Threshold Program," Millennium Challenge Corporation, accessed July 12, 2012, www.mcc.gov/pages/countries/program/zambia-threshold-program.

21. "Strong EU Commitment Needed to Get MDGs Back on Track," Plenary Session 14–17 June, European Parliament, www.europarl.europa.eu/news/en/headlines/content/20100607FCS75591/7/html/Strong-EU-commitment-needed-to-get-MDGs-back-on-track.

22. "Development and Cooperation—EuropeAid, Achieving the MDGs," European Commission, February 17, 2012, ec.europa.eu/development/how/achieving_mdg_en.cfm.

23. "EU Official Development Aid Reaches Record €53.8 Billion in 2010," European Union @ United Nations, www.eu-un.europa.eu/articles/fr/article_10900_fr.htm.

24. "The Millennium Development Goals Report 2012," United Nations, www.un.org/millenniumgoals/pdf/MDG%20Report%202012.pdf, 30.

25. "Severe Acute Respiratory Syndrome (SARS)," A.D.A.M. Medical Encyclopedia, PubMed Health, February 19, 2011, www.ncbi.nlm.nih.gov/pubmedhealth/PMH0004460/.

26. "The Millennium Development Goals Report 2012," United Nations, www.un.org/millenniumgoals/pdf/MDG%20Report%202012.pdf, 39.

27. "Impact of Malaria," Centers for Disease Control and Prevention, accessed August 7, 2012, www.cdc.gov/malaria/malaria_worldwide/impact.html.

28. "About the Campaign," Nothing But Nets, 2012, www.nothingbutnets.net/about-us/.

29. "About WHO," World Health Organization, 2012, www.who.int/about/en/.

30. "Human Rights Basics," Amnesty International USA, 2012, www.amnestyusa.org/research/human-rights-basics.

31. "Quotations by Eleanor Roosevelt," The Eleanor Roosevelt Papers Project, George Washington University, accessed July 12, 2012, www.gwu.edu/~erpapers/aboute leanor/er-quotes/.

32. "Female Genital Mutilation," World Health Organization, February 2012, www.who.int/mediacentre/ factsheets/fs241/en/.

33. Rachel Brown, "French MPs Vote to Ban the Burka," ABC News Australia, July 14, 2010, www.abc .net.au/news/stories/2010/07/14/2952787.htm? section=world.

34. Ibid.

35. Lorena Galliot, "Wearing Full Islamic Veil Could Land Women in 'Citizenship' School," France24, May 19, 2010, www.france24.com/en/20100518-france-full-islamic-veil-burqa-niqab-ban-citizenship-courses-alliot-marie.

36. "Six Women Fined under French Burqa Laws," The Australian, January 3, 2012, www.theaustralian .com.au/news/world/six-women-fined-under-french-burqa-laws/story-e6frg6so-1226235329079.

37. Josh Kron, "Resentment toward the West Bolsters Uganda's New Anti-Gay Bill," The New York Times, February 28, 2012, www.nytimes.com/2012/02/29/ world/africa/ugandan-lawmakers-push-anti-homo sexuality-bill-again.html?scp=2&sq=uganda&st=cse.

38. Jim Yardley, "Maid's Cries Cast Light on Child Labor in India," The New York Times, April 4, 2012, www .nytimes.com/2012/04/05/world/asia/india-shaken-by-plight-of-13-year-old-maid.html.

39. "About the ILO," International Labour Organization, www.ilo.org/global/about-the-ilo/lang--en/index .htm.

40. Charles Duhigg and Steven Greenhouse, "Electronic Giant Vowing Reforms in China Plants," The New York Times, March 29, 2012, www.nytimes.com/2012/ 03/30/business/apple-supplier-in-china-pledges-changes-in-working-conditions.html.

41. "About Us," Human Rights Watch, 2012, www .hrw.org/en/about.

42. "About Us," Freedom House, accessed August 11, 2012, www.freedomhouse.org/.

43. Hakan Altinay, "Global Governance: A Work in Progress," YaleGlobal, January 26, 2010, yaleglobal.yale.edu/about/ altinay.jsp.

44. Global Governance Watch, www.globalgovernance watch.org/.

45. Paul Wolfowitz, Mark Palmer, and Patrick Glen, "Wolfowitz: UN Needs Millennium Governance Goals," American Enterprise Institute, April 2, 2012, www .aei.org/press/foreign-and-defense-policy/international-organizations/wolfowitz-un-needs-millennium-gover-nance-goals-release/.

46. "Global Governance 2025: At a Critical Juncture," US National Security Council and the European Union Institute for Security Studies, September 2010, www.dni.gov/nic/ PDF_2025/2025_Global_Governance.pdf.

47. Stephen Krasner, International Regimes (Ithaca, NY: Cornell University Press, 1983).

48. "What is CITES?" Convention on International Trade in Endangered Species of Wild Fauna and Flora, accessed July 25, 2012, www.cites.org/eng/disc/what.php.

49. Margaret Keck and Kathryn Sikkink, Activists beyond Borders: Advocacy Networks in International Politics (Ithaca, NY: Cornell University Press, 1998).

50. "About," OccupyWallStreet, accessed July 25, 2012, occupywallst.org/about/.

CHAPTER 12
CONNECTING TO THE WORLD

1. Kate Gustafson, "I Would Do It All Again in a Second," Transitions Abroad Magazine (March/April 2004), www. transitionsabroad.com/publications/magazine/ 0403/beyond_the_comfort_zone.shtml.

2. Marcelo M. Suarez- Orozco, "Wanted: Global Citizens," Educational Leadership, 64, no. 7 (April 2007), 58–62.

3. Gustafson, "I Would Do It All Again," 2004.

4. "Fast Facts," Institute of International Education, Open Doors 2011. www.iie.org/Research-and-Publications/ Open-Doors/Data/Fast-Facts.

5. Ibid.

6. Ibid.

7. Jeffrey S. Lantis and Jessica DuPlaga, The Global Classroom (Boulder, CO: Paradigm, 2010), 95.

8. Kristina Bergan, "A Non-Profit Experience," paper submitted to fulfill requirements for internship at International House, UNC Charlotte, May 2009.

9. Tamar Lewin, "Rarely Win at Trivial Pursuit? An Embassy Door Opens," The New York Times, December 17, 2006, nytimes.com/2006/12/17/weekinreview/171ewin .html?pagewanted=print.

10. "Careers Representing America," US Department of State, accessed July 25, 2012, www.careers.state.gov.

11. Matthew McManus, "Careers in the U.S. Government," in Maria Pinto Carland and Candace Faber, eds., Careers in International Affairs, 8th ed., (Washington, DC: Georgetown University Press, 2008), 53–102.

12. Denis McDonough, "Careers on Capitol Hill," in Carland and Faber, Careers, 126–130.

13. "International Business," Washington State Department of Commerce, 2010, www.choosewashington .com/business/international/Pages/default.aspx.

14. "Fast Facts," Peace Corps, www.peacecorps.gov/about/fastfacts/.

15. See www.un.org/en/employment for an overview of UN career information and careers.un.org/lbw/Home.aspx for a more detailed discussion and actual job openings.

16. Kristi Ragan, "Careers in International Development," in Carland and Faber, *Careers,* 324.

17. Global Volunteer Network Foundation, www.gvnfoundation.org/.

18. Kevin Gill, global director of staffing for Honeywell, quoted by Bill Clabby in "Proving that Study Abroad is Worth it—Conclusions from Research on Real Benefits of the Experience," presentation at CIBER Short-Term Study Abroad Conference, Provo, Utah, 2009, marriottschool.byu.edu/conferences/ciberstsa/presentations.

19. Association of American Colleges and Universities, "What Is Liberal Education?" 2012, www.aacu.org/leap/What_is_liberal_education.cfm.

20. Rutgers University offers a PhD (as well as an MS) in global affairs on its Newark campus through its Division of Global Affairs. The Global and International Studies Program at the University of California Santa Barbara offers a global emphasis as part of PhD programs of participating departments. See dga.rutgers.edu and www.global.ucsb.edu/phd/about.html for more information.

21. See the Association of Professional Schools of International Affairs, www.apsia.org/apsia/index.php.

22. Robert G. Blanton, "Surveying International Studies Programs: Where Do We Stand?" *International Studies Perspectives* 10, no. 2 (2009): 224–240; Marijke Breuning and John Ishiyama, "International Studies Programs: For What Purpose and For Whom?" *International Studies Perspectives* 5, no. 4, (November 2004): 400–402; Marijke Breuning and John Ishiyama, "Marketing the International Studies Major: Claims and Content of Programs at Primarily Undergraduate Institutions in the Midwest," *International Studies Perspectives* 8, no. 1 (February 2007): 121–133; Jeanne A.K. Hey, "Can International Studies Research Be the Basis for an Undergraduate International Studies Curriculum?" *International Studies Perspectives* 5, no. 4 (November 2004): 395–399; James C. Hendrix, "Globalizing the Curriculum," *Clearing House* 71, no. 5 (May/June 1998): 305–309; Heidi H. Hobbs, Harry I. Chernotsky, and Darin H. Van Tassell, "International Studies and the Global Community: Transforming the Agenda," in Robert A. Denemark, ed., *The International Studies Encyclopedia*, vol. 7 (Hoboken, NJ, Wiley-Blackwell, 2010), 4598–4609; Ann Kelleher, "Does International Studies Have a Common Core: An Analysis of Seventy-Three Curriculum Programs?" Presentation at the annual meeting of the International Studies Association, Honolulu, Hawaii, March 4, 2005.

23. Robert G. Hanvey, "An Attainable Global Perspective," *Theory Into Practice* 21, no. 3 (1982), reprinted in Patrick O'Meara, Howard D. Mehlinger, and Roxana Ma Newman, eds., *Changing Perspectives on International Education* (Bloomington: Indiana University Press, 2001), 244–279.

24. Maryann Cusimano Love, *Beyond Sovereignty: Issues for a Global Agenda*, (Belmont, CA: Thomson Higher Education, 2007).

25. Darla K. Deardorff, "The Identification and Assessment of Intercultural Competence as a Student Outcome of Internationalization at Institutions of Higher Education in the United States." EdD thesis, North Carolina State University, 2004.

TUESDAY RAVEN

Janet Lorimer

SADDLEBACK PAGETURNERS

• SPY •

PAGETURNERS

SPY

A Deadly Game
An Eye for an Eye
I Spy, e-Spy
Scavenger Hunt
Tuesday Raven

SCIENCE FICTION

Bugged!
Escape From Earth
Flashback
Murray's Nightmare
Under Siege

ADVENTURE

A Horse Called
  Courage
Planet Doom
The Terrible Orchid Sky
Up Rattler Mountain
Who Has Seen
  the Beast?

MYSTERY

The Hunter
Once Upon a Crime
Whatever Happened
  to Megan Marie?
When Sleeping
  Dogs Awaken
Where's Dudley?

Development and Production: Laurel Associates, Inc.
Cover Illustrator: Black Eagle Productions

SADDLEBACK
PUBLISHING • INC.
Three Watson
Irvine, CA 92618-2767

Website: www.sdlback.com

ISBN 1-56254-140-4

Printed in the United States of America
05   9 8 7 6 5 4 3 2 1

CONTENTS

Chapter 1

Jenn Maxwell paused outside the restaurant to shake out her wet umbrella. As she closed the umbrella, she glanced up at the sign over the door. It read *The Sherlock Holmes*. Just over the words was a picture of the famous English detective. Jenn smiled. Sherlock Holmes and his faithful sidekick Dr. John Watson had never really existed, of course. But people still loved the stories about them.

"Londoners *love* tradition. Leave it to them to name a restaurant after a make-believe detective," Jenn thought. "And leave it to my old friend Rob to choose this place for us to meet."

The door flew open and a young couple burst out onto the wet sidewalk. Music, laughter, and light spilled out on the street as Jenn hurried inside.

The restaurant was crowded and noisy. Jenn wondered if this was a favorite place for Londoners or just another tourist trap. Then she heard the accents of people talking. Again she smiled. Most of the customers seemed to be Americans like herself.

Jenn felt a tap on her shoulder. She turned and saw Rob Gray's welcoming smile. "Hello, Jennifer. I've got a table reserved for us at the back," he said in his clipped British accent.

As they threaded their way through the crowd, Jenn thought, "It's been five years since we saw each other, but it's almost as if we never said goodbye."

Jenn worked for the CIA, America's Central Intelligence Agency, while Rob worked for British Intelligence. Both of them were agents who specialized in hunting down terrorists. They had worked well together on several earlier cases. Jenn was more than a little curious about their new assignment together.

After they ordered, Rob smiled across the table. "You're looking good, Jenn. I'm glad you're here."

She smiled. "You look good, too. A little older, but still the same old Rob. So tell me—just why *am* I here?"

Rob raised an eyebrow. "You mean, no one's told you?"

Jenn shook her head. "Yesterday morning I was in Los Angeles wrapping up another case. Then my boss called from Virginia. He told me to pack my passport and get to London. What's up?"

At that moment, the waitress set plates of steaming fish and chips in front of them. Jenn loved this dish. She knew that fish and chips are as dear to the British as hamburgers and French fries are to Americans.

Jenn bit into a piece of crisp, hot fish. "So, what's up? Are we on a case?" she asked. "Something top secret?"

Rob grinned. "Same old Jenn.

Questions, questions. Yes, we're on a case as of yesterday. Top secret? Not really. It's just something we need to take care of as quickly as possible. Tell me—does the name Hal Lambert mean anything to you?"

Jenn looked at him in surprise. "Lambert? The last I heard he was behind bars in the States."

"Well, he must have done his time, because he showed up in London a few days ago," Rob said.

He sprinkled malt vinegar on his helping of chips. To Jenn, chips were still French fries, no matter what anybody called them. Like most Americans, she ate hers with ketchup. The British liked theirs with malt vinegar.

Jenn frowned. "Lambert is pretty much just a small-time thief, Rob. I'm sure Scotland Yard can handle him."

Rob nodded. "I agree with you. And so did Scotland Yard—until yesterday. That's when Lambert was found stabbed near the Tower of London. But here's the interesting thing! Just before they took him to the hospital, he said two words—Tuesday Raven."

Rob gazed at Jenn, his blue eyes searching her face. Jenn dropped her fork with a clatter, and her brown eyes widened. *"Raven?"* she said. "Are you sure that's what he said?"

Rob nodded. "Can you believe it? It's been five years since we ran into the Raven. Remember?"

Despite the heat in the room, Jenn shivered. "How could I ever forget? Thanks to the Raven, I almost died!"

Chapter 2

Five years before, Jenn and Rob had worked on a very tough case. They'd been assigned to hunt down a terrorist group led by a man named Jeffrey Graham—code name, *Raven*.

Rob called the group a hit-and-run mob. The terrorists' MO, or method of operation, was to plant a bomb, set it off, and then escape to another part of the city. It was a good scheme. While Scotland Yard's police were busy at the site of the first bomb, the terrorists would launch another attack somewhere else. The police were soon spread too thin to be effective.

"We spent all our time mopping up after each attack," Rob said bitterly. "Raven was a clever chap, all right. He never left any clues. Do you remember?"

"I remember," Jenn said, nodding. "Then, when we did find him, it was purely accidental."

"That's right," Rob said. "He'd been hurt. Actually, he'd injured himself while he was making a bomb. Served the bloke right, I say."

"I'll never forget it. We caught up with him in a nasty little hotel down near the docks," Jenn said.

"We got a tip from an informer, remember? He said the leader of the terrorists was in the hotel. That's when you and I went after him."

Jenn gazed at her plate, reliving that terrible day when she'd come so close to death. "We called for backup because we were afraid Raven would get away," she said.

"You went up the front stairs, as I recall. I went up the back," Rob said. "Then I heard a shot—"

"You heard it, but I *felt* it," Jenn said

quickly. "If that bullet had been half an inch closer—"

Rob reached out and squeezed her hand. "I thought we'd lost you!"

"It was my own darned fault," she replied angrily. "I didn't give Raven enough credit."

"You got a look at him when he ran by you," Rob said. "No one else had ever seen Raven. After we caught him, you were able to testify against him so we could put him away for . . ."

Rob's voice trailed away. He saw the frown on Jenn's face. "Someone must have tipped Raven off that we were coming," she said slowly. "You know, Rob, I've been thinking about that day for five years. I hate to say this—but the person who tipped Raven had to be someone we were working with."

Rob drew back, his face cold. "What? You're saying it was a copper?"

Jenn nodded. She waited, knowing how her friend would react. Rob was very proud of Scotland Yard, London's internationally respected police force.

"You have no *proof* it was a copper," he said slowly.

"No—but think about it. Who else knew we were going after Raven?"

"The person who gave us the tip," Rob said. "That was an anonymous tip, wasn't it?"

"Yeah," Jenn said. She picked up her fork and pushed the cold chips around on her plate. All of a sudden she wasn't hungry anymore. "At first, we thought it was someone in Raven's group, another terrorist. But later, when I had more time to think about it, I realized it might also have been a cop."

"Maybe we'll never know," Rob said. "Raven would never talk about his organization." He flagged down the waitress to get the check.

"What about Lambert?" Jenn asked, folding her napkin. "Has he said anything else?"

Rob shook his head. "The bloke's still out of it, I'm afraid. He still hasn't regained consciousness."

"Will he make it?" Jenn asked.

Rob shrugged his shoulders. "The doctors don't know. But he's being guarded around the clock."

"So what's our next move?" Jenn asked, pushing back her chair.

"Let's go for a little stroll," Rob said. "I could use some fresh air."

When they stepped outside, they found that the rain had stopped. The air was crisp and cold.

Jenn took a deep breath. "Hard to believe it's been five years since I was here," she said. "But London doesn't change much, does it?"

For a while they walked down the street in companionable silence. Rob was remembering cases they had worked on together. Jenn was musing about the history of London. United States history was just a few hundred years old, but

England's history dated back more than two thousand years!

Jenn looked up and saw lights dancing on water. "The River Thames," she said with a smile. "I haven't been near the Thames since that day I got shot." She shuddered. "Speaking of Raven—how's he doing these days? Still plotting to blow up London?"

Rob shook his head and glanced over at her. "I guess I forgot to tell you. Raven is no longer in prison."

Chapter 3

Jenn stopped in her tracks. "Raven isn't behind bars? But I thought—"

"I know. So did I," Rob said sourly. "I only found out when I called the prison this morning to check up on him. They told me he was released a few months ago."

"But the man is a *terrorist!*" Jenn gasped. "How could they set him free?"

Rob shrugged. "I wasn't told, but I'm guessing that he was let out for good behavior. The warden had always said he was a model prisoner."

Jenn groaned. They crossed the street and stared out across the Thames. A full moon had risen just above the horizon. She leaned on the waist-high, concrete wall and gazed out at the river.

"We have to assume that Raven might be up to his old tricks," she said. "Suppose Lambert found out about it. Maybe that was why he got stabbed. He might have threatened to turn Raven in."

But even as she talked, Jenn could see that the theory she was spinning out didn't hold up. "Do you know where Raven is now?" she asked Rob.

"No, but I have his daughter's address," Rob said. "Tomorrow morning we'll go see what she knows."

Jenn choked back a laugh. "Why, I'd forgotten that! I always found it so hard to believe that the Raven, a cold-blooded criminal, was also a family man."

Rob glanced at his watch. "Oh, dear. It's getting late. After your long flight, you must be tired," he said.

They began walking toward the nearest underground train station— better known to the British as "the tube."

Rob frowned. "Raven had a wife and two daughters," he said, picking up the conversation. "His wife died a few years ago, but I gather the daughters are quite fond of their old dad. Sarah, the oldest, has a good job in London. But it seems that the youngest—Lilah—is hellbent on following in her father's footsteps. The girl's been in and out of trouble since she hit her teens."

"I'm sorry to hear that," Jenn said. "Is it possible that she's taken over her father's organization?"

Rob shrugged. "Maybe. Although I wonder if a bunch of aging terrorists would be willing to take orders from a woman—and a young one at that!"

Jenn grinned. "Do you know where Raven's followers are?"

As they descended into the station, Rob said, "Raven would never tell us who worked for him, so we weren't able to arrest anyone else. I'm guessing that most of them left England. Some might have ended up in America."

Jenn made a face. "Thanks a lot. But

that might be how Lambert learned about Raven. Tomorrow I'll call my office to find out."

While Rob bought their tickets, Jenn gazed around. London's underground train system was the oldest in the world. The tube stations were always busy as people traveled about the huge city.

Jenn followed Rob as they hurried through the station. Finally they reached the platform where they could catch their train. A large crowd of people were standing around, waiting.

"Come on, Jenn," Rob shouted, as he pushed through the crowd. But as she tried to follow, a tall, stout man in a plaid raincoat shoved between them. By standing on tiptoe to see over the man's shoulder, she could see Rob just ahead of her. She called out his name, but Rob couldn't hear her over the noise of the crowd. Jenn gritted her teeth and tried to push by the bulky man in the plaid raincoat. But there was no room to move.

"Excuse me," Jenn called out loudly. She nudged the man as she tried to get by, but he acted as if he didn't hear her. "How rude! He probably doesn't want me getting on the train in front of him," she thought angrily.

Peering over the man's shoulder, she saw a redheaded girl wearing a pink hat step behind Rob. Something about the girl made the hair on the back of Jenn's neck stand up. In horror, Jenn saw the redhead's hands come up as if she was about to give Rob a shove. He was so close to the edge of the platform, he'd surely fall onto the electrified rails!

Then Jenn heard the whistle of an approaching train. Thinking fast, she jabbed her closed umbrella into the ribs of the man in the plaid raincoat. When he cried out and stumbled sideways, Jenn threw herself forward, grabbing for the redhead. But the girl had already given Rob a hard push.

Chapter 4

Rob teetered on the edge of the platform. Then, as the train roared into the station, two people standing next to Rob managed to grab his coat. They yanked him back to his feet just in time.

At that very moment, the redhead kicked Jenn hard and broke free. And before Jenn could stop her, the girl took off running and vanished into the crowd.

The doors of the train slid open. The passengers inside poured onto the platform as passengers on the platform shoved their way into the cars.

Jenn reached Rob a second later. He was white-faced and shaking. "Want to sit down for a moment?" she said. "We can wait for the next train."

Rob shook his head. "No, no, I'm

quite all right. Let's ride this one."

As they stepped into the car, Jenn glanced around. She didn't see either the plaid raincoat or the pink hat anywhere on the platform or in the train car.

"I suppose they could have gotten into a different car," Jenn thought, "but somehow I doubt it."

The doors shut with a *whoosh*, and the train slid forward. As it rushed through the dark tunnel, Rob and Jenn gazed silently at each other. But they didn't speak a word until they reached Paddington Station.

"I'll walk you to your hotel," Rob said. "Then I think I'll catch a taxi home. My knees still feel a bit rubbery."

"That was a close call," Jenn said.

"Stupid of me, standing so close to the edge like that," Rob scolded himself. "I know better."

"Hold on," Jenn said. She told him about the man in the plaid raincoat and the girl in the pink hat. "I could be wrong about the man. Maybe he really *was* just being rude. But somehow I got the feeling that the two of them were working together. It seemed that he was deliberately blocking me so she could push you off the edge."

Rob shivered. "If you're right, then we're being watched and followed."

"Yes. And it also means that those two must be involved in this case somehow," Jenn said softly. "Unless—can you think of anyone else who might have it in for you?"

Rob grinned sourly. "I should say so. How about every criminal I've ever put behind bars?"

Jenn sighed. "Great! Well, for the time being, we've got to assume it's the Raven case. We know that *something* is going on, Raven is involved, and I guess whatever it is will happen Tuesday—the day after tomorrow."

By now they had reached Sussex Gardens and a row of small bed-and-breakfast-type hotels. Rob told Jenn he'd pick her up at 10:00 the next morning.

As she crawled into bed, Jenn tried to figure out what it was that Raven was up to. More bomb attacks? Or something even worse? But she was too tired to think clearly. Before she could come up with anymore questions, she fell asleep.

Monday dawned clear and bright. Jenn ate a hearty English breakfast of fried eggs, Canadian bacon, grilled tomato slices, and toast. The hearty meal cheered her up. Even though she and Rob had only 24 hours to solve this case, Jenn felt certain she could handle a dozen Ravens!

Rob was right on time, waiting patiently. As she always did in England, Jenn felt funny slipping into the passenger side of the car. It was the exact opposite of an American car. The driver sat on the *right* side and drove on the *left* side of the road!

As Rob pulled into traffic, Jenn said,

"I called my office this morning. They're going to find out who Hal Lambert shared a cell with. I'm willing to bet you it was one of Raven's pals."

"No bet," Rob grinned. "I'm sure you're right. Here." He handed her a slip of paper with a name and address.

"Sarah Graham," Jenn read. "Raven's older daughter."

"That's right. Sarah always seemed like a decent sort of person," he said.

Jenn nodded. "I remember her from the trial. She had a steady job and she did seem like a law-abiding citizen."

Sarah Graham lived in a small brick house on the outskirts of London. As the agents got out of their car, they saw her come out of the house. Neatly dressed in a blue suit, she looked as if she were leaving for work. When she saw the agents approaching, she waited for them.

Rob pulled out his identification and explained what he and Jenn wanted. Sarah gazed coldly from one agent to the other. "So you want to know where my father is," she said in a flat voice.

"If you'll just give us an address," Jenn said pleasantly, "we'll be on our way, Ms. Graham."

A sour smile twitched at Sarah's lips. "As a matter of fact, I was going there myself," she said after a moment. "You can come along. I'll take you."

"There's no need—" Jenn started to say, but Sarah had already climbed into the front seat of Rob's car. Jenn sighed and got into the back seat.

Sarah directed Rob to drive back into London. But aside from giving him directions, she would say nothing more about her father. All she said was, "You'll see for yourselves."

After about 20 minutes, Sarah told Rob to park in front of a large, two-story building. Jenn saw nurses coming in and going out. This was clearly a nursing home of some kind.

"This way," Sarah said, her heels

clicking sharply on the cold linoleum. She led them down a hallway, finally stopping in front of an open door. In the room beyond, a thin, pale man with a shock of white hair lay in a narrow hospital bed. His eyes were closed, as if he were sleeping. At first, Jenn didn't recognize the man. Then she drew in her breath sharply. It was Raven!

"I'm sorry, Sarah. What's happened to him?" Jenn said softly.

Sarah smiled at the uncomfortable look on Jenn's face. "He's very ill—as you can see. The doctors give him only a few weeks to live. Do you want to see his medical records?"

Jenn shook her head. She didn't need a medical chart to tell her that this was why Raven had been let out of prison.

Chapter 5

Sarah stepped back into the hall, closing the door of her father's room behind her. "Thanks for the ride," she said to Rob in a sarcastic voice. "I was on my way to see Dad when you two drove up. I go to see him every day on my way to work."

"I—I'm so sorry," Jenn mumbled.

Sarah let out an ugly little laugh and shook her head. "No, you're not. I know you people. You're thinking that once Raven is dead, you'll have one less criminal to worry about."

Rob's mouth tightened angrily. "Now look here, miss," he started to say. But Jenn signaled him to be quiet.

"Sarah, we think someone may be trying to start up your father's old gang again. Can you help us out?"

Sarah rolled her eyes. "Oh, *please!*"

"Do you know what happened to the rest of your father's mob?" Rob asked.

Sarah shrugged. "How should I know? Those chaps aren't the type to send us Christmas cards."

"Where's your sister these days?" Jenn asked.

Sarah shrugged again. "My sister and I don't exactly think alike. The fact is that she's gone her way, and I've gone mine. Now if you'll excuse me—"

"Do you know where we can find Lilah?" Jenn asked.

Clearly annoyed, Sarah shook her head. "What's the world coming to when you coppers don't know how to find the criminals?" She laughed again and went back into her father's room.

Rob and Jenn exchanged looks. "Back to square one," Jenn said.

As they left the nursing home, Rob said, "This is my fault. I was so sure it had to be Raven up to his old tricks! It never occurred to me that—"

"Don't blame yourself," Jenn said. "Let's concentrate on what we *do* know."

Rob started the car and pulled onto the road. Jenn recited the facts they were sure of so far. "We don't have much to go on," she said at last. "We know that Lambert is a petty thief."

"Which means he was probably planning to steal something," Rob added.

"He was found stabbed near the Tower of London. Do you think he might have tried to double-cross someone?"

Rob nodded. "Anything is possible. All I know is that Lambert said 'Raven' and 'Tuesday'."

"So it's reasonable to assume that something is going to happen there Tuesday—tomorrow," Jenn said.

"At the Tower?" Rob asked.

Jenn shrugged. "It's as good a guess as any. He must have been there for a reason. At least it's some place to start,

Rob. Let's go take a look around."

The Tower of London was one of the most popular tourist attractions in the country. Jenn knew the castle was more than 900 years old. At one time it had been used as a prison, and many famous people had been jailed there. The "Tower" was actually a huge fortress made up of *many* towers inside the walls.

Even though she'd visited the Tower before, Jenn never grew tired of seeing the tall stone towers looming up over the moat. The moat was no longer filled with water, of course. And prisoners were no longer beheaded inside the castle walls. But every time she came to London, her first view of the Tower was always a thrill.

After finding a place to park the car, Rob led Jenn to a bench outside the Tower. "Lambert was sprawled out right here on this bench," Rob said. "I guess people thought he was just taking a nap. But then Lambert groaned, someone saw blood, and they called Scotland Yard."

Jenn gazed down at the bench, which was now roped off with the yellow plastic tape used by the police. She could see dark stains on the bench's wooden seat.

"But people are walking by here all the time. Wouldn't you have thought someone might have *seen* the stabbing take place?" she said.

"Maybe—but a professional killer would know how to make it quick and silent," Rob said.

"Which means that it wasn't just a spur-of-the-moment crime," Jenn said. "This stabbing was well thought out."

Thinking hard, she looked up from the bench to the Tower itself. The light brown stone turrets stood out starkly against the clear blue sky.

Then Jenn suddenly thought of something else. "Rob," she exclaimed, "what about the Crown Jewels? Could *they* be what Lambert was after?"

Chapter 6

England's Crown Jewels had been on public display inside the Tower of London for more than 300 years. Of course, the famous collection included the crowns and scepters worn by Britain's kings and queens. But there were also sets of priceless dishes and numerous other antique items made of gold and silver.

Rob frowned. "Do you know how well the Crown Jewels are guarded? It would take a highly skilled group of thieves to even *think* about stealing them. As far as we know, Hal Lambert was just a penny-ante thief. He wouldn't have stood a chance!"

Jenn's shoulders slumped. "You're right," she said. "Lambert was small-time—but not stupid." She shook her head. "Still, there had to be *some* reason for him to be in London. I can't believe he was just playing tourist."

"I agree," Rob said. "Tell you what, Jenn. Let's take a quick tour of the Tower. Maybe something will come to us, and we'll be able to figure out what Lambert was after."

Rob and Jenn hurried to the main entrance. Visitors from all over the world were lined up to see the Tower.

Jenn and Rob showed their badges to one of the Tower Guards, a Yeoman Warder. The Warders were nicknamed "Beefeaters." Jenn had heard that no one was sure where the Warders had gotten that name. Some people thought it was because, many years ago, the Tower guards had been given meat to eat when few other people could afford it.

Jenn wasn't surprised when one of the Warders insisted on searching her backpack. She remembered that a terrorist bomb had been set off inside the Tower of London many years before. Ever since then, purses, backpacks, and other bags had to be searched.

Rob and Jenn had to walk through the gates of several towers before they were inside the fortress itself. Just ahead, one of the Warders was talking to a group of tourists about the history of the Tower. Jenn stopped for a moment to listen. The uniformed Warder was telling his listeners about all the people who'd had their heads cut off in the Tower.

"Good grief! The Tower of London certainly has a bloody history," Jenn whispered with a shudder.

"Makes me glad I'm alive now," Rob murmured, "instead of back then."

As they strolled along one of the paths, Jenn said, "I can't imagine what Lambert would have been able to steal here. As you say, this place is much too well-guarded."

They took their time, examining each

tower that was open to the public.

"I need to sit down," Jenn said at last. She and Rob dropped onto a bench bordering the lawn of Tower Green.

Jenn saw an English raven hopping about on the grass. The shiny black bird was quite large. As Jenn watched, a small child ran toward the big black bird. A Beefeater stopped the child just in time. "Easy there, miss! You'd better not try to pet him. He's not a very friendly fellow, I'm afraid," the Warder said. "Sometimes the ravens bite people."

The child scampered away to find her mother. Jenn watched the girl go, wishing her life were that simple.

"We can safely say that Lambert was here to steal something—but what is it?" Rob said, breaking into Jenn's thoughts. "We've crossed off the Crown Jewels. Too hard for someone like Lambert. There are displays of historical artifacts in every tower, but why would Lambert be interested in those things?"

"I agree. And he wouldn't be able to pawn anything he stole from the Tower, either," Jenn said.

"A private collector might buy from him," Rob said. "But we still have the problem of how Lambert would get past the guards. Don't forget this place was designed to be a *fortress*."

Then, as another thought struck him, Rob groaned. "Jenn, I think perhaps we've made a mistake. We just might have assumed something we should not have taken for granted."

She turned to him with a puzzled frown. "And that is—?"

"We've assumed that Lambert was trying to steal something from *inside* the Tower of London. But the fact is that he was found stabbed *outside* the Tower."

She still looked puzzled. "And your point is—?" she asked again.

"Maybe he was after something *close* to the Tower," Rob said, "but not *in* it."

Jenn sighed. "Any bright ideas?"

Rob pulled a map from his pocket and spread it out between them. "Look, Jenn, we're here," he said. "Why don't we check out the grounds around the Tower?"

Jenn nodded. "Okay, I'm on. But first, let's get some lunch. It's way past noon, and I'm starved. Besides, I need to call the States to find out who Lambert's cellmate was."

"There's a place near here where we can buy sandwiches," Rob said.

As they left the Tower, Rob led her toward a cafeteria. Jenn pulled a tiny cell phone from her backpack and made her call. She was still talking when Rob returned, carrying sandwiches and paper cups of hot tea to a park bench.

"Hope you don't mind cucumber and watercress sandwiches," he said after she hung up. "That was all they had."

Jenn bit into her sandwich. "Very tasty! Guess who Lambert shared a cell with in the States?" she said. Rob shrugged and shook his head. "A small-time loser named Buzzy Malloy," Jenn said with a grin. "And who do you think Buzzy Malloy's girlfriend is?"

Rob looked blank. "I haven't a clue. But I've got a feeling you're about to tell me," he said.

Jenn's grin widened. "A young Englishwoman named Lilah Graham!"

Chapter 7

Rob looked shocked. "Once again, we're back where we started!" he exclaimed. "So there *is* a link between Lambert and Raven." Then he frowned as a new thought struck him. "On the other hand, I never heard that Raven's mob was into stealing. As far as I knew, they were only interested in acts of terrorism."

Jenn shrugged. "Well, there certainly is a link between Lambert and Raven's family," Jenn said. "I think it's safe to bet that Lambert was in London to steal something—and that Buzzy and Lilah were involved somehow. But what could have gone wrong? Who stabbed Lambert? And why?"

"I think we should stick to our plan,"

Rob insisted. "Let's check out the area around the Tower. If Lambert really was 'casing the joint,' as you Yanks would say, maybe we'll find what he was looking for. Could be a jewelry store. Or it might even be—"

"Wait a minute," Jenn said. "First, let's pick up a copy of that events magazine of yours. What's it called?"

"*Time Out*," Rob said. "Good idea. The datebook listings might give us an idea of what Lambert was after."

They headed toward Tower Hill. As they walked, Jenn glanced about. She was still hoping to spot something—*anything*—that might have attracted Lambert to this place.

On their right, Jenn saw Tower Hill. It was the exact spot where most of the Tower's prisoners had been beheaded. She remembered reading that only seven people had been executed inside the Tower, but literally hundreds had been executed at Tower Hill.

On their left was the Church of All Hallows. Jenn knew that a church of one kind or another had stood on that site for 1,300 years. Amazingly, the church that stood there today contained some bricks that dated back to the Roman occupation of Britain.

"What could he have been after? I see historical buildings everywhere," she said to Rob. "I see plenty of shops and tourist attractions. But I don't see anything that would interest a thief *and* a group of terrorists. Are we making bad guesses again?"

"*Tuesday*," Rob said thoughtfully. He stopped and gazed at Jenn. "Whatever Lambert had planned, it wasn't going to take place until Tuesday."

"So?" She frowned, puzzled.

"So far, we're guessing that Lambert wanted to break in some place to steal something, right?" Jenn nodded. "But what if he planned to break in for another reason? What if he was looking for a place where Raven's group could rig a bomb? Or maybe set a fire?"

Jenn stared at him in horror. "Then it could be any place where people gather—*if* that's what Raven's group is really after." She thought for a moment. "It doesn't make sense. Lambert never tried to get into places that had a lot of security. If Raven's group wanted to rig up a bomb in a public place, why would they use Lambert, of all people?"

Rob looked worried. "We'd better get a copy of *Time Out*," he said.

They hurried to the nearest shop that sold newspapers. They found everything there from gum to postcards to packages of cookies—which the British call *biscuits*. Jenn was amused at how different the English language could be, depending on who was speaking it.

Jenn bought a copy of *Time Out*. Then she and Rob went into a nearby pub and ordered cups of hot tea. Jenn gave half the pages of *Time Out* to Rob.

"If you see something interesting, circle it," she said. "When we finish, we can compare notes."

For a while they read in silence. Then all of a sudden, Jenn yelped. "Found something?" Rob asked.

Jenn gave him a troubled look. "Are you absolutely sure Lambert said the word *Raven*?" she asked.

Rob nodded. "Yes, I think so."

"You *think* so?" Her troubled look became even more troubled.

"Well, that's what I was told," Rob said uneasily. "Why?"

"What if Lambert's job had nothing to do with the Tower? What if the word he said was *Craven*?" Jenn asked.

Rob frowned. "I—I don't know. I guess I could call Scotland Yard. Maybe the copper who overheard Lambert would remember exactly. Why?"

Jenn turned the page around so Rob could see it. She jabbed at a datebook entry with her finger. Rob leaned forward to read the listing out loud.

The British Museum is pleased to announce a new exhibit of rare and priceless jewels. This must-see display will be open to the viewing public for three weeks only, beginning Tuesday.

Rob glanced up at Jenn. She nodded in encouragement, and he read on.

The jewels in this fantastic exhibit are on loan from American businessman Wesley Craven.

Chapter 8

While Jenn finished her tea, Rob went to make a phone call. When he returned, he said, "The copper I talked to wasn't absolutely sure if Lambert said 'Raven' or 'Craven.' So you may be right."

Jenn glanced at her watch. "The museum will be closing soon," she said. "We'd better get going!"

They hurried to Rob's car. As he pulled out of the parking lot and into traffic, Jenn let out a sudden yelp.

"What's wrong?" Rob exclaimed.

"Oh, no!" she wailed. "I just saw a billboard with an ad for a new play. It's called *The Raven*."

Rob groaned. "I'm going to be seeing that word—"

He slammed on his brakes as a small

yellow car cut in front of them. Rob cursed, downshifted, and stomped on the gas. The tires screamed as rubber bit into pavement and the car took off.

Jenn was thrown back against the seat. "Thank goodness for seatbelts," she muttered as they tore through traffic.

She closed her eyes as they spun around a corner. When her eyes snapped open, she took a good, long look at the canary-yellow compact car they were following. It was veering dangerously from one lane to the next.

Jenn tried to read the license plate, but it was completely covered with a layer of mud. Then Jenn caught a glimpse of the driver and gasped.

"Rob, I know who—"

"Hold on!" he roared, narrowly missing a big delivery truck coming across the road. Ahead of them, the yellow car suddenly swerved into a narrow side street. Before Rob could follow, a big red double-decker bus came from the opposite direction. It stopped in traffic and blocked their way.

Rob beat on the horn in frustration, but the bus was also pinned in. Neither vehicle could move.

Jenn put her hand on his arm. "Take it easy," she said softly. "The yellow car is long gone by now."

Rob slumped back against the seat. "I'd just noticed that we were being followed when the little yellow car whipped around me," he said angrily. "I'd give anything to know who the driver was."

"Well, I can't give you a name," Jenn said. "But I can tell you that the driver was the girl in the pink hat!"

"The girl in the pink hat," Rob said. "The one who tried to push me onto the tracks in the tube station? Did you get a good look at her?"

Jenn shook her head. "I wasn't paying attention until she cut in front of us," she said, checking her watch.

"We're too late for the museum now," she went on. "Why don't we go talk to Lilah Graham? Scotland Yard must have an address on file."

Scotland Yard did have an address. Lilah Graham's place turned out to be a seamy boarding house in White Chapel. Jenn waited in the car while Rob talked to the manager of the boarding house. While she waited, Jenn glanced up and down the street.

The district wasn't as bad today as it had been a century ago. Jenn had read that in the late 1800s, White Chapel had been a notorious slum. The people there had lived in cruel poverty. About half the children born in White Chapel died before reaching the age of five.

Today, most people remembered the district for another reason. In the late 1800s, White Chapel had been the hunting ground of the vicious serial killer known as Jack the Ripper. To this day, no one was absolutely certain of

Jack the Ripper's real identity.

Rob finally came out of the boarding house and walked down the front steps. "No luck at all," he said. "Lilah Graham moved out a week ago. The manager said she left in a big hurry—without leaving a forwarding address. Looks like she's disappeared."

Jenn rubbed her tired eyes. "We keep going round and round. What was Lambert after? What's going to happen tomorrow? And where?"

Chapter 9

When Jenn opened her eyes the next morning, her first waking thought was, "Oh, no, it's Tuesday!" She groaned, wanting to pull the covers over her head until Wednesday. "Lambert, you little rat, why didn't you give us more to go on?" she thought crossly as she crawled out of bed.

After Rob picked her up, they drove across London to the British Museum. No matter how many times she visited the museum, Jenn always felt a sense of awe when she climbed the front steps.

The British Museum was a great treasure house nearly 250 years old. It contained fantastic artifacts of all kinds, from Greek sculpture and Egyptian mummies to fine art and rare jewels.

Within the museum's walls were priceless riches from all over the world.

As Rob and Jenn entered the main hall, they saw visitors hurrying from one part of the museum to another. Tourists, as well as British citizens of all ages, flocked to the museum every day.

In the museum bookshop, Rob picked up a brochure that told about current displays. "The Craven display is on the second floor," he said.

The agents climbed the wide marble staircase to the upper level. There they used their badges to get into the big hall where the Craven jewels were on display. The display wasn't due to open officially for another hour.

Jenn explained their purpose to the curator and the chief of security. She said they weren't sure if *anything* was going to happen. "We're just trying to cover all the bases," she said. "We want to take a look around and make sure you have enough security."

While Rob and the security chief double-checked the alarm system, Jenn examined the displays. Around the walls of the long gallery, glass cases had been set up to display the Craven jewels.

Jenn drew her breath in sharply at the dazzling beauty of the gems and their settings. A ruby as big as a hen's egg was set in a heavy gold necklace. A diamond ring seemed to flash blue and white fire. Emeralds spilled green light across white velvet.

"This is just the kind of thing that would certainly tempt Hal Lambert," Jenn thought. "At the same time, it's a bit ambitious for him. As I recall, his targets were small stores, not huge, well-guarded museums."

After she and Rob had carefully checked every part of the exhibit, they headed for the stairs.

"I don't see how Lambert could have planned to break in here," Jenn said. "The security is too high-tech for him."

"I agree," Rob said. "And here's something else to think about. What do you suppose Raven's group will do now—with Lambert in the hospital?"

Jenn thought about that as they walked downstairs. "Good question. Will they cancel their plans, or will they hire someone to replace him?" She sighed. "All we seem to come up with are more questions, Rob. We aren't—"

"*Look out!*" Rob yelled, throwing himself at Jenn. In a split second he tackled her, throwing her to one side.

Jenn fell on the stairs, then rolled down the last four steps, landing with a thump at the bottom. Just before she stopped rolling, something fell from above and crashed next to her.

Jenn looked up. She caught a flash of plaid at the top of the stairs!

As she struggled to sit up, a guard hurried to her side. "Are you all right, miss?" he asked worriedly as a crowd of startled onlookers began to gather.

Jenn nodded and looked around. She knew she was probably bruised—but nothing seemed to be broken. "What happened?" she asked.

Before the guard could answer, Rob pushed through the crowd. He and the guard helped Jenn to her feet. While another guard chased the onlookers away, Jenn limped to a nearby bench.

"That was your friend in the plaid raincoat," Rob said. "I looked up just as he tried to drop a big stone bowl on you. If I hadn't pushed you out of the way, you would have been flattened!"

Chapter 10

"You saved my life," Jenn said in a shaky voice.

"Ah, but what are friends for?" Rob said with a grin. Then he grew serious. "I hate to tell you this, Jenn—but unfortunately, Mr. Plaid Raincoat got away."

"What about the girl in the pink hat?" Jenn asked.

Rob shook his head. "Sorry, old girl. I didn't see her."

Jenn groaned. "I'm sick and tired of those two hounding us. It's high time we went after *them* instead! Maybe they have the answers we want."

"Could be," Rob said. "They certainly aren't shy about wanting to get rid of us." He leaned back against the bench.

"Plaid Raincoat took a big chance today. It's only by luck he was able to get out of the museum without being caught."

"How *did* he get out?" Jenn asked.

"First, he got rid of the raincoat," Rob said. "One of the guards found it in an upstairs rubbish bin. After that, our suspect looked just like everybody else. No doubt he easily blended in with the crowd and simply walked away."

"Sure," Jenn said, "I get it. That plaid raincoat was like a red flag. If he had gone on wearing it, he would have been caught for sure." Then she stopped talking, drawing her breath in sharply. "Oh, Rob, maybe that's *it!*"

"What?"

"Just think about it. That bright pink hat. The plaid raincoat. That canary-yellow car." Jenn ticked off each item on her fingers. "Don't you see? They were *meant* to be noticed. Our attackers were practically waving flags to make sure they got our attention."

"But why?" Rob still looked puzzled.

"To draw us away from—" She frowned. "They must think we're a whole lot closer to solving this puzzle than we really are."

"What is it they think we know?" Rob wondered aloud. He started to pace up and down. "Let's go through it again. All we know is that *something* is going to happen today. And we know that it is somehow related to ravens."

"And it may take place at the Tower," Jenn said. "Ravens at the Tower—*that's it!*" In a burst of excitement she jumped to her feet, but then howled in pain.

Rob rushed to her side. "You're hurt, Jenn! You should see a doctor."

"No time," she said through gritted teeth. "It's just my shoulder. I bet it's black and blue, but we have to get out of here. I think I know what Raven's group is after."

"What?" Rob demanded as they hurried to the entrance.

"It's so simple," Jenn said. "It was right there—right under our noses the whole time!"

"What?" Rob roared in frustration as they raced down the front steps.

"The ravens at the Tower," Jenn said. "Surely you know the legend. I heard it the first time I toured the Tower of London. Then yesterday, while we were walking around the grounds, I heard one of the Beefeaters telling the story to a group of tourists."

"Of course I know the legend!" Rob said crossly as they climbed into his car. "I'm sure every schoolchild in England has heard it. The ravens who live at the Tower are protected for just one reason. According to the story, if the ravens ever left the Tower, the kingdom would fall."

Jenn nodded. "And that's why the ravens' wings are clipped, right? So they can't fly away."

"Well, yes," Rob said, "but I don't see—" He started the car.

"What would happen if the Tower ravens were *kidnapped*?" Jenn asked.

Rob frowned. "I never thought much about it. After all, it's just a *legend*!"

"I don't believe the kingdom would fall," Jenn said. "On the other hand, I think there would be a huge uproar. People would be very upset. After all, the ravens are a national symbol. They've been living at the Tower of London for centuries! As I understand it, no one knows when the first ravens arrived."

"That's true," Rob said. "So what you're suggesting is that the terrorists plan to kidnap the Tower ravens?"

"And hold them for ransom," Jenn said. "The kidnappers would be killing two birds with one stone—no pun intended. The kidnapping would cause a lot of chaos, *and* they'd make some money out of the crime."

Rob looked at Jenn as if she'd lost her mind. "You can't be serious! Only an idiot would consider it. Imagine trying to kidnap a flock of fierce birds from inside that well-guarded castle!"

"I didn't say the kidnappers were terribly smart," Jenn said.

"Jenn, that isn't just stupid, it's—it's downright *insane*!" Rob exclaimed.

"Why?"

"Well, for one thing, the Tower is securely guarded by both the Beefeaters and a military guard." Rob pulled carefully into traffic. "It's not like everyone there goes home at night. About 150 people still live inside the Tower walls."

"Really?" Jenn looked surprised. "I had no idea—"

"Most of them are the Beefeaters and their families," Rob explained.

"What happens at the Tower after the visitors leave at the end of the day?" Jenn asked.

"The outer gates of the fortress are locked, and the keys are handed over to the Resident Governor of the Tower," Rob said. "It's quite a ceremony."

Jenn was silent for a moment. "So maybe the terrorists *aren't* going to wait until after dark. Maybe they plan to kidnap the ravens during the day."

"That's ridiculous," Rob hooted, shaking his head. "They'd never get away with it."

"They just might—*if* that's the last thing anyone would expect," Jenn said.

When they reached the Tower, Rob pulled one of the Beefeaters aside. He quickly told him what he and Jenn suspected. Jenn saw the Beefeater's eyes crinkle up with laughter.

"Kidnap the *what*?" The man's mouth twitched.

Jenn took a deep breath. "I know it sounds crazy, but it's the only thing that makes sense. We've checked out every other lead we can think of that relates to the word 'raven'."

"We'll just take a quick look around,"

Rob said. "It will only take us a few minutes."

"Speaking of looking," Jenn added, "there are a couple of people we think might be in on the plot." She did her best to describe the man in the plaid raincoat and the girl in the pink hat.

The Beefeater listened carefully. "Not a lot to go on, miss," he said at last. "That description is a bit vague."

"I know," said Jenn with a sigh. "But if you do see them—"

"I'll be sure to pass the word along to the other Warders," the guard promised her. "In the meantime, miss, if you need any help checking on the ravens—" He couldn't resist grinning.

Chapter 11

Inside the Tower, Rob and Jenn strolled up and down the paths. They didn't want to attract attention, so they tried to look like any other pair of visitors. But unlike other tourists, they were on the lookout for deadly terrorists.

"Who takes care of the ravens?" Jenn asked. "Is that someone's special job?" She pulled a Tower brochure from her backpack and studied the map carefully.

"The Ravenmaster," Rob said. "What are you looking for on that map?"

Jenn gasped with laughter. "Listen to this," she said. "It says here that the ravens' *lodgings* are adjacent to the Wakefield Tower."

Rob raised one eyebrow. "What's so funny about that? It just means that the lodgings are *near* the Wakefield Tower."

"I know what 'adjacent' means," Jenn said. "I'm talking about the ravens' *lodgings*. Don't you think it sounds funny to talk about *lodgings* for birds? It sounds like condos for crows." She couldn't resist chuckling at the absurd idea.

Rob sighed. "Oh, you Americans. I suppose you'd just say *cages*."

He pointed just ahead. On the grass about 20 feet away, Jenn saw several large birdcages. A slender young worker wearing navy blue coveralls and a gray cap was cleaning the inside of one of the cages. Several ravens were perched on top of the cage or hopping about on the grass. Jenn guessed that they might have just been fed.

As Jenn and Rob looked on, a raven hopping about on the lawn suddenly seemed to lose its balance. It began to stagger from side to side. Jenn's smile disappeared. "Look, Rob. Something's wrong with that bird," she whispered.

The worker looked up. Just as Jenn climbed over the low iron fence that was meant to keep people off the grass, the raven fell on its back. Jenn got to the raven at the same time the worker did. She reached out to pick up the bird, but the worker grabbed her arm.

"Watch out there, miss," the worker warned, "you might get pecked. Those birds are mean."

Jenn drew back. She saw how sharp the raven's beak was. "Wait, Rob," Jenn said, turning to her partner. "Do you know if there's a special veterinarian who takes care of the ravens?"

"I'll go find a Warder," Rob said as he turned and walked away.

"You're thinking of the Ravenmaster, miss," said the worker. "That's who you want. Here, I've got a cloth. I'll wrap the bird up and take it to the Ravenmaster myself." The worker carefully bundled up the bird in a dirty-looking towel.

Jenn's eyes suddenly narrowed. She

reached out and pulled off the worker's cap. Long red curls fell to the worker's shoulders. *"You!"* Jenn yelled.

The girl's fist struck out, hitting the startled agent on her sore shoulder. Jenn let out a cry of pain. Then, with the raven under her arm, the redhead leaped over the fence and took off running.

"Stop that woman!" Jenn yelled as she ran after her.

The redhead plowed through the groups of visitors like a football player running for a touchdown.

The distance between Jenn and the kidnapper widened. Then Jenn saw Rob and a couple of Beefeaters walking toward her and the kidnapper. She yelled at Rob to stop the redhead. He immediately crouched down on the pathway, blocking the girl's path. She couldn't stop herself in time. When she stumbled over Rob, the two Beefeaters reached out. One of them grabbed her and the other rescued the raven.

By the time Jenn reached the group, she saw a Warder checking the raven. Rob introduced the man as the Ravenmaster. "The bird seems to be all right," he said. "But I think it may have been drugged."

Jenn and Rob exchanged looks. "The water? The food?" Jenn said. "Someone needs to check them, too."

The Ravenmaster looked worried. "We'd better try to round up the rest of the ravens," he said. "We need to make sure we have them all and that they haven't been harmed."

"It might be a good idea to close down the Tower until we find the other kidnappers," Rob said.

One of the Warders helped Jenn handcuff the redhead. In a few moments the prisoner was taken to a small office out of the public's sight.

"I'm pretty sure this is the woman in the pink hat," Jenn said to Rob. "I never did get a good look at her face, but I certainly remember the red hair."

"It's Lilah Graham," Rob cried. "This is the woman we've been looking for. I'll call Scotland Yard. They'll send a car around to pick her up."

"I need to get back out there to help search for the other ravens," the Warder told Jenn. "Will you be all right here on your own?"

"I'll be fine," Jenn said. "And while you're at it, check on your employees. The other kidnappers are probably disguised as Tower workers, too."

As soon as the Warder left, Jenn shoved the prisoner into a chair. Then she perched on a corner of the desk and glared down at the redhead. "Lilah Graham," Jenn said. The redhead said nothing, but she grinned boldly.

"Following in your father's footsteps, Lilah?" Still, there was no response. "Where's Buzzy?" Jenn asked. "Where's your buddy in the plaid raincoat? And who else was in on this caper?"

Lilah sneered. "You're asking *me*? You want them, you *find* them, copper!"

Jenn smiled thoughtfully. "Is that the way you want to play it? Well, if you're all we've got, I guess we can book *you* for attempted murder, attempted kidnapping, terrorism—"

The sneer vanished. Now Lilah glared back at Jenn. "What murder?" the redhead snapped.

"Oh, please," Jenn said. "You stabbed Hal Lambert a few days ago. Trouble is, he lived and he fingered you! If you're going to do a job, Lilah, do it right! There's nothing worse than sloppy—"

The insults worked. "I never tried to knock him off," Lilah exclaimed. "It was—" Her mouth snapped shut.

"The man in the plaid raincoat?" Jenn guessed. But from the look on Lilah's face, Jenn knew that it wasn't.

"Not the plaid raincoat? Then how about Buzzy?" Jenn said. When Lilah didn't answer, Jenn grinned. "Thanks for your help, Lilah. Your silence tells me everything I needed to know."

Lilah just looked away.

"Why *did* you people want to kill Hal, anyway?" Jenn asked.

Lilah took a deep breath. "Because the little weasel got cold feet. He took one look at the size of the Tower and the number of guards and he got scared. We were afraid he'd turn on us." She smiled. "But me and Buzzy have alibis for the day Lambert was stabbed."

"I bet you do," Jenn said.

"The most you can get us for is attempted kidnapping. But I know a good lawyer and we'll cut a deal."

At that moment there was a brisk knock on the door. Then the door opened, and Jenn glanced around. A woman officer from Scotland Yard entered the office. "I'm here to pick up the prisoner," the officer said, pulling out a gun.

Jenn spun about, her fist slamming

down hard on the woman's gun hand. The woman cried out as the gun flew into a corner of the room.

At that moment, Rob came running into the office. He gazed in confusion as Jenn grabbed the officer and pulled her arms behind her back.

"Hold on to her," Jenn said. "This is no Scotland Yard copper."

While Rob held the officer's arms behind her back, Jenn pulled off the woman's disguise. She wore a wig, dark glasses, and sponge rubber padding to make her cheeks puff out.

"*Sarah Graham!*" Rob exclaimed. "Jenn, how did you guess?"

"Even I know that most cops in England don't carry guns," Jenn said. "It was a dead giveaway."

"So she must have been in on the plan from the very beginning," Rob said as he handcuffed Sarah.

"That's right," Jenn said. "Meet the well-mannered, neatly dressed, hard-working head of the terrorist mob."

Sarah glared at Jenn and Rob. "We almost pulled it off," she snarled defiantly. "Next time—"

"There won't *be* a next time for you, Sarah," Jenn said. "I just realized why Lilah didn't protest when I suggested that either she or her boyfriend had stabbed Lambert. That's because Lilah knew all the time that it was you."

"Prove it!" Sarah snapped.

"Hal Lambert will be happy to help us prove it," Rob said. "When I called Scotland Yard, they told me he'd just been taken off the critical list."

Soon a pair of real Scotland Yard officers arrived to take the prisoners away. Rob and Jenn wandered outside.

"I owe you an apology," Jenn said softly. When Rob raised a questioning eyebrow, she explained. "The other night I said I thought a copper had tipped off Raven five years ago. I was wrong. It was Sarah Graham. She was the one who called us that day to tell us where her father was hiding. And then she called her father to warn him that we were coming to arrest him."

"But why would she do that?" Rob asked, scratching his head.

"She probably hoped that we'd all end up killing each other," Jenn said. "She wanted to take over her father's organization. By the way, how are the ravens?"

"In great form," Rob said with a grin. "And all accounted for. Buzzy Malloy and the man in the plaid raincoat were picked up on Tower Green. They were trying to catch more of the ravens. But the birds were pecking the kidnappers so badly that they had to let them go."

Jenn laughed. "Well, Rob, forgive my little joke—but I can honestly say that this case has been for the birds."

COMPREHENSION QUESTIONS

RECALL

1. What kind of work did Rob and Jenn do? What was their specialty?

2. Where could you go to see England's Crown Jewels?

3. What two words did Hal Lambert whisper after he had been stabbed?

NOTING DETAIL

1. What *almost* happened to Rob as he waited for the train?

2. What were the names of the Raven's two daughters?

ANALYZING CHARACTERS

1. Which two words could describe Lilah Graham? Explain your thinking.
   - *suspicious* ● *harmless* ● *bitter*

2. Which two words could describe Rob Gray? Give examples.
   - *cowardly* ● *professional* ● *determined*

VOCABULARY

1. Many historical *artifacts* are in the British Museum. What is an *artifact*?

2. Jenn said that Hal Lambert had *fingered* Lilah. What does that word mean?

3. What name do Americans use for the food that the British call *chips*?

4. What do Londoners call their *subway*?

CAUSE AND EFFECT

1. Rob saved Jenn from getting hit in the head with a heavy stone bowl. What *effect* did his rescue effort have on her?

2. What did Jenn do to *cause* the man in the plaid raincoat to step aside?

3. In England, what *caused* Jenn to feel funny about sitting on the passenger side of a car?

DRAWING CONCLUSIONS

1. Why did Rob think it was unlikely that Hal Lambert was planning to steal the Crown Jewels?

2. What did Jenn discover that linked Hal Lambert and the Raven?